WOMEN AND ISLAMIC REVIVAL IN A WEST AFRICAN TOWN

WOMEN AND ISLAMIC REVIVAL IN A WEST AFRICAN TOWN

ADELINE MASQUELIER

INDIANA UNIVERSITY PRESS
BLOOMINGTON AND INDIANAPOLIS

This book is a publication of

Indiana University Press
601 North Morton Street
Bloomington, IN 47404-3797 USA

www.iupress.indiana.edu

Telephone orders   800-842-6796
Fax orders   812-855-7931
Orders by e-mail   iuporder@indiana.edu

2009 by Adeline Masquelier

♾The paper used in this publication meets the
minimum requirements of the American National
Standard for Information Sciences—Permanence of
Paper for Printed Library Materials, ANSI
Z39.48-1992.

Manufactured in the United States of America

Library of Congress Cataloging-in-Publication Data

Masquelier, Adeline Marie, [date]
  Women and Islamic revival in a West African
town / Adeline Masquelier.
    p. cm.
  Includes bibliographical references and index.
    ISBN 978-0-253-35366-5 (cloth : alk. paper) —
ISBN 978-0-253-21513-0 (pbk : alk. paper)
  1. Muslim women—Niger—Dogondoutchi—
Social conditions.   2. Women—Niger—
Dogondoutchi—Social conditions.   3. Islam—Niger—
Dogondoutchi.   4. Dogondoutchi (Niger)—Social
conditions.   I. Title.
    HQ1812.Z9D663 2009
    305.48'697096626—dc22

                                          2009010072

2   3   4   5   14   13   12   11   10

For Bill

Power, and resistance, are . . .
intrinsic to the development and
exercise of any traditional practice.
                                TALAL ASAD,
"The Idea of an Anthropology of Islam"

CONTENTS

PREFACE

It is impossible for [Nigérien] women to conduct themselves in the same manner as European women. They are in the dark, they know nothing. One cannot get rid of traditions too fast, it would not work. One has to do things progressively. Secluding [Nigérien] women is the best alternative. They are immature and ignorant, this is why they must be controlled. Once they become educated, it's different; they have the maturity and intelligence to act responsibly.

I used to live in Saudi Arabia. Over there, you can spend two years without seeing a girl give birth to a child out of wedlock. Here, there are many unwed mothers. This is why seclusion is better for women who have no maturity. We are protecting them from themselves. If you don't teach a woman how to behave responsibly and to have a profession, you don't help her by setting her free. Here, society can't afford to treat its women like in America or in France where women are educated and have employment. You must work with people's traditions. You can't take away their customs all at once. [Doing so] only creates confusion.

It's like when you guide a crippled man on the path. At some point, he gets stuck, he can't go either forward or backward. Are you helping him by pushing him? There are people here who cannot even count the days of the week. It's very hard to change people, you must go slowly. Each country had its own climate and customs. Here we seclude women.

Seated in a lavishly furnished parlor, I was listening to Malam (Teacher) Awal expound his views on Muslim women's place in contemporary Nigérien society. Upon my return to the small provincial town of Dogondoutchi, Niger, after a six-year absence, local friends had assured me that my new ethnographic project on the current Islamic revival sweeping Niger should include a discussion of the controversial Mahamane Awal—or Shehu (Shaykh) Muhammadu Awalu, as he is officially referred to in Hausa. A charismatic Sufi personality reputedly blessed with extraordinary powers, he had changed the lives of many, I had been told of the preacher who had recently taken up residence in my old neighborhood. Not everyone thought well of him, however. Known among the country's urban elite as "*le marabout de Doutchi*" (the

Qur'anic teacher of Doutchi),[1] the preacher had been embroiled in scandal and controversy ever since his arrival in town. "You must meet him, you must find out why they call him *malamin mata* (the teacher of women)," my assistant Mahamadou insisted after I told him I was interested in learning about the changing place of Islam in women's lives. Several days later the two of us (Mahamadou in pants and shirt of Western inspiration, and I, wearing a veil and a skirt down to my ankles) made our way to Awal's home. A man standing at the door ushered us in without ceremony after learning that I wished to be granted an audience with the prominent preacher. To my surprise, he turned out to be Awal himself. I expected a taller, considerably older man, whose wisdom and charisma would be more readily apparent.

A slightly built and plainly attired man in his early thirties, Malam Awal nonetheless radiated grace and confidence. "In what language would you like to conduct the interview? English, French, or Hausa?" he asked after I explained the purpose of my visit. I was astonished. It was not just the linguistic choices Malam Awal presented to me that were so remarkable (only a minority of town residents can claim fluency in French and virtually none speaks more than a few words of English) but also what these choices implied about the image my interlocutor consciously wanted to project. He was, his question intimated, a sophisticated man who welcomed inquiries from external observers; his mastery of French and English was proof of refinement, experience, and a life of travel. The preacher, I soon found out, was uncommonly skilled at marketing himself for audience consumption: our taped conversation (which lasted close to four hours and was conducted in Hausa) became a forum through which Awal made a show of his polished erudition, his cosmopolitanism, his wisdom, and his virtue—all for my personal benefit.

Malam Awal was one of those "new" Sufis (Soares 2007a:76) whose mission was to teach people the "true" meaning of Islam and reinvigorate the faith at a time when numerous Muslims throughout the country felt threatened by the loss of moral and spiritual values. He channeled his charismatic energy toward the creation of a community of loyal followers who, through their renewed engagement with God's word, learned to be supposedly proper Muslims. Although he claimed to be working within a long-established Sufi tradition, he borrowed liberally from the doctrines of local Muslim reformists who condemned the ways that Islam had been traditionally practiced in this part of Africa. To bolster his legitimacy, the preacher routinely latched onto women as both the custodians of an inherited (and un-Islamic) tradition and the symbol of a newly configured morality the definition of which he enunciated at length in his sermons. Women who pledged their loyalty to Malam Awal embodied, through dress and deportment, marriage and domesticity, a new kind of piety characterized by conscious and conscientious commitment to the Qur'anic message. In addition to dressing modestly, they spent thriftily, married soon after puberty, and thereafter abstained from leaving the marital compound, except to pursue their religious education.

When I asked him why he promoted women's seclusion, Awal responded that he did so because the women of Niger were "immature and ignorant" and therefore, as he made clear in the statement (extracted from our conversation) quoted at the opening of this book, in need of control. Much like veiling, seclusion, he explained, was but a temporary measure—part of the moral scaffolding needed to guide local women on the path to reformation. Once they had acquired, through religious training and discipline, the maturity their Western counterparts already exhibited, Nigérien women would be freed from such confinement and constraints, he informed me. I was fascinated by the diplomacy (bordering on obsequiousness) of Awal's responses and especially by his intimation that the form of religiosity he promoted was not a reaction to Western modernism; this rhetoric sharply contradicted the preacher's caustic denunciation of Western immorality in his sermons.

However, it is not his attempts to flatter my Euro-feminist sensibilities so much as his claims that each country had "its own climate and customs" that I found both troubling and compelling for what it suggested about the preacher's vision of his own mission. Faced with the challenge of reforming the moral conduct of "superstitious" and uneducated masses, Awal spoke of the changes he was implementing as a move forward away from ignorance. If this progressive break with tradition was meant to normativize the Muslim practices of Dogondoutchi residents and align them with a purportedly universalist Islam, ultimately Awal's Islamic revival was profoundly shaped by the socio-religious context in which it unfolded. Indeed, as I argue in this book, its success was largely owing to the artful way in which it combined innovation with adherence to familiar forms of religiosity. By rooting his message in an apparent concern for the preservation of local "customs," Malam Awal endeared himself to a population that had grown wary of the radical Islamic reformism so prevalent in this and other regions of Niger. He understood that it was by "work[ing] with people's traditions," as he put it, that he would successfully legitimize his Sufi movement and earn his rightful place as a saintly figure in the community.

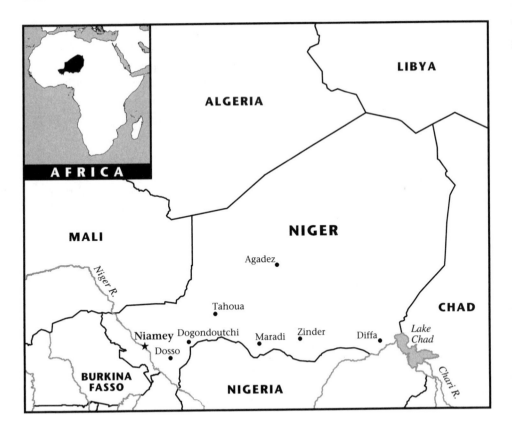

Map 1. Niger.

This book explores the particular forms that this project of Islamic reform has taken, its costs and consequences, as well as the possibilities it has
generated for women seeking to embrace, or alternatively, resist, Awal's vision of Islam. The setting for my exploration is Dogondoutchi, a small Sahelian town located about 25 kilometers from the Nigerian border. At the time
of my 2004 research, the population of Dogondoutchi and the neighboring
villages that together make up the commune of Dogondoutchi was estimated
to be over 45,000. Most of the town's inhabitants identify as Mawri. The rest
identify as Fulani, Tuareg, Hausa,[2] or Zarma. The Mawri are a local sub-
group of the much larger Hausa ethno-linguistic entity located chiefly in
southern Niger and northern Nigeria.[3] Traditionally recognized by their
"ethnic" marks, two scars that cut their cheek from the corner of the mouth
to the ear on each side, Hausaphone Mawri are a largely heterogeneous

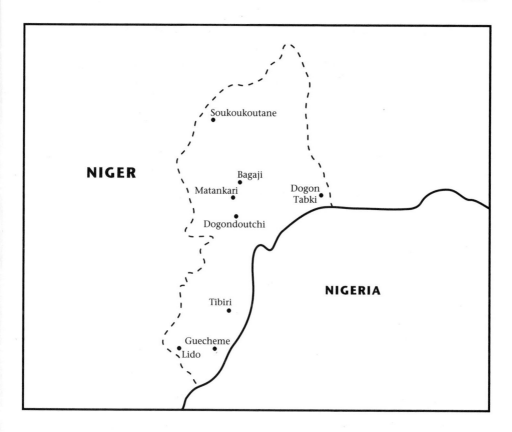

Map 2. *Département* of Dogondoutchi. The region is also known as Arewa.

population of 250,000 people. They occupy Arewa, a region of semiarid grasslands, savannas, and thorn shrublands situated on the western edge of Niger's Hausa-speaking region. Since the restructuring of Niger's administrative districts in 2004, Dogondoutchi has become the administrative seat of the *département* bearing its name. Despite its status as *capitale départementale*, Dogondoutchi has no paved streets save for the pot-holed front road that cuts through the administrative sector; electricity is unevenly distributed across the neighborhoods; and, with the latest rounds of budget restrictions, trash collection is sporadic at best. The town has retained the quaint look of a large village nestled at the foot of a picturesque cluster of hills, which are fossilized remnants of an ancient valley. The old neighborhoods, with their rambling webs of dirt streets lined with mud walls, are densely populated, noisy, and busy. During the day, street stalls are set up offering anything from matches and medicines to spices to soap and kerosene for sale; old men sitting together under the shade provided by neem and tamarind trees chew kola nuts and share news while young men zoom through on noisy motorcycles and small children play with toys made of cardboard boxes, metal wire, or millet stalks. Inside the walled-in compounds, women attend to their domestic chores, sweeping courtyards, pounding grains, or frying snacks to be sold to neighbors. To the west and the south lie the more recent, fancier neighborhoods. There the townscape is dotted with the modern *villas* (cement houses with metal roofs) of civil servants and prosperous merchants. In these new *quartiers* that have sprouted up on what once was either farmland or grasslands, the streets are wider and straighter and the walled compounds less densely distributed, giving the place a more urban feel.

In Dogondoutchi, as in the rest of Niger, Islam is now equated with status, power, and *arziki* (a word evoking notions of wealth, prosperity, and well-being). Although some Dogondoutchi residents—particularly women— often secretly continue to rely on spirits as more powerful mediators with a distant God than Arabic prayers, they are nonetheless forced by circumstances to acknowledge the benefits of becoming Muslim. Since prosperity is viewed as an undeniable sign of God's goodwill, the wealth and success of respected *alhazai* (persons who have accomplished the pilgrimage to Mecca) provide a powerful incentive to turn to prayer (*salla*). That the term *alhazai* (the plural form of *alhaji*) refers to successful merchants (assuming that, thanks to their wealth, they have accomplished the *haji* [pilgrimage]) further testifies to the intricate connections between religious identity and wealth.

A few generations ago, the large majority of local residents relied exclusively on farming for their subsistence. They must now supplement the income they derive from the sale of millet, sorghum, beans, and ground nuts with other sources of cash such as petty trading and transport. Over the years, drought, deforestation, and land degradation have increased local farmers' vulnerability to the environment, forcing many to migrate to larger cities in search of employment. Local youths, who are largely unemployed regardless of their degree of education, are bitter and disillusioned about their future prospects. When they do not disparage farming altogether, most young men tend to see it as an unreliable source of income; some want nothing to do with it, hoping instead to secure a civil service position or, for the less literate, steady employment in the growing transport industry or in commerce. But the failure of structural adjustment programs originally aimed at boosting local economies has quashed most dreams of social advancement and, with them, processes of social reproduction that were once taken for granted.

Amid dwindling economic opportunities, severe land shortages, and growing feelings of disempowerment, competing Islamic visions of moral order
have found eager support among those who believe that Niger's economic
problems are rooted in immorality and that widespread moral reforms must
be instituted before the debilitating effects of poverty and underdevelopment
can be reversed. Thus *bori* spirit possession, which was once a central dimension of health-seeking practices and a popular form of entertainment as well
as a wellspring of political resistance (Masquelier 2001b), is now severely
condemned by all Muslims as a source of evil and corruption.

Singing, dancing, drumming, and praise-singing have similarly been
identified as un-Islamic traditions that must be purged from the repertoire of
local practices if society is to survive the serious ills currently afflicting it.
As elsewhere in the world, Islam has recently taken on new meanings for
Dogondoutchi residents searching for viable alternatives to the perceived
failure of Western models of gender, family, and society. New modes of religiosity, new expressions of piety, and new definitions of morality have
emerged in past decades to affirm the centrality of Islam in public and private
life. With the spread of foreign Muslim ideologies, imported from Nigeria
but often modeled after Saudi, Egyptian, or even Iranian forms of religiosity,
local ways of being Muslim are subject to increased public scrutiny—though,
as we shall see, the reforms advocated by religious leaders cannot be understood as purely foreign imports that wipe away locally existing practices.

For the women of Dogondoutchi, Malam Awal's Sufi revitalization and
the larger Islamic revival of which it is a part have been experienced as mixed
blessings. Although the women have gained new rights and understandings
of their place in Muslim society, they have also lost some autonomy and
sources of value, as new gender dynamics and patterns of authority, wealth
management, and sociality have emerged out of the ongoing debates over
what is and what is not part of Islam. Continuing struggles over the definition of an Islamic modernity and the terms of society's "re-moralization"
have translated into acute concerns about women's visibility, sexuality, and
propriety. As "bearers of Western contagion" (Cooper 2006:39) or, conversely,
as symbols of ignorance and backwardness, women are made to embody all
that has gone wrong with development and modernity. In his sermons, Awal
routinely focused on women's lack of piety, their supposedly dissolute conduct,
and, more generally, the moral failings they displayed through their alleged
carelessness and lack of discipline. Regulation of women's visibility and autonomy is also a key component of the moralizing discourses of other Muslim
activists (which scholars variously refer to as fundamentalists, Islamists, or

reformists) for whom the perceived spread of immorality can be directly traced to society's failure to contain female sexuality. This book is an attempt to document how Muslim practices in Dogondoutchi, literally and symbolically, fashion sociopolitical, religious, and economic spaces around women, their bodies, and their sexuality.

Although they are the privileged targets of moralizing Islamic discourses, women in Dogondoutchi are not passive pawns in local contests over the definition of Muslim identity. Admittedly current debates about religious truth, authority, and authenticity are ostensibly controlled by men who are perceived to know Islam better than women do, aside from possessing the worldly knowledge that insures economic independence. As social actors, women nonetheless contribute significantly to the construction of Muslim tradition and the formation of religious identities. Whether they resist marriage reforms that threaten their social position, defy husbandly authority to attend sermons, ignore altogether certain injunctions from religious leaders, or embody, through dress and public conduct, a particular form (or absence) of piety, they actively participate in an economy of representations and practices increasingly structured in Islamic terms.

Originally I had not intended to center so much of my analysis around Awal and his impact on the Muslim community in Dogondoutchi. Yet, as I became better acquainted with the preacher, his mission, and his methods, I realized that Awal's conception of religion and reform would have to be included in my discussion if I wanted to capture the "discursive texture" (Bowen 1993:11) of the Muslim experience in Dogondoutchi and evoke the "spaces of dissension" (Foucault 1972:152) that divergent ideologies have helped create. Like other Muslim perspectives currently debated and contested, Awal's interpretation of Islam is part of a constantly evolving discursive field whose heterogeneity and complexity I have tried to convey through a discussion of some of the incidents and controversies, sermons and conversations, rumors and reminiscences that I witnessed during my successive research trips to Niger.

My presentation here of the "syncretic dynamism" (Bernal 1994:39) of Muslim discourses and practices in Dogondoutchi is by no means a complete picture; much had to be left out. Rather, this discussion reflects my attempts to come to grips with certain dimensions of Muslim life in Dogondoutchi, particularly women's endorsement of religious undertakings that appear to reinforce their subordination to male authority. I am still struggling to articulate this issue in terms that highlight both women's agency and their commitment to traditionally sanctioned virtues. Some chapters grew out of my own involvement in the lives of people I have known and cared about for many years. As a whole, they provide an account of the growing importance of Islam in the lives of Dogondoutchi residents. Granted, not everyone in Dogondoutchi displays the same dedication in the performance of religious duties. Whereas some pray five times a day and engage in conscious acts of piety, others do not. Nonetheless, Islam can be said to "set the widest stage for their actions" by specifying the kind of world they inhabit and the "kind of actions that are compatible with that world" (Delaney 1990:514).

The opening chapter discusses the theoretical and methodological issues that bear on my research. It situates my analysis of changing Muslim ideas and practices in Dogondoutchi within the anthropology of Islam and as part of a rising scholarly interest in the study of Muslim women in Africa. Chapter 2 presents a historical overview of the profound changes that took place in the area in and around Dogondoutchi in the aftermath of the French conquest, focusing on the development of Islam in the context of *la politique musulmane* (colonial policies toward Muslims). It also documents the development and transformation of Muslim practices in the early postcolonial period, when Dogondoutchi residents massively abandoned spirit-centered forms of worship and embraced the more "cosmopolitan" values of Islam.

If French (and later Nigérien) policies paved the way for the unprecedented spread of Islam in Arewa, the recent political liberalization and the emergence of a public space where Muslims could debate the merits of various forms of religiosity has radically transformed the ways that Nigériens imagine themselves as part of the *umma,* the global Muslim community. It has also encouraged the spread of ideas on how to reform Islam. Chapter 3 opens with a confrontation between two Muslim factions vying for control of the Friday mosque in Dogondoutchi—one wanting to preserve local Muslim practices and the other pushing for reforms. The chapter traces the spread of reformist ideas about Islam and situates the confrontation in the mosque within the context of the deregulation of Niger's one-party regime and the emergence of a public sphere. Key to my approach in this and subsequent chapters is an effort to highlight the diversity of historically specific Muslim discourses and practices in Dogondoutchi and the limitations of conventional understandings of Islam in Africa as either Sufi or anti-Sufi in orientation. Chapter 4 chronicles the rise to prominence of Malam Awal. Focusing on a religious ceremony held in March 2000 to mark the day Awal first set foot in the town three years earlier, I explore how the preacher initially rallied support and (at least for a few years) maintained his clout. Aside from publicly demonstrating the size and devotion of his following, I argue that the event was part of a concerted strategy to revitalize a spiritually weakened community by turning Dogondoutchi into the devotional capital of Niger.

With the rise of Muslim reformism, the spirit-centered practices so central to women's marital and reproductive lives have been increasingly dismissed as "superstition," a product of ignorance and confusion. After Malam Awal began to preach, however, talk of the threat that spirits posed to humans resurfaced, for rather than treating spirits as outmoded, parochial expressions of culture, Malam Awal took them (and their powers) seriously. Chapter 5 describes Awal's confrontation with a spirit who hindered the construction of his mosque. By casting the spirit as a creature of Satan who must be vigorously combated, Awal demonstrated that spirits continued to play a role in the constitution of the moral order. His victory over the spirit—concretized by the erection of a mosque on the very place where the spirit resided—signaled to all that one could affirm one's commitment to Islam without entirely abandoning "old" beliefs. Islam, the incident made clear, remained thoroughly dependent on pre-Islamic cosmologies for legitimizing its own authority.

In the chapters that follow, the focus shifts to the lives and practices of women. Chapter 6 explores recent transformations in the matrimonial economy and describes the strategies women use to challenge the visions of frugal domesticity promoted by both Malam Awal and the Muslim reformists he so virulently criticizes. At a time of anxious questioning about wealth management, women's role in society, and, more generally, the relevance of Islam in the lives of ordinary Muslims, women for whom prosperity is not antithetical to Islamic piety have resisted the call to austerity. Senior women in Muslim households that oppose Muslim reformists continue to equip their daughters with the latest trappings of modern domesticity when they leave the parental home as young brides to join their husbands' households. In this chapter I discuss a young woman's insistence on receiving an expensive bed as a wedding gift from her impoverished mother, and I examine how the acquisition of this item is implicated in the creation of social worth and the definition of moral domesticity for Mawri women.

In Niger, much of the debate over what constitutes propriety and piety has centered on women's dress and visibility. In recent years many women have noticeably modified their veiling habits and their visiting patterns in response to injunctions that they dress modestly and stay home. Yet, as I argue in chapter 7, women's experience of head coverings has a long history of marking Muslimhood in this region and complicates the conventional assumption of an emerging conception of the female body as repository of a newly prescribed Islamic morality. For some women, covering one's head and upper body is an experience that is embodied rather than articulated in terms of what the veil signifies. It is rooted in a notion of modesty that predates the current rhetoric surrounding female morality. Although said to be new, current styles of head dress are elaborations of already existing practices whose own embodied consequences must be critically interrogated rather than being taken for granted. Wearing modest attire and eschewing clothes of Western provenance does not mean rejecting fashion altogether, especially for a younger generation attracted to new and foreign dress styles. I also trace some intersections between fashion and piety through a focus on changing sartorial practices and the domestication of global stylistic forms. My discussion underlines the highly diverse and personalized strategies through which women balance the sometimes conflicting demands of trend-setting fashions and Muslim norms and how, in the process, they reformulate both the "fashionable" and the "moral."

Partly because of their limited access to literacy and education, Mawri women have often been characterized as ignorant and wedded to tradition. Women, I heard men say in the late 1980s, were too caught up in their veneration of *bori* spirits to commit to Islam. The recent emphasis on religious education spearheaded by Muslim activists of various stripes has enabled women to shape themselves as moral agents and as privileged vehicles of society's spiritual reformation. Paradoxically, renewed concerns about women's moral conduct have paved the way for the devalorization of women, as Malam Awal made clear during our conversation through his insistent focus on women's alleged immaturity and immorality. Chapter 8 examines how the preacher targeted women's supposed lack of virtue and how women reacted by ultimately rejecting him. Local women's responses to the stigmatization of their identities demonstrate a capacity for reflective and thoughtful engagement with Islam and Muslim practice. I argue that women's ability to critically assess Malam Awal's rhetoric was shaped by the very lessons the Sufi preacher taught them. In my closing remarks I revisit some conclusions reached in preceding chapters to insist on the contingent and contested nature of local women's understanding of Islam. Through a brief look at reproductive politics, I show that if women in Dogondoutchi have felt increasingly pressured to emulate a more "orthodox" and allegedly universal Muslim tradition, they nevertheless have found ways to authorize the very practices that are categorized as un-Islamic by promoters of moral reforms even as they strive to live a Muslim life.

In the end, Mawri women in Dogondoutchi have displayed diverse responses to local efforts to redefine womanhood in Muslim terms. In the process of contesting the rules and restrictions imposed on them, ignoring them, or, alternatively, embracing them through new comportment and consumption practices, they have devised multiple ways of being Muslim. This book is an account of how women negotiate their place as daughters, wives, and mothers in an increasingly complex and diversified religious economy. In her study of a Shi'a community in Beirut, Deeb (2006:5) notes that much has been made of the impact of Islamization on national and international politics but comparatively little has been written on how new understandings of Islam have become part of people's lives. By attending to women's experience of the Islamic revival in Dogondoutchi, I have tried to answer Deeb's (2006:6) call for a sustained engagement with the way Muslims regularly "practice and perform piety" in contexts of religious reforms. In Dogondoutchi, women grapple daily with the problem of how to adjust their actions so as to live their lives according to certain moral standards without sacrificing practicality or "wisdom." Their attempts to adhere to Muslim conduct are fraught with inconsistencies and ambiguities. Confronted with multiple ways of "being Muslim," they struggle as they must decide what it means, in practical terms, to lead a Muslim life. Those struggles and the highly personalized ways in which women sometimes go about living a Muslim life are precisely what I document in this book.

A final point: as a small provincial town in what is now the poorest country on earth, Dogondoutchi would not be seen as a place that *matters* in conventional analyses of Islam. Urban elites and foreign observers generally describe "Doutchi" as a quiet, unchanging town at some remove from today's centers of power and commodity production. Certainly, of course, the place bears all the hallmarks of African "tradition": subsistence agriculture, mud homes, illiteracy, spirit possession, and so on. Indeed, because the town is primarily known for the once vibrant practices of spirit devotion and spirit possession taking place in its midst, its overwhelmingly Muslim population is treated as "peripheral to wider trends in Islamic disputation, thought and identity" (Marsden 2005:255). One could even describe it as no more than a blip on the map of the Muslim world. Yet it would be a mistake to characterize Dogondoutchi as an isolated community whose residents are unaware of wider trends—a cultural backwater devoid of significance. Like other "out-of-the-way places" whose multidimensional forms of engagement with the global world have been documented by anthropologists (Piot 1999; Shaw 2002; Tsing 1993), Dogondoutchi has been powerfully shaped by wider processes of transformation. It provides a vibrant and constantly changing context for the negotiation of Muslim identities.

Save for a few notable exceptions (Bowen 1993; Marsden 2005), anthropological studies of Islamic revival movements have largely focused on urban areas where Muslims are assumed to be more cosmopolitan, better educated, and generally more capable of critically engaging with the teachings of Muslim reformists than their rural counterparts. I argue, however, that mapping out rural movements of Islamic reform and revival is crucial to our understanding of the contemporary Muslim world. As Marsden (2005) has convincingly demonstrated for the Chitral region of northern Pakistan, village and small-town Muslims are neither naive nor all accepting in the face of pressing demands that they align their lives more closely with the principles of the Qur'an. In-depth studies of "rural" Muslims should be an essential part of the wider picture of Islamic revivalist movements, because these Muslims, too, are "capable of critical intellectual exchange, and it is through such complex processes that their opinions and, importantly, attitudes have an impact on the societies and networks of which they form an integral part" (Marsden 2005:255). In what follows I portray Dogondoutchi as a setting of competing and contradictory forces, where current discussions and debates over what constitutes Islam speak to larger concerns arising from local residents' uneasy, often uneven, incorporation into global processes of social transformation. It is my hope that *Women and Islamic Revival in a West African Town* not only provides a fresh picture of the generative dynamics of Muslim life in West Africa but also contributes to our understanding of how global forces of change affect local communities by standardizing cultural forms even as they reinforce diversity and promote parochialism.

ACKNOWLEDGMENTS

Much of this ethnography was written in the aftermath of Hurricane Katrina, when, after a two-month stay in Lancaster, Pennsylvania, I returned to
my devastated hometown of New Orleans in October 2005 hoping to simultaneously complete my study and contribute to the rebuilding of the city. As
I now sit back and ponder on all that has happened in the intervening years,
I cannot help but wonder about the form this book might have taken had
Katrina not laid waste to the Gulf Coast. Try as I may, my experience of
writing *Women and Islamic Revival in a West African Town* cannot be dis-
sociated from my life in the immediate post-Katrina period, when everything
that New Orleans returnees did, from gutting homes to collecting trash and
debris from the streets to buying books at local bookshops, was a form of
engagement and a way to participate in the reconstruction of the city and its
economy. Writing can be a lonely and anguishing process. In the midst of my
self-imposed solitude, the feeling of being vested with a mission helped enormously: not unlike the pizzeria owner in my neighborhood who, upon re-
opening his establishment, put up a banner signaling that he was "Rebuilding New Orleans One Pizza at a Time," I convinced myself that every page I
wrote was also part of the collective rebuilding effort. Writing gave me a
sense of purpose that was heightened by the knowledge that Tulane University, my academic home, was facing enormous challenges in the post-Katrina
period. It was my hope that authoring this book would provide a sign (surely,
one of many) that despite the losses it had sustained and the new obstacles it
was confronting, Tulane remained a place of intellectual ferment and scholarship, where research was conducted and books were written.

Although I must ultimately claim authorship, this book belongs to many
others. Almost all its pages bear the traces of encounters, small and large.
The numerous conversations I had with Dogondoutchi residents, some of
whom I have known for more than twenty years, the stimulating feedback
friends and colleagues provided, readers' suggestions, a student's pointed

question, and the insights gleaned from other studies have enriched the text immeasurably. For each and every one of these encounters, I remain deeply grateful.

Fieldwork on *bori* spirit possession conducted in 1988–89 provided the foundation upon which I built the subsequent research project that has resulted in this book. Successive research trips to Dogondoutchi, Niger, in 1994, 2000, 2004, and 2006 were funded by Tulane University's Committee on Research, the Newcomb Foundation at Tulane University, and the Netherlands Ministry of Foreign Affairs. I thank the Nigérien Ministère de l'Enseignment Supérieur, de la Recherche et de la Technologie, for granting me permission to conduct research in Niger. To the people of Dogondoutchi who invited me into their lives and helped me make sense of it all, I cannot begin to convey the extent of my gratitude. I hope I may be forgiven for offering particular appreciation to a limited few: Alhaji Boubacar, Babban Liman, Alhaji Yacoubou, Malam Dubu Amadou "Jimi" Lawal, Malam Buge and his family, Malam Nayoussa, Hajiya Fatima, Hajiya Mariama, Tabagoudou, Fati Moïse Jamila Bassirou, Mariama Awali, and Saadi Nassirou. Adizatou (Dije) Akaki has been a caring friend and a precious source of insight into the lives and struggles of Mawri women. I admire her spirit and resilience. Thanks also to Mahamadou Noma, who assisted me during my 1994 and 2000 fieldworks. On the day I returned to Dogondoutchi in December 2004, I met Salifou Hamidou. His help, support, and friendship proved critical to the success of my project. Salifou worked tirelessly to make my research at once possible and pleasurable; research in Dogondoutchi would be unthinkable without him. I have relied greatly on the assistance offered by members of his family, known in town as the Moïse family, and I am thankful to them. I must also signal my gratitude to Henriette and Gabriel Mayaki for their generous hospitality and for their warm friendship. None of the individuals I met in Dogondoutchi asked me to withhold their names, but I have nevertheless done so to protect their anonymity. Therefore, except for individuals such as the founder of the Awaliyya who are public figures, I have used pseudonyms for the persons who appear in these pages.

The writing of this book was made possible by a fellowship from the American Council of Learned Societies in 2004–2005 and a fellowship from the National Endowment for the Humanities in 2005–2006. In the course of writing this book I have incurred a considerable debt of gratitude to those who have sustained me through sometimes difficult times: aside from extending unlimited support and encouragement, Misty Bastian and Brad

Weiss have nourished me intellectually over the years. When my family and I needed a home, after Katrina made our city uninhabitable, Misty and her husband, John Svatek, opened their home to us, providing critical logistical and emotional assistance and helping us to get back on our feet. Brad, like Misty, has offered insightful commentary on select chapters. Benjamin Soares read chapters 2 and 4 closely and provided much needed criticism and sage advice. Barbara Cooper's suggestions for improving chapter 7 have been immensely helpful. Behrooz Moazami's and Liz McMahon's close readings of chapter 4 have been beneficial as well; if I have not always followed their sensible editorial advice, I am nonetheless grateful to them for pointing out issues that required clarification, and also for their rigorous feedback. Numerous book editors and anonymous readers have read earlier versions of some chapters and left their imprint on them, helping make this a much better book. Many other friends, teachers, and colleagues have offered encouragement, guidance, and insight: Ralph Austen, Janice Boddy, Tim Burke, Conerly Casey, Jean Comaroff, John Comaroff, Debbie Durham, Karen Tranberg Hansen, John Hanson, Do Hodgson, Michael Lambek, Boube Namaiwa, Steven Pierce, Steve Selka, Rosalind Shaw, Abdoulaye Sounaye, Wim van Binsbergen, Rijk van Dijk, and Luise White.

Over the years I have presented drafts of various chapters at Bard College, Tulane University, the University of Toronto, the University of Chicago, the University of Helsinki, Louisiana State University, the International Institute for the Study of Islam in the Modern World in Leiden, Indiana University, Leiden University, and the University of Lisbon; discussants and audiences at these presentations provided invigorating feedback. At Indiana University Press, Dee Mortensen was a supportive editor, expertly shepherding the manuscript through the review and editing process. In their capacity as reviewers for the press, Barbara Cooper and Robert Launay offered valuable and perceptive comments. They identified inconsistencies and ambiguities that had crept into the narrative and gently pushed me to rethink a concept or rephrase an argument. This would not be the book it is without their tremendous help.

I reserve my deepest gratitude for my husband, Bill More. He has supported me in crucial ways, at times sacrificing his own interests to ensure that I could bring this project to fruition. I dedicate this book to him. My daughters Margaux, Éléonore, and Julia have shown more patience and indulgence toward my book writing than I could ever have hoped for. Knowing that they share my commitment with social justice and my involvement in scholarship has been a source of joy and satisfaction. Finally, although this book has drawn heavily from the input of others, I alone am responsible for any remaining shortcomings. I hope that the book does justice to those who so generously helped me and guided me as I explored their world and their lives.

*   *   *

Two of the chapters were published elsewhere in a different version. Chapter 3 appeared as "Debating Muslims, Disputed Practices: Struggles for the Realization of an Alternative Moral Order in Niger," in John and Jean Comaroff's edited volume *Civil Society and the Political Imagination in Africa: Critical Perspectives* (University of Chicago Press, 1999). Chapter 7 appeared as "How Is a Girl to Marry without a Bed? Women's Value, Wealth, and Domesticity in Niger," in Wim van Binsbergen and Rijk van Dijk's edited volume *Situating Globality: African Agency in the Appropriation of Global Culture* (Brill, 2004). A portion of chapter 5 appeared as "Witchcraft, Blood-Sucking Spirits, and the Demonization of Islam in Dogondoutchi, Niger" in *Cahiers d'Études Africaines* 189–190 (2008): 131–160. Permission to publish this material here is gratefully acknowledged.

WOMEN AND ISLAMIC REVIVAL
IN A WEST AFRICAN TOWN

GENDER AND ISLAM IN
DOGONDOUTCHI

1

Sai da addini aka ci gaba—Only with Islam can you develop.
—*Izala preacher, Dogondoutchi, 2004*

The things we did before, Islam now forbids. Like permitting women to leave their homes so that men can see them. That is wrong, that is not what Muslim women do.
—*Muslim scholar and critic of Izala, Dogondoutchi, 2004*

Diatribes booming from strategically placed loudspeakers have become familiar fixtures in Dogondoutchi ever since the early 1990s. Whether accusing youth of debauchery, castigating women for ostentatious spending patterns, or urging tradition-bound Muslims to abandon their allegedly incorrect practices, the raspy voices of Muslim clerics remonstrating the faithful are heard in every neighborhood. Throughout Niger, this intensification of sermon delivery coincided with the emergence of an independent anti-Sufi movement of Nigerian origin, the Jama'atu Izalat al-Bid'a wa Iqamat al-Sunna (Society for the Removal of Innovation and the Restoration of Tradition), referred to as Izala, in what had been, until then, a country ostensibly oriented toward Sufism (Meunier 1998). In West Africa, Sufism has been conventionally understood through the hierarchical relation between a charismatic religious guide, referred to as *shayk* (or *marabout* in French colonial parlance), and his disciples. In Senegal, where the majority of Muslims identify as Sufis, Sufi religious leaders have not only initiated disciples into the order and provided guidance in religious matters, but they have also played an important role in local politics and society. Largely because of the prominent position they occupy in the politico-religious landscape, Sufi orders in Senegal have been the object of extraordinary scholarly scrutiny.[1] The attention received particularly by the Mourides has helped reinforce the problematic notion that they typify the experience of Sufis elsewhere in Africa. Yet, as Launay (1992) and Otayek (1988) have pointed out for Côte d'Ivoire and Burkina Fasso, respectively, Sufism in West Africa is not exemplified by the Senegalese case, where there is a prevailing sense of corporate identity among members of the same order and rivalry between orders. Moreover, the conventional wisdom that Islam in Africa is essentially Sufi has blinded scholars to the diversity of Muslim discourses and practices in the region (Otayek and Soares 2007). Although Sufi orders clearly have exerted considerable influence on Islam in Africa, it is important to recognize that they do not enjoy everywhere the visibility that orders such as the Mourides enjoy in Senegal. Writing about Islam and Muslims in contemporary Africa therefore implies thinking "beyond the long-standing and ongoing preoccupation with Sufi orders" (Soares 2007b:320) and attending to the fluid, shifting, and heterogeneous nature of Muslim discourses and practices.

In Dogondoutchi, membership in Sufi orders is restricted to a select few who assemble in the evening around a white cloth to engage in the recitation of a special litany of prayers following the performance of the sunset prayer, *mangariba*. They tend to be Qur'anic scholars, though they need not be. In fact, not all local Qur'anic teachers are affiliated with an order. Aside from encouraging the recitation of *zikiri* (recitation of the names of God), Sufis approve the use of Qur'anic amulets (typically, verses of the Qur'an written on slips of papers folded and wrapped in leather) and the performance of certain rituals (such as the celebration of the Prophet's birthday). They promote, along with the veneration of saintly figures, the redistributive ethos around which much of everyday life is ordered in local communities.

Although few Muslims formally follow the Sufi path (*darika*), many are loosely identified as 'yan darika (members of a Sufi order)[2] partly because they ostensibly adhere to practices that—in the absence of a clearly defined sense of collective Sufi identity—are loosely defined as Sufi but also, and more important, because they oppose Izala reformism. They cannot be said to share a unified vision of Islam and, in fact, exist as a group only in the context of their opposition to Izala reformists. Some see themselves as representing the religious orthodoxy currently threatened primarily by Izala reforms and also by Malam Awal's own revivalist project. Although I have tried not to lump all those outside the revivalist circles under one designation, I refer to them as "traditionalist" Muslims—those who claim to follow inherited religious traditions and reject "new" ones—when it seems relevant to underscore that their criticisms of reformist Muslims routinely invoke tradition when they are compelled to articulate what "being Muslim" means to them. Put differently, their religious orientation as traditionalists acquires salience precisely when they voice their objections to the Izala vision of Islam and Muslim society, because in so doing they give shape to their own conceptions of Islam as inherited traditions. Elsewhere I use the designation "*'yan darika*" not because I wish to treat the clusters of diversely affiliated Muslims collectively, but because it is the term used by Hausa-speakers to identify Muslims who are not part of the Izala community. Here, again, identification as a *'dan darika* (member of a Sufi order) is predicated not on a shared vision of Islam but on people's antagonistic relation toward Izala. In other words, one is a *'dan darika* based not on what one is but on what one is *not*. In this context, defining someone as a *'dan darika* says remarkably little about the form of religiosity this person may engage in—if at all. Not all individuals classified as *'yan darika* by local observers are observant Muslims, even if, as often occurs, being Muslim is integral to their identity. The difficulties I faced in trying to describe the diversity of Muslim orientations in Dogondoutchi suggest the slipperiness of religious identities while reminding us of the inadequacy of our analytical concepts (such as "traditionalist" Islam) to capture the complexity and fluidity of religious affiliations.

The two major Sufi orders in Niger are the Tijaniyya and the Qadiriyya. Usman 'dan Fodio, who in the 1800s led a *jihad* against the Islamicized Hausa states and founded the Sokoto Caliphate, was a member of the Qadiriyya.[3] Many of the wealthiest merchants of Niger belong to this order, whose members are locally referred to as *'yan sadalu* because they pray with their arms at their sides (a position known as *sadalu*). The Tijaniyya, founded in Algeria by Sheikh Ahmad al-Tijani in the eighteenth century, was later introduced in Niger in the 1950s by members of the Niassiyya branch from Kano, Nigeria. Because they pray with their arms crossed on their chests (in the *kabalu* position), members of the Tijaniyya were henceforth known as *'yan kabalu*. Initially a controversy surfaced between *'yan kabalu* and *'yan sadalu* over prayer styles. The Muslim community became polarized over whether one ought to pray with arms crossed or outstretched. Eventually *'yan kabalu* and *'yan sadalu* resolved their differences. The current absence of rivalry between them, and their lack of a corporate sense of identity, means that few residents are able to differentiate a Niassiyya Tijani from a Qadiri. Some people told me that the two orders merged after resolving their disagreement over prayer styles, but this is far from the case. Members of each *darika* (Sufi order) must engage in the group recitation of prayers particular to that *darika*. Niassiyya Tijanis thus perform the *wazifa* (chanted phrases, including the ninety-nine names of God) daily and the *hadra* (including the recitation of the Qur'an and other devotional texts) on Fridays.

To counter the supposedly corrupting influence of Sufism, the Jama'atu Izalat al-Bid'a wa Iqamat al-Sunna (henceforth, Izala) emerged in northern Nigeria, later expanding into Niger via the Hausa commercial networks straddling the Niger-Nigeria border. As its name indicates, Izala advocates a return to a "pure" Islam and promotes conservative moral standards.[4] 'Yan Izala (members of Izala), believing that current troubles are a consequence of the failure to live a proper Muslim life, condemn the perceived syncretism of local Sufi orders and their "incorrect" readings of the Qur'an. In an effort to align themselves with a putatively universal Islamic tradition anchored in the Middle East, they urge everyone to reject indigenous traditions as well as Western values on the basis that practices not mentioned in the Qur'an are cultural contaminations. Regardless of whether they have a formal Sufi affiliation, all opponents of their reforms are identified as *'yan darika* (members of a Sufi order).

Aside from claiming that there is no traditional culture outside Islam, *'yan* Izala have criticized the Nigérien government for failing to solve social problems which they believe are caused by irreligious behavior. What the country needs, *'yan* Izala argue, is a return to God's ethical commandments for social organization and personal conduct. Their criticism of the state and of their religious opponents' Muslim practices endeared them to Muslims dissatisfied with the status quo. The reformist movement spread quickly thanks to its ability to present itself as a solution to the country's problems. Izala's vision of a lost golden age was fervently embraced by devout Muslim elites, but it is largely among disenchanted youths that the movement secured its following. Some of these youths were educated young men with some Western-style secondary schooling whose professional aspirations were frustrated by a shrinking labor market unable to absorb the growing numbers of job seekers. Others were illiterate youths who saw their future imperiled by economic decline, land shortages, and shrinking prospects, and for whom Izala provided the vision of a possible future.

Those who perceived the sweeping anti-Sufi reforms to be intrusive attacks against long-established Muslim traditions emphatically opposed *'yan* Izala's attempts to align local religious practices with a supposedly universal Islamic model. Prior to the emergence of Izala, Muslims in Dogondoutchi, whether or not they accomplished the daily prayers, rarely questioned the dictates of a faith that had come to define the status quo for most Nigériens. Izala's call to reform generated conflicts and anxiety over the definition of Muslim identity and compelled many to reconsider what being Muslim meant even as they resisted Izala views. In May 1997, within this context of intensified questioning, while adversaries remained locked in a struggle over the authoritative use of Islam, Mahamane Awal arrived in town.

A preacher of wide renown, Mahamane Awal—usually referred to as Malam Awal (Malam meaning "Teacher," a respectful term of address)—had been summoned by local "orthodox" elites anxious to cut short Izala's nascent success and reenergize a deeply divided Muslim community. Thanks to his reputation as a ruthless critic of Izala, his formidable rhetorical skills, and his magnetic personality, he was a highly solicited guest among Nigérien elites throughout the country who hoped to revitalize the roots of Islam. On the day of his arrival in Dogondoutchi, Malam Awal quickly launched a vitriolic diatribe against the Izala ethos, accusing local reformists of misusing the Qur'an through their ignorance, selfishness, and dishonesty. Those who expected the distinguished visitor to support the vision of Islam shared by the anti-Izala factions were mistaken, however. Within days, it became abundantly clear to everyone that the reformist project would not be the sole target of Awal's denunciatory sermons.

The preacher found much to criticize in the practices of traditionalist clerics whom he accused of greed and incompetence. While alarm and outrage spread among traditionalist ranks, crowds listening to the preacher's captivating sermons grew daily. For ordinary Muslims caught between the rigid intolerance of Izala preachers and the burdensome financial demands of traditionalist clerics, Malam Awal's message was uniquely attractive: it encouraged the performance of Sufi rituals deemed central to the faith while freeing them from the supposedly abusive authority of Muslim clerics. Resonating with Izala efforts to redefine female virtue, the message focused on women as repositories of a newly prescribed Islamic morality. Numerous Mawri women embraced Awal's revivalist message and deployed, through dress and deportment, moral imperatives that defined them as upholders of purity and as members of what soon became known as the Awaliyya order. Others defiantly resisted Malam Awal's design of a new "sacred architecture" of sexuality (Mernissi 1987:xvi), viewing it as a menace to their autonomy and religious identity. Meanwhile, issues regarding women's access to education and income, rights to divorce, and the mobility and visibility they should be permitted were vigorously discussed.

In the early 1990s Izala's success in promoting religious rationalism appeared to signal the decline of certain Sufi-related practices such as the veneration of saintly Muslim leaders, the chanting of *zikiri,* and the use of Qur'anic *materia medica* for healing and protection. The coming of Malam

Awal changed all that. His presence in Dogondoutchi, the preacher told everyone, had been mandated by God who wished to make Dogondoutchi the hub of a new Sufi order where "true" Islam would flourish. In his sermons Awal strove for spectacular performances aimed to arouse people's moral imagination and draw them into the Awaliyya community. Owing to his eloquence and audacity, he rapidly emerged as a pivotal figure of the local politico-religious landscape.

Though he clearly followed in the footsteps of his Sufi predecessors, Malam Awal was not what could be called a traditionalist Muslim. On the contrary, he was an innovative and iconoclastic leader. He confronted the "corrupt" elitism of local Muslim leaders, helping foster the notion, already popularized by 'yan Izala, that onerous social obligations, such as gifts of money to Muslim religious specialists after the birth of one's child, victimized the poor and should be abandoned. Yet at the same time he opposed Izala's egalitarianism which he saw as misguided, revolutionary, and altogether un-Islamic. By promoting himself as a leader and a visionary, he reanimated the notion of the Sufi master who received unconditional devotion from his followers. Muslims, Hoffman (1995:3) notes, have developed "a nostalgia for the past" as well as a perception that the generation of the Prophet Muhammad and his companions represented the pinnacle of spirituality and morality for humanity. Each succeeding generation contributes further to the decline of the Muslim community, the effects of which can be mitigated only by the presence of a "renewer" once every hundred years. For many Dogondoutchi residents, Awal was the renewer who had come to revitalize the local Muslim community.

Countering the reformists' efforts to banish "magic" and other un-Islamic practices, Malam Awal convinced many that ritual control of the occult was a vital dimension of Muslim authority—an authority he claimed solely for himself as the performer of miracles and the blessed leader of the Awaliyya order. He taught adepts how to worship and how to perform the long prayers and spiritual exercises that he had composed; he instructed them to be patient, honest, and charitable; and he spoke at length about the need to resist the devil's temptations. The reforms he instituted to rid society of corruption stretched far beyond the domain of worship, penetrating deep into the experiential fabric of everyday life. From dress to domestic life, from sexuality to the semantics of civility,[5] he set out to reform, cleanse, and control the community, thereby supposedly saving it from moral depravity. Dressed in immaculate white, Awal's adepts were generally recognizable from afar. At the urging of the religious leader, they wore their prayer beads around their necks, in direct contravention of Izala and *darika* teachings.[6]

The preacher campaigned, paradoxically, in favor of moderate bride-wealth payments, promoted women's education, and encouraged frugality, thereby joining with the reformists whose model of utilitarian moral economy he had originally been invited to criticize. Like Muslim reformists, he required women to cover their bodies and promoted the seclusion of women, he opposed the implementation of a Family Code (aimed at protecting the rights of women and children in matters of divorce, inheritance, etc.), and he lectured at length about the dangers of female permissiveness. At first his attacks on "corrupt" scholarly elites and his urging of moral restraint and frugality found wide support among local Muslims eager to relinquish burdensome social obligations yet wary of the joylessness of Izala life. Muslims, he never tired of telling his supporters, should devote their lives to serving God through, among other things, the performance of religious chants. Serving God also meant looking to Sufi scholars for enlightenment and inspiration. By appearing to personify, through his life path, the trajectory of other saintly figures of Islamic history, Awal rejuvenated Sufi traditions while enhancing his appeal as a world renouncer. Thanks to his clever use of technology (rituals were videotaped and sermons tape-recorded to be broadcast at opportune moments), he emerged as something of a media personality—a religious "superstar" (Birman 2006; Soares 2004a:43) as well as a defender of truth and justice who had set out to re-moralize a society riddled with conflict, misery, and impiety.

Within a few years, however, tales of spiritual trickery, financial deceits, and sexual exploitation surfaced, and some of Awal's disciples came to see their leader in a less positive light. Feeling that they had been misled by the preacher's message of renewal, they progressively left the Awaliyya to reintegrate the clusters of diversely situated Muslims whose "group" identity only emerges in the context of their opposition to 'yan Izala. Malam Awal was not the person he pretended to be, they declared to justify their shifting loyalties, thereby echoing the claims of Nigérien secularists who characterized the controversial preacher as a charlatan and the epitome of all they found objectionable in "traditional" or "folk" Islam.[7] Among the disillusioned were many senior women who had originally championed the charismatic leader's vision of a reinvigorated moral order and who had worked tirelessly to support his mission and promote his reforms.

Less than a decade after his triumphant beginnings as a renewer of the faith, the once powerful Awal had lost much of the support he initially enjoyed among the town's residents. By 2005 his caustic admonishments that Muslims shed their sinful habits and follow the righteous path were no longer transmitted daily by the loudspeakers of the Awaliyya mosque. Still, the preacher continued to garner considerable attention for his flamboyant demeanor and controversial interventions in public life. His appeals that followers resist the state-sponsored vaccination campaigns against polio in 2003 and 2004 (discussed briefly below) were but an instance of the kind of influence Mahamane Awal continued to exert on local "Muslim politics" (Eickelman and Piscatori 1996). Whether we can agree with those who believe that his career as a holy man is essentially over, in the last decade Malam Awal certainly has had a profound impact on the local religious scene, helping to frame various debates centering on questions of Islamic practice (which traditions are part of Islam and which are not), the boundaries of Muslim virtue, and the definition of pious womanhood. It is precisely around the much publicized, though short-lived, career of Mahamane Awal as a religious leader that my account of gender and religious practice in Dogondoutchi unfolds.

The wondrous tales Malam Awal told about his life, the stories of miracles his followers circulated, the controversies provoked by his views on marriage, health care, and domesticity, and the accusations of chicanery and charlatanism that contributed to the decline of his popularity are not simply about the man who managed to capture the moral imagination of an entire town. They are, more fundamentally, also discussions about Islam, and they underscore major concerns of this book. With the spread of Izala, and the subsequent inception of the Awaliyya order, religious institutions in Dogondoutchi have undergone significant transformations, leading to the emergence of new ways of being Muslim and new modes of defining what is "Islamic" and what is not. In the context of these transformations, Muslims have become acutely aware of divergences between their beliefs and practices, and the beliefs and practices of others, Muslim or not. Many attribute these differences to ignorance (*jahilci*) based on the notion that Islam is superior to all other religions and that only one conception of Islam—usually their own—is correct. However, the complex unfolding of allegiances and rivalries over time also suggests that religious identities, far from being stable, are shifting, temporal, and emergent. How Dogondoutchi residents, and more specifically female residents, negotiate their position as social actors and moral agents in the ever fluctuating and tangled field of Muslim identities is the analytical focus of this book.

My exploration of Islam and Muslim practices in Dogondoutchi has been inspired by Talad Asad's concept of "discursive tradition." According to Asad (1986:14), Islam is "neither a distinctive social structure nor a hetero-

geneous collection of beliefs, artifacts, customs, and morals. It is a tradition."
Anthropologists writing about Islam must therefore begin, "as Muslims do,
from the concept of a discursive tradition that includes and relates itself to
the founding texts of the Qur'an and the Hadith [the preserved records of the
Prophet's words and deeds]" (Asad 1986:14). This means essentially acknowledging that Islam consists of discourses "that seek to instruct practitioners
regarding the correct form and purpose of a given practice, that precisely
because it is established, has a history" (Asad 1986:14). Tradition here is not
an unchanging set of cultural prescriptions, a mere repetition of old forms
that buffers its practitioners from a threatening modernity; instead it is a set
of discourses that instruct how a practice is best secured and provides justification for why it should be maintained, modified, or rejected. In other words,
Islam is about "the practitioners' conceptions of what is *apt performance*"
(Asad 1986:15). Asad's concept of discursive tradition enables us to move
beyond the problematic distinction between "orthodox" and "folk" Islam, and
consider what Islam might mean to ordinary Muslims, regardless of their degree of literacy and education and their religious ideologies. What makes a
practice Islamic, Asad argues (1986:15), is that it is "authorized by the discursive traditions of Islam, and is so taught to Muslims." From this perspective, the competing modes of religious discourses that have emerged in
Dogondoutchi are all Islamic. Far from being frozen in time, these traditions
are continually reformulated, and the practices they authorize acquire significance insofar as they are thought to be historical, established, and authentic. In this book I explore how Islamic tradition is discursively shaped in the
context of emerging arguments about how to define "true" Islam.

Ever since Izala's moralizing rhetoric about the "political economy of
contested symbols and meanings" (Peletz 1993:68), competing discourses
about "true" Islam have played out their disagreements on the contested ter-
rains of gender and domesticity. Amid intensified concerns that the introduction of Western mores has produced corrupt lifestyles and provoked a loss
of spiritual values, women in Dogondoutchi have become the privileged
vehicles for expressing the aspirations, anxieties, and ambivalence associated
with changing perceptions of social realities. The sartorial aspects of modesty, the rules governing women's education, and the format weddings should
take have become the focal points of verbal and visual debates within the
Muslim community. If women are seen by some as vessels of tradition, they
can also be viewed as the prime embodiment of Muslim revival (Ong 1995).
Although women of any age, status, and religious affiliation are increasingly
compelled to deploy through dress and demeanor the changing signs of piety

and modesty signifying their Muslim identity, many find subtle, and some-times not so subtle, ways to resist the increasingly strict norms that have come to define the moral woman in Niger.

By centering on the emerging transformations in gender roles and modes of religiosity in the provincial town of Dogondoutchi, this book explores three interrelated issues: (1) how Islam, at a time of growing awareness of alternative interpretations of the Qur'an, functions as the privileged vehicle for the invention and sustenance of a moral order; (2) how Mawri women have become central to the moral order in Dogondoutchi; and (3) how women themselves actively participate in ongoing debates about Muslim woman-hood, at times resisting emerging redefinitions of their roles that, allegedly, are based on closer readings of the Qur'an. In a country where the recent lib-eralization of politics, markets, and media has led to the proliferation of reli-gious debates, disagreements over the management of wealth, the ritual and sartorial dimensions of piety, and the ordering of social spaces underscore wider concerns about changing definitions of gendered realities. Gender politics, in turn, crystallizes more diffuse but still pervasive anxieties about the shifting boundaries of the moral community. In this book I examine how newly emerging Muslim ideologies of gender, power, and domesticity have enabled Dogondoutchi women to securely anchor their religious identity as guardians of moral and spiritual values while at the same time limiting their powers of autonomy and self-expression.

Muslim Identities in Dogondoutchi: Definitions and Boundaries

Islam, in the Arewa region of Niger, is a fairly new import. The historical record suggests that this region remained impervious to the influences of commerce and religion much longer than the surrounding Hausa-speaking regions, and that only in the last century did Mawri people turn to Islam. These changes were not without costs. Elderly informants proudly recounted how, as children, they had to fight their own parents to attend Qur'anic school. Because they were the first in their families to convert to Islam, they faced ostracism and endured mistreatment. In those days Qur'anic education took place at night, by wood fires students would light (both to keep warm and to break the veil of darkness) and at dawn, before elders could make de-mands on their labor. In compensation for the education they received, Qur'anic students also worked in their teacher's fields, assisting with sowing, weeding, and harvesting.

Partly because it has only recently been Islamized, Dogondoutchi remains known throughout Niger as a bastion of "fetishism," much to the chagrin of pious Muslims who are loathe to revisit the region's pre-Islamic past. When tradition and cultural heritage are discussed in newspapers addressed to French-educated elites, "*les féticheurs de Doutchi*" tend to figure prominently in these accounts. In recent years, however, religious practices subsumed under the rubric of "fetishism" have become marginalized by the growing ascendancy of Islam. Increasingly fewer residents participate in the spirit possession performances known as *bori*. In every neighborhood, the amplified call to prayer periodically interrupts daily activities with its gritty, piercing sounds, "permeat[ing] the consciousness of believer and nonbeliever alike" (Delaney 1990:516) and setting the tempo of daily life. Many men publicly accomplish the five daily prayers. Following ritual ablutions, they join friends and neighbors for prayer at one of the neighborhood mosques, often nothing but a humble prayer ground delimited by a neat row of stones and on which plastic mats have been placed. Muslim women pray in the confines of their homes, if and when they are not busy with domestic chores. Though postmenopausal women are allowed to take part in public worship, they never do. If they manage to retreat to an isolated corner of the compound to perform their ablutions and prayer, younger women who cannot so easily disengage themselves from daily preoccupations often skip prayer altogether. Whereas five times a day men generally set aside a time and place away from worldly concerns, women, especially those with young children, often pray in noisy, distracting conditions. Consequently, "there is undeniably a difference in the experience of *salla* [prayer] for women and men; for women, it is less associated with collective times and spaces, it is often performed alone, and it is imbued with the distractions of daily life" (Cooper 2006:380).

Because of how it punctuates the texture and rhythm of life in Muslim communities, *salla* has become synonymous with Islam. Regardless of whether they actually perform the five daily prayers, Muslims are known as *masu salla* (those who pray) as distinct from "those who sacrifice" (referred to as *masutsafa*, fetishists, or *'yan bori*—members of *bori*). Because *salla* has come to designate exclusively Muslim prayers, Christians generally do not use the word when referring to their own forms of worship. Muslims "pray," whereas Christians "read." Muslims worship in *masallatai*—houses of prayer; Christians, in contrast, attend services in churches, which local residents uniformly refer to as *l'église*.[8] In recent years mosques have sprouted up in almost every street, motivated by the widely held belief that building a mosque facilitates access to paradise. Wealthy merchants finance elaborate constructions, complete with minarets, domes, and columns (inspired at times by the Saudi architecture they admired during the pilgrimage to Mecca), and others invest in more modest structures, a simple shelter made of thatch and wood. In Dogondoutchi, prayer grounds now dot the townscape with startling regularity. They far outnumber the spirit shrines that remain scattered about as durable relics of a time when local people expressed their commitment to the *iskoki* (spirits) by shedding sacrificial blood for them.[9]

Within the Muslim community, the past is self-consciously invoked as a time of backwardness, impiety, and ignorance—*jahiliyya*. "Backwardness" is not simply the province of *bori* and other spirit-centered practices, however. Under its new connotation as illiteracy, it has become part of Islam as well. "In the past," local residents occasionally admit with a twinge of discomfort, Muslims prayed the wrong way, indulged in "un-Islamic" activities, and did not know that women had to cover their bodies. Because, like other Muslims elsewhere, they largely assumed "to be Muslim was to be like them" (Bernal 1994:50), they did not entertain the possibility that their tradition was not part of the orthodoxy. These mistakes, people swiftly point out, have since been corrected. "Today" Muslims know how to worship properly, because they have access to knowledge (*ilimi*) and education (*tarbiyya*). Whether they discuss doctrinal matters or ritual practices, members of Izala routinely affirm their own convictions in light of past religious errors. Because most Muslims in Niger have limited training in Arabic, they (like their opponents) do not focus on the exegesis of Islamic texts in their debates about Islam but on the fine points of ritual performance.

Because their main obligation is to convince those who call themselves Muslims to abandon all heresy and conform to the sacred Scriptures, these reform-minded Muslims are referred to as fundamentalists or Islamists by scholars and commentators who see "family resemblances" between the Izala project and Islamic movements elsewhere. Fundamentalism can be broadly defined as a militant desire to defend religion against the onslaught of modern, secular culture, based on the assumption of a fixed truth that has its source in the Scriptures. Besides referring to a belief in the inviolability of sacred texts, however, the term "fundamentalism" connotes fanaticism and bigotry. Rather than clarifying the Izala conception of Islam, the word reflects our hostility toward movements of this sort (Munson 1993:152). It also breeds misconceptions. Fundamentalism is inevitably associated with conservative ideologies of gender, family, and society, which, in the Izala case, only inadequately recapitulate key values and attitudes. Mindful of the cautionary notes sounded by Harris (1994) and others on the use of the term "fundamentalism," I refer to 'yan Izala as reformist Muslims in order to transcend the well-worn dichotomy between "modernist" and "conservative" Islam, and to stress the ambiguities inherent in the Izala vision of Muslim society.

Elsewhere the term "Islamist" has been invoked as a generic concept referring to individuals or organizations aiming to renew and reform existing social conditions (Hodgkin 1998; Westerlund 1997). Although it might appear more neutral than "fundamentalist," "Islamist" is not a designation Nigérien Izala members employ when speaking of themselves, whereas the term "reformist" reflects an Izala self-designating concept that refers to the suppression of certain undesirable innovations and a return to the golden age of Islam. 'Yan Izala, whom French-educated, secular Muslim Nigériens often refer to as "*Izalistes*" or "*intégristes*," are at times identified as "Wahhabi." In French West Africa, "Wahhabi" is a label French colonials somewhat indiscriminately attached to Muslim leaders whom they perceived as a potential threat to their administration. As Brenner (2001) notes, the term was used pejoratively, connoting fanaticism and danger. When French administrators intent on curbing the progress of Islam used the term, it mattered little whether those they labeled "Wahhabi" were followers of Muhammad b. 'Abd al-Wahhab, the founder of what is today the dominant form of Islam in Saudi Arabia and Qatar. Although 'yan Izala generally look to Saudi Arabia for inspiration and consider as a key text the *Kitab al-tawhid* (written by Muhammad b. 'Abd al-Wahhab to expose the Salafi doctrine), in Dogondoutchi they do not speak of themselves as Wahhabi.[10] In fact, few Dogondoutchi residents know the precise history of the Izala movement, which is currently, the largest Islamic reform movement in West Africa, with newly established centers in Cameroon and Benin.

Because, as noted above, they routinely invoke inherited tradition to legitimize their ritual practices and justify their opposition to Izala, I refer to self-described Sufis and defenders of Sufi-inspired religious practices as "traditionalists" whenever appropriate. Included in this category are individuals who do not necessarily share a unified vision of Islam. Nor can they be said to constitute a well-defined group with distinguishable institutions, practices, agendas, and ideological claims. For one thing, many Dogondoutchi residents who call themselves Muslim possess a minimal knowledge of the Qur'an. Their limited understanding of the Qur'an and ignorance of Arabic in no way reflects their degree of sincerity and piety. Nonetheless, if some Mawri appear to be very devout Muslims, others are less so. Thus Dogondoutchi residents exhibit remarkable diversity in the intensity of their religious commitment and the expression of their Muslim identity. In recent years new forms of Muslim religiosity have emerged in tandem with new models of personhood and public life, and new patterns of consumption, thereby further contributing to the plurality of religious expressions. Paradoxically this religious diversity has been countered, in part, by the recent polarization of the Islamic field. The spread of Izala, as Kane (2003) rightfully notes, has largely contributed to the hardening of doctrinal differences and the sharpening of religious identities, with the result that the majority of Dogondoutchi residents are identified as either 'yan darika (regardless of whether they belong to a Sufi order) or 'yan Izala. Upon Awal's arrival, as we saw, a third faction, the 'yan Awaliyya, emerged in the late 1990s, complicating the neat opposition between Sufis and anti-Sufis in the local religious vernacular.

Since its inception, Izala in Nigeria has splintered into several hostile factions (see Umar 2001).[11] On the other side of the border, in Niger, the association has managed to keep a more united front, gathering into its fold all those who challenge the authority of Muslim elites and seek to align local religious practices with what they define as "correct" Islam. This hardly means that Nigérien 'yan Izala are unified behind a common vision of Muslim society, however. Within the association, disagreements are common, regarding, for instance, whether women should be allowed to work outside the home. Educated reformist Muslims who tend to have fairly liberal views on the "woman question" are criticized by their more conservative counterparts who seclude their wives, believing that female permissiveness leads to adultery and, by implication, to society's downfall. Thus neither among 'yan Izala nor among those who challenge them can we speak of a Muslim community unified by a consensus, although members of each faction will close rank when "one of theirs" is targeted by opponents' criticisms.

If the emergence of reformist Islam has promoted the polarization of identities, it remains that some Muslims who consider Islam a personal religion rather than a social movement cannot easily be identified as members of either the traditionalists, the reformists, or the Awaliyya faction. Meunier (1998) refers to this population of mostly French-educated Muslims as "rationalists." I prefer to call them "secularists," a term that bears none of the negative implications that "rationalist" connotes for those outside that category who, by default, are defined as lacking rationality. In Dogondoutchi, the secularists, most of whom are civil servants transplanted to this region, remain a distinct minority. In my experience they are generally reluctant to become involved in local religious debates; they have plenty to say, however, about the diverse array of "heroic fighters" (Öncü 2006:242) and charismatic figures, such as Malam Awal, who have surfaced with the liberalization of the religious economy. They speak critically of Muslim religious leaders who challenge the state.

Like other media-savvy religious activists who package Islam as an alternative basis for community construction (Schulz 2006; Soares 2007a), Malam Awal attracted controversy for his vociferous criticisms of prominent clerics and his denunciation of state-sponsored health programs. When the state, in partnership with the World Health Organization and the United Nations Foundation, dispatched health workers to inoculate children against polio in 2003 and 2004, Awal instructed his followers to bar them from their homes. These health campaigns, he warned, were part of a Western plot to sterilize Muslims; instead of promoting public interest, he claimed, the Nigérien government was following the dictates of foreign administrations looking to lower the fertility of Muslim girls and ultimately weaken Muslims worldwide.[12] Awal's implication was that public servants and health care workers were dangerous agents of foreign powers and should not be trusted. Their claim to serve the health needs of the community was simply a ploy to earn the trust of unsuspecting parents and facilitate the sterilization process. At a time of growing disillusion with state-sponsored programs loudly proclaiming commitment to the national good, the preacher's unsettling message provided an effective critique of Western-based models of public health. It exposed the cost of blindly embracing technologies, such as contraception, that, for many Muslims, are synonymous with immorality and a loss of spiritual values. Aside from affording unparalleled insight into the fashioning of religious authority, Awal's actions—which local religious leaders strongly condemned—point to the limitations of assuming that the dissemination of media contributes uniformly to the standardization of Islamic tradition (Eickelman and Anderson 1999). Indeed, as scholars have noted (Eickelman and Piscatori 1996), the use of media technology has enabled a new generation of Muslim preachers and activists to promote religious agendas that directly contradict Muslim orthodoxy. Awal is one of these media-savvy *mala-mai* (Qur'anic teachers) who call into question the authority of the *ulama* (Muslim scholars), thereby contributing to the further diversification of the Islamic landscape. Note also that fertility—and the disciplinary apparatus controlling it—appears to be a central trope in Malam Awal's vision of moral order, an issue I return to later. Aside from spreading alarmist claims about the endangered fertility of young Muslim girls, the preacher routinely spoke out against family planning. In his opinion, those who resorted to contraception to limit the size of their families only demonstrated their lack of faith in

God and in His ability to provide for His people. There was nothing in the Qur'an, Awal insisted, relating to birth spacing, and therefore contraceptives were *haram* (forbidden).

Regardless of the religious affiliation they claim, Muslims in Dogondoutchi are increasingly concerned with moral reform and improvement. Although the Izala rhetoric of reform and purification did not convince everyone to abandon their supposedly incorrect ways of being Muslim, it has nevertheless pushed many Muslims to "Islamicize" their own discourses, thereby underscoring the notion of a widespread return to Islam (Otayek and Soares 2007:23). Now even those who reject the Izala project speak of seclusion and veiling as remedies against immorality. Non-Izala girls now wear the *hijabi* (veil), once an index of reformist identity. Reformist Muslims for their part appear to have progressively relaxed the restrictive ethos they initially established to rescue society from moral degradation. The once strict rules governing Izala marriage celebrations have been loosened, and so it is harder to trace the distinctive contours of Izala and *darika* identities, flexible, changing, and intersecting as they have become. This suggests that the opposition between reformist and anti-reformist Muslims (or, for that matter, *'yan* Awaliyya) vastly oversimplifies the fragmented, yet also fluid, nature of the religious landscape in Niger.[13] Although analyzable as distinct domains of experience, each with its defining characteristics, Izala reformism, the Awaliyya, and the practices of those who oppose both Izala and the Awaliyya have actually undergone significant transformations, as individuals on every side of the religious split negotiate (and renegotiate) their positions within these competing ideological formations. Rather than characterizing the religious field as a clean break between three opposite camps, we must understand the complex ways in which people in Dogondoutchi selectively draw from these various orientations at different times to forge new Muslim identities. This book is an effort to map the new configurations that have resulted from these creative recombinations. Note that although Nigérien society as a whole does not fall neatly into opposed blocs, such as reformist and traditionalist, still it is in terms of opposition that people in Niger define religious difference and account for the disagreements that have surfaced about the definition of Islamic tradition. Whether they come from the country or the city, the Zarma-speaking western region or the Hausaphone East, ordinary Nigériens tend to characterize Muslims as either reform-minded *'yan* Izala or tradition-bound *'yan darika*. As I hope to show, the reality on the ground is far more complex.

Islam in Anthropology

Based on Marx's and Weber's theories, many anthropologists have long assumed that modernization would lead to a worldwide progressive decline in religion, or at least its withdrawal to the private arena. An icon of tradition, religion in the so-called Third World was to be increasingly washed away by a rising tide of education and urbanization. From this perspective, not only were religion and modernization incompatible but secularization was a sine qua non for modernization. The assumption that religion is a major hindrance to development, however, has proved generally invalid. Far from fading under the onslaught of colonial rule and later the rise of the modern state, people's spiritual perceptions of the world have been key trajectories of modernization (Comaroff and Comaroff 1993; Geschiere 1997; Masquelier 2000, 2002; Meyer and Pels 2003; Moore and Sanders 2001; Shaw 2002; Weiss 1998; White 2000).

Contrary to predictions that, with modernization, colonial and postcolonial societies would emulate the secularized West, religion in many places has not only resisted the impact of modernity but has also furnished a prominent stage for the elaboration of multiple strategies of resistance and innovation (Behrend 1999; Comaroff 1985; Lan 1985; Meyer 1998a; Masquelier 2001b). Rather than a hostage to the past, religion often becomes a way to face the present, a source of symbolic capital that can bring about economic and social advancement (Cooper 2001; Grégoire 1993; O'Brien 1999; Masquelier 1993; Soares 2005). As attested by the ethnographic record, religion routinely provides metaphysical explanations for hardships resulting from social, political, and economic change (Ashforth 1998; Corten and Marshall-Fratani 2001; Geschiere 1997; Sanders 2001; Smith 2001; Smith 2004). Religion, in short, plays an active role in shaping modernity everywhere.

The recent recognition that involvement in religion signals an attempt to "retool culturally familiar technologies as new means for new ends" (Comaroff and Comaroff 1999:284) has fostered renewed interest in religious revival and in "fundamentalist" interpretations of sacred texts, whether Christian, Muslim, Hindu, Sikh, Buddhist, Confucian, or Jewish. Islamic revival, in particular, has been the focus of intense academic attention. In its various manifestations as state-centered political reforms, intensified expressions of religiosity, or both, Islamic resurgence has become a popular concept for exploring the potency of Islam as a global force and its troubled historical relations with the West. Much attention has been given to religious activism in the form of reformist, anti-Sufi movements and associations but considerably less has been paid to freelance charismatic figures that have attracted wide followings by providing alternative moral frameworks for rethinking people's place in society. I have chosen to focus my analysis on one of those self-styled religious leaders partly to correct this imbalance and counter the argument that Muslim saints, often described as "quintessentially traditional religious figures" (Soares 2005:79; Werbner and Basu 1998), have become irrelevant in the face of reformist Islam's sober, text-based message.

According to Gellner (1981), the emergence of more "modern," urban-centered Islamic reform movements has accelerated the marginalization of Muslim saints.[14] Geertz (1968:104), in *Islam Observed,* similarly noted that the secularization of thought characterizes the Muslim world. Ironically, though anthropologists have now abandoned such Weberian models of rationalization in their analyses of religion, the field of Islamic studies remains based on the assumption that modernization led to an "intellectualization" of the Qur'anic message and to the subsequent decline of "unorthodox" practices such as those associated with Muslim saints in Sufism (Crapanzano 1973; Eickelman 1976; Gellner 1981; Gilsenan 1973). Fortunately there are exceptions to this trend. In their studies of Sufi saints, Ewing (1997) and Werbner (2003) provide ample evidence that Sufism in its various incarnations is a vibrant, if contested, institution. They also demonstrate that Sufi practices cannot easily be characterized as traditional, given the complex ways in which they have been impacted by colonization, nation building, and other modernizing processes. As Werbner (2003:6–7) notes,

> Sufism is not an oppositional movement in any simple sense. Rather than rejecting modernity, a case can be made for the continued vitality of Sufism as a positive response to modernity. Sufi fraternities and saintly blessings legitimize and support worldly achievements [. . .] This is not to argue that Sufis are "moderns," who are simply living out an alternative modernity. Sufism rejects ideas of individual religious agency, autonomy, and rationality which are the bedrock of liberal modernity, stressing instead the embodied charisma, perfection and transcendence of the Sufi master, whose spiritual intimacy with God leads to the magical enchantment of the world.

In West Africa evidence suggests that far from progressively eroding under the combined impact of education and technology, the prestige of Sufi religious specialists is expanding. As the work of Schulz (2003) and Soares (2004a) in neighboring Mali demonstrates, modernization in the guise of economic liberalization has facilitated the privatization and personification of charisma in self-authorized preachers, some of whom have become key actors in local religious economies. As bearers of divinely attributed knowledge and dispensers of blessings, these often striking figures base their authority not on direct relationship to the Scriptures but on their supposed closeness to God. People flock to them hoping to receive the blessings that will facilitate access to riches. However reprehensible the practices of these "religious entrepreneurs" (Soares 2004a:94) may appear to literate elites who espouse more sober views of divinity and authority, their surging popularity nonetheless testifies to the pivotal role they play in a world where relations between production and value, work and wealth, are increasingly mystified. By focusing on a specific manifestation of what Gaffney (1994:37), following Weber, terms "priest-magicians," this book stresses the relevance of Sufism in places supposedly overrun by the puritan logic of reformist Islam and draws attention to the agentive character of a religious tradition that has been conventionally characterized as unchanging, static, and tradition-bound.

Returning for a moment to the issue of Islamic reformism, the divergent forms of this resurgence in both public and private life have, with notable exceptions, rarely been examined critically. The Iranian revolution of the late 1970s and the mobilization of Islamic activism in Egypt, Sudan, Afghanistan, Indonesia, or, say, Malaysia have focused attention on the vigor of militant Islam and its potential to ignite countercultural movements. Because they often assume the existence of a monolithic Islamic "fundamentalism"— characterized as a return to the past—political analyses of resurgent Islam have fueled popular views that Islam and the West are on an inevitable collision course (Huntington 1996). Their characterization of the Islamic revival as a sweeping movement that irreversibly changes the place of religion in society is problematic at best (Kepel 2002; Roy 1994). It is predicated on the concept of "political Islam" which involves the illegitimate irruption of Islamic tradition in the secular domain of politics. As Hirschkind argues (1997:4), this concept is inadequate, as it translates religious experience into "a posited distortion or corruption of properly religious practice." Analytical models based on the notion of "political Islam" fail to account for the various ways that Muslims respond to the call to reform Islam, and they ignore how these responses further contribute to the diversification of the religious landscape.

Precisely this kind of sweeping generalization about Islam as a menace to the New World Order enabled the United States, in 2003, to officially accuse Niger, an overwhelmingly Muslim country, of having supplied yellow cake uranium to Iraq in direct violation of U.N.–leveled sanctions against that "rogue" and equally Islamized state. In his January 2003 State of the Union address, George W. Bush informed Americans that "the British government ha[d] learned that Saddam Hussein recently sought significant quantities of uranium from Africa" (Bush 2003). At a time when the U.S. administration was attempting to enlist support for its policy to disarm Iraq on the presumption that it possessed weapons of mass destruction, any evidence of the threat that Saddam Hussein's government constituted should be heard loud and clear, the president's advisers reckoned.

In December of the preceding year, in a report on an alleged attempt by Iraq to buy yellow cake, Niger was identified as the supplier—the country with some of the largest deposits of uranium ore in the world—based on earlier European intelligence. The nature of that intelligence was highly doubtful, however. Members of the U.S. intelligence had long suspected that the documents brandished as proof of an Iraqi attempt to buy uranium ore from Niger were fraudulent. Further reports eventually revealed that, by early 2002, both the CIA and the State Department found that the documents were inauthentic. Despite incontrovertible evidence that the story of the uranium purchase was pure fabrication, George Bush, in his State of the Union address, spoke as if it had really happened in order to paint Iraq as a threat to global security. In March 2003, as the United States was invading Iraq supposedly to preempt a nuclear threat, the head of the International Atomic Energy Agency (assigned to the task of uncovering any trace or evidence of weapons of mass destruction [WMDs] in Iraq) reported to the UN Security Council that the documents had been forged. No matter that ultimately the government of Niger was discretely exonerated; the very fact that, despite ample evidence to the contrary, this impoverished West African nation was even suspected of such treachery demonstrates how stubborn the notion of a unified Islamic threat remains in some quarters.[15]

In their attempt to question the concept of an unchanging and homogeneous Muslim "civilization," anthropologists have grappled with issues that their predecessors, concerned with "primitive" or "traditional" religions, did not face. Conventionally anthropological analyses focused on the religion of particular societies, regions, or communities. As Launay (1992) perceptively notes, although different religious configurations were seen as comparable, it is now largely recognized that they often had little in common save for the labels ("witchcraft," "animism," and so on) that anthropologists assigned to them. There is, on the other hand, only one Islam. To deny or doubt it is, most Muslims would agree, tantamount to blasphemy. The question then becomes how to document the diversity of Muslim societies and trace the development of Islam in the context of specific cultural and historical conditions, without violating the unitary nature of Islam. One should ask, "how can the very diverse—if not diverging—religious beliefs and practices of Muslims be comprehended within a single idea of 'Islam'?" (Launay 1992:5; see also Gaffney 1994; Lambek 1993; and Soares 2005). Muslims in Dogondoutchi may disagree vehemently about what "Islam" is, but they do agree about Islam's singularity. The very nature of their disagreement, in fact, is rooted in the notion that there is only one "true" Islam—and therefore there is only one "correct" way of being Muslim.

Because their studies are ethnographic, anthropologists typically treat the ensemble of practices subsumed under the heading of "religion" as social phenomena whose meanings and manifest characteristics emerge in specific cultural settings. Because Islam, by definition, transcends locality and history, it has defied scholarly attempts to enshrine its practices as "organic products of the particular, if not peculiar, features of a specific locality" (Launay 1992:6). This is largely why the study of Islam long remained the province of Orientalists who distilled the substance of the faith from normative elements, such as the traditions of the Prophet, and the laws derived from them. In their "search for an anthropology of Islam" (el-Zein 1977:227) that would concern contexts rather than texts, scholars including Geertz (1968) and Gellner (1981) accounted for the tremendous variability they observed at the local level by characterizing it as expressions of popular Islam, as distinct from the scripture-centered, urban-based practices that constituted the normative core of Islam.

Borrowing from Redfield's model of the "great tradition" of urban centers versus the "little tradition" of rural communities, scholars reified Muslim practices according to a folk/urban distinction that saw Islamic orthodoxy flowing outward from centers of knowledge to become parochialized (and syncretized) in rural peripheries. Aside from the theologically problematic implications of distinguishing between "high" and "low" Islam, analyses emphasizing the pluralistic, localized character of Islam at the expense of its global dimensions tended to overlook the historical connections between Muslim societies (Bowen 1993; Marsden 2005; Soares 2005). In their concern for localized expressions of religiosity, anthropologists often focused on elements that distinguished the societies they were studying, while ignoring what they shared with other Muslims. Muslim practices were reduced to cultural idiosyncrasy, which only reinforced urban elites' perceptions that their "religion" could be distinguished from "folk" Islam.

As Antoun (1989) points out, Redfield's perspective generally dismisses or at least oversimplifies these complex so-called traditions while reifying the characteristics that differentiate them. It would be tempting, for instance, to categorize the Muslim practices that Izala condemns as part of "folk" tradition, and thus see reformist Islam as the expression of a "great tradition" based merely on how Dogondoutchi residents themselves describe religious diversity in their town. People routinely allude to the fact that the advent of *salla* (prayer) in Dogondoutchi is relatively new, and that until recently local knowledge of the Qur'an remained weak. In fact, *'yan* Izala justify their embrace of reformism precisely by claiming that it offers a corrective to religious practices that mix up *al'ada* (tradition) with *addini* (religion).[16] However, some practices that *'yan* Izala have introduced on the grounds that "they are mentioned in the Qur'an" are contemporary Muslim inventions. Consider, for instance, Muslim women's adoption of the *hijabi* (veil) which *'yan* Izala insist are expressions of Islamic authenticity. The potency of veiling resides in its ability to "restore a link with past traditions; it signifies the immutability of religion and nonsecular time" (Göle 2002:183). Yet, as I argue in chapter 7, these expressions of so-called Islamic dress are essentially innovative attempts to fashion female identities in accordance with newly emerging notions of morality and piety. As such, they exemplify the extent to which Muslims in Dogondoutchi interpret the Qur'an as they see fit even as they reassert the rootedness of their practices in an unchanging Islamic past.

Compared to their opponents, *'yan* Izala allege to be more knowledgeable and adhere more closely to the rules enunciated in the Qur'an , but their claims are routinely contested. Traditionalist scholarly elites frequently disparage the training of Muslim reformists, insisting, at times justifiably, that their knowledge of Islam is superficial at best and that they cannot present themselves as experts, for example, in matters of Islamic jurisprudence. Questions about what constitutes religious knowledge—and how one defines religious expertise—are central to the current dispute between *'yan darika* and *'yan* Izala. Yet, despite vehement affirmations by reformists and their opponents of the mutual disparity of their doctrinal views, the appeal of what Eickelman (1989) characterized as a "generic" Islam has helped standardize to some extent external signs of religiosity. This does not mean that we should gloss over what may be very real disagreements between *'yan* Izala (or *'yan* Awaliyya) and Muslims who reject Izala reforms, but it should sensitize us to the dangers of overrating the differences between these communities. Mindful that "any religion encompasses a number of traditions that are in some degree in conflict" (Laitin 1986:24), in this book I trace the distinct strands of debates through which women in Dogondoutchi variously affirm their identities as Muslims at the same time that I stress the underlying coherence in the joint claim that all Muslims are part of the *umma*, the global Muslim community.

Studying Islam in Africa

On the West African "periphery" where Islam has frequently been described in the ethnographic record as flexible, accommodating, and syncretic, French scholars and colonial administrators traditionally relied on the concept of *Islam noir* (Black Islam) to characterize the religious practices they encountered. In the colonial lexicon, "Black Islam" was an indigenized form of Islam that had been weakened through its incorporation of indigenous elements (Arnaud 1912; Marty 1917). Through this process of dilution, the religion was believed to acquire a tame "individuality" (Arnaud 1912:128) that made it particularly attractive to colonial administrators wary of the perils of pan-Islamism and pan-Arabism. Far from replacing indigenous practices, *Islam noir* accommodated them, as the following excerpt from a 1950 report makes clear:

> The so-called "Islamized" masses have only been superficially converted. The great strength of Islam is above all its flexibility, its amazing capacity of adaptation and decomposition; in many places, animism has found its refuge, and one could almost say, its revenge within a nominal Islam.[17]

To some extent, because Islam in this part of the continent was characterized as a watered down version of the true religion, ethnographies of West African societies did not generally focus on Muslim institutions as the main topic of their investigations. In-depth examinations of Muslim tradition and practice in West Africa were the preserve of historians and Orientalists concerned with Islamic development.[18] Trimingham (1959) and Fisher (1973), for instance, advanced developmental models of progressive Islamization to chronicle the successive engagement of Islamic civilization with indigenous religion in West Africa. And while important studies of Islam in West Africa appeared in the 1960s and 1970s (Hiskett 1973; Last 1967; Levtzion 1968; Trimingham 1962), the great majority were written by Anglophone scholars. Few scholarly works address Islam in the former French colonies: in its "blackened" and politicized expression, Islam was apparently of little interest to students of religion. Moreover, as Cooper (2006) perceptively notes, studying religion in Africa at the time almost always meant studying Christianity—or those indigenous religions that had provided the moral framework for the adoption of Christianity.

More recently, ethnographically richer studies of Muslim practices in West Africa were prompted by the recognition that practices described by literate elites as "fringe" or "marginal" Islam often turn out to be intimately connected with "core" Islam (Lewis 1986:96). In his engaging ethnography of Muslim traders in Koko, a small provincial town of northern Côte d'Ivoire, Launay (1992) offers an illuminating account of how members of the Muslim community define and redefine what it means to be part of the *umma* through the debates, concessions, and confrontations they engage in with various degrees of conviction. Soares's (2005) study of what he calls the "prayer economy" of Nioro du Sahel is an equally lucid and meticulous analysis of changing understandings of the role of Islam in a Malian town during a period from the eve of the French colonization to recent times. Launay and Soares are careful not to reify the emerging divisions in the Muslim communities they studied; they stress that tension between Islamic unity and expressions of sectarian difference manifests itself as an awareness of the consistency of religious tradition side by side with evolving religious practice. In the end, they both demonstrate convincingly the limitations of dividing Islam into "orthodox" and "un-orthodox" traditions. This book similarly seeks to transcend the distinction between high doctrine and popular belief that has guided previous analyses of Islam in Africa. Through an in-depth examination of the "political economy of meaning" (Roff 1987) that makes up the field of Muslim practices in Dogondoutchi, I discuss key features of what Muslims variously define as unchanging (or universal) Islamic elements within the framework of shifting engagement between local realities and global contexts.

As noted above, the concept of "discursive tradition" articulated by Talal Asad (1986) has been most helpful in guiding my examination of the conflict between the notion of Islam as a way of unifying the *umma* and the potential of Islamic ideology to generate powerful expressions of difference. Understanding Islam as a discursive tradition implies seeing it as historically evolving discourses through which the foundational texts (the Qur'an and *hadith* collections) and other related narratives are reinterpreted to respond to the conditions of a changing world. Tradition, viewed in this way, is a malleable concept. Although it implies the existence of immutable guiding principles, its form and substance are still routinely reinterpreted to enable the boundaries of the forbidden (*haram*) and the permissible (*hallak*) that are at the heart of Islam to accommodate Muslim communities' shifting contexts of engagement with social realities. Unlike the "invention of tradition" model that legitimizes the presence of a new practice by formal reference to the past (Hobsbawn

1983:4–5), the concept of "discursive tradition" allows scholars to consider how Muslims discursively engage with and reflect on the past to articulate meaningful formulations of the problems and possibilities of the present without appearing to reject past traditions or invent new ones (Asad 1986). Because it retains the notion of orthodoxy (defined as correct practice) even as it recognizes the changing constitution of orthodoxy, Asad's formulation encourages analyses of the debates through which Muslims variously relate local religious practices to the Scriptures and, ultimately, specify which practices are acceptable and which are not (see Bowen 1993; Fischer and Abedi 1990; and Mahmood 2005).

Muslim Women in Africa

A quick survey of the literature on Islam reveals how conventional studies of Muslim culture have tended to make women appear primarily as objects of reform and manipulation molded from above by a universal Islam (Mernissi 1987). In analyses of Muslim societies, Islam has often been defined as the "primary agent of women's definition" (Bernal 1994:37) and the main obstacle to social and economic advancement. The counter perspective has focused on women's engagement in processes of resistance, but it has done so by often assuming the existence of homogeneous forms of oppression and generalized female responses to women's devaluation. This book challenges both views by addressing the culturally specific and personalized strategies through which Mawri women caught in polemics about cultural and religious authenticity shape their world and define the contours of their religious identities. By focusing on actors rather than institutions and by tracing the meanings Islam has for people instead of assuming that Islam always determines their choices and constraints, my study seeks to illuminate how women relate to doctrine in practical ways and how they selectively use Islam now that Muslim identity is central to the ways that Mawri people constitute themselves as pious persons. Inspired by recent studies on the personal experience of Muslim women (Abu-Lughod 1998b; Cooper 1997a; Deeb 2006; Hale 1996; Hefner and Horvatich 1997; Mahmood 2005), I try to particularize Mawri women's understanding of Islam and ground the dynamics of gender in specific contexts, histories, and processes.

Despite a vigorous focus on gender in West African studies, ethnographies specifically addressing the condition of Muslim women in West Africa are rare, partly because, save for some notable exceptions (Alidou 2005; Callaway 1987; Coles and Mack 1991; Cooper 1997a; Popenoe 2004; Saunders

1978), the study of Muslim women's issues is overwhelmingly directed at Middle Eastern or South Asian societies. In comparative works on women in the Muslim world, Muslim women of Sub-Saharan Africa are generally omitted from the analysis unless they live in Sudan or Mauritania—nations identified as "Arabic." It is as if Muslim women from other parts of Africa were somehow irrelevant, a hint perhaps that the field of Islamic studies still largely operates under the premise that African Islam is not "real" Islam. By describing Mawri women's engagement with Islam in the context of emerging debates over Muslim identity and practice, I intend to correct the misperception that African women are not really Muslim.

This book also counters the Orientalist view that Islam is monolithic and rigid, a timeless piece of the cultural heritage shaping women's lives for better or for worse. In Dogondoutchi, the last half-century has seen tremendous changes in local patterns of religious practice. For those who converted to Islam in the first decades after Independence, there was never any question about the definition and boundaries of Islam and Muslim practice. In recent years, Muslims in Dogondoutchi (and in the rest of Niger) have become increasingly aware that their own way of life, refracted as it is through the critical gaze of others, may not correspond to what they once believed was orthodoxy. Because they have conventionally been associated with "superstition," spirit veneration, and other practices that orthodox Islam rejects as un-Islamic, women are particularly eager to present themselves as proper Muslims. Women's engagement with Islam and, more specifically, their attempts to claim a connection to religious knowledge and enjoy the recognition denied to non-Muslims provides an ideal case for examining how Muslim practice is constructed and reconstructed in the context of gender relations. Islam and gender "intertwine in complex ways," Bernal (1994:56) points out in her analysis of changing Muslim traditions in northern Sudan. I try to illuminate this intertwining of gender and religion by investigating how, in daily life as well as in institutional settings, Dogondoutchi residents manipulate symbolic and material resources to address gender-specific needs, concerns, and aspirations.

Because they are largely poor, unschooled, and living in semi-rural conditions, the women I spent time with in Dogondoutchi have little in common with the literate and highly articulate female subjects of other studies of the Hausa-speaking region (see Boyd 1989; Boyd and Last 1985; and Mack and Boyd 2000). Boyd and Last (1985) argued, justifiably, that the scholarly focus on African women's activities in *zar* and *bori* practices has highlighted instances of noncompliance with normative Islam at the expense of women's active history of engagement with Islamic tradition.[19] Following the conquest of the Hausa states by Usman 'dan Fodio in the early nineteenth century, women of the ruling class actively contributed to the spread of the religion and the forging of a Muslim identity in the Sokoto Caliphate. In addition to producing an abundant literature, women like 'dan Fodio's daughter, Nana Asma'u, played a central role as teachers, mentors, and role models to other women in newly converted communities (Boyd and Mack 1997; Mack and Boyd 2000).

If Mawri women can be said to have been *"agents religieux"* (Boyd and Last 1985:283), it is largely because of their participation in *aznanci* (veneration of tutelary spirits) and in *bori,* not their contribution to Islam. Partly because Arewa remained unaffected by the wave of Islamic proselytism even after the Sokoto Caliphate established suzerainty over many of the Hausa states, Mawri women did not benefit from the legacy of Nana Asma'u's teachings.[20] Few women in Dogondoutchi ever heard of the gifted teacher, activist, and poetess. Fewer still know that in neighboring Nigeria her legacy is kept alive in learning centers where, thanks to the training they receive from educated female teachers, ordinary Muslim women learn to read, memorize, and recite the Qur'an.

For the majority of Nigérien women, access to Islamic literacy and scholarship has traditionally been restricted (Alidou 2005; Cooper 1997a; Dunbar 1991). In the late 1980s, girls I met who attended *makaranta allo* (Qur'anic school) did not go beyond the first stage of Qur'anic studies, during which they would commit the entire content of the Qur'an to memory but not learn the meaning of the words they recited. Since the emergence of Izala, much has been done in urban areas to facilitate women's access to Islamic education through the creation of schools for female students, the appointment of female teachers, and, more rarely, the recognition of female religious authority. Alidou (2005) thus reports the proliferation of female-based Qur'anic literacy classes in Niamey in recent years. Because they provide spaces where women can meet away from home without fearing opprobrium, these schools are valuable for conducting extra-Qur'anic activities. In Dogondoutchi, by contrast, women's Islamic education has not made significant strides. Its format, content, and accessibility remain controlled by men, who generally express limited interest in generating female solidarity and fostering the kind of female-centered social and spiritual reflection that goes on elsewhere.[21] As we shall see, despite—or perhaps because of—limitations in the current Qur'anic educational system, women in Dogondoutchi have found alternative means of accessing spiritual capital, which they use to justify their own practices or disparage the practices of other Muslims.

Researching and Writing about Islam in Dogondoutchi

Although the understanding I gained of gender and Islam during eighteen months of doctoral fieldwork in the late 1980s informs much of my discussion, the material for much of this book was collected during four subsequent periods of research totaling almost seven months in 1994, 2000, 2004, and 2006. When I set out, in 1994, to do research on Muslims in Dogondoutchi, I had in mind an exploration of women's daily life and domestic values that would shed light on the complicated relation between Muslim identity and *bori* activities. Few of the Muslim women I met during my initial research trip prayed regularly, and even fewer had attended Qur'anic school. Most of them discreetly visited *bori* healers, even though their husbands largely discouraged their participation in spirit-centered activities and forbade attendance at *bori* performances altogether. They did not listen to the Friday sermon delivered by the local imam—attending sermons was a man's thing—and would often invoke ignorance when I questioned them about the Qur'an. They simply showed limited interest in Islamic matters, and yet they saw themselves as practicing Muslims because they fasted during *azumi* (the month of fasting) and regularly gave alms. As women, however, their commitment to Islam remained undervalued, and their sense of Muslimhood was blurred and poorly defined. Because generally more emphasis was placed on the transgressions they committed (such as visiting *bori* healers or sacrificing to the spirits) than on the Muslim religious duties (*ibada*) they performed, women were often seen as "inferior Muslims" (Cooper 2001:98). They were expected to be less disciplined, and less pious—in short, less Muslim.[22]

On returning to Dogondoutchi in June 1994, I found that women's attitudes toward religion had changed radically. The country was in great turmoil following the emergence of Izala, and families were torn apart by religious strife. People argued passionately over the right way to pray, socialize, celebrate a happy event, and generally conduct themselves as Muslims. They had become increasingly conscious that their choices of dress, marriage partners, or entertainment had important implications for the way they would be perceived as Muslims. Documenting changing modes of religious expression thus assumed a sense of urgency. This meant reconfiguring the focus of my research and rethinking my lines of questioning as well as the concepts and categories that framed my inquiry. In the process my relations to certain town residents changed radically: men who had previously given me hearty handshakes now avoided all physical contact; touching between members of the opposite sex, they told me, was forbidden. They addressed me with a noncommittal "*salamu alaikum*" instead of reciting the seemingly interminable list of conventional Hausa greetings I was accustomed to. They also objected to my handing them small gifts of cash "to buy meat for the children," as I had routinely done in the past. As members of Izala, they could not accept payment for teaching me *addini* (Islam). Still, they were more than happy to instruct me about the "correct" practice of Islam. At times this meant listening to lengthy lectures about the inadequacy of my head coverings (which often slipped backward, exposing my hair) or the immodesty of my overall attire, an unpleasant process that was mitigated by the information I took in about the politics of dress and the poetics of concealment.

The conversations I had with women, young and old, reflected their newfound attitudes toward religion. Aside from actively claiming their place in the newly configured moral order, women had become considerably more vocal about what being Muslim meant to them. Except for the few times *'yan* Izala denied me access to the family compound because they worried about the potentially damaging influence I could exert on their wives, the women I spoke with generally welcomed my questions about Muslim identity and practice, no doubt because they saw in our encounters an opportunity to "set the record straight." They were eager to make Islam the focus of our conversations and to educate me by paraphrasing preachers, playing taped sermons, and sharing opinions. My conversations with older women generally yielded richer material than with their younger counterparts, probably because young women had fewer experiences to recount. In keeping with local norms of reserve governing female conduct, young women (especially if they were recently married) tended to be less vocal and less eager to discuss religious matters. Western-educated young women were a notable exception to this trend, no doubt because of the confidence fostered in them by the classroom's more egalitarian environment.

During my two-month stay in Niger that year, I rarely slept. The country was paralyzed by a general strike and, save for the soccer matches featured in the evening (it was the World Cup, and Nigériens were cheering for Cameroon), there was no television programming. Far from returning to the stillness of pre–oral media times, however, Dogondoutchi was abuzz with the shrill sounds of amplified Muslim oratorical performances. In their struggle to control an emerging Islamic public space, reformists and their religious opponents confronted each other through loudspeakers and cassette recordings in oral/aural battles that radically redefined the local soundscape. I was living next to a Qur'anic teacher who resented the Izala preachers' intrusion into his sonic world. After the much awaited birth of his first male child, he bought an amplifier to broadcast his nightly performance of *zikiri* (the chanted repetition of God's names). From midnight until just before the dawn prayer, he kept the whole neighborhood awake with his high-pitched, strained recitations. He wished to thank God for giving him a son, he claimed. I suspect that he was also trying to drown out the voices of Izala preachers emanating from nearby loudspeakers by engaging in precisely what Islamic reformism forbade.

As I learned more about the Izala vision of a reformed society, I began to worry about the repercussions that talks of implementing *sharia* (Islamic law), a central goal of Muslim reformists, could have on the lives of Nigérien women. Young women dressed in "skimpy" attire had been attacked and stripped by angry Muslim reformists in the cities of Maradi and Zinder. In Dogondoutchi, scores of young girls had been beaten and their clothing ripped off their bodies by 'yan Izala. On one occasion, it was the girls' singing (an activity Izala reformists reject as un-Islamic) next to an Izala mosque that prompted their tormentors to chase and "punish" them. In Niamey the government's attempts to draft a Family Code, which was to include legal protection for Nigérien women, had been quashed by Muslim reformists who objected to state interference in matters that, in their opinion, should be regulated by Islam. What impact could emergent violence and prejudice—much of it targeted at women—have in a country previously known for its relative tolerance of religious difference? Men I knew had been wounded in bloody confrontations with religious foes. Speculation abounded in some quarters as to whether the clashes between 'yan Izala and 'yan *darika* foreshadowed more ominous events. "When Nigeria has a cold, Niger coughs," people say when they wish to describe the formidable cultural, religious, and economic influence that oil-rich Nigeria exerts on its northern neighbor. If there was any truth to the saying, how long, I wondered, could Niger remain immune to the kind of intercommunal violence infecting Nigeria?

While the last decade of the twentieth century was framed by severe outbreaks of violence involving Muslim reformists, by the time I returned to Dogondoutchi, in February 2000, tensions between reformists and those who once stood resolutely against Izala had abated. The previous farming season had been disastrous—excessive rainfall had flooded villages and neighborhoods, washing away homes, soaking fields, and turning dirt roads into mud baths. People worried about surviving *la période de soudure*, the "hungry" period that precedes the harvests and during which granaries are empty and food prices are at their highest. Malam Awal's presence and formidable charisma helped allay the anxieties of many residents: by making war on immorality and ignorance, they figured, the preacher would also confront the sources of their economic troubles.

Thanks to Belgian funding, the once decrepit town dispensary had been entirely refurbished. It graduated to the rank of district hospital, generating great pride among local residents who liked to boast of its expanded, newly equipped facilities. Meanwhile, the construction of a new Friday mosque sponsored by Izala had come to a halt after funds provided by external donors (allegedly from Kuwait and the neighboring town of Maradi) had dried up. There were other changes as well. New neighborhoods had sprouted up to accommodate the town's rapid demographic expansion. Everyone relied on a new system of transportation, the *kabu kabu* (motorcycle taxi), to move more speedily across town; oddly enough no one seemed to think twice about women with calves exposed who zoomed through town hugging tightly to the waists of the motorbike drivers—men unrelated to them. And despite warnings by preachers of the dangers of foreign cultural productions, Indian videos with their dancing and singing heroines and action-packed scripts had reached a new pinnacle of popularity among youthful audiences.

In late 2004, when the country was in the throes of the presidential and legislative elections, I visited Dogondoutchi for six weeks. There was much to talk about with old and new acquaintances: the attacks on the World Trade Center and the subsequent invasion of Afghanistan and Iraq, Malam Awal's waning popularity, new trends and fashions, and, as always, the failure of the Nigérien state to provide for its people. Young men were up in arms about rising unemployment, continuing inflation of wedding expenses, and government corruption. They spoke of immigrating to America, becoming hip-hop artists, and marrying "for love," as they assembled with members of their *fada* (youth gathering) to drink heavily sweetened tea and listen to music late into the night. Meanwhile, young women oblivious to preachers' admonitions that they espouse frugality and sobriety made strenuous demands for gifts of all kinds on their paramours (including cell phones with which to evade parental control). They spent much time watching foreign drama series on television and discussing with one another the latest in sartorial styles and decorative interiors.

I spent my 2006 fieldwork almost exclusively exploring what being Muslim meant for local youths, many of whom were facing unemployment, boredom, and disillusion. Regardless of which side of the religious divide they supported, young men in particular were concerned with issues of moral responsibility and ethical improvement. Against the background of economic decline and punitive structural adjustment systems, they found ways to make religion socially and ethically compatible with newly emerging models of personhood, success, and fashionability. Although most embraced a Muslim identity, a distinct minority turned to Christianity, specifically Protestantism. At a time when the Catholic population was waning, more and more people in Dogondoutchi were joining Protestant churches despite the disapproval they exposed themselves to by doing so. Protestantism may only have a tenuous hold in this predominantly Muslim town, but as Cooper (2006) notes in her account of Evangelical Christianity in Maradi, its significance in contemporary Nigerien society cannot be understated.

During my successive fieldworks, I listened to numerous sermons and attended Muslim celebrations ranging from naming ceremonies to weddings to Sufi rituals. I conducted formal interviews (with religious and civic leaders, for instance) that supplied valuable information about the social and religious history of the community. Complementary data were assembled from conversations with Qur'anic scholars and schoolteachers, as well as farmers, traders, and artisans. A great portion of my time was spent visiting women in their compounds and observing and participating in their daily activities. Additional archival research was conducted in the Archives Nationales in Niamey; the Institut de Recherches en Sciences Humaines (IRSH) in Niamey; the Centre des Archives d'Outre-Mer (CAOM) in Aix-en-Provence, France; and the holdings of the University of Chicago, Tulane University, and the Africana Library at Northwestern University. If interviews provided much needed material, some of my most valuable insights often arose during casual meetings, chance encounters, or impromptu conversations. The data generated through these experiences have informed substantially the format and content of this book.

In Dogondoutchi my daily routine varied little. I often spent the morning visiting women in their homes (and men in their shops and offices), came home and transcribed taped conversations during the early afternoon when most people rested, and then ventured out again when the heat had abated and women were busy preparing the evening meal. The rooms I rented each time in a different family compound afforded me the opportunity to witness both the daily routines of household members and the small dramas that inevitably punctuate life in these multigenerational settings. On Thursday and Sunday evenings I often attended Izala (and Awaliyya) sermons with some of my female neighbors. Other evenings were devoted to watching videos at one of the local "theaters" (stools and mats assembled in rows behind a television and video or DVD player set in a family compound) that charged 50 CFA francs (10 cents) for admission. At night there were also wedding receptions and theatrical performances to attend, as well as special Sufi celebrations or Izala rallies. These were not as taxing as the *bori* performances I previously attended in 1988–89 which lasted until the wee hours, but they still left me exhausted and wishing at times for quieter, less eventful evenings.

Some people chided me for asking questions whose answers, they would point out, I already knew. I ask the same questions, I would explain, because I want to know if everyone has the same answer. I also told them that I was interested in how people phrased their responses to my questions. Friends familiar with my research knew that I collected words and wordings, that I was interested in the ways that Hausa speakers played with language to communicate experience. Words are more than an expression of what they describe; they are also associated with the speaker's or audience's experience of what the words describe. Moreover, when people speak of something, the (often multivalent) words they use illuminate a constellation of related concepts beyond the specified referent. In the way that they resonate with other experiences, words help anthropologists map out local conceptions of the world. At other times a wordless action, such as a woman's body language in the presence of her husband, could prove just as helpful to trace culturally shaped patterns of experience.

During these successive research trips, I relied on the support of several individuals who assisted closely with various tasks, including setting up appointments and helping with transcriptions: Mahamadou Noma early on helped me navigate deftly the treacherous waters of religious affiliations when I worried that being identified with one Muslim faction would mean that no member of another faction would be available for consultation.[23] His marital woes, dreams of social advancement, and personal squabbles with former friends who had joined Izala greatly helped clarify for me how the Islamic revival affected ordinary Muslim men. Hadiza Akaki, my friend of more than twenty years, provided insight, logistical assistance, gossip, and much more. She could always be relied on for help with transcriptions, and her own struggles to make sense of Izala sermons were deeply illuminating. Salifou Hamidou worked closely with me in 2004 and 2006, helping me with all aspects of the research. His knowledge of Dogondoutchi as well as his social skills and personal interests in issues of faith and religion proved invaluable.

Although reformist attitudes toward the female body and sexuality have substantially impacted existing patterns of gender dynamics, they have rarely translated into men's refusal to converse with me. If anything, Izala men, in particular, were even more eager to engage me in conversation and convert me to Islam. Thanks to my anomalous status as a comparatively wealthy woman, a Christian, and a foreigner, I enjoyed considerable latitude in my comings and goings. As the mother of teenage daughters, I also eventually acquired the kind of respectability that only elder, mature women enjoy. Over the years I have grown deeply attached to Dogondoutchi and to the people who live there. In 2004 a seventeen-year-old boy was astonished to learn from one of his neighbors that the white woman who had just greeted his mother—a longtime friend—had once tied him to her own back when he was an infant. Returning every so often to the same community has been immensely beneficial. It has helped me gain a valuable longitudinal perspective on a constantly evolving Muslim community whose fractures and mending along religious lines would otherwise have not been so readily apparent.

Although I consider many in Dogondoutchi my dear friends, Malam Awal is not one of them. The four-hour conversation I had with him (I was later told he never granted interviews)[24] and my subsequent invitation to an important celebration that very evening (see chapter 4) were part of the chance encounters I just alluded to. Had I not personally met the preacher, this book would have taken a different form—a potent reminder of the contingent nature of field learning and of the situational quality of what we call "data." Inspired by Abu-Lughod's (1991:138) advice that we start "writing against culture" to produce what she calls "ethnographies of the particular," I devote several chapters of the book to a discussion of Malam Awal. Mahamane Awal's Sufi persona was irreducibly particular yet also exemplary. As a unique and extraordinary preacher, he was hardly representative of the kind of *malamai* (Qur'anic teachers) to which Dogondoutchi residents were accustomed. Yet not only did he become a part of the religious history of the town but, at least for a while, he also personified knowledge and piety for a large segment of the Muslim community. The particulars in which we live, Abu-Lughod (1991:158) perceptively notes,

> suggest that others live as we perceive ourselves living, not as robots programmed with "cultural" rules, but as people going through life agonizing over decisions, making mistakes, trying to make themselves look good, enduring tragedies and personal losses, enjoying others, and finding moments of happiness.

By focusing on women's long and winding "conversation" with a Muslim preacher, on their dreams of a fairer, kinder world, their disillusions, and their struggles, I have tried to convey some of the "flux and contradiction[s]" (Abu-Lughod 1991:158) inherent in the life of a human community.

As I wove Awal's story into that of the town and its people, I faced some conundrums. At a time of widespread Western antipathy toward Muslims, would writing about Malam Awal's perversions and patriarchal stance be seen as an attempt to characterize him as a "bad Muslim" (Mamdani 2004)? On the other hand, how should I present the preacher as the pivotal cultural broker that he was without appearing to make a hero out of him? More important, perhaps, could I write of Awaliyya women's veneration for the man without making them look excessively naive or helpless in the face of such potent misogyny? Writing chapter 8, where I discuss local women's progressive disenchantment with the preacher and their ensuing disengagement with the Awaliyya, was my way out of these challenges. It allowed me to portray women as more than just victims of Malam Awal's predatory schemes while conveying a sense of the humanity and frailties of the Muslim preacher.

Throughout the book I have tried to highlight the historical specificity of religious discourses in Dogondoutchi without losing track of the wider context of Islamic awareness within which they are anchored. The town's rich and complex religious history has created conditions for the possibility of multiple ways of being Muslim; however, that multiplicity has a specific configuration that generates a particular dynamic of potentiality and limitation, of inclusion and exclusion. Although some of the themes that have emerged in local Muslim discourses and that I examine in this book are manifestations of broader concerns and will be familiar to many readers, other themes speak to the irreducibly unique nature of the religious terrain in Dogondoutchi. The chapters that follow represent my attempts to make sense of how, in their quest for religious conformity and ethical improvement, Dogondoutchi's female residents struggle to reconcile the particularistic ethos that many claim is part of their Muslim heritage with the supposedly universal norms that govern Muslim conduct in the wider world.

"THOSE WHO PRAY":
RELIGIOUS
TRANSFORMATIONS IN THE
COLONIAL AND EARLY
POSTCOLONIAL PERIOD

2

Fetishism is the most powerful obstacle that the development of Islam can meet.
—*Commandant du Cercle de Dogondoutchi*, Droit Musulman et
Coutumes Indigènes

What was to become the colony of Niger was first explored by the French during an expedition headed by Captain Louis-Parfait Monteil in 1891 (Fuglestad 1983). Monteil secured treaties with various chiefs before reaching the Lake Chad area by way of territories that were largely either under the yoke of the Sokoto Caliphate or paying tribute to the Tuareg, a population of nomadic pastoralists who had successfully established their domination over sedentary populations in southern Niger. Although Niger was virtually conquered by 1908, the French took another decade and a half to defeat Tuareg resistance and definitively claim all the colony's territories. France's occupation of Niger had been a military exercise characterized by impatience toward the treaty-making process and swift resort to military action (Crowder 1968:70). Once the territories were "pacified," the French realized that Niger, like the rest of the West African hinterland, was no Eldorado. Niger, wrote Lieutenant-Colonel Noël in 1903, "is a territory of sacrifices, an ill forced upon us which we must bear perhaps so that we can escape a greater ill."[1] In a 1913 report, a local administrator, Capitaine Mahant, noted that "the richness of this country never existed except in the minds of bluffers. The country is poor, really poor."[2] In the view of the French administration, the territory's only value resided in its strategic location: it was a link joining French territories to the north, the west, and the east, and shielding these territories from Nigeria's influence (Idrissa 2001).

Unwilling to invest too heavily in a colony that appeared to have little economic potential, the French government left the local administration to muddle through with a limited supply of men and resources. Understaffed and short of funds, the colonial regime was weak, always depending on the support of local populations for its survival. As a result, Niger was considered by some to be "*le pays le plus dur de l'AOF*" ("the toughest country in French West Africa") (Fuglestad 1983:23). In some quarters it earned the reputation of being a "penitentiary" colony, where only undesirable administrators would be sent.[3] As one of the most remote and barren of the eight colonial divisions of the federation of West Africa, Niger would remain neglected.

Whereas across the southern border, roads, hospitals, and schools were introduced into what had become British Hausaland (northern Nigeria) as part of Britain's indirect rule, in Niger infrastructure developed erratically, if at all (Cooper 1997a; Miles 1994).[4] Intent upon minimizing administrative costs and consolidating their control, the French inflicted a heavy tax burden on colonized populations and at the same time imposed peace and abolished slavery, thereby ruining the political and economic bases of the ruling aristocracy. These reforms profoundly upset the elaborate networks of alliance and rivalries, exchanges and redistribution, that constituted the existing social order. As the administrative grip on the region tightened after the 1920s, colonial exactions in the form of taxes intensified, severely straining farmers' ability to make ends meet.[5] At the same time that villagers were increasingly unable to secure stable profits, they could no longer turn to the aristocracy during years of poor harvest. Appointed rulers who enjoyed limited political legitimacy often compensated for their precarious position by plundering villages or enforcing their own rules when it came to tax collection or labor requisition. Consequently crop failures periodically turned into famines of massive proportions and provoked substantial migrations to Nigeria—where farmers could evade French policies (de Latour Dejean 1980).

Under British colonial jurisdiction, Islamic institutions in the territory of the former Sokoto Caliphate were allowed to prosper, but this was not the case in Niger where administrators were largely concerned with curbing the advance of Islam. French administrators knew little about the beliefs or practices of Islam or its relation to other African religions (Labouret 1931). They were often misinformed and wrote disparaging reports on the forms of religiosity they witnessed. Most striking to the colonists on their arrival was the incidence of Islam in one region and religious practices known, in colonial parlance as "fetishism" or "animism," in another.[6] Niger, like the rest of West

(not a settler colony)

Africa, seemed to be divided between two religions, though a closer look would reveal how closely these seemingly distinct traditions converged and intersected. Arewa was one of the regions apparently untouched by Muslim proselytism. Throughout the colonial period, French authorities would work hard to preserve Mawri populations from what they perceived as the corrupting influence of Islam. How and why they did so, and what the consequences of these policies were, is the focus of this chapter. The French presence in Arewa resulted in a complete realignment of the balance of power: by upsetting the generative dynamics of local politico-religious orders, restructuring economic networks, and preventing armed resistance to Muslim presence, the French administration unwittingly paved the way for the widespread diffusion of Islam—precisely what the administration wished to avoid. Even while they systematically discouraged Qur'anic education and proselytism, Islam spread steadily. The first Friday mosque was built in Dogondoutchi in 1938, a testament to the dramatic religious changes sweeping the region at the time. In what follows I consider some of the images, perceptions, and prejudices that shaped the colonial regime's experience of Islam, Muslims, and non-Muslims in Arewa, for they provide a backdrop for the unfolding contemporary debates on religious identity. Wherever it implanted itself, Islam adapted to the local cultural landscape. The absorption of indigenous elements into Muslim epistemologies greatly contributed to the diversity of Islam as a localized practice, a process that would become the focus of colonial scrutiny as the French hammered out the details of their *politique musulmane* (policies toward Islam and Muslims). As we shall see in chapter 3, it is precisely the syncretized dimension of Islam, so meticulously documented by an earlier generation of colonial observers, which Izala reformists currently wish to expunge because it is allegedly not part of Islamic tradition. Izala reformists argue that many of the religious practices of local Muslims are part of "African culture," not Islam. In denouncing the supposedly un-Islamic practices of those who manufacture or make use of *gris-gris* (amulets), engage in "fetishism" (the worship of a "fetish," or ritual object), or follow the teachings of "charlatans," they borrow freely from the French colonial lexicon from which some of these conceptual categories originate.

At Independence, and, more specifically, after the 1974 coup during which Colonel Seyni Kountché took the reins of government, conversion to Islam intensified in and around Dogondoutchi. Ostensibly pressured by local religious leaders to abandon their ancestors' "backward" ways, Arewa residents massively turned to the Muslim faith and culture. They started to "pray" and invited Muslim clerics to "tie" marriages. They adopted Muslim attire, stopped scarifying babies, and gave their children Muslim names. They stopped attending public rituals aimed at cultivating the support of spirits and sent their children to Qur'anic school. The adoption of a Muslim identity was especially pronounced among the residents of Dogondoutchi, which by then had become a town of several thousand inhabitants. In neighboring villages, meanwhile, participation in spirit-centered practices remained strong, although there, too, adherence to Islam would eventually become the norm, and spirit devotees would be relegated to the margins of the social order.

In short, the spread of Islam in Arewa occurred largely during the second half of the twentieth century. Within that period, one can isolate two waves of Islamization, the first after World War II, when talk of independence was gaining momentum, and the second during the presidency of Seyni Kountché, when ties to the Muslim world were cultivated by the government to finance the country's development. This chapter discusses the development of Islam from the advent of French rule until the first few decades of Independence, highlighting, first, the main features of *la politique musulmane* during the colonial period and, second, the ways that Islam was increasingly promoted as a pivotal element of Nigérien identity in the second decade following Independence. My treatment of history here is more descriptive than analytical, as the discussion is intended only to provide a setting for the current Islamic revival. It is worth noting that although the colonial period constituted an important moment in the Islamization of Arewa, it is after Independence that the spread of Islam intensified most dramatically throughout the region. Official declarations about the separation of state and religion notwithstanding, Islam became at that time the de facto religion of the Nigérien people. In Dogondoutchi, this translated into the heightened visibility of Muslim practices such as naming ceremonies, weddings, and burials, all central to the definition of "being Muslim." In exploring what being Muslim meant at the time for Dogondoutchi residents, I consider briefly how burials emerged as central for affirming distinctions between Muslims and non-Muslims.

French Policy toward Islam

French policies toward Islam and Muslims in West Africa were far from consistent over time,[7] conditioned as they were by both local political circumstances and wider relations of power. Overwhelming evidence nonetheless suggests that they reflected a deep ambivalence toward Islam. This ambivalence, tainted at times with frank hostility, was rooted in a republican spirit inherited from the French Revolution and guaranteed the separation of church and state (Triaud 2000). Following their longtime confrontation with the Roman Catholic Church, republican and radical secularists saw in Islam another agent of obscurantism that needed to be vigorously combated for the sake of *laïcité* (secularism). Although, in theory, French rule guaranteed freedom of religion, it did not prevent colonial administrators from intervening in local Muslim affairs whenever they saw them as a disruption of public order. Because they constituted "an intolerable attack on the secular religion of 'progress'" (Cholvy, in Triaud 2000:170), such affairs called for administrative and political measures against anyone who could be identified as a threat to colonial rule. Under the guise of preserving order, democracy, and progress, French authorities thus routinely targeted religious figures or organizations suspected of spreading "superstition" among African populations.

French suspicion of Muslim Africans was also rooted in the earlier conquest of North Africa, when colonial administrators discovered the Sufi orders. These were promptly identified as "secret societies," which, like their European Christian counterparts such as the Jesuits, constituted a menace to the colonial order (Triaud 2000). During the conquest of Niger and Chad, the Sanusiyya, a Cyrenaic order that began to extend its influence into regions of Chad and Niger in the last decades of the nineteenth century, was the focus of renewed French anxiety over the militancy of Islam (Fuglestad 1983). The Sanusi-led Tuareg resistance to colonial occupation in Niger as well as in Chad for more than a decade only confirmed in the eyes of the French the image they had previously formed of the Sanusiyya as a "militant, anti-French, and anti-Christian sect of fanatics" (Vikør 2000:457).[8] In their concern to diffuse a potential threat to the stability of the French empire, local administrators zeroed in on the activities of Muslim religious specialists, known as *marabouts* in colonial parlance, based on their supposed affiliation with a Sufi order.[9] Recall that the Sufi orders were not as developed and prominent in Niger as in Senegal.[10] Nevertheless, and despite whether they had ties to a particular *darika* (literally, "path"; Sufi order), Muslim preachers were widely suspected of using Islam to abuse people and satisfy their thirst for power. A 1912 political report from Niger thus mentions the presence of "errant *marabouts* more interested in temporal than spiritual affairs and whose privileged occupation consists of taking advantage of people's credulity."[11]

The establishment of the *paix coloniale* increased security and facilitated the mobility of individuals across West Africa. The circulation of Muslim clerics outside their specific districts was a particular concern for French authorities. Because they traveled widely and had the potential to unify Muslim populations behind a cause, itinerant preachers were considered a menace to the colonial power. Monitoring their comings and goings and curbing their activities was thought to help minimize the possibility of subversion. A number of administrative decrees were thus issued throughout West Africa aimed at gathering information on the status, sphere of influence, and traveling routes of these "foreign" Muslims. The activities of these individuals, whether they were Qur'anic teachers, preachers, or amulet makers, were carefully recorded and at times restricted (Arnaud 1912).

With the start of World War I, colonial suspicion of Muslim religious specialists took the form of a veritable obsession about the possible emergence of pan-Islamic movements and their redirection against French powers (Cruise O'Brien 1967): there was, in particular, deep concern about possible links between Muslims in West Africa and those under the jurisdiction of the Ottoman Sultan (at the time an ally of Germany) and how this might be a possible menace for the French administration. Individuals suspected of disseminating anti-French propaganda or engaging in what could be described as "subversive activities" were arrested[12] and, in some cases, exiled.[13] By the same token, applications for the construction of mosques and the creation of Qur'anic schools were routinely denied. By localizing Islam, containing its impact on non-Muslim populations, and isolating Muslim communities from one another through various administrative and political measures, French authorities tried to minimize what they saw as potential threats to the stability of the colonial order in West Africa. In so doing, they instituted a disciplinary regime in which any and all Muslim activity was carefully policed not only by French authorities but also by Muslims themselves (Brenner 2001; Soares 2005).

Concerned that Muslim groups, despite these measures, could rapidly unite and turn against their colonial masters, the administration resolved to "know its enemies" (Cruise O'Brien 1967:311). Local administrators were ordered to gather intelligence on Muslim populations and Muslim religious specialists to identify potentially disruptive elements. During World War I French authorities invested scholars with the mission to evaluate the risks of propaganda coming from Turkey and elsewhere.[14] The main objective of these studies was to determine the extent of "inter-territorial communication for religious purposes" through the circulation of pamphlets and newspapers, the organization of Sufi orders, and the sermons of traveling preachers (Cruise O'Brien 1967:309). Also worried about the possible emergence of Mahdism, administrators were constantly watching for signs of impending revolt. Individuals suspected of entertaining contacts with other Muslims in

Cairo or Khartoum were kept under vigilant surveillance and all intercepted documents originating from these cities were systematically confiscated.

Certainly not all Muslims were identified as potential opponents of the colonial administration.[15] In regions where they did not encounter resistance from Muslim populations, colonial authorities were more inclined to build alliances with local Muslim leaders rather than keep them under surveillance, especially when these individuals proved to be valuable administrative, political, and military assistants. Indeed, even in regions of West Africa where considerable effort was devoted to regulating the performance of Muslim activities, the administration was careful to reward those identified as "loyal" friends of France. The cooperation of Muslim elites, it became obvious to French authorities early on, was essential to the stability of their colonial possessions. The trend to enlist cooperation coincided partly with the end of World War I and the defeat of Germany, after Muslim troops proved their courage and loyalty on the battlefields.[16] From then on, Islam lost some of its dangerous character, and dealing with the Muslim question became a matter of minimizing the significance of Islam while enlisting the support of Muslim populations. Muslim subjects who demonstrated their allegiance to the colonial regime were thus gratified with special privileges such as the construction of mosques, paid passages to Mecca, or the protection of the administration.

By cultivating the goodwill of Muslim subjects, even as it curtailed the activities of "charlatans," "vagabonds," and other supposedly subversive Muslim leaders, French authorities hoped to create a "controlled, malleable, pliable Islam that they could twist and bend to serve their purpose" (Clarke 1982:190). To that end, they also tried to gain control over Muslim education by setting up a qualifying examination for teachers. Qur'anic teachers who spent two hours a day teaching French to their students would, under a special policy, be rewarded with a subsidy (Cruise O'Brien 1967).[17] The brutal repression of the Hamawiyya, a Sufi order that originated in Mali, was an important exception to the general climate of compromise and collaboration that characterized the interwar period (see Soares 2005).[18] However, it underscores the extent to which the French authorities remained determined to stamp out any attempt by the Muslim leadership to evade colonial control (Triaud 2000).

After World War II relations between French authorities and their colonial subjects changed substantially, as the colonies became part of the republic and Africans were called upon to participate in the shaping of their future by electing representatives to Parliament. Despite this climate of political liberalization, however, the notion that Islam potentially threatened the colonial order was fueled by the inflammatory rhetoric of young *arabisants* returning from their studies in Libya, Egypt, Sudan, or Saudi Arabia, and criticizing local Muslim elites for their supposed ignorance and lack of belief (Brenner 2001; Kaba 1974). This was a time of dramatic changes in the Muslim world: nationalism was sweeping the Arab world (it was the period of Nasser), and Pakistan and India, and later Indonesia, and Libya gained their respective independence. In 1954 the Algerian war erupted. Fearful of the threat of pan-Islamism and pan-Arabism, the French resolved to curb the influence of young preachers who promoted a supposedly Wahhabi interpretation of Islam; not only did the so-called Wahhabis accuse local Muslims of "idolatry" and irreligiosity, they also advocated the end of colonialism, thereby directly menacing French authority.[19] But times had changed, the era of decolonization was looming, and repression generally did not extend beyond the stage of bureaucratic maneuvers (Triaud 2000).

The Colonial Agenda: Preserving Indigenous Religion

In the immediate aftermath of the conquest of the interior of West Africa, colonial officials hoped that Islam could be used to raise Africans from the depth of their alleged ignorance and "primitiveness." On the Eurocentric scale of judgment used to evaluate the development of different colonial societies, Islam was generally situated between "civilized" Christianity and "primitive" religion. From this perspective, Africans who had been Islamized were assumed to have ascended halfway up the ladder of intellectual, social, and material progress, and to be somewhat closer to "enlightened" Europeans than their "pagan" brethren. Despite having been substantially "blackened" through its incorporation of indigenous practices and resources, Islam was believed by some to have had a positive effect on converted African populations: besides fighting alcoholism and the "barbarous" practice of human sacrifice, it was thought to have instilled in the African psyche the notions of work, order, and economy (Quellien 1910). If Africans could emerge from their "backward" state through conversion to Islam, then it followed that the Islamization of Africa was a positive step in the evolution of the continent (Launay and Soares 1999). From this perspective, colonial authorities should therefore encourage the spread of Islam among colonized populations.

The notion that Islamization was a necessary stage in the evolution of Africans was not widely shared, however. Indeed, many in the colonial administration doubted Islam's potential to discipline (and ultimately redeem)

Africans. For one thing, it was not at all clear that Islam was adapted to the specific "genius" of the African. There was the risk that Islam would tamper with the "African essence" of new converts and lead them on the wrong evolutionary path. Further, promoting Islamization in the colonies essentially meant giving Muslim clerics a license to spread the faith. This was an inherently risky proposition, given how quickly proselytizing was known to turn into fanaticism. On the other hand, the so-called fetishism of non-Muslim populations was thought to be more malleable than Islam. It was the ideal foundation upon which to lay the scaffold of French culture and civility. With the appointment of William Ponty as Governor-General of French West Africa in 1908, the notion that Islam was maladapted to African needs would prevail and suspicion toward Muslim clerics would intensify.

Ponty believed that Islam had been allowed to spread unchecked, and often at the expense of indigenous religions. If left unchallenged, it could become a growing impairment to French rule. Because non-Muslim Africans, in Ponty's opinion, were more flexible and less likely to resist colonial policies than Muslims, everything should be done to halt the progress of Islam in their midst and help them set out along the path to French civilization (Brenner 2001:154–55). To safeguard French interests and guarantee stability in the colonies, Ponty implemented a program, along the lines of the Berber policy followed in North Africa, to keep non-Muslim Africans free from the religious and political domination of neighboring Muslims; overall, the program required "opposing Islamism with the counterweight of organized fetishism" (Brevié 1923:256).

The administrative measures Governor Ponty set in motion to hold Islam in check and protect the rights of non-Muslim people were predicated on what he called a *politique des races,* a policy that ensured ethnic particularism by enabling each "race" to have chiefs appointed from its own people (Amselle 1998; Cruise O'Brien 1967). In accordance with this policy, administrators were ordered to carefully prevent the diffusion of Islam in non-Muslim societies, although they should nevertheless cultivate the loyalty of those who had already adopted Islam. At the practical level, this implied demonstrating more deference toward the so-called fetishism of Africans than in the past, as well as recognizing the legal status of non-Muslims. As noted above, Muslim preachers were to be watched closely, and any attempts at proselytizing were to be systematically discouraged. Opposing the spread of Islam also translated into measures designed to combat the spread of Arabic, the language of the Qur'an. To that end, the teaching of French in both secular and Christian mission schools was to be intensified (Brenner 2001). Ponty's successor,

Governor-General Clozel, similarly tried to contain Muslim expansion and protect indigenous practices believed to have been stifled by Islam. Because Islam should be prevented from claiming new converts, the "particularistic instincts" of indigenous populations that had not been Islamized were to be carefully channeled to "build a barrier" against the spread of Islam.[20] The concept of a barrier to prevent Islam from contaminating non-Muslim populations was widely adopted until the end of the colonial period. In Arewa, as we shall see, the French policy of insulating "fetishist" populations from supposedly destructive Muslim influence effectively hastened the collapse of the local politico-religious order and ultimately paved the way for the emergence of Islam.

The first occupants of Arewa, led by a queen priestess, the Sarauniya, settled there in the sixteenth century and were said to have come from the East. As hunters and gatherers, the Gubawa, as they were known, lacked a centralized political organization and delegated the propitiation of land spirits to priest elders known as 'yan 'kasa (masters of the earth). One of these 'yan 'kasa, known as the Baura, attained a central political position after he married the daughter of Sarauniya (de Latour 1987). As other groups settled in the area and intermixed with Gubawa, their descendants, who recognized the Sarauniya's leadership, came to be known as Azna. The term "Azna" refers not to some notion of ethnicity so much as to the socio-religious order around which these populations had united (de Latour 1987). Often applied indiscriminately to any non-Muslims by the colonial administration (Séré de Rivières 1946), the term remains widely used today to differentiate the members of a handful of surviving 'yan 'kasa lineages from both the pockets of 'yan bori (bori devotees) and the largely Muslim residents of Arewa. Throughout the area, the number of Azna has dwindled in the face of Muslim expansion. Their role as ritual experts and guardians of local "heritage" (gado) has largely been eclipsed by the part that 'yan bori play in the religious affairs of Arewa communities, even as bori activities themselves become increasingly marginal.

When a group of Bornuan warriors, led by their chief Ari, conquered the area soon after the first Gubawa settlements were built, the Gubawa were forced to acknowledge the political suzerainty of the newcomers. Government became the responsibility of the Arewa, the descendants of Ari, while the "masters of the earth" retained ritual control over the land (Piault 1970). The founder of the Arewa dynasty, a product of Ari's union with the Baura's daughter, took the title of Sarkin ("Chief of") Arewa, thereby initiating the mode of exchanges and alliances that from then on insured the warrior group's political legitimacy. Despite their military supremacy, the Arewa

45

(and the later populations who pledged allegiance to them upon settling in the region), depended on the Azna and their ritual sanctioning of the Arewa leader's power. Azna propitiation of tutelary spirits also insured the health and prosperity of Arewa communities, as well as their protection from enemy invasion.

Military preparations and war (a central source of wealth and power for the aristocracy) brought Azna and Arewa together as they requested the support of the spirits. Yet relations between the two groups were far from peaceful. Mawri oral tradition is replete with references to disputes between the people of Lougou—the village of the Sarauniya and the seat of Azna power—and the people of Matankari, the seat of the Arewa leadership. Such quasi-permanent instability preserved Azna autonomy while enabling the Arewa to compete freely for power (de Latour 1987). These various groups and identities later became subsumed under the ethnic marker *Mawri,* a term originally used by Zarma-speaking people (and later adopted by the French) to refer to the populations of Arewa. From the outside, the latter appeared homogeneous enough, organized as they were around a centralizing political power, which enabled their Zarma neighbors to identify them as Mawri (de Latour 1987). Yet far from being homogeneous, the identities that have been lumped together under this designation are a disparate set whose diverse composition betrays the region's complex history of invasion, migration, alliances, and rivalries.

By the turn of the nineteenth century the Sokoto Caliphate had gained control over many of the neighboring Hausa states; but Arewa, a region of subsistence agriculture, remained largely insulated from the influence of Islam.[21] The Mawri's reputation for fierceness and violence kept would-be proselytizers at bay. The French were determined to keep it that way. As the epigraph to this chapter suggests, they hoped that the non-Muslim region of Arewa would serve as a buffer against Muslim expansion. They implemented explicitly anti-Islamic measures, carefully monitoring the comings and goings of the few "foreign" preachers who ventured into these territories, discouraging them from setting up Qur'anic schools, and arresting them whenever they were seen to be taking advantage of local populations. They also actively supported Azna religious practices, going so far as financing annual sacrificial ceremonies held to seek the protection of local spirits. The stated aim of the French was to prevent Muslim proselytizing from destroying indigenous mores. This is how seventy-year-old Alhaji Adamou, a third-generation Muslim, described the French administration's unequal treatment of Muslims and non-Muslims in the region:

The French, they did not like Muslims. Early on they were forcing people to work. When they heard that you were a Qur'anic student, they would automatically take you for *corvée* [forced labor.] They did not prevent you from praying, of course. But the 'yan bori [bori devotees], if they asked the commandant for a contribution to buy an ox, he would give them the money and they would sacrifice the ox on the *doutchi* [literally, "stone"; rocky formation after which the town of Doutchi is named].

The Mawri exerted romantic fascination over colonial observers at the same time that they conveniently bridged the gap between Europe and Africa, civilization and savagery. The French, trained to identify the distinctions between one "race" and another, saw the people of Arewa as uncommonly brave, strongly attached to their land, reluctant to travel, and prone to pick a fight. Having long resisted the encroachment of Islam, they were also categorized as "fetishists"—and it was in the interest of the colonial administration that they remained so. Although the Mawri's so-called fetishism was described as a "fierce and bloody religion based on human and animal sacrifice,"[22] its brutal impact was believed to have been undercut by the colonial conquest. This was all for the good, of course. The advent of *la paix coloniale* meant that agriculture and commerce would now flourish. Increased security, by the same token, would facilitate travel and communication across the region. If the intensification of the movement of goods and people across Arewa was encouraged by the French looking to develop commercial routes, there was also concern that the newly established peace would attract itinerant Muslim clerics eager to propagate Islam. It was therefore essential to bolster local religious practices so as to preserve the balance of power that had emerged between colonial authorities and colonized populations. As the administrator Mahant put it, Islam "may have weakened [Islamized populations'] destructive instincts" but "the evil it carries far outweighs the good it can produce."[23]

For those who shared Mahant's ambivalence toward Islam, Muslim preachers represented more of a threat to local populations than to the French administration. Although the likelihood of an Islamic movement directed at the colonial administration was occasionally mentioned in local reports, a more important concern was Islam's incompatibility with Mawri society. By all accounts, the Mawri were fervently attached to their "fetishes" and wanted nothing to do with Islam. They marked their contempt for the Muslim faith, the French duly noted, by burning the sites where itinerant preachers had prostrated themselves during worship: by spreading thatch on the ground and setting it on fire, they purified the land from the "polluting" influence of Islam. While local administrators wrote with evident satisfaction about the limited influence that foreign Muslim teachers ostensibly enjoyed in Dogondoutchi, they nonetheless frequently mentioned the need to preserve the non-Muslim "customs" of local populations from Muslim influence.

In the early years of colonial rule, a possible Muslim expansion in the region seemed of no particular concern. For one thing, the only Muslims in Arewa in the 1910s, apparently "foreign merchants and travelers from Nigeria,"[24] were merely passing through. Further, local populations were believed to be "totally indifferent to things that were not related to their material well-being,"[25] so, in the eyes of the French, there was little danger that they might embrace a religion requiring discipline, commitment, abstinence, and the timely performance of duties. Despite the presence of a few Qur'anic teachers in the area, Islam was reported to have "had little influence on the indigenous soul."[26] People's resistance to Islam, combined with their material ambitions and successful agricultural pursuits, made Mawri society the perfect terrain in which to sow the seeds of progress and civilization. In the words of a local French official, "it will be the honor of our civilization to succeed where Islam has failed."[27]

Early on the French noticed the tensions in Arewa between a handful of Muslims (whom they routinely identified as "Fulani" or as "foreigners from Nigeria") and the majority of so-called fetishists. "The animosity of Mawri-Azna for Muslims is real and it is in our utmost interest to capitalize on this feeling,"[28] an administrator reported in 1912. Worried that certain measures they had taken had been "very detrimental to the fetishist society,"[29] the French resolved to protect these populations from the putative evils of Islamization. Despite the reputation they enjoyed as "blood-thirsty" warriors, the Mawri were seen by the local administration as relatively docile colonial subjects. In contrast, Muslims who infiltrated the region were routinely described as potentially disruptive agents, looking to build their power. Their commitment to Islam was generally dismissed as vacuous and insincere; this was, needless to say, a problematic view of the situation.

The decidedly anti-Muslim stance tingeing administrative reports on the Mawri is rooted in the work of Maurice Delafosse and Jules Brevié, two colonial ethnographers who dismissed the supposed benefits of Islamization among African societies and insisted that indigenous religious practices were the foundation of African culture. In their pursuit of the "degree zero of paganism" (Amselle 1998:118), devoid of foreign influence, Delafosse and Brevié explicitly stated that Islam, described as the "religion of the Semites," was incompatible with the values of black Africans and should play only a minor role in France's African colonies. Islam was a "religion of travelers and nomadic shepherds" (Brevié 1923:145), ill-adapted to the needs of sedentary hunters and farmers on the African continent. Owing to the incompatibility between Islam and African society, Africans "had remained virtually naturist," Brevié insisted (1923:145).[30]

From this perspective, Islam spread only when it was forcibly imposed on local populations. Islamization, Brevié argued (1923:116), was "synonymous with social desegregation among black Africans." Non-Muslim Africans, by resisting Islamic incursion, "only obeyed their instinct of conservation" (Brevié 1923:xi). Delafosse, a protégé of Governor-General Clozel, similarly defended what he called "*l'âme nègre*" ("the Negro soul") (1922). In his attempt to rehabilitate African religions, he criticized the widespread use of the term "fetishism" to refer to non-Muslim religions. Because he felt that the word was derogatory, he opted instead for the supposedly less demeaning term "animism." Brevié, on the other hand, preferred the concept of "naturism," which he defined as "the type of civilization encountered among Sudanese peoples, because they are still close to the natural state of primitives and also because, to them, man is the center of the natural world and sees it as being in relation only to him" (1923:vii).

Far from amounting to "a crusade against Islam," French attitudes toward colonial subjects, Brevié insisted, should reflect consistent efforts to develop "ethnic" religions:

> Based on what the lessons of the past and the present have taught us, we believe that Muslim civilization responds neither to the aspirations nor to the needs of black societies which have their own civilization that suits them better than any other because it is the logical product of their normal evolution. (1923:x)[31] [my translation]

The ideas sown by Delafosse, Brevié, and others through their published work found a fertile soil in regions like Arewa, where colonial authorities wished to preserve flourishing indigenous practices from the supposedly corrupting influence of Islam. No longer seen as the epitome of "barbarism," as had originally been the case, "animism" emerged from a moral standpoint as "at least as fruitful as Islam and from the political standpoint, more malleable, accessible, and hospitable, and less prone to dangerous propaganda" (Hardy 1940:83).

At first the French policy of favoring non-Muslim practices at the expense of Islam appeared to be working. In 1914 the subdivision of Dogondoutchi counted no more than 289 Muslims out of a total of 47,000 residents according to a colonial survey.[32] Some twenty years later Islam had won reportedly only a limited number of adherents in the town itself:

> In the midst of the Islamized Zarma, Tuareg and Hausa races, the Mawri constitute a fetishist stronghold against which Islam has had limited success. The only *marabout* enjoying some prestige in Dogondoutchi is Mamgadou Malle, originally from the Sudan [modern day Mali] who arrived in the region on the heels of the Voulet-Chanoine Mission.[33] Despite all his efforts, he has never managed to establish a school. He does appear to have some influence on the *chef de canton* [customary chief] of Dogondoutchi, Arzika, a nominal Muslim. The only practicing Muslims are Fulani and Zarma. (République du Niger 1936)

Though French authorities, by the mid-1930s, were successfully curbing the activities of Muslim clerics, some ten years later the number of itinerant preachers had grown noticeably along with those who identified as Muslim. Among the 15,551 individuals recorded in the May 1946 census of the *canton* of Dogondoutchi, 1,786 were listed as "Islamized," 8,767 as "animist," and 4,998 as "practicing no religion" (Séré de Rivières 1946). The growing number of converts to Islam was a source of concern for the French administration: "The Mawri had until now remained fierce fetishists. Their resistance is starting to weaken," a local official noted at the time (Séré de Rivières 1946).

Even as they encouraged local resistance to Muslim proselytism, the French dealt a blow to Azna authority by barring the *'yan 'kasa* from occupying any leadership position in the new colonial order. When it came to political matters, they dealt strictly with the Arewa chieftaincy, whose methods of governance appeared to be more efficacious and in step with local social realities. In addition, as the French started selecting the chiefs, the *'yan 'kasa* lost their ritual control over the process. By integrating the *sarki* (chief), often converted to Islam, and not the Azna leadership in the colonial administration, the French favored the rise of a relatively structured form of Islam (de Latour 1987, 1992). The religion of the Prophet was becoming associated with the social advantages that the colonial administration bestowed upon Arewa leaders. The authority of *'yan 'kasa*, already made vulnerable by the terrible defeat of the Sarauniya by the infamous Voulet-Chanoine expedition in 1899, was eroding.[34] The "masters of the earth" seemed ill-adapted to the new order based on technology and the written word (de Latour 1982, 1987).

In the years that followed, the rates of conversion to Islam grew steadily. The start of World War II, during which colonial subjects fought to defend the "free world," helped Islam become less threatening as the interests of colonial France appeared to coincide with Muslim aspirations (de Latour 1987; Triaud 1974). This was a time of relative prosperity and optimism. If colonial administrators now tolerated Islam because in spreading among Mawri populations it allegedly lost its bellicose character, they nonetheless continued to promote and protect non-Muslim religious practices. It is significant that most of the early conversions to Islam took place among the peasantry. Only after the war did local elites convert massively to the religion of the Prophet. By then, the progress of Islam in Arewa had become quite discernible even if the proportion of Muslims to non-Muslims remained low compared to other regions of Niger.

Islam Noir: Colonial Constructions of Islam in Dogondoutchi

In perhaps the earliest census taken in Niger, French officials were able to assert in 1912 that a great majority of the population of the Territoire Militaire was Muslim. Of 930,000 inhabitants, 718,000 declared they were Muslims, and the remaining 212,000 identified as "fetishists."[35] The practice of Islam was hardly uniform across the colony, however. As one local official noted in his report to the governor of French West Africa, "there is no Islamic unity in the Territory and customs vary from one district, or rather from one race to another."[36] The wide variation in Muslim practice from one region to the next occurred, colonial observers believed, because wherever it took root, Islam adapted to its new cultural milieu. Because of the diversity they witnessed, the French tended to evaluate the Muslim situation of each district separately: they were reluctant to make generalizations about Muslim practice in Niger, even though they were prone to generalize extensively about "African Islam." Nourished as it was by the different *terroirs* it grew on, Islam ostensibly took on "an infinity of personalities that var[ied] with the *mentalité* specific to each different race; there [was] in reality as many different Islams in French West Africa as there [were] Islamized people."[37] Despite being tinged by local cultures, Islam was still seen as a "foreign" faith, generically distinct from "fetishism" and the array of cultural practices that the French, in their attempt to classify Africans, associated with each specific "race."

In Arewa, as previously noted, Muslims early on were scant in number. Historical sources identify Malam Malley (or Malle) as the first Qur'anic teacher to have had an impact, however minimal, on the Dogondoutchi community. The year was 1890. Malley had come from the West to spread the Qur'anic message. He first made several visits to what at the time was only a small village, but eventually he settled in an area known as Sarkin Noma, now one of the central neighborhoods of Dogondoutchi (Mertens and Frigola 2002). Contrary to what is asserted in colonial reports, he was apparently not the only scholar hoping to make conversions in the area at the time. At the end of the nineteenth century Malam Bunkayaou, a cleric from Nigeria, built a prayer ground with thatched walls in another neighborhood. He translated the Qur'an into Hausa to help local Muslims better understand the meaning of God's message (Mertens and Frigola 2002). Around 1900 a mud-walled mosque, the first of its kind, was erected by Amadou Daoura 'dan Katsina, followed by another one in 1933. A third mosque, the first Friday mosque in town, was built in 1938 by Malam Oumarou 'dan Itace who became the first imam of Dogondoutchi.

Until then, the institution of the Friday prayer was reportedly unknown in Dogondoutchi (Mertens and Frigola 2002), as well as in many other West African communities. The construction of the Friday mosque was a significant milestone in the development of Islam in Dogondoutchi, as it was a response to the needs of an officially constituted Muslim community. Unfortunately details surrounding the event are scarce. The presence of this mosque does indicate, however, that the local practice of Islam was becoming more standardized, with Muslims of diverse origins and social status assembling for the midday prayer every Friday. The Friday mosque constitutes the symbolic heart of the Muslim community. There, the faithful unite behind the imam who leads the prayer. The erection of a Friday mosque in town is evidence that, in converting to Islam, people adopted more normative ritual practices such as regular prayer.

If French authorities in Dogondoutchi did not, as far as I can tell, prevent the construction of the Friday mosque, they nonetheless remained dismissive of the religious pretensions of local Muslims whom they routinely characterized as lazy, ignorant, and undisciplined. They described conversion to Islam as a superficial process that did not prevent new Muslims from remaining engaged in "fetishism." This was a clear indication that the French seriously misunderstood the complex and intricate ways in which Islam and the array of practices glossed as "animism" or "fetishism" intersected and influenced one another. French officials believed that Mawri villagers turned to Islam for reasons of convenience (and because they had decided to follow a particular Muslim cleric) and that they did so only as long as their religious duties did not interfere with the exigencies of daily life.

In contrast to their "fetishist" counterparts who were characterized as sincere, steady, and committed, local Muslims supposedly lacked religious zeal. According to French reports, they prayed irregularly and only when they were not engaged in some previous activity at the time of prayer. "One rarely sees the natives leaving momentarily their occupations to go to the mosque or accomplish the prayer on the very spot where they find themselves," a district officer from the neighboring town of Dosso noted.[38] Because Muslims performed the prayer with little or no understanding of the words, their public affirmations of piety were seen by the French as hollow. As one local administrator put it, "for the majority of the Muslims, prayer is nothing but a mechanical act of propriety, one recites meaningless sentences while performing ritual gestures with much seriousness and solemnity, but without fervor and simply because everyone else is doing it."[39] Even though they fasted and gave alms to the poor, ordinary Muslims in Dogondoutchi were thought to be relatively uninformed about basic Qur'anic principles. To the dismay of one French administrator stationed there in 1914, apparently none had ever heard of Mecca or had any desire to travel there.[40]

Muslim clerics themselves did not escape criticism. According to French reports, they had limited scholarly training, spoke no Arabic, lacked religious fervor, and were generally more motivated by the attraction of financial gain (through the sale of amulets and other services) than by the prospects of making converts. In the early years of the colonial period, Qur'anic teachers who appeared in Arewa were foreigners schooled in northern Nigeria who sought to make a living through their teaching and the performance of divination, healing, protection, and so on. Most of them were neither theologians nor literate teachers but were amulet makers. The French contemptuously referred to them as "charlatans." They were thought to have no influence over local populations.[41] Their relative lack of success in attracting followers, the French surmised, owed as much to their questionable knowledge of Islam as to the indifference of Mawri populations for religions other than their own. Villagers in Arewa were reportedly suspicious of these individuals, an attitude encouraged by colonial authorities:

> The prestige of *marabouts* is insignificant because they do not fool anyone about their knowledge and the role they play. Local populations tolerate them and use them as long as they confine themselves to religious activities and participate as little as possible in the private or public life of residents.[42]

On the other hand, when a Muslim religious specialist acquired a substantial following, his success was explained by colonial observers in terms of the reputation he had earned as a "sorcerer endowed with superior powers" (Brevié 1923:187). Aside from disparaging the credentials of local Muslim scholars, such claims reveal how ingrained the notion was among colonial administrators that *Islam noir* was closer to "animism" than to its putatively "white" and purer counterpart.

Whether or not they successfully attracted local villagers to their faith, Muslim preachers were thought to produce shallow conversions prompted by a modicum of instruction and requiring limited commitment: "African" Islam was but a varnish under which an African mentality remained—the mentality of the "sedentary peasant" concerned above all with his relationship to the natural world (Hardy 1940:86–87). Local converts were routinely described as nominal Muslims who accomplished the prayer in a perfunctory way when they remembered to do it at all: "Some who have converted to Islam easily forget to perform the prayer, others driven more by pride than by fanaticism ostensibly accomplish the prayer, but do so by mispronouncing words the meaning of which they do not know."[43] To French observers, the converts' lack of literacy betrayed their lack of faith. That they simply went through the motions as they performed prayers whose literal meaning they did not understand could only mean that Islam was a mere façade, hiding a continued immersion in the "authentic" world of spirits and sacrifice that so fascinated colonial observers. In 1947, according to the district chief,

> the old animist customs are disappearing following the considerable progress of Islam in this region. Nevertheless, even the Islamized Mawri retains a certain affection for his old beliefs, and if he accomplishes the *salam* [prayer], he does not forget to perform sacrifices in the purest animist fashion.[44]

In another report, the same district chief went on to note that just because "animism" was losing ground to Islam, "one should not assume that a rigid barrier is emerging between Islam and animism, for many of those who claim to be Islamized keep in their hearts and minds a primordial attachment to their former religion and they are more afraid of *bori* spirits than of Allah."[45]

Whereas in the colonial imagination "animism" remained pure and strong because it was essentially frozen in tradition, Islam, on the other hand, had been deeply colored by "*la religion du terroir*" (Cardaire 1954:3). Through its absorption of indigenous elements, this "blackened" Islam had become less threatening and more susceptible to French control. It was therefore preferable to the purer, yet also more politically potent form of Islam that the French supposedly encountered in North Africa.

Despite the absence of highly trained religious specialists, Islam was progressing steadily in Dogondoutchi. As noted earlier, this had little to do, in the opinion of local administrators, with the quality of Qur'anic education.

Islam was gaining ground, one administrator surmised, because "although the *marabouts* were not knowledgeable, they were both numerous and patient."[46] The schools they opened attracted students. The French did nothing to oppose the opening of local Qur'anic schools, but they also did nothing to encourage Islamic education. Indeed some of their policies suggest that they obstructed local attempts to promote knowledge of the Qu'ran and Muslim practices. Recall that those who studied the Qur'an were apparently singled out for *corvée* (forced labor). Paradoxically, the French were rather dismissive of local Qur'anic teachers' educational aspirations: the latter were reported to limit their teachings to the first few verses of the Qur'an. Students thus spent more time engaging in physical labor for the benefits of their teachers than learning the Qur'an. The alleged illiteracy of Muslim clerics also meant that the risks of dissemination of anti-French propaganda via newspapers, pamphlets, and other written documents were minimal. Still, French administrators were suspicious of the *malamai*'s motives; the future of the French colonial enterprise seemed increasingly precarious and any threat to its stability had to be averted. Until their departure at Independence, French administrators would continue to distrust both Muslim religious specialists and ordinary Muslims, even though they relied on them for administrative purposes.

Independence: The Intensification of Conversions to Islam

Although the propagation of Islam in Arewa was largely the result of colonial policies that often unwittingly stimulated religious conversion, it was only after Independence that adherence to the Muslim faith intensified dramatically. Following the end of colonial rule, a number of Qur'anic schools opened in Dogondoutchi and the surrounding villages to meet the growing demand for Islamic education. From the 1970s on, an increasing number of girls received a Qur'anic education, which had previously been reserved for boys. The great majority of local children at the time remained unschooled, however. According to the 1962 census, more non-Muslims than Muslims populated most Dogondoutchi neighborhoods (Mertens and Frigola 2002). The town as a whole counted few mosques, and not until 1968 was a new Friday mosque built, with contributions from Muslims throughout the region, to replace the then dilapidated edifice built in 1938 by Malam Oumarou 'dan Itace.

During the first fourteen years of independence, no concerted effort was made to turn Islam into the common denominator between the various ethnic groups that made up the country's population. When Hamani Diori was elected president of the newly independent nation, he inherited the colonial regime's concerns to "take the reality of Islam in hand and seek to structure it" (Triaud 1981:13). Following in the footsteps of the French administration, Diori officially ran the country as a secular state. This meant primarily that he did not interfere with the country's religious institutional structure. Leaving Islam in the hands of Muslim clerics, Diori attempted to unify the country by concentrating instead on the issues of literacy, road construction, and economic development (Horowitz et al. 1983). Meanwhile, the legal system underwent a formal laicization, and religious education was co-opted through the implementation of state-run *medersa* schools (French-Arabic schools where French language and culture are taught alongside Arabic and Islamic sciences) (Miles 1994).

Although Hamani Diori did not promote Islam as a central element of Nigérien national identity, the religion of the Prophet nevertheless expanded rapidly during his presidency. Even before Independence, Islam was already solidly entrenched among the *évolués,* those colonial subjects who had acquired the accoutrements of French culture—language, dress, and education—and thus could petition for French citizenship and were exempt from forced labor. Many of them joined the *Rassemblement Démocratique Africain* (RDA), a parent organization of what would become the ruling party. Known as the "Muslims' party," the RDA contributed to the construction of mosques and promoted the pilgrimage to Mecca (de Latour 1992). As an increasing number of educated people turned to the Muslim faith and culture, Muslim identity became synonymous with power, wealth, and success. In Dogondoutchi many people continued to seek the spirits' assistance when illness or disaster struck, but they could not ignore the various advantages that local Muslims appeared to enjoy (Masquelier 1993). Prosperity, it was widely believed, was a blessing God bestowed upon his creatures. Wealthy *alhazai*—pilgrims from Mecca—who engaged in public acts of piety became models to emulate for those longing for status and affluence. While spirit devotees remained centrally implicated in the production of local cosmology and morality, the *malamai* played an increasingly important role in the community.

Despite the significant expansion of Islam, it was paradoxically the Catholic Church that appeared to enjoy official support. In 1961 the first stone of the cathedral of Niamey was put in place, some two years before the construction of the capital's *grande mosquée* would begin (Triaud 1981). Still, as Miles (1994) points out, Diori was a Muslim, as were the great majority of his countrymen. He sought to remind Nigériens of this by engaging in public demonstrations of piety. In 1962 he went on the pilgrimage to Mecca. The trip was intended to assert his legitimacy as president of a predominantly Muslim country more than to promote Islamic values (Triaud 1981). Only after Colonel Seyni Kountché seized power in a 1974 coup was Islam used to forge a nationalistic consciousness among the nation's disparate ethnic elements. Through the patronage of the pilgrimage to Mecca, the construction of mosques, and the establishment of a Muslim university in Say, concerted efforts were made to unify Nigérien people under the banner of Islam. In some cases, this unification took a literal form. In Niamey, billboards were posted proclaiming "Our God, Allah; Our Book, the Qur'an; Our Prophet, Mohamed" (Horowitz et al. 1983).

A few months after becoming president Kountché founded the *Association Islamique du Niger* (AIN), ostensibly to facilitate communication between the central administration and the Nigérien population. Clearly, however, the creation of this institution was primarily motivated by a desire to fundamentally restructure the role of Islam in the public sphere and establish a shared national identity for the citizens of Niger. Until then, Muslims were organized into private associations, the Muslim community was often divided by doctrinal and territorial disputes (Triaud 1981), and a local sense of ethnic identity prevailed over one's sense of being Muslim. With the creation of the AIN, Kountché sought to promote Islam as *the* religion of the Nigérien people. In a speech to the representatives of AIN on the day of the formal constitution of the association, the president solemnly remarked:

> Before April 15 [the date of the coup], religion was disorganized in our country essentially because structures were out-of-date and tattered. They reflected neither the Islamic face of our country, nor the aspirations of a people who has almost totally submitted to Islam. (Triaud 1981:37)

The establishment of the AIN would change all this. From then on, appointed delegates participated fully in the administrative life of the country, providing a vital link between the government and private citizens. The AIN's stated goals were to promote respect for the precepts of the Qur'an, to extend Islamic education, "to unite Muslims of the two sexes, and to work for the creation and development of libraries" (Sahel Hebdo, in Dunbar 1991:83). The association soon became, in Nicolas's words, "one of the pillars of the regime" (1978:42). As a powerful counterforce to any maraboutic attempt to reform the country's social and political order, the AIN also protected the state from the potential development of militant Islam (Triaud 1981).

After the disastrous impact of the 1973 oil crisis on the economy of many African countries, the Nigérien administration made a concerted effort to cultivate ties to the Arab world. Kountché hoped to obtain additional political and economic support from oil-exporting states and garner legitimacy at home as a Muslim leader by implementing a pro-Islamic policy, in Niger's *Charte Nationale,* a pre-Constitution, for supporting the Palestinian cause and denouncing Zionism as racism (Charlick 1991). Over the following years Niger received assistance from Arab states but not enough to offset the country's dependence on Western developmental aid. Since much of this assistance went to build mosques and cultural centers, finance radio programs, provide scholarships to Arab universities, and support local Muslim associations, Niger's alignment with the Muslim world ultimately resulted in an intensification of religious education (Nicolas 1987). The Islamic University of Say was created, for instance, thanks to the contributions Niger secured from Libya and the Islamic Conference.[47]

Kountché's public recognition of Islam as the national religion of the Nigérien people set off a strong wave of proselytizing in Dogondoutchi in the late 1970s. The AIN did not have a direct hand in the Islamization of the region even though the association was well represented among the local religious elite. Instead, Muslim leaders were invited to participate in the *Société de Développement* (Development Society), an ambitious restructuring of society into a series of councils aimed at channeling input from civil society to government, a role that appears to have had a greater impact. Invested with new visibility, Muslim leaders exhorted those who did not pray to move on to the right "path" (meaning the Islamic path) and send their children to Qur'anic school. Meanwhile, the 'yan 'kasa were further excluded from the political scene, a process that originated when the French administration, anxious in part to protect their religious legitimacy, shut them out of local power negotiations and effectively reduced their ascendency over the terms of *commandement.* With the 'yan 'kasa no longer centrally implicated in the well-being and survival of communities, local residents increasingly turned to the local administration when economic crises and environmental disasters struck.

As the state strengthened its administrative grip over the country, it took charge of installing new *chefs de canton* (customary chiefs). Chiefs therefore no longer needed the sanction of the Azna leadership to buttress their legitimacy. In this regard, the *naden sarauta* (turbaning ceremony)[48] of Amadou Gao, who in 1981 succeeded his brother, Soumana, as *Sarkin* ("chief of") Arewa, is revealing of the changes taking place in the region (de Latour 1987). Unlike Soumana, whose involvement in *bori* activities was well known,

Sarki Amadou was Muslim and intended to give Muslim clerics pride of place in his administration. To avoid alienating the many people in his district who were Azna, he renewed tradition just as a facade. On the eve of the installment ceremony, he summoned the Azna priesthood in Matankari, the former capital of the Arewa chiefs, and gave them an ox to sacrifice to the spirits (de Latour 1987). Instead of reviving tradition, however, his gesture definitively broke with it: in the past, *'yan 'kasa* were never summoned by the *Sarkin* Arewa. Rather, he himself rode to Bagaji—where the supreme priest, the Baura, resided—to receive the nomination for the chieftaincy. In the place of the *'yan 'kasa*, the Préfet (head of the *département* of Dosso, a district that included Arewa), would from then on preside at the turbaning ceremony of the *Sarkin* Arewa (de Latour 1987). With power (*iko*) now on the side of Islam, the *'yan 'kasa* had become irrelevant to the political life of Arewa. As one of de Latour's (1992:132) informants explained to her:

> [Islam] is something strange for us. We see that our beliefs have not managed to stop Islam and that everyone is more and more influenced by this religion, so we too have adopted it. The problem is also that our priests no longer have strength.

Throughout Arewa, those who had so far resisted conversion were pressured to abandon their "backward" ways. Spirit-centered practices were no good, preachers in Dogondoutchi warned audiences during their Friday sermons. To induce people to leave the spirits and turn to Islam, local Muslim leaders made it known that they would no longer attend the burial of those who "did not pray." Muslims, they admonished their audiences, should no more eat with *kafirai* (pagans) than they should participate in the burial of non-Muslims even if that person happened to be their neighbor. The imam of Dogondoutchi himself reminded the faithful assembled for the Friday prayer "not to attend the burial of those who did not pray" (Koutoudi 1988:47). Anxious to avoid ostracism, growing numbers of residents identified as Muslims: "We do the prayer because one must be buried by a *marabout:* people are not respected if they don't pray," a Mawri villager told de Latour (1992:132) in 1973.

Dogondoutchi residents also told me that they, or members of their family, had stopped sacrificing to the spirits because they wanted to be buried by *malamai* when they died.[49] By then Muslim identity had become an indispensable ingredient of social and economic success. Prayer, a conspicuous element of daily life, was virtually synonymous with Muslim practice. To be recognized as a Muslim, simply calling oneself a Muslim was no longer enough. One had to prove it by engaging in public acts of worship. This requirement applied strictly to men, since women prayed in their homes. "Do you pray?" was a standard question that *malamai* asked of those requesting their services. Because those who did not pray were not Muslim, they could not aspire to the moral capital attached to a Muslim identity. More important, they could not avail themselves of the services of Muslim clerics in times of mourning or celebrations. The dread of being rejected by the Muslim community after the birth of one's child, the death of one's kin, or at one's funeral (when the presence of people and the supply of *gudummawa*—help offered in the form of money and gifts—demonstrated the strength of social ties) was a powerful incentive for men to attend prayer sessions and visibly demonstrate their engagement with Islam.

To be buried with *malamai* in attendance confirmed one's status as a pious Muslim and a member of the Muslim community, and was also a reward for a lifetime (or even a few years) of demonstrated commitment to the faith. As Muslims were urged to engage in public displays of religious devotion, burials became privileged arenas for the performance of Muslimhood. Marriage and naming ceremonies, too, were a central locus for the ritual management of identity. *Malamai* played a prominent role at these events. By presiding over the "tying" of the marriage (during which an initial bridewealth transfer is made), they marked the ritual as "Muslim," thereby designating the bride and groom and their families as Muslim—and reminding us that there is a fundamental relation between the theatrical and the sociological notion of role in ritual (Launay 1992).[50] Conversely, the absence of *malamai* at a funeral, the "tying" of a marriage, or a naming ceremony was interpreted to mean that the households involved were not Muslim and that they could not secure the recognition, rights, and services available to "rightful" members of the Muslim community. Such an eventuality was a disgrace that most people who were not dedicated *'yan bori* were keen to avoid even if paradoxically they were likely to complain about the excessive fees levied by *malamai* in exchange for their services. Harouna, a mechanic and father of four, described the Islamization of the 1970s as follows:

> Those *malamai*, they came from Nigeria, to preach and to convert people. When people asked them to "tie" the marriage, they would ask, "do you pray?" If people answered "no," they would refuse to "tie" the marriage. *Babu ruwansu*—they didn't care. For the naming ceremony, too, they would refuse to do it if people didn't pray. Because of this, now people pray even if they do *bori*. This way, they can make sure a *malami* will come to "tie" the marriage, attend the naming ceremony, and bury their children when they die.

Note that, according to Harouna, the Islamization of Dogondoutchi at that time should be attributed to the proselytizing efforts of outsiders who crossed the Nigerian border in search of would-be converts. Whether or not this can be verified, a concerted effort certainly was made by Muslim religious elites to standardize Muslim practices and distinguish them from non-Muslim traditions.[51] As great pressure was placed upon people to identify as either Muslim or spirit devotees, it became important to display one's membership in the Muslim community by performing certain "Islamic" practices. Funerals and other rituals thus emerged as important sites for the dramatization of Muslim identity. By being buried in Muslim fashion, one demonstrated that one had not sacrificed to the spirits during one's life, at least not publicly.[52] As Harouna makes clear, however, people did not simply defer to these demands to demarcate Muslims from non-Muslims in the Dogondoutchi community. In many cases, they sought the assistance of spirits in times of crisis, even as they fashioned new Muslim identities.

This is not to say, of course, that faith and piety played no role in these conversions. On the contrary, learning to live a proper Muslim life was often an important dimension of one's change of religious identity. All the same, by embracing Islam, people did not abandon previous beliefs so much as they adopted new practices that visibly marked them as Muslim. Conversion to Islam is too often assumed to be a total and uncompromising process, a sweeping rejection of the "old." The equation of "belief" with homogeneous, systemized, and neatly bounded cosmology led scholars to neglect the conversation between Islam and what is conventionally categorized as "traditional" religion. Mawri women may combine forms of spirituality and religious identity generally understood to be incompatible even as they claim to conduct their life according to strict Muslim principles. The range of ways in which they live their lives as Muslims invites us to reconsider these religious categories. This book is an attempt to explore how women in Dogondoutchi go about living their lives as Muslims in their irreducible complexities.

Dogondoutchi: A Heterogeneous Muslim Community

As is the case elsewhere, Muslims in Dogondoutchi are expected to perform the religious duties recognized as the Five Pillars of Islam: the profession of faith, the five daily prayers, the fast, alms giving, and, for those who can afford it, the pilgrimage to Mecca. The performance of some of these duties underscores the gender segregation on which Muslim life is based. As noted earlier, men tend to pray in public. Women, on the other hand, are expected to satisfy their religious obligations within their homes. Older women past childbearing age may, theoretically, join the men in prayer but they rarely, if ever, do.

For both Mawri men and women, the construction of one's identity as Muslim involves donning Muslim attire, the terms of which are currently subject to great debate. Being a Muslim in theory also means abstaining from alcohol, tobacco, and ritually unclean meats,[53] as well as engaging in a vast array of practices both at the individual and communal levels that make up the total way of life that is Islam. Because Islam regulates human activities ranging from the most minute and intimate acts of daily living (such as shaving, defecating, or having sex) to the most public and elaborate rituals of communal life (such as the celebration of the Prophet's birthday), it has been characterized as an "orthopraxy" (Smith 1957:28), which puts an emphasis on conduct through which unlettered Muslims can distinguish themselves from non-Muslims and construct themselves as moral persons. From morning till night, through the ways that it carefully and fastidiously prescribes how the body should be treated, groomed, oriented, or presented, Islam is the "very context in which daily life unfolds" (Delaney 1991:25). Being Muslim also means relating to other members of one's household and one's community in a morally responsible and religiously prescribed manner—although the line between religious requirement and mere custom (*al'ada*) can be a fine one, as demonstrated by the ongoing discussions and debates about what is and what is not "Islamic."

By subjecting to painful regulations everything from the way one performs ablutions to how one relates to members of the opposite gender, Islam has contributed substantially to the texture, rhythm, and sounds of life in Mawri communities. This does not mean that all Islamic norms are known, or even followed. Some, quite simply, have no relevance for local Muslims. Nonetheless, many dimensions of daily existence acquire their particular quality thanks to the myriad prescriptions that people follow, at least some of the time, as they go about their occupations. It is important to note that Muslims are not the only ones who invest their activities, mundane and otherwise, with the stamp of Islamic morality and sociality. Today even *bori* devotees expect *malamai* to attend the naming ceremonies of their children and to "tie" their marriages—a testament to the prestige Islam enjoys and the breadth of its influence on Mawri society. They reckon time by the five daily prayers that punctuate the life of their Muslim neighbors with clockwork regularity. And they also routinely frame their activities with pious enunciations: one utters *Bismillah* (In the name of God) to invite a guest to sit down and *'Al-hamdu lillahi* (Praise be to God) to signal praise and satisfaction. *Bori* prayers, themselves, are replete with references to Allah, who, as the Supreme Being, rules over the spirits and delegates powers to them.

Islam may have penetrated into every nook and cranny of Mawri society, helping to structure, rationalize, and moralize countless aspects of it, but it does not mean that all Muslims lead the same kind of Muslim life. Instead, people's commitment to Islam and their contributions to what might be called an Islamic tradition have various expressions. To begin with, not all those who identify as Muslims pray or fast. A significant number of Muslim men—and some women, who are identified as *karuwai* (prostitutes)—consume alcoholic beverages at the local bars, even though abstention from alcohol is an important hallmark of Muslim identity. Others engage in forms of religiosity (including attending church in the company of Christians) which their neighbors disapprove of. Although the influx of Muslim teachers trained in northern Nigeria, Sudan, or elsewhere has helped standardize local practices to some extent, the range of ways of being Muslim remains wide. Muslims have divergent views on how they should relate to the spirits (*aljanu*) that invade their spaces and occasionally their bodies. As a result, they disagree on the legitimacy of the spirit-centered practices of *bori*. For some individuals, especially women, *bori* is neither antithetical to nor easily distinguishable from practices more widely recognized as Islamic. For most Muslim men, on the other hand, it is a remnant of ancestral custom that must be rejected because it is a form of "idolatry" (*shirka*) practiced by unbelievers (*kafirai*). In recent years spirit mediums have become the object of increasing opprobrium, a trend that discourages would-be adepts from joining *bori* and publicizing their involvement in spirit-centered activities.

With the rise of Izala, other previously unquestioned issues became controversial and fostered antagonism between Muslims. Not everyone has joined in the controversies, however. Liberal Muslims, many of whom are the products of state-sponsored education, are proud of the religious freedom Nigériens ostensibly enjoy. They are fiercely critical of preachers who, through their inflammatory rhetoric, promote dissent in their communities and incite crowds to violence (against scantily clad women or prostitutes, who allegedly symbolize the threat society must guard itself against, for instance). Young people, too, are strikingly broadminded when it comes to religious attitudes and values even if in certain contexts they may vocally claim to support Izala values or, conversely, reject them. Most of them today want nothing to do with the sectarian disputes that absorbed their elders' attention in the last decade of the twentieth century. They may not agree on issues such as whether married women should be secluded or whether listening to music is un-Islamic, but these issues are rarely a prelude to wider disagreements. With rates of unemployment soaring and with increasing rural poverty, they face more pressing problems. Unlike the previous generation, for whom Izala's swift rise and emerging public debates over the authenticity of certain modes of religious expressions had divisive outcomes, youth are generally less rigid in the styles of spirituality they adopt and more tolerant of differences in Muslim practice. For these young people, being Muslim is about making pragmatic compromises (about dress or lifestyle, for example) that they can justify by invoking their immaturity or state of impoverishment, and by ignoring the condemnation of "narrow-minded" preachers and critical elders. Regardless of their degree of religious devotion, they are keenly aware that they belong to a global community that (ideally, at least) transcends geographical, ethnic, and class distinctions (Masquelier 2007).

It is fair to say that this was not always so. Although in the early years of Independence, Islam helped somewhat to minimize sectarian competition and promote a sense of shared identity among Nigériens, it did not have the power to draw connections across ethnic boundaries. Thus rivalries between Zarma-speaking populations and the numerically dominant Hausa-speakers (with whom Mawri people identify) intensified as large numbers of educated Zarma successfully integrated into the emerging urban bureaucracy after the French departed. Today, despite evidence to the contrary, the perception lingers among the Mawri peasantry that Zarma people have been favored by the successive Nigérien governments. Although babies are no longer scarified at birth, most Nigériens born before the 1980s can be identified by their "ethnic" facial scars; in the past, these scars as well as people's language and cultural identity often divided them more effectively than Islam could unite them. Thus Fulani herders who settled long ago in the area around Dogondoutchi do not mingle with town residents. In the late 1980s Fulani men were described as devious, dishonest, and generally untrustworthy. Although they, too, were Muslim, their fair complexion set them apart and their "ways" were thought to be fundamentally at odds with local traditions.[54] To this day, Fulani residents arouse suspicion. Although they are entrusted cattle, goats, and sheep for daily care and enjoy rights of access to grazing areas, including cultivated land, they are still seen as "foreigners" by local farmers wary of the damage an unsupervised herd of cattle can inflict on a millet field before the harvest.[55]

In conclusion, the post-Independence Islamization movement did not succeed in homogenizing local forms of religious experience and morality. Even if Muslims adopted increasingly standardized practices, one cannot characterize some of the transformations discussed in this chapter as a one-dimensional progression toward a single, dominant, and uncontested model of religious and moral behavior derived from the teachings of *malamai*. People in Dogondoutchi responded variously to the pressure to Islamize. Some rigorously followed the Qur'anic principles they had learned, and others lived with significant compromises, even though all claimed a Muslim status and wore recognizably Muslim attire. Simply put, being a Muslim meant different things to different people. Through the recognition of these numerous distinctions, we can appreciate how postcolonial identities have been multiplied, transformed, and circulated (Mbembe 1992) amid the impact of religious debates within the Muslim diaspora in Niger. The next chapter explores the recent emergence of a public sphere, where Muslims can converse and disagree about the role of religion in society. I show that such public debate is not simply about the power of the Muslim collectivity against the state, but also about the coexistence of multiple and competing Muslim voices struggling to be heard in the rising cacophony.

DEBATING MUSLIMS,
DISPUTED PRACTICES:
THE NEW PUBLIC
FACE OF ISLAM

3

Relations between Tijaniyya and Izala are like relations between co-wives.
This is why on both sides people gossip and speak ill of each other.
—*Abdou Magaji, Dogondoutchi, 1994*

In 1992 a violent dispute erupted between 'yan Izala and 'yan Tijaniyya
(members of the Tijaniyya order) in the Friday mosque of Dogondoutchi.
Foreign proselytizers who had come to stimulate the religious fervor of Izala
followers, but inadvertently offended their religious opponents, spurred a furi-
ous commotion one afternoon, as Muslims assembled on the prayer grounds.
It started as a heated argument between members of the two Muslim factions but soon escalated into physical confrontation, and before the police
could intervene, men were fighting with knives, clubs, and machetes on the
prayer grounds. When the police finally disarmed some of the assailants,
many had been wounded, though no one was critically injured. Several individuals were escorted to police headquarters and detained there, but apparently no formal charges were made. Mamane, a thirty-year-old butcher and
member of Izala, recounted the incident for me two years later:

> I was with some visitors [and members of Izala] who had just arrived from Ni-
> geria, having been authorized by the state to preach. *Sarkin* Arewa [the custom-
> ary chief] was absent. We went to see the town chief to let him know that we
> had some guests. It was a Saturday. The Tijaniyya clerics were informed that
> 'yan Izala would preach. It was time for the four o'clock prayer. The 'yan Izala
> decided to go to the main mosque and pray. They parked their car inside the
> mosque grounds to protect it from any damage [at the hands of opponents of
> Izala]. But Tijaniyya clerics told the neighborhood hoodlums [about the Izala's
> presence] and they started to throw stones at the car, warning the 'yan Izala to
> get out of the mosque because it wasn't their parents' mosque. The 'yan Izala re-
> alized that the hoodlums had been acting on the orders of the *malamai*. The

police arrived to settle things. The 'yan Izala got in touch with the mayor and the town chief, and they visited one of the Tijaniyya leaders to ask for reparations. Things were settled, and the 'yan Izala were authorized by the mayor's office, the town chief, and the police to preach wherever they wanted.

In his version of events in the mosque, Mamane does not mention the scuffle that ensued between members of the two Muslim factions. He depicts Izala followers as the innocent victims of parochialism and prejudice.

According to Mina, a young woman who allegedly witnessed the incident, the fight erupted after the 'yan Izala argued that half the *masallaci juma'a* (Friday mosque) was rightfully theirs because they, too, were Muslims and therefore just as legitimately entitled to the prayer grounds as their opponents. It happened on a Friday, market day in Dogondoutchi. The 'yan Izala, who had just arrived in town from Nigeria, parked their car in the mosque grounds. The 'yan darika, who had assembled there for the Friday prayer, were outraged by what they perceived as disrespectful behavior by the foreign visitors. They told them to leave. "Why do you enter the mosque in your car? Who are you to do such a thing?" they supposedly asked. The 'yan Izala answered that they wanted half the mosque in which to pray, that it was theirs as much as the 'yan Tijaniyya's. It was then, Mina told me, that the fighting began. The 'yan Izala were soon outnumbered and tried to leave the premises, but their car wouldn't start. It was said that Malam Boubakar, a powerful cleric, had used his medicines to pin their car to the ground. The 'yan Izala tried in vain to start their car. Eventually the town chief, himself a 'dan Izala, offered excuses to Malam Boubakar just as his Nigerian guests were able to start their automobile and, precipitously, leave the scene.

Contradicting Mamane's and Mina's reports, other versions of the incident portrayed Izala followers as mean, aggressive, and intolerant individuals whose sarcastic—often merciless—critiques of mainstream Islam only fostered friction, and whose thoughtless acts led to violence. According to opponents of the Izala association with whom I spoke, the 'yan Izala only entered the mosque to cause trouble: they parked their car within the walls of the mosque in order to provoke the 'yan darika, and so they got what they deserved for trespassing sacred grounds with an automobile. In these versions of the affair, a *malami* (scholar) spoke harshly of Izala during his preaching, allegedly claiming that if the corpse of a 'dan Izala was disinterred the day following the burial, one would find the carcass of a donkey in place of human remains. The preacher also challenged 'yan Izala to swear on the Qur'an—presumably to test their faith in the doctrine they were preaching and defending. In response, one 'dan Izala, an elderly respectable man, allegedly agreed to put his faith to the test despite warnings that he would die if he dared. But before he was able to approach the Qur'an, his daughter begged him to desist. The old man came closer but did not actually touch the Holy Book; other 'yan Izala had intervened. They were then jostled by 'yan darika eager to witness the old man's humiliation and unnerved by his supporters' attempts to protect him. This, reportedly, led to the violent fight that jolted Dogondoutchi— a town where previous religious debates typically pitted Muslims as a group against *bori* devotees.

Even if, in the end, no one was charged with destroying property or endangering life and nothing on the ground was visibly changed, the fight at the mosque was a watershed in the history of Dogondoutchi's religious politics, as it ushered in a new era of debate and division over Muslim identity, knowledge, and authority. Many of those who previously had not taken sides now felt public pressure to acknowledge their views on matters of religion. That the versions of the incident apparently all disagree on what prompted the violence, how it ended, and how those who had taken part were affected is itself indicative of the many perspectives and wide-reaching tensions dividing the local community.[1]

According to Rabi, who had joined Izala three years earlier to follow her husband, the old man was actually assaulted by his opponents, who had never intended to let him prove his faith. When he returned home after quiet had been restored, concerned kin reprimanded him for having risked his life. As Rabi put it, "Why did he go there at all? He had no friends, no neighbors [to watch out for him]. The 'yan darika could have killed him." Rabi's anguished statement highlights the violent hatred that colored the relationship between 'yan Izala and 'yan darika, a loathing, some said, that could lead a man to stand by and watch his brother die if the two belonged to opposite Muslim factions. It was believed that 'yan Izala carried knives, aggravating the anxiety of many residents already pessimistic about the outcome of the growing rivalry. Stories of fathers mercilessly beating their newly converted sons with clubs and rumors of 'yan Izala surreptitiously feeding people "medicine" (allegedly made with the blood of drowned kittens) to induce conversion were legion in Muslim circles.

The incident at the mosque, predictably, was followed by other disputes pitting reformists against critics of Izala, brothers against brothers, fathers against sons. Contested in these disputes were the nature of Islamic knowledge and the legitimization of Muslim authority. Despite their often divisive outcomes, most significant about these confrontations is that they would not have occurred had there not been a breakthrough in Islamic consciousness in

Niger allowing multiple perspectives to emerge. This new awareness, the debates it spawned, and the divergent perspectives that emerged are explored in this chapter by focusing on Izala, the reformist movement whose rapid spread in Niger sparked intense struggles over the definition of Muslim identity and the correct practice of Islam. Like Muslims elsewhere, Dogondoutchi residents, ever since Izala appeared, have been continually arguing about how to relate the Scriptures properly to local social practices and forms of religiosity. Whether the Qur'an is one or many, for instance, was a burning issue for Dogondoutchi residents in the early 1990s. Some followers of the Prophet were attracted to the notion that there were many Qur'ans, for this would justify the emergence of several Muslim traditions and facilitate their peaceful coexistence within one community. With this came the prospect of legitimizing access to different truths—each Qur'an defining its own particular brand—easing the current competition to define what constituted Islamic tradition.

The problem of only one book for all Muslims was not always so hotly debated. Until recently Dogondoutchi residents knew one kind of Islam exclusively and rarely questioned the dictates of a faith that had come to define the status quo for most Nigériens, regardless of their degree of wealth and education or their gender and social status. Communities were split by religious debate, but the arguments were primarily about the nature of spirit-human relationships. Muslims would generally argue that if spirits intervened in people's lives, they should be ignored. *Azna* and *bori* devotees disagreed, claiming that spirits were a necessary—and largely inevitable—presence in people's lives and that driving them away merely compounded difficulties. In the late 1980s the local chief of *bori* often criticized *malamai* for insulting spirit devotees during their preaching, and bitter confrontations would erupt between the followers of the Prophet and the 'yan bori. Rumors about the allegedly deceitful and manipulative practices of local *malamai* were rampant in the *bori* community (Masquelier 1992, 2001b).

But the situation was not a clear-cut divide. Although, in the past, Muslims and *bori* adepts have fought, scorned, or offended each other, their visions of the world were not irreconcilable. The identities of Muslims and non-Muslims, as I have argued elsewhere, have been fluid, multilayered, and often overlapping (Masquelier 2001b). For Muslim women, for example, *bori* was a valuable resource in dealing with the vicissitudes of marriage and the troubles associated with reproduction, and so, for them, *bori* and *salla* (prayer) were not incompatible. Muslim men also found spirit-centered practices useful as a foil against which they stressed their superiority over parochial *bori* adepts. Preachers criticized *bori* practices in their sermons and urged spirit devotees to abandon their "sinful" ways. Muslim elites, when not forbidding their performance altogether, pressured *bori* leaders to stop holding un-Islamic rites. At the same time, when Islam seemed bent on repressing what was locally referred to as "traditional" culture, evidence emerged that *bori* had evolved in conjunction with Islam (Masquelier 2001b).

Despite the intensity of earlier confrontations, the long-standing moral debates pitting *bori* values against Muslim conventions appeared less relevant with the emergence of Izala. Local residents' ongoing attempts to debase *bori* were eclipsed, at least initially, by Muslims attacking Muslims. The disputes now centered on the source and content of Islamic knowledge, the correct practice of Islam, the public expression of religious devotion, and the appropriate conduct of women in society. All this emerged with the sweeping reforms instituted in the early 1990s by what was then a minority of 'yan Izala eager to purify Islam and free itself from the control of Muslim elders. In only a few years Izala reformists, calling themselves "particular kinds of Muslims" (Brenner 1993a:3), managed to carve out a niche for themselves in their attempts to impress upon Nigérien communities an alternative moral order based on what they claimed was a literal reading of the Qur'an. The rapid spread of this Izala movement led to the polarization of the religious field, with the reformers referred to as 'yan Izala and anyone else, including Sufis, as 'yan darika.

This chapter focuses on the continuing struggles between 'yan Izala and their critics for the control of truth to illuminate how public Islam acquired a new momentum as a source of moral order. These struggles occurred in the context of profound transformations in the social basis of religious authority largely facilitated by the state's retreat from civic life, the spread of accessible, affordable media technologies, and the sharp sense of "abjection" (Ferguson 1999:236) experienced by youths who felt cheated by the false promises of post-Independence governments. By democratizing access to religious knowledge and encouraging personal interpretation, Izala reforms also forced Muslims of all persuasions to adopt a particular perspective and publicly articulate their individual convictions. The question of what it meant to be a Muslim acquired a new salience in these debates. Muslims on either side of the religious divide were compelled to think more critically about the arguments they invoked to justify their ways of living a Muslim life. Through their contributions to public debates in which they spoke *as* Muslims, Nigériens had a discernable impact on shaping an Islamic public sphere, even if they disagreed, sometimes violently, on the particular form it would take.

The Public Face of Islam

In his analysis of the Maitatsine movement in northern Nigeria, Watts notes that wherever Islam provides the moral framework for the elaboration of an oppositional culture aimed at challenging dominant hegemonies, it acts "as both an alternative political and economic platform to the state and a critical oppositional discourse" (1996:284). The Maitatsine movement emerged in the 1970s under the leadership of the Muslim scholar Muhammad Marwa, who claimed to have had divine revelations superseding those of the Prophet Muhammad. In his sermons the controversial preacher (whose Hausa nickname was Mai Tatsine, "the master of condemnation") vigorously attacked materialism and forbid the use of Western consumer goods such as watches and bicycles. He also prohibited certain indigenous practices, such as using baobab leaves for sauces, based on his unorthodox interpretation of the Qur'an. Maintaining that the Qur'an was the only acceptable source of guidance for Muslims (Hiskett 1987; Loimeier 1997b), he criticized the corruption of political leaders and Muslim scholarly elites, and encouraged his disciples to defy the law. In December 1980, following a series of clashes with the police, Marwa's increasingly restless followers (mostly frustrated Qur'anic students and poverty-stricken urban migrants) tried to occupy the central mosque in Kano. Their ensuing conflict, first with security forces and later with the Nigerian army, left some six thousand people dead, among them Muhammad Marwa (Hiskett 1987; Isichei 1987; Lubeck 1985). Like other reformist movements in West Africa and elsewhere that spring from the constant negotiation of Muslim tradition, Maitatsine compels us to critically rethink the relation between state and society. The Kano riots brought attention to the worsening predicament of migrants and Qur'anic students from the rural hinterland, whose growing numbers could no longer be absorbed by Kano's economic and religious networks (Loimeier 1997b). At a time when political parties were still banned, that Marwa mobilized the political energies of Kano's malcontents under the banner of Islam, successfully channeling them into expressions of social unrest, suggests the extent to which Islam in its most messianic forms can provide an effective critique of the state and the status quo.

Though substantially different from the Maitatsine movement in scope and substance,[2] Izala similarly contributes a "utopian vision of civil society" (Watts 1996:255) that challenges the normative functions of the secular state. Because, like the 'yan Tatsine, 'yan Izala engaged in vociferous attacks against traditionalist *malamai*, Qur'anic teachers, and religious leaders, as well as criticizing many Muslim traditions as un-Islamic, their public declarations generated counterattacks by the disparaged parties eager to reassert the legitimacy of their interpretation of Islamic tradition. As traditionalist and reformist adversaries struggled to articulate bits and pieces of Islamic knowledge to demonstrate the superiority of their own perspective, they constructed themselves in contrast to their opponents; because both claimed a Muslim status, this was the only way to highlight their own Muslim distinctiveness. Like other reformist visions that have emerged in the context of salient oppositions between Muslim factions throughout Sub-Saharan Africa (Al-Karsani 1993; Brenner 1993b; Dilley 2004; O'Fahey 1993; Thorold 1993; Westerlund and Rosander 1997), Izala conceptions of Islam became defined "not so much by consensus among their adherents, as by the cleavages that distinguish[ed] them from other recognized and rejected alternatives" (Launay 1992:9). In this regard, one should resist overemphasizing the homogeneity of the reformist movement. Indeed, 'yan Izala disagree among themselves on many issues. French-educated 'yan Izala tend to be in favor of contraception and a woman's right to work outside the home in contrast to their Arabic-educated counterparts, who insist that women should stick to domestic tasks and that contraception is an affront to God.

Most notable about these conflicts is that, through their negotiations of what constitutes "Islam," Muslims on either side of the debate engaged in critical discussions of society and culture. Though ostensibly arguing about religious matters, they ultimately came to "rethink how they ordered their lives" (Bowen 1993:326) and to cultivate a new consciousness about their place as Muslims in the Nigérien nation-state. Similar to the Indonesian case described by Bowen in which Gayo villagers came to debate all matters Islamic from worship to work to the music they should listen to (if at all), Dogondoutchi residents contributed to a "public sphere of discourse that combine[d] religious, social, and political messages" (Bowen 1993:325).

If these religious debates offer a valuable perspective from which to consider the form civil society takes in postcolonial Africa, they also signal the limitations of conventional formulations of civility that have enjoyed wide currency in academic analyses of citizenship and society (Comaroff and Comaroff 1999; Launay and Soares 1999; Soares 2004b). In addition to the fact that the bourgeois public sphere described by Habermas (1989) excludes religion,[3] the problem with an idealized formulation of civil society is that it presupposes egalitarian, democratic, and rational exchanges of ideas. Moreover, it contributes a fairly narrow vision of the forms that resistance to state hegemony might take. The debates in Niger concerning public arenas not fully controlled by the postcolonial state are, of course, emancipating to some extent, but they are also oppressive. In Fatton's words, they are "neither homogenous, nor unitary [but rather] fragmented by the contradictory historical alternatives of competing social actors, institutions, and beliefs" (1995:73).

Like other increasingly prominent religious reforms elsewhere that compel us to rethink the state's articulation of local moralities (Lehmann and Siebzehner 2006; Meyer 2006; Schulz 2003), the successful spread of Izala forces us to understand civil society in broader terms, as a social space where issues of freedom, power, and responsibility can be entertained in the context of utopian visions designed to challenge what 'yan Izala in Dogondoutchi perceive as oppressive and un-Islamic institutions, relations, and ideas. Disagreements surrounding matters as diverse as worship, education, commensalism, and the dispersal of wealth highlight how contentious issues—themselves an index of the cleavages that emerge within society—provide an effective means through which some Muslims can reinvent themselves as custodians of endangered Muslim values by adopting alternative strategies of self-presentation and political contestation. As we shall see, 'yan Izala's vision of an alternative Muslim civil society that promotes a philosophy of "each man for himself," stresses education for all, and redefines women's roles provides a privileged vantage point from which to explore the role of Islam in its mediation of state-society relations. The rise of religious activism in Niger, as elsewhere in the world, coincides with the sharp decline of the state, rapid population growth, rising economic inequalities, and an accelerated exodus from rural areas (Eickelman 1997:29). Although Izala originated as a critique of Sufi doctrine, it also gave voice to a host of concerns that arose out of the profound sociopolitical and economic transformations of the last decades (Umar 1993). Its appeal, therefore, must be largely understood in terms of the movement's ability to offer disenfranchised populations a revitalized sense of identity and a framework for collective action in the face of the state's growing inability to provide for its citizens.

Civil Society and Islam in Contemporary Niger

For Nigériens who participated in the country's first multiparty election in 1993 and then witnessed the return of military rule in their virtually bankrupt country less than three years later, the path to democracy has been bumpy and filled with disappointments. During its early years as an independent state, the country was run by a single-party civilian government under the presidency of Hamani Diori. This was a favorable period for Nigérien agriculture, the ground-nut–based export economy expanded, and, as a result, rural discontent was minimal (Charlick 1991:57). In 1974 a devastating drought, combined with accusations of corrupt management of food relief, prompted Colonel Seyni Kountché to oust Diori and install a military regime. During much of Kountché's presidency, Niger enjoyed a prosperity brought by uranium revenues at a time when the price of uranium was high. The state invested heavily in agriculture and health care, and expanded the size of its bureaucracy. For a brief period, literate Nigériens could obtain jobs as civil servants in the newly expanded administrative sector. With the 1985 collapse of uranium prices on the world market, however, prosperity ended as the government found itself increasingly unable to meet its obligations. Upon Kountché's death in 1987, his successor, Colonel Ali Saïbou, was faced with a growing deficit, rising unemployment, and intensifying dissatisfaction among certain sectors of the population. Pressured by foreign donors to undertake reforms, he released political prisoners, promulgated a new constitution, and liberalized some of the country's laws and policies. The liberalization he inaugurated became known as *la décrispation* (the loosening of tension). New political parties and civic associations sprang up after Saïbou gave in to union and student demands that he institute a multiparty democratic system. In July 1991 a National Conference was convened to pave the way for the adoption of a new constitution and multiparty elections. The conference was the setting of vigorous debates about the role Islam should play in the definition of the state, pitting young liberals who defended the vision of a secular state against reformist Muslims who argued for a more central role for Islam in Nigérien affairs. Though much was accomplished during the transition to multiparty politics (such as the adoption of electoral and rural codes), the economy continued to worsen.

In 1993 Ousmane was elected democratically as president of Niger. However, rivalries within the ruling coalition eventually brought the government to a virtual standstill, which prompted Ibrahim Baré Maïnassara to depose Mahamane in January 1996. After the drafting of a constitution for a Fourth Republic, fraudulent presidential elections installed the coup leader as commander of the nation in July 1996, thereby effectively disenfranchising much of the Nigérien electorate. International donors immediately stopped multilateral and bilateral economic assistance. Thereafter the government's human rights record worsened considerably: opposition leaders were jailed, journalists were routinely intimidated or deported by the military, and the offices of independent media were burned or raided each time they criticized the regime. Persistent drought, soil degradation, high import prices, a flat uranium market, and burdensome debts further weakened the already troubled economy. On April 9, 1999, in a coup led by Major Daouda Malam Wanké, Baré was killed by his own guards. A National Reconciliation Council was established to oversee new presidential elections, and in November 1999 Tandja Mamadou won the presidency. Soon after, foreign aid resumed.[4] In December 2004 Tandja was elected to his second presidential term.

Despite the resumption of foreign aid, the return to democracy has not brought an immediate solution to the country's most burning fiscal problems. Since uranium was the country's chief export, major domains of economic and civic enterprise came to a standstill with the slump in uranium prices. Tax revenues were reduced to 9 percent of the GNP. Intent on maintaining public expenditures at their boom level despite an inexorably shrinking tax base, the government was unable to pay bills submitted by local suppliers or to finance an adequate level of public service. Niger's external debt more than doubled during 1984–88, and the payment of state employees' salaries was routinely delayed. Attempts to generate revenues by raising tax rates and strengthening enforcement met with failure. While some civil servants were philosophical about receiving their April salaries in May or June, the armed forces occasionally reacted with mutiny. Throughout much of the 1990s, growing discontent, fostered by the further withholding of government workers' salaries, led to a series of strikes, crippling public services and causing major disruptions throughout the country, particularly in the national educational system, with most students spending more days outside than inside the schools.

In the wake of escalating fiscal deficit, and on the urging of international donors to undertake thorough reforms, the Nigérien government resorted to desperate stopgap measures that only resulted in a transfer of civic operations out of the formal sector, commonly referred to as *la fuite vers l'informel* (the flight toward the informal sector) (Barlow and Snyder 1993). Desperately needed social services such as health care and education were drastically curtailed, and unemployment rose. While Niger's participation in the artificially maintained franc zone protected the country from currency fluctuation, the fixity of the CFA franc to French currency for more than forty years also abetted the slow but consistent impoverishment of a population encouraged to buy French imported goods. In 1994 the CFA franc, the currency of the *Communauté Financière Africaine* (African Financial Community), was devalued to increase domestic production and investment by boosting exports. Overnight, Nigériens saw their living standards decline steadily and had to pay twice what they used to for many of the imports they had come to depend on. Owing to its dismal literacy rates, low life expectancy, and abysmal standard of living, Niger ranked 173rd out of 174 countries on the UN's Human Development Index in the early 2000s. In 2005 the UN assessment of the well-being of Nigériens dipped even lower, and Niger was ranked the poorest country in the world.

It is probably too early to offer a prognosis on the impact of recent events on Niger's path to democracy and pluralism. What is certain is that the *décrispation* introduced in the late 1980s to facilitate Niger's transition to a civilian, democratically elected regime has promoted an upsurge of popular ambitions and fostered the emergence of new forms of social protest—some taking distinctly religious forms. Among other things, the democratization promoted by former president Ali Saïbou ushered in an era of public debate on politics and policy through the introduction of two new independent newspapers, *Le Républicain* and *Haske* (light, in Hausa) that challenged the government-controlled *Sahel* by offering readers previously suppressed information on various topics. Since then, scores of newspapers, some fiercely critical of the regime, have been published by political parties or independent actors. Even more important, some one hundred local radio stations have been created that provide news, discussions, and entertainment in local languages for the majority of the non–French-speaking population.

Liberalization and the recognition of civic rights notwithstanding, criticizing the government is not without risks. Even democratically elected leaders have occasionally taken action to limit freedom of the press and stifle political discussions through intimidation, harassment, and detention. Radio stations, widely popular among the largely illiterate population, are not immune to this censorship. Indeed, it has been suggested that the post-Kountché military regimes of Saïbou, Baré, and Wanké were more tolerant of Muslim reformists than were the democratically elected regimes of Ousmane and Tandja (Sounaye 2006). Despite efforts by these successive regimes to control media content, however, the local independent press—now comprising more than twenty privately owned newspapers—has remained relatively assertive in protesting government actions.[5]

Although civic and political organizations were banned from holding gatherings during Baré's presidency, people throughout the country became increasingly aware nonetheless that they belonged to specific groups and needed to organize to defend their interests. According to *Voice of America* Hausa broadcaster Aliyu Mustaphawas (1991:1, 4), the new openness that characterized talk about politics and the state in Niger in the early 1990s was largely owing to the National Conference that was deliberating the country's political future in 1991. His description of the new climate in the capital is revealing of the changes the whole country was experiencing at the time:

> If you have been away from the city of Niamey for say two or more years, you would feel the change immediately, as soon as you arrive in town. You will observe right away the change in people's facial expressions, and they talk a little louder than before. [. . .] It looks like virtually everyone is involved in one activity or the other, from politicians, academicians, members of the business community to workers, students, and women. Everyone, that is, except the military. One gets the feeling that the entire country has suddenly become politically alive, in sharp contrast with the past when Niamey used to be politically boring. (Mustaphawas 1991:4)

These mechanisms of self-determination reflect the many forms that postcolonial public opinion takes when it emerges in broad daylight. From the five-year Tuareg struggle for secession[6] to the students' demonstrations in the 1990s to the rejection of the government's Family Code by reformist Muslim associations, one witnessed a complete transformation of the political process (Monga 1995). For Nigériens who, in 1996, lost—or perhaps never had—rights to full participation in the civil and political life of their nation, and who suffered an austere authoritarian regime until the late 1980s, these movements of social protest were a means of reclaiming the right of self-expression, previously usurped by the government (Monga 1995). Thus, for instance, between 1994 and 2000, the number of officially recognized Islamic associations went from five to more than forty (Sounaye 2006).

Against this background, I highlight some defining characteristics of the Izala doctrine and its success in channeling communal discontent to show how the reformist movement has contributed in its own way to the affirmation of social identity in Dogondoutchi. Because its members faced the threat of imprisonment for subversive activity, the Izala movement remained in its embryonic stage until 1992, when its leaders felt it was safe to emerge from the shadows.[7] It now operates in a climate conducive to identity-based politics. Although they sometimes spoke of transforming Niger into an Islamic republic on the Iranian model,[8] 'yan Izala did not, at first, play a determining role in the political life of the country.[9] In recent years, bolstered by popular support, Izala activists have gained strength and poise on the political scene. Their opposition to the state has grown bolder, thereby "contributing to the erosion of its tenuous legitimacy" (Charlick 2004:99). The Tandja government has responded cautiously to the Izala challenge, even if it has occasionally cracked down on those who openly defied the state's authority. More recently, however, despite the obvious political costs, the crackdown on Izala will apparently remain part of Tandja's policy, mandated partly by Niger's partnership with the U.S. administration in its "war on terrorism" (Charlick 2004).

Truth, Authority, and Authenticity

'Yan Izala professed to liberate Muslims and "animists" alike from the shackles of superstition and idolatry through education and enlightenment. But their virulent denunciation of Sufism and its founders virtually ostracized them from the rest of the Muslim community (Masquelier in press). They angered local Muslim clerics by relentlessly accusing them of quackery and denouncing them as parasites living off a credulous and ignorant population, as they themselves were castigated by those who objected to their novel conceptions of society and sociality. They made enemies of former friends by contesting the scheduling and length of daily prayers,[10] and by promoting an ethic of frugal commensality that contradicted important social values based on generosity and ostentation. Their widely disseminated, cleverly advertised doctrines also raised passionate resentment among devout Muslims, who saw themselves as having followed the precepts of the Qur'an long before 'yan Izala undertook their reformist mission. In the eyes of Muslim elites, 'yan Izala who claimed to know the Qur'an well were nothing but impostors with limited training and no expertise in Qur'anic law.

In the past, the official promotion of an admittedly liberal Islam helped minimize sectarian tensions and promote national unity. More recently, the confrontation between anti-Izala and reformist factions suggests that Islam has become a medium for expressing ideological, political, and even socioeconomic cleavages (Al-Karsani 1993). It is no surprise that Izala was seen by many of its opponents as a subversive force backed by foreign Muslim powers who wished to transform the country into one of their satellites. An individual need only attend one of the semiweekly preaching sessions organized by Izala to assess the divisive effects of the movement in Dogondoutchi. Rather than giving voice to shared values, the words of Izala preachers widened oppositions and sharpened rivalries. In challenging state authority and redefining their place in society, 'yan Izala thus contributed to the emergence of a civil society that was "neither homogenous, nor wholly emancipatory [but rather] contradictory, exhibiting both democratic and despotic tendencies" (Fatton 1995:93).

Despite their insistence that all that came after Muhammad is *haram* (forbidden), Izala's call for a return to the pristine Islam of the Prophet is not a rejection of modernity. Rather, like reformists and "modernists" in Malaysia, Trinidad, and elsewhere (Bowen 1997; Peletz 1997; Thaiss 1994), Izala followers tried to find a middle path between Islam and modernity. Although reformist movements describe their doctrine as a return to the roots of Islam, the general effect, Brenner (2001:144) points out, is

> to create a doctrinal *tabula rasa* that allows for the complete legal reinterpretation of Islam. This break with the past in turn allows for the "modernization" of Islam, in the sense of refashioning its legal constraints to conform with contemporary social, political, and economic conditions. In fact, the process involves a reinterpretation of the past in order better to confront the present.

In Niger, Muslim reformists so far have had more impact on the performance of devotional practices and the fashioning of modest personas than on the transformation of legal institutions. By forcing those who call themselves Muslims to abandon all innovations, learn to read and write Arabic, and conform more strictly to the Scriptures, Izala followers have forged a Muslim modernity that responds to the aspirations of certain segments of society without seeking inspiration in Western notions of authority and accountability. In this alternative modernity, innovations that effectively promote the cause of Izala by facilitating the spread of its message are deemed acceptable. Loudspeakers, cassettes, and radios are thus part of the innovative technological infrastructure necessitated by the breadth and urgency of the Izala mission.[11]

As is the case elsewhere, the use of broadcast technology by Izala reformists initiated a dramatic shift in the forms that knowledge took as well as in the ways in which knowledge was expressed and transmitted. In the process of assessing differing truths or defending the superiority of one over another, Muslims on either side of the religious divide explored and questioned the whole notion of *ilimi* (knowledge), its sources, forms, and substance, in ways that they never had before. For much of what was taken for granted as Islamic doctrine now had to withstand the light of scrutiny. Much of what had been embodied now had to be objectified to justify its legitimacy. What had been known as common sense now had to be articulated as knowledge. Practices that were justified by an appeal to tradition had to find justification in Qur'anic sources. Knowledge, while remaining the stuff of everyday social life, also became progressively more sacralized. No longer was it sufficient simply to distinguish knowledge from common sense.

More than ever knowledge had become "linked to doing and its embodied signs; objectified knowledge [must be] displayed and legitimated in practice" (Lambek 1993:25).

Because the Izala message of reform circulated within spaces of doubts and ambiguity even as it exposed the supposed fallacy of previously unquestioned traditions, it failed at times to provide answers, generating instead confusion and ambivalence. Some Muslims in Dogondoutchi thus wondered whether the process of translating the book from Arabic into Hausa or Tamasheq might have introduced disparities between the original and the translations. This would explain why Muslims disagreed about many issues even though they all used the Qur'an as the source of their knowledge. Confronted with the multiplicity of arguments against or in favor of a particular religious practice allegedly based on the Scriptures, they felt confused. Current debates about the nature of Islamic knowledge forced them to question previously axiomatic truths and traditions (Masquelier in press).

The Qur'an remains the ultimate reference for those who seek to legitimize practices that were once justified by a simple appeal to tradition. As self-appointed custodians of the truth, Izala reformers constantly invoked the holy book in their criticism of a faith allegedly corrupted by syncretism and innovation. They therefore condemned the wearing of *layu* (amulets) because the Qur'an made no mention of protective charms. Amulets are routinely purchased as protection against disease, witchcraft, and spiritual attacks or for curative purposes. People also purchase amulets and other Qur'anic medicines to obtain success in school, at work, or in love. Amulets can also protect against theft, automobile accidents, and the schemes of a jealous co-wife[12] or an overambitious colleague.[13] In the face of Izala's condemnation of *layu*, ordinary Muslims, many of whom wore amulets or bought them for their children, insisted, along with an appeal to timeless traditions, that their faith, too, was based on a thorough knowledge of the Qur'an.[14] Thus we see how doctrinal debates between Muslim reformists and anti-Izala Muslims operated "within a context which ultimately reduce[d] all argumentation to a demonstration that the content of a given doctrinal position constitute[d] a better reading than its competitors of the fundamental Islamic texts" (Brenner 2001:135).

For those reluctant to acknowledge the superiority of one doctrinal position over another, widely divergent views could only mean that more than one holy book must exist. Those committed to the uniqueness of the Qur'an invoked practical sources of difference; for example, one man told me that doctrinal discrepancies between 'yan darika and 'yan Izala originated because Abubakar Gumi, one of the founders of Izala in Nigeria, had translated the Qur'an from Arabic to French and then to Hausa, and his different rendering of key terms led to diverging understandings of Islamic precepts and practices. For others, doctrinal differences stemmed from the fact that, although some had actually read and memorized the word of God, others simply pretended to have done so. From the Izala perspective, Islam was one, and to suggest otherwise was blasphemy: 'yan Izala may disagree with anti-Izala Muslims over what was or was not "Islamic," but their disagreement assumed the existence of a single Islam (Launay 1992:5). Yet others, less textual in their view of the truth, insisted that their book resided not on paper but in their hearts, having been thoroughly memorized; the written book was but an imperfect transcript. For them, engaging in Qur'anic discussions was an intimate part of how one lived one's life as a Muslim. Islamic truth laid less in doctrinal debate than in lived practice.

That the Qur'an should generate such confusion about its ontological status is hardly surprising. It is, as Fischer and Abedi noted, "a profoundly enigmatic text. For Muslims, it is the word of God, divine in both its meanings and its language, infinite, beyond human capacity for definitive exegesis" (1990:97). At the same time, the very structure of Qur'an and hadith, "a fun house of mirrors playing upon appearances and resemblances [mutashabih] that may or may not be grounded" (Fischer and Abedi 1990:100), lays in being open to debate, dialogue, and reinterpretation. The manner in which the text itself is held to relate to actual everyday practice also changes over time and space. To understand the reformist movement currently sweeping through Muslim communities in Arewa and elsewhere requires that we pay close attention to the interpretive and dialogic tradition that is at the very heart of Islam. Only by acknowledging the current struggles for the definition of truth and the control of knowledge can we begin to approach the multiplicity and richness of expression that have emerged out of universalist Islamic principles. Note that Islam's long history of revival and reform is not simply rooted in its own traditions. It is also responding to Westernization and secularization. Anti-Sufism, in its most recent incarnation as Izala, promotes an alternative moral and political order that contests the legacies of Western colonialism. This is what makes Islamic reform movements in Africa and elsewhere so relevant to discussions of postcolonial identity and modernity. For, in such cases, Islam becomes the vehicle for the articulation and sustenance of new traditions as well as the idiom in which a culturally convincing critique of the postcolonial state can be shaped.

Origins of the Izala Movement

Although Shaykh Abubakar Gumi is widely regarded as the originator of what is referred to as "anti-Sufism" in Nigeria, conventional social history suggests that the Izala movement was founded by Malam Ismaila Idris[15] with the support of Gumi, who had close ties with Saudi Arabia, Kuwait, and the Muslim Students Society (Ibrahim 1991). Originally associated with the Qadiriyya, Gumi started developing an anti-Sufi perspective in the emergent context of local elites' opposition to colonialism. British domination was believed to foster religious ignorance through inadequate Islamic education. Aside from generally condemning ignorance and "superstition," Gumi blamed colonialism for undermining Islamic learning. In the 1940s he developed a sustained critique of the doctrine of Sufism (Umar 1993). After being appointed Grand Kadi of northern Nigeria he had more opportunities to shape governmental policies on Islamic matters, although his denunciations of Sufi-based practices remained muted largely because of northern Nigerian leader Ahmadu Bello's reluctance to antagonize the Sufi orders. Thus only after the assassination of Bello in 1966 was Gumi—no longer restrained by the premier's vision of Muslim unity—able to widely publicize his views on education, worship, and the supposedly un-Islamic nature of Sufism. With the popularization of Gumi's views of Sufism, reformist Islam was "transformed into a mass social movement" (Umar 1993:163).

As Sufi orders began to unite in opposition to what they saw as a serious threat to their legitimacy, Gumi's close followers felt the need to create an organized forum for the continuation of their leader's anti-Sufism. In March 1978 in Jos, Nigeria, they founded the Jama'atu Izalat al-Bid'a wa Iqamat al-Sunna (Society for the Removal of Innovation and the Restoration of Tradition). Thus Izala was born. The Izala vision of a better society was the product of, and response to, particular forces and events in Nigerian society, but it also emerged from global concerns about the nature and future of Muslim practice, as attested by the multiplicity of Islamic movements whose agendas call for similarly far-reaching reforms.

The movement spread quickly through the distribution of taped cassettes of Gumi's sermons and the preaching of his doctrine throughout the country. To promote his message Shaykh Gumi also made strategic use of Radio Kaduna,[16] the Nigerian Television Authority, and the Hausa language newspaper *Gaskiya ta fi Kwabo* (Watts 1996:275). The history of Izala in Nigeria is well documented, but less is known about the early beginnings of the movement in Niger,[17] and particularly in Dogondoutchi. In the 1980s, when the town of Maradi was fast becoming an Izala stronghold (Grégoire 1992, 1993), local leaders had no visible following in Dogondoutchi. They kept their meetings secret for fear of being jailed on charges of conspiracy. Some were imprisoned on at least two occasions at the urging of *malamai* who had denounced them as criminals intent upon causing harm to local residents. Both times they were later freed when the charges against them could not be substantiated. Meanwhile, increasing numbers of local Muslims attended their preaching sessions and later became 'yan Izala themselves. Women predictably took no visible part in these developments.

Joining Izala was an informal affair. One only had to accomplish *salla* at an Izala prayer ground, familiarize oneself with the Izala ethos, and adopt the visible signs of Izala identity—the beard, the turban, and the modest *jaba* (a knee-length, long-sleeved shirt worn over drawstring pants). Issa, a *'dan* Izala and high school teacher, recounted in 1994 how the movement took root in Dogondoutchi:

> Izala has existed for a long time but, in Doutchi, no one knew about it. No one knew the leaders of the association. Those who belonged to Izala would leave for [the village of] Matankari for the Friday prayer and the police would arrest them. They were forbidden to practice their brand of Islam. This is because everyone was afraid of this new religion. Later the government and everybody else understood what it was about. The government then issued an authorization that allowed [Izala members] to practice their religion. We have even been granted a plot of land to build our mosque.

The project of building a new place of worship on land granted by the local administration developed after the fight in the *grande mosquée*, when 'yan Izala realized that, to insure the growth of the movement and to make concrete their opposition to the 'yan darika, they would need a mosque of their own. Knowing full well that they would not be granted subsidies to finance the construction of the building, Izala members decided they would all pitch in: the mosque not only would be a place to attend prayers and sermons; it would also symbolize Izala's vitality and be a tangible reminder of the Izala community's resiliency for generations to come. The urgency of their mission to build a mosque was heightened by the fact that in the nearby village of Matankari, an Izala *masallaci juma'a* (Friday mosque) already stood, and its construction had been sponsored by a prosperous Niamey-based merchant eager to promote the Izala message in his native village. If the Izala community of Matankari—where the association had long enjoyed a visible though discreet following—could boast a Friday mosque, then surely, many told me, the 'yan Izala of Dogondoutchi should have their own place of worship. More than a question of demographics—'yan Izala in Dogondoutchi far outnumbered their counterparts in Matankari—above all it was a point of honor.[18]

In the early days of the reformist movement, the sermons of Izala preachers, as noted, incited widespread suspicion. Izala leaders were accused by traditionalist Muslim elites of having started a new and dangerous religion that would contribute to the community's moral downfall. 'Yan Izala actively denied having introduced a new faith, claiming instead that Izala was the "true" Islam and that Muslims who did not follow Izala were *kafirai* (unbelievers). Eventually they learned to temper their criticisms of traditionalist Islam and focus on rallying Muslims to their cause. Rather than further alienating those who were hostile to the Izala message from the start, some focused on the notion that all Muslims should learn to worship correctly. As one 'dan Izala put it, "Izala is not a religion, it's an association.[19] All those who say 'Allah akbar' are Muslims. There is only one God, and one religion, Islam. The 'yan darika may want to fight with the 'yan Izala but in the end, they are all Muslim."

Significantly, and regardless of how they felt toward the reformist doctrine, few Dogondoutchi residents I questioned in 1994 were even dimly aware of the origins of Izala. One 'dan darika, a prosperous trader, knew of Abubakar Gumi, the charismatic leader of Izala who died in 1992. "Abubakar started Izala," he told me, "but before he [Abubakar] died, he reconverted to Islam [*sic*]. He told everyone, [Izala] isn't a true religion." According to a local butcher who had been a member of the organization for three years, the founder of Izala was "a man like everyone else, a Moroccan. Tijani is his name." Other Dogondoutchi residents believed the movement had no specific origin. To them, Izala was but a moral and spiritual philosophy based on the rigorous application of Qur'anic precepts. As one of them, a wealthy entrepreneur in his fifties, put it, "those who know how to properly abide by the principles of the Qur'an are 'yan Izala."

One man, who described himself as a "*true* Muslim,[20] not a 'dan Izala," offered the following opinion:

> Izala comes from Sokoto [Nigeria]. Over there, they fight. ['Yan Izala there] have killed more than one hundred people. But here [in Dogondoutchi], we prevent the people from fighting among themselves—especially after the fight at the mosque where people came with axes, bows, and clubs.

Most striking in this testimony is the emphasis on the aggressive nature of the organization whose members allegedly "killed more than one hundred people" in the name of Islamic authenticity and piety. True, no fewer than thirty-four clashes involving Izala and the Tijaniyya and Qadiriyya orders occurred between June 1978 and December 1980 in Plateau State Nigeria—and most of them "called for the intervention of the Police and often resulted in loss of life and damage to vehicles or properties" (Umar 1993:169). By no means is this violence specific to anti-Sufism, however.[21] It also characterizes previous disputes between the now reconciled Sufi orders. Thus the intense rivalry between the followers of the Qadiriyya and Tijaniyya occasionally led to violent clashes in the 1950s and 1960s in Nigeria and elsewhere (Loimeier 1997a; Paden 1973; Umar 1993; see also Launay 1992). Recall that, in Dogondoutchi, members of the Reformed Tijaniyya who followed the teachings of Shaykh Ibrahim Niass of Senegal and members of the Qadiriyya previously disagreed over the correct posture to adopt during prayer. Niassiyya Tijanis, known as 'yan kabalu, crossed their arms on their chests while they stood during worship, whereas Qadiris or 'yan sadalu dropped their arms by their side. Today, such disputes are the stuff of memory. With the emergence of Izala, 'yan kabalu and 'yan sadalu everywhere set aside their differences and joined forces to oppose Izala reformists (Grégoire 1992; Paden 1973).

Of Donkeys and Twins: Rumors of Inhumanity and Hypocrisy

Although the Izala message of reform appealed to many, especially youth whose social mobility was increasingly blocked by the country's worsening economic situation, it was resisted vigorously by a significant number of Muslim elders who saw it as a threat to the established order. Aside from denouncing 'yan Izala as agitators who fomented disputes in what had previously been peaceful communities, many Muslim preachers derided them in their sermons. When 'yan Izala were not accused of poisoning communal wells, they were ridiculed for wearing long, pointed beards and jokingly referred to as masu geme (the bearded ones). This is particularly ironic given that the designation is traditionally reserved for Christian missionaries. A host of rumors circulated about the inhumanity and avidity of 'yan Izala, fueled by rising concerns that the reforms they advertized jeopardized not only moral identities but also the strong communitarian traditions that had long regulated social relations in Dogondoutchi. One type of rumor was the notion that when they died, 'yan Izala turned into donkeys. In 1994 I was told many times that anyone exhuming what they thought was the body of a deceased 'dan Izala would invariably find the carcass of an ass instead.

Stories of fathers killing their sons over doctrinal disagreements and later witnessing their transformation into pack animals surely indicated a deeply troubled community, wracked by fear and prejudice. In 1992 a respected lo-cal religious leader provoked members of the Izala association as they as-sembled for prayer at the Friday mosque, warning them that if anyone dared touch his Qur'an, he would die. He then declared that if anyone dug up the corpse of a *'dan* Izala a day or so after the burial, he would find a donkey in the dead man's tomb. "This is because they turn into animals as soon as they die," he explained. His provocative statement implied that despite their de-termined efforts to claim exclusive access to truth, and therefore to blissful eternity, *'yan* Izala would never enter paradise. They were, after all, nothing but beasts.

Those who declared allegiance to Izala were scornfully derided by their adversaries for wearing short pants—the longer pants worn by their oppo-nents, the reformists argued, picked up dirt from the ground and signaled disrespect for God at prayer time—and for incompletely wrapping their tur-bans around their heads, letting the tip of the turban hang loosely behind their backs in the alleged manner of Muslims in the Middle East.[22] They were the targets of satirical songs making fun of their attempts to emulate the pious look—the beard, the turban, and so on—of Saudi Muslims. Their wives and daughters were likewise denounced for hypocritically hiding their "flawed" virtue behind veils.

'Yan Izala were also accused of cursing twin births. In Mawri communi-ties, twin babies have been traditionally welcomed by their parents as a gift from God, even if, paradoxically, they also represent an excess of fertility whose consequences must be mitigated by specific practices (Masquelier 2001a). They are powerful, dangerous beings endowed with extraordinary abilities. They are also quite vulnerable by virtue of their "abnormality" and require special treatment in order to function as "full" human beings. In the early 1990s local practices that aimed at insuring the well-being of these spe-cial babies became the target of Izala efforts to eradicate "superstition" and standardize Muslim practices. These traditions were *haram* and had to be abandoned, *'yan* Izala claimed. Soon after, rumors began to circulate that *'yan* Izala systematically killed the firstborn of twins at birth. They did this, I was told by *'yan darika,* to erase the taint of immorality associated with that in-fant. For Izala devotees, so their adversaries conjectured, twins were not a gift from God but the unmistakable mark of sin: a woman who gave birth to two children at once was believed to have engaged in adultery. If the second-born was the product of her legitimate and morally sanctioned union to her husband, the firstborn resulted from her sinful liaison with another man. From this perspective, the only way to lessen the humiliation of a cuckold

husband was to kill the infant whose existence stood as a painful reminder of its mother's wantonness.

Although 'yan Izala I spoke with categorically denied engaging in such cruel practices or knowing anyone else who did, these new preoccupations with twin births suggest the extent to which the 'yan Izala's concern to restore purity and piety centers on women as repositories of Islamic morality. According to 'yan Izala, respectable Muslim women should stay home and refrain from having any contact with men other than their husbands and close kin. Here, control over women's sexuality takes the shape of a strategic redefinition of twin births, the anomalous dyad having become a measure of the new mother's depravity and deviation from Qur'anic principles. Although the dispute may have started over the proper way to celebrate the birth of twins, it evolved into a full-fledged controversy about the contested boundaries of Muslim womanhood and domesticity. Ultimately the rumors linking 'yan Izala to dead donkeys and infanticide reveal that contested religious identities fueled controversies over the definitions of Islamic practice as much as they were shaped by them.

These rumors also articulated emerging anxieties about social reproduction and must be situated against the backdrop of the International Monetary Fund (IMF) and World Bank–mandated neoliberal policies aimed at controlling demographic growth. Amid concerns that the country's projected population explosion threatens developmental gains, the Nigérien government has focused on regulating births.[23] The government's attempts to curb population expansion has met with ferocious opposition by reformist Muslim associations advocating an Islamic approach to family and reproductive issues. As we shall see, Izala leaders especially condemn family planning, equating contraception with "killing the fetus." Those who take measures to limit the size of their families go against God's will, they warn. 'Yan Izala also reject the use of condoms to contain the spread of AIDS, believing that it promotes sexual promiscuity and encourages young people to engage in premarital sex. Emerging in the context of controversies over the legitimacy of contraception, the recent preoccupation over twin births suggests that fertility has become ever more central to the Muslim definition of moral order. Aside from articulating a critique of Izala views of family and society, alleged reports of infanticide gave shape to a community's emergent fears of moral chaos. The discursive space opened up by the rumors of Izala wrongdoing made room for Dogondoutchi residents to consider new ways of being Muslim, which entailed a heightened scrutiny over the terms of reproduction and the definition of fertility.

Other stories told how, despite claims that they rejected amulets as un-Islamic, *'yan* Izala, like everyone else, made wide use of them.[24] In 1994 the rumor spread that, after an Izala leader had been mortally wounded during a major scuffle between Izala and anti-Izala factions in the country's capital, more than one hundred amulets were found on his body when it was prepared for burial. This proved, Dogondoutchi residents insisted, that members of Izala were liars and could not be trusted. These attacks on the validity of Izala views suggest that even as the Izala movement promoted discussions over long-established social and moral orthodoxies, it generated rage, hostility, and enmity. Rather than democratically imparting enlightenment and opportunities, the civil space that emerged out of intra-Muslim debates was often "the domain of profoundly inegalitarian and obscurantist institutions and lifestyles" (Fatton 1995:77) that fueled widespread tension and bitter conflicts.

In recent years the rumors have quieted down and the tensions have lessened. Almost two decades after the introduction of reformist Islam in Arewa, Izala leaders enjoy a broad popularity, most notably among younger Muslims who, at least originally, were particularly receptive to the reformist ban on conspicuous consumption. The movement also counts wealthy entrepreneurs among its constituency. In contrast to both the Nigerian situation (where many of the followers of Malam Idris are poor) (Isichei 1987) and the context described by Grégoire (1993:114) in Maradi, where Izala seems to attract "young rich kids," adherence in Dogondoutchi cuts across all social strata. Izala has been construed as a form of protest against Sufi corruption, and against the redistributive ethos around which much of everyday life is ordered in Mawri communities given the centrality of gifts in forging or cementing social relationships. Although it has clearly provided a forum for pursuing political objectives and airing grievances in the absence of other outlets, the movement is more adequately understood in relation to profound existential changes in the lives of its devotees. Its impact must therefore be assessed in the context of a "reorientation from a communal to an individualistic mode of religiosity [that] seems to be more in tune with the rugged individualism of capitalist social relations" (Umar 1993:178).

Individuality, Equality, and Frugality in Izala Discourse

Because *'yan* Izala believe that the Muslim world is "in a state of decline" (Esposito 1992:19) and that the ills of the present are a consequence of the failure to follow proper Qur'anic principles, they urge all followers of the Prophet to return to an authentic Islam, devoid of heathenism and innovations.

Local practices that have become an integral part of Muslim life such as wearing amulets, practicing divination, or drinking the ink used to write Qur'anic verses are declared *haram*. Because, according to 'yan Izala, the troubles of the modern world originate from people's lack of devotion and deviation from "true" Islam, practices that appeared after the death of the Prophet are considered *bidi'a* (innovations) that must be eradicated. From this perspective, Sufi orders are not part of Islam because they appeared after the Prophet's death. Instead, they are "a new religion standing on its own" (Umar 1993:168). Practices associated with Sufism such as the celebration of the Prophet's birthday, the invocation of God's names, the veneration of living Muslim saints (religious specialists believed to be blessed with God's grace), and other devotional practices are condemned for leading to *shirka* ("idolatry"). Only God should be invoked in prayer, Izala members maintain, and neither saints nor the Prophet should be the object of religious veneration.[25]

A return to the pristine Islam of the Prophet and caliphs is also a call to frugality, 'yan Izala insist, repeating tirelessly the Prophet's admonition against spending more than one can afford. Thus, whereas Sufi elders and neighbors engage in ostentatious gift giving among kin, friends, and neighbors, and redistribute their resources widely among dependent clients, Muslim clerics and the indigent, members of Izala preach individualism, conservation, and the rational utilization of resources. This means that, in the mid-1990s, 10,000 CFA francs ($20) was regarded as a sufficient sum to pay bridewealth instead of the customary 100,000 or 200,000 CFA francs ($200 or $400). It also means, as one charismatic Izala leader put it, that "for the naming ceremony [of your infant], all you need to slaughter the ram is a sharp knife." This ironic referent is the conspicuous (and, in his opinion, needless) distribution of money, kola nuts, and other gifts when a child is given a name on the seventh day of its life. The simpler, the better: if you cannot afford a ram, a chicken will do; it is more in accord with the teachings of the Prophet to economize than go heavily into debt.

Because 'yan Izala claim that one's chief responsibility is to care for immediate dependents, not to entertain neighbors, they have earned a reputation for being tight-fisted, selfish individuals who turn their back on social obligations. In a society that has traditionally condemned the private accumulation of wealth, the Izala ban on conspicuous consumption has angered many for whom generosity is inseparable from friendliness, moral engagement, and sociality. In contrast, those who have embraced the tenets of Izala philosophy are mostly young men, who, at a time when most people struggle to make ends meet, welcome the movement's injunction against needless expenditure. Note that hiring young men as drivers, laborers, traders, and clerks was an effective way through which local businessmen recruited new adherents to Izala. To obtain a job or secure patronage from prominent Izala merchants, one must first and foremost join the reformist association.

Generational divisions have grown in recent years. As the extended family has splintered under the impact of increasingly individualistic modes of farming, individuals are no longer able to depend so extensively on shared family resources and must fend for themselves (deLatour Dejean 1980; Sutter 1979). Households are still multigenerational but young men have become largely responsible for providing for their wives and children. Although this growing individuation has freed the younger generation from the control of a gerontocracy often perceived as abusive, increasing economic privatization has not, in fact, relieved people of social and economic obligations. On the contrary, the social and financial pressures placed on salaried workers, seasonal laborers, and heads of households have become more acute. The demands for money placed on those who have the good fortune to enjoy a regular income often far exceed the meager supply. Endless requests for cash—to celebrate the birth of a child, buy new outfits for the family, help a friend in need, make donations to *malamai,* or entertain important guests—flow in from the social networks that pull against an increasingly bureaucratic, urban-centered economy. Amid falling standards of living, rising unemployment, and disintegrating family support, the Izala endorsement of frugality has provided a publicly sanctioned avenue of escape for young men reluctant to burden themselves with costly traditions yet also unwilling to appear disrespectful of them.[26]

In the 1990s it was said that *'yan* Izala brought a calabash of milk to their mothers when reaching adulthood to compensate for the *nono* (breast milk) their mothers had nourished them with as infants. By "paying" for the milk that had sustained them, they signified their radical disengagement from the tight web of kin-based exchanges of which they had been a part since childhood. To become further disentangled from the multigenerational households that, as grown men, they were expected to help maintain, *'yan* Izala were rumored to bring rams to their fathers as reimbursement for the animals that had been purchased at their naming ceremonies. By means of these extraordinarily callous gestures, which spoke loudly of their "selfish" intentions, young reformists were believed to buy both their freedom from the paternal household and the right to be financially free of obligations to its members. Over the past few years, however, critics of Izala have conceded, grudgingly, that rumors of milk payments and reimbursements in the form of rams were unfounded. No one, it turns out, was ever caught engaging in this offensive behavior. Nor does anyone claim to have witnessed the transformation of a *'dan* Izala into a donkey. There is widespread agreement that such defamatory gossip was itself the product of troubled times during which ignorance and fear of change led people to engage in malicious and characteristically uncharitable conduct.[27]

In addition to advocating a different way of managing one's wealth, Izala followers also promulgate conceptions of society and social relations that contrast sharply with those of most Muslim elders, exacerbating latent intergenerational conflicts. Until quite recently, or so Izala critics would have us believe, Mawri sons rarely questioned the authority of their fathers who, by definition, knew better about issues ranging from marriage to Muslim practice to wealth management. In the 1990s sons left their fathers' households never to return, believing that following the dictates of non-Izala elders meant violating Muslim principles and leading a sinful life. While family obligations and loyalty to one's parents were morally sanctioned, loyalty to the *umma,* the community of Muslims united in submission to God, must take clear precedence. Preachers who want to remind their audiences of these principles invoke the story of Abraham's willingness to sacrifice his son Isma'il, and Isma'il's willingness to be sacrificed: although undeniably strong, the father-son relationship "was subordinated to God's wishes" (Eickleman and Piscatori 1996:82). Thus, for *'yan* Izala, it was acceptable to ask one's son for advice if one knew little about Islam. As I was told by Karimou, a staunch *'dan* Izala who worked hard to reunite a divided Muslim community: "One should not feel shame. One should simply want to learn."

Izala efforts to forge a community of believers united in the common struggle against profligacy and immorality exemplifies how civil society can become the source of a counter-hegemonic social movement directed not so much against the state but also against local-level community and family structures: through their insistence that a son's primary allegiance is to his God rather than his father, *'yan* Izala actively question the moral legitimacy of parental authority, especially when, as they often claim, it is based on decidedly un-Islamic principles. Their rejection of patrilineage, in tandem with the subversion of local religious authorities, suggests that we cannot simply analyze Nigérien politics of emerging identities, power, and self-representation in terms of conventional state-society oppositions. The Izala message exploited the doubt and ambiguity introduced by the *décrispation* of the late 1980s over the constantly negotiated meanings of truth, legitimacy, and tradition. In this context, then, we can understand how, for instance, local competition for control of the main mosque in a West African town contributed to an emerging critical consciousness about Muslim identity.

Arguing that distinctions in ethnic origin or social status have no place in Islam, 'yan Izala oppose all practices—from saint worship to Sufi ritual—that presume a differential basis of power and authority among believers. In their opinion Mawri society—and, by extension, Nigérien society in general—is too hierarchical. No one, they insist, should be at the mercy of elders, especially if, through their ignorance and lack of piety, the latter perpetuate a system of values that betrays Qur'anic principles. This position is consistent with the Izala view of education, characterized by a fairly egalitarian ethos. To critics of Izala, however, this concept is unacceptable, as seen in the following comment by Malam Ibrahim, a Qur'anic scholar about forty years old:

> The followers of Izala, they don't believe in hierarchy, but the whole world can see that there are differences between leaders and followers. One must respect one's superior. If you think that everyone is equal to everyone else, you cannot do the prayer. Why even put an imam in front to lead the prayer?

Because 'yan Izala repeatedly challenge the authority of their elders, their religious opponents perceive them as youthful rebels bent on abolishing the status quo and revolutionizing the social order. Their mantra, that innovation must be eradicated, justifies their abolishment of Sufi-related traditions such as the veneration of saints—a move 'yan darika vigorously condemn as misguided. Again, in the words of Malam Ibrahim:

> Izala people lie when they say that waliyyai [saints] do not exist. It is saints who pray and whose prayer God hears easily. God says: "Innovations are not permitted and those who engage in innovations are going to hell." But it is not our way which is full of innovations. What God does not like is the following: setting up a shelter to play music, meeting with people and gambling, those are the kinds of meeting God does not approve.

The concept of innovations per se is not what critics of Izala object to, Malam Ibrahim suggests, but rather what Izala designates as innovations. To many Muslims, music making and gambling, for example, are un-Islamic and therefore objectionable; the tradition of saint worship, on the other hand, is intrinsic to Islam. The scholar's comments, like those of other Dogondoutchi residents, exemplify how the emergence of Izala and the heightened consciousness it spurred have prompted Muslims to characterize Islam as a systematized entity distinct from other religions (Eickelman and Piscatori 1996).

Returning to the egalitarian values shaping the Izala ethos, it is note-worthy that the reformist preachers' appeal to followers to abstain from con-tact with kin who fail to obey Muhammad's teachings has translated into severe family crises. For example, 'yan Izala refuse to eat with kin who have not embraced the reformist message, for it is sinful to sit down with an "un-believer" even if it happens to be one's father. Further, they do not kneel in the presence of father, mother, father-in-law, mother-in-law, or anyone else whose age or social status traditionally dictates that they must be shown def-erence (Grégoire 1993:112; Loimeier 1997a). For many opponents of the Izala revival, showing respect to one's parents, whatever the circumstances, is an essential personal obligation: those who do not fulfill this social duty are simply power-hungry, selfish individuals whose total disregard for social tra-dition erodes their humanity (Masquelier in press). 'Yan Izala are troubled by 'yan darika's claim, widely publicized in the mid-1990s, that, as one young man put it, "those who belong to Izala do not like their fathers, mothers, brothers, or sisters." In their own defense, 'yan Izala insist that following the Prophet's teaching to the letter—which may mean alienating oneself from one's kin—is more important to Allah than upholding traditions that simply strengthen the power of the local gerontocracy.

Even more offensive to their Muslim opponents is the Izala claim that Muhammad was human like everyone else and ought to be remembered as such. Though he led an exemplary life, Izala preachers insist, the Prophet was not an intercessor and his role in the Muslim community "should be limited to that of a transmitter of the revelation" (Loimeier 1997b:199). Traditionalist Muslims, like their predecessors who saw the Prophet as a "lawgiver with the authority of a God" (ibid.), assert that Muhammad is above humanity and can-not be treated as a simple messenger. As a young trader exclaimed angrily dur-ing a conversation we were having about the reformist doctrine: "They do not believe in prophets and they say that Muhammad is just a man. If there are no prophets, then who brought the Muslim religion?" In the eyes of many Mus-lims, a lack of respect for prophets both predisposes one to join Izala and typifies "Izalaness." To Hajiya Bibata, a loquacious and successful trader whose views coincided with many of her neighbors, such radical egalitarianism was treason:

> They [the 'yan Izala] have betrayed the Muslim religion by saying that the Prophet is a man like other men. Everyone knows he is God's messenger. God sent him so he would teach people how to serve him. And since the 'yan Izala serve him wrong, he [God] punishes them and they become donkeys. I will never give my daughter to a 'dan Izala. The people of bori follow God better than 'yan Izala do.

To maintain, as Hajiya Bibata does, that those who engage in spirit possession—an activity deemed sinful and anti-Muslim by followers of the Prophet—are actually more pious than Muslim reformists is a serious insult. It also indicates the tremendous ire the reformist message provoked, at least initially, among many Muslims for whom Izala's assertive individualism and egalitarianism were a threat to society and family. Yet the lack of filial piety and altruism is precisely what attracted many young Mawri to the reformist movement.

The unparalleled appeal to youth of the 'yan Izala campaign for an "order of rectitude" (Al-Azmeh 1993:25) harking back to the time of Muhammad has also given rise to local speculation concerning the movement's legitimacy. A common opinion is that 'yan Izala tempt would-be converts with offers of money, using funds funneled in from Saudi Arabia, Egypt, Libya, Kuwait, and Nigeria. Clearly outsiders closely associate the power of the movement with the management of wealth. In 1994 'yan Izala retorted bitterly to those accusing them of "buying" converts with foreign funds that local leaders received nothing but Qur'ans from Saudi Arabia, although they invested their energies tirelessly in teaching the *sunna* (the code of conduct modeled on the Prophet as told in the *hadith*) and recruiting new members. That they eventually managed to build a spacious Friday mosque where the Izala community now congregates for the Friday prayer testifies to the global connections Izala leaders have been able to forge across West Africa and beyond.[28]

Literacy and Enlightenment for All

The Izala movement has also intervened in the discussion of how to define knowledge and its control. Very few Muslims in this region of Niger completed Islamic studies or even learned how to read Arabic. Although the number of children attending Qur'anic school has grown substantially since Independence, students typically do not progress beyond oral recitation of the Qur'an in Arabic. The relative absence of educated Muslim scholars thoroughly initiated in the Scriptures long insured that, save for an occasional confrontation with members of the *bori*, the authority of *malamai* went unchallenged. 'Yan Izala deplore this situation and are determined to eradicate quackery and ignorance. They have striven to give Muslims a chance to learn about Islam on their own, and they insist that education must be accessible to all, regardless of age, gender, or social status. Rather than send their children to Qur'anic school, they set up their own educational centers to provide an intensive education in Arabic. Izala children thus attend school from 8 AM to 12 PM and from 4 PM to 6 PM. Although the content and format of Izala teaching differs from those of "standard" Qur'anic education ('yan Izala discourage rote memorization of the Qur'an and, in theory at least, insist on the importance of learning Arabic), the most visible distinction between Izala and other Qur'anic schools is in the teacher-student relationship: whereas Qur'anic teachers customarily take in children from rural villages who have to beg for food because their parents cannot provide for them, 'yan Izala point out that children should neither work for their teachers (to compensate for the instruction they receive) nor beg for food. Parents, they insist, are responsible for their own children and should provide for them; begging is demeaning and against God's will. In recent years the melodic chanting of *almajirai* (Qur'anic students) who requested *sadaka sabo da Allah* (alms for the sake of God) and received leftover food from neighboring households has grown scarce. In the eyes of 'yan Izala, this is a positive step. Children who spend much of their days begging for food, 'yan Izala claims, are not only being exploited by their teachers but they have little time left for learning.

Education is not simply for children, however. In an attempt to promote their vision of an enlightened *umma* (Muslim community), 'yan Izala singled out *jahilci* (ignorance about Islam and Muslim practice) as one of the targets of their reformist mission. *Jahilci* has become imbued with moral overtones which imply that ignorance of Islam is a sin that can be overcome by exposure to the salvational effects of Qur'anic education. In more secular contexts, *jahilci* can be taken to mean "illiteracy," yet the strong Islamic resonance remains (Cooper 2006). Accusations of *jahilci*, therefore, generally imply not simply ignorance but also impiety. In their efforts to promote knowledge and ultimately contribute to the "re-Islamization of society" (Sounaye n.d.:1), Izala scholars attempt to teach certain modern skills in addition to religious instruction (Westerlund 1997). As noted earlier, whereas in traditional Qur'anic schools run by traditionalist *malamai*, children were simply taught basic ritual obligations and memorized the Qur'an phonetically, Izala schools encourage students to learn Arabic as a way to pursue independent Islamic studies (Sounaye n.d.; Westerlund 1997). Precisely because they perceive knowledge as potentially accessible to all, 'yan Izala have been especially critical of religious leaders who define *ilimi* as esoteric or mystical knowledge and use their control of it to justify their status as possessors of "blessings." In a sermon delivered in June 1994, an Izala preacher declared:

> You must protect yourself from bad *malamai*. God said, "Leave those bad *malamai*. I am going to protect you. Those who have much knowledge but who haven't used it properly, leave them. I am going to punish them. I don't want their prayers. I will reject them like I rejected Satan."

Knowledge is for all, Izala leaders routinely argue, and individuals who claim to have special spiritual powers to control the occult should not be trusted. In their rhetorical battles with other Muslims, Izala reformists accuse amulet manufacturers and providers of *rubutu* (liquid Qur'anic verses that one drinks) of quackery and deceit. Clerics, they say, use secrecy as a front to cover up their lack of education and to exploit gullible clients in need of reassuring advice when they should earn their living through honest work. In the eyes of Muslim reformists, these clerics are "bad" Muslims.

People's (and specifically women's) alleged gullibility and willingness to trust the powers of *malamai* is rooted in the fetishization of the written word. Literacy remains a fairly mysterious capacity for Dogondoutchi residents who did not attend school. The patent effectiveness of writing as a way to communicate that defies temporal and spatial boundaries makes it a privileged candidate for use in intercourse between people and distant deities. Goody (1968, 1987) suggests that writing, as embodied speech, has often been valued more by illiterate peoples for its role in superhuman than in human communication, and that the initial appeal of Islam to outsiders is tied to the power of inscription. Whether or not this applies to the Mawri case, local people tap into the reservoir of power vested in sacred texts.[29] As demonstrated by the debate on whether more than one Qur'an exists, few individuals have access to the holy book, and even fewer can decipher it. As happens when literacy is primarily religious, "the Book becomes less a means to further enquiry, a step in the accumulation of knowledge, than an end itself, the timeless depository of all knowledge" (Goody 1968:237).

By democratizing literacy,[30] 'yan Izala not only demoted *malamai* from their position as guardians of sacred and restricted knowledge; they also reconceptualized Muslims' entire relationship to the holy book—and, ultimately, to the written word. Qur'anic verses, the 'yan Izala vehemently argued, were not meant to be written so that their power could be manipulated and absorbed through charms and *rubutu*. Such practices mistakenly attributed god-like powers to the Scriptures that they did not have. In the eyes of 'yan Izala, Qur'anic verses should not be fetishized in this way because, ultimately, only God has the power to heal. The aim of Muslim leaders should be to demystify religious texts by empowering believers with Qur'anic knowledge, not capitalizing on ignorance and belief in magical powers. The Scriptures, the 'yan Izala insisted, only has one set of correct interpretations; people must be taught them so that they could ignore all else (see Bowen 1993).

Izala promotion of women's rights to education has allowed them to counter their opponents' claims that they seek to deprive women of their freedom. Women should be schooled, Izala followers assert, because they are invested with the sacred task of educating their children and taking care of their household. Because this activity should have topmost priority, women should be given the necessary tools (i.e., an Islamic education) to carry out this important task successfully. After all, the future of the Muslim community is in their hands. "Women are queens, it says so in the Qur'an," volunteered a local Izala preacher. Even as they glorify the role women play in Muslim society, Izala leaders insist that women should stay home, as that enables women to devote themselves fully to their children' education. Disputing accusations that they strip women of their autonomy, 'yan Izala often stress that women have the noblest of missions—that of edifying the next generation.

Seclusion, Mobility, and Autonomy

In Islam, morality translates into a set of rules that prescribe male and female action and the presentation of the body. In the reformist discourses of Izala, women's bodies in particular have become the focus of meticulous attention. As is the case elsewhere in the Muslim world (Abu-Lughod 1986; Bauer 1985; Delaney 1991; Gaspard and Khosrokhavar 1995; Hawley and Proudfoot 1994; Mernissi 1987; Ong 1995; Rugh 1986), much of the debate over what constitutes respectability, piety, and modesty centers on women's dress and deportment and the creation of "docile bodies" (Foucault 1977). For wives and daughters of 'yan Izala, membership in the reformist movement means wearing the *hijabi*—a veil that ideally covers much of their bodies—and living in total or partial seclusion.

By championing veiling, seclusion, and other practices aimed at curtailing women's autonomy, 'yan Izala initially collided with other Muslims who resented Izala contestations of the previously unquestioned conventions governing women's movements and visibility. Seclusion is not an exclusive Izala practice, however. Not all secluded women belong to Izala households even though most do. Conventional Muslim views on female mobility and visibility are increasingly matching those of 'yan Izala. Home is where Muslim women belong, I was told in 2004 by a number of non-Izala household heads. This is not surprising considering the extent to which, as Mack (2004:7) noted for northern Nigeria, "Muslim Hausa culture is focused inward, with the family at its core and the wife and mother as overseer of this context." From this perspective, seclusion helps reassert the centrality of the notion of interiority by focusing on enclosure.

Despite the role of seclusion in the affirmation of productive domesticity (see chapter 6), its recent popularity cannot be understood simply in terms of the notion of interiority, however. At a time when a significant number of Nigérien women are enjoying greater mobility than in the past thanks to the development of state-sponsored education and infrastructure, the growing prominence of seclusion must be assessed in the context of emerging debates about morality and the role of Islam in people's lives.[31] In this context, the promotion of seclusion is not so much about transforming women's conditions as it is about defining the boundaries of religious identity. In the Muslim community, the curtailment of women's mobility is seen as an index of progress, marking the boundaries between today's world of Muslim values and a pre-Islamic past characterized by "backwardness." As the traditionalist imam of Dogondoutchi explained:

> *Masu zuwa kasuwa* [women who go to the market], it's a sin. God told us to keep women in their homes. Before Islam, women went everywhere. Now they don't come out unless they have to go to the dispensary or visit their families. Even a young girl who is not yet married shouldn't walk around. She should not see men, and men should not see her.

Many men in Dogondoutchi would agree with this view regardless of whether they favor the Izala agenda. A young university student currently unemployed told me, in 2006, that when he married, he would provide for his wife and insure that she remained home, away from the prying eyes of male neighbors. As he saw it, women should be spared the burden of earning a living: this was a man's responsibility. Moreover, women could not be trusted; restricting their mobility both eased their domestic burden and limited the possibility of seductive encounters.

Several degrees of seclusion exist in Dogondoutchi. Women who live under the most rigorous seclusion are permitted to exit their compound only when they need medical assistance. For the vast majority of secluded women, however, the rules governing *kubli* (seclusion) are more flexible. These secluded wives are allowed to visit neighbors and kin after nightfall, when obscurity makes them less likely to be noticed by potential admirers. Moreover, remaining secluded, even under the strictest conditions, does not imply total isolation. During the day women are rarely alone for very long. Besides perhaps having co-wives, they often receive visits from neighboring women. They also rely on a constant stream of young female visitors in and out of their compounds for news, errands, and company. Women who are not secluded, on the other hand, may leave the marital compound. This implies, in theory, that they enjoy more mobility. That they generally cannot do so before securing their husband's approval often means that many largely stay home. When rigorously enforced, Dunbar (1991) notes, the principle that wives must ask their husbands for permission before going out is more likely to impact women's mobility and autonomy than the less commonly instituted practice of seclusion.

Prior to the emergence of Izala, *kubli* in Dogondoutchi was reserved for the wives of the pious, the wealthy, and the elites. Except for rare cases, seclusion did not mean that wives were strictly sheltered. They had opportunities for entertainment as well as evening visits to neighbors, kin, and mourning households. The terms of seclusion could also be negotiated. In 1989 a husband whose wife, a close friend of mine, was secluded had agreed on several occasions to let her ride in my car when I traveled to Niamey so she could visit her sister there. In his eyes, the inside of my Peugeot 504 was a contained space, so that while she was traveling, his wife remained protected by the "portable seclusion" the car provided. Farming, however, was off-limits. In theory at least, secluded women do not work in the fields. Ordinary women, on the other hand, play a significant role in agriculture. In fact, it is precisely because their labor in the field is needed that they cannot be secluded (Dunbar 1991).

On joining the ranks of Izala, men curtailed their wives' mobility more strictly on the advice of reformist Muslim leaders, even though the *hijabi* (veil) which all Izala women were enjoined to wear was meant to enable them to enter public spaces without calling attention to themselves. Keeping their wives at home meant that Izala women did not enter public spaces, at least not without wearing a veil. As one *'dan* Izala put it:

> [Women] should not work in the fields. It is also men who must provide water and wood supplies for the household. It is *haram* to take one's wife to the fields and put her to work. But women can become teachers, nurses, midwives, office clerks [as long as] they cover their bodies before stepping out of the house.

Education and seclusion should ideally encourage the creation of a society where women are honored, favored, and free of the struggle for survival. I have heard *'yan* Izala say that the Prophet himself, when asked about women's distinct tasks, replied along these lines: "to manage a house well, to keep a husband happy, and behave appropriately was equal to anything men might do" (Metcalf 1987:148). From this perspective, staying at home and attending to domestic chores are the best ways for a woman to earn respect. But keeping one's wife at home does not mean that she should be ignorant of religious laws and principles. In fact, Izala preachers maintain, it is a husband's responsibility to ensure that his wife is properly taught, because knowing the precepts of Islam is the best way to serve God.

Seclusion also requires that a servant is hired to accomplish the wifely chores—getting water at the neighborhood tap, for example—that involve leaving the compound during the day. As noted above, it also implies freedom from farm work—and the added financial burden of having to hire day laborers at harvest time—although I have met secluded women who, in desperate times, participated in the millet harvest alongside their husband and children because not doing so would have meant starvation, or at least privation, the following year. A man who secludes his wives accrues prestige—and, some say, divine rewards. Men anxious to display their religious commitment may resort to these domestic arrangements even when it is not economically practical. I was told of a man in Dogondoutchi whose intensely pious dispositions led him to seclude his wife. Because he could not afford to hire a young girl to perform household duties in place of his wife, he brought water from the pump himself. The performance of these humble female tasks by a man, my female friends agreed, was a true sign of piety.

When a man's financial situation changes dramatically, however, he may be forced to grant his wives greater autonomy and make use of their labor, if only to stop having to pay for the servant bringing in water and firewood when no children are available. Malam Arji, a devout 'dan Izala who owned a prosperous transport business, was compelled to ease the restrictions imposed on his three wives' mobility after his truck broke down and his earnings declined. Although the water faucet he had installed earlier in the compound solved the problem of having to hire help to bring in water from the neighborhood pump, he now lacked the funds to employ laborers to work on his farm. Despite his strong wish to shield his wives from the outside world, Malam Arji needed their labor to insure the timely harvesting of the crops that would guarantee the household's economic survival in the coming year (all the more so now that the farm was their sole means of livelihood). His inability to keep his wives in *kubli* was perceived by neighboring women, many of them overburdened with domestic chores themselves, as a significant drop in social status. Although most of these women were fiercely critical of Izala reforms that centered on bridewealth and wedding expenditures and had ridiculed Izala veils in the past, they nonetheless sympathized with Malam Arji's wives and the undesirable situation they currently were in. Poverty was one thing they all could relate to.[32]

For many men and women, seclusion meant primarily that wives were barred from entering public spaces. Yet consensus was widespread that regardless of whether they were in *kubli,* women (especially if they were young and married) should stay home and avoid being seen in the *kasuwa* (the marketplace), for example, where many people converge each week to engage in commercial transactions and also socialize and gather news. Except for educated elites who encourage their wives and daughters to pursue careers outside the home, many Muslim husbands, regardless of their religious allegiances, believe that a woman should remain within the walls of her compound, even if seclusion is not an option. Even *bori* leaders made it clear to me in the late 1980s that their wives did not enter the public arena of possession performances unless they were past their child-bearing years; if they were, they served as hosts to spirits. *Bori* performances were not only considered conducive to romantic encounters, they were also the epitome of lasciviousness, unrestraint, and immodesty. In short, these were places to be avoided if one wished to preserve one's reputation as a modest and honorable wife. Young women—especially if they were married—who dared attend possession ceremonies were assumed to lack virtue and were identified as prostitutes. *Bori* devotees may thus disagree with Muslims about the role spirits play in people's lives, but they agree that a woman's place is within the marital compound.

The widely shared view that home is where women belong suggests that, in many cases, the debates centering around the legitimacy of *kubli* may have more to do with the enunciation of doctrinal difference—Izala versus *darika* identity, Muslim versus non-Muslim practice—than with instituting dramatic changes to women's status. In other words, although most women in Dogondoutchi saw their mobility curtailed once they married, the secluded lifestyle of Izala wives was more visibly enunciated in daily practice—and more formally associated with the reformist ethos—than was the case for the wives of 'yan darika and non-Muslims. At the same time, even men who did not officially seclude their wives spoke of the need for *kubli.* In the eyes of a number of Muslim husbands with whom I spoke in 2004, *kubli* was not so much a choice as a duty. As one of them explained: "All Muslims should keep their wives in seclusion. Even if they are very poor. But women should be able to go the dispensary at night; or visit their families. If they ask for permission." From this perspective, women are technically allowed to socialize but only in the evening—when their features are hidden by darkness—and at the discretion of their husbands. Those who are spotted in unlikely places such as the marketplace are automatically suspected of having violated their husband's trust. After all, no husband—unless he belongs to the educated class—would ever permit his wife to enter the public space of the weekly market: doing so would be tantamount to admitting his failure to control her whereabouts, in addition to signaling to all her lack of virtue. As Callaway notes in her study of Hausa society in northern Nigeria, women are perceived as "inherently crafty and promiscuous" (1987:44). If they escape their husband's control to enter the marketplace, it probably is not to purchase things so much as to attract the attention of other men. "Why else would they be dressed in their best clothes and wear makeup?" a senior woman once asked rhetorically as we were discussing young wives "going places." Her question required no answer. Everyone there knew that the presence of an elegantly dressed married woman at the market meant she was up to no good.

Even if they do not seclude their wives per se, men can drastically limit their autonomy by simply denying them the right to meet friends or attend gatherings. Without first asking her husband's approval, a woman cannot, for example, visit a new mother on the day of her infant's naming ceremony, call on an ailing kin, or seek a doctor's services. Although most of the married women of child-bearing age whom I met were not in *kubli*, they spent much of their time engaging in domestic chores, while insisting they could go anywhere—with their husband's permission. A couple of schoolgirls told me in 2004 that they were hoping to attend a university after graduating from secondary school. They both had plans to pursue ambitious careers. When I brought up the topic of marriage, however, one of them remarked that, once married, she would defer to her husband in all things—as was expected of her. By this she meant that she would give up any plans of a professional career if her husband did not want his wife to work outside the home.

Although the notion of romantic love is making its way into the Mawri moral imagination, prospective brides, raised as they are in Muslim households where spouses rarely interact publicly, do not expect to spend much time with their husbands—even if courtship absorbs a great deal of their attention. In this deeply gender-segregated society, the eagerly anticipated state of marriage is, for them, more about motherhood, domestic life, and economic survival than about companionship or intimacy. In addition to being modest and "showing evidence of domestic skills" (Callaway 1987:41), a good wife obeys her husband. If *budurwoyi* (unmarried girls) enjoy the freedom to come and go, all this ends with marriage—unless they come from educated families where women are often expected, upon finishing their schooling, to find employment as civil servants or in the private sector. Yet even educated girls know that careers do not replace marriage. Everyone must marry, and, in the eyes of some, the sooner, the better, given the alleged rise of sexual promiscuity among unsupervised youths.

Because men spend most of their days outside the home conducting business, socializing, or traveling, they are rarely home to grant their wives permission. Thus some women are known to sneak out without securing their husband's consent, occasionally enlisting the support of a co-wife to cover their tracks or provide an alibi if their absence is discovered. This is hardly the norm, of course. Women spend most of their time within their compounds, especially if they are married to wealthy men who can afford to limit their involvement in domestic and farming activities. By claiming that a woman's place is in her home, reformist preachers have helped popularize the notion of seclusion—or partial seclusion—even among their opponents. Despite the resentment they feel for Izala activists, the latter implicitly agree with them that, ideally, a woman should stay home—at least during her reproductive years. Still, it is important to clarify that these emerging concerns about *kubli*, containment, and morality are not entirely new, despite Izala preachers' insistence that, before the emergence of the reformist association, women lived unprincipled, shameless lives. Moreover, the 'yan Izala I met did not agree as to what *kubli* actually entailed at the practical level. For some, imposing seclusion on married women meant that they should not be seen outside their homes during the day. For others, it simply meant that women should remain mostly in the marital compound, but it did not exclude an occasional visit to a neighbor or a new mother celebrating the birth of her child. For yet others, it meant that women could leave their homes regularly so long as they were veiled and had their husband's permission. During the 2004 presidential elections, I saw a significant number of veiled Izala women walk toward the public school classroom where voting was taking place. Many of them probably rarely left their homes on ordinary days, but on Election Day it was their duty to vote, even if it involved walking across half the town to get to their destination.

My discussion of Izala's position on *kubli* raises the question of the reformist movement's vision of femininity and domesticity within the larger debate about women's rights in Muslim societies. Studies of conservative Islamic movements have often revealed that control over women's sexuality, and over their social and economic roles, is one of the cornerstones of the Muslim reformist agenda. The rhetoric of many of these movements joins a condemnation of women's aspirations for greater freedom to a broader critique of the pernicious effects of European and U.S. social and political institutions on the Muslim world (Awn 1994). In Iran, one of the first measures taken by Khomeini's government was to pressure women into wearing the chador (cloak) in an attempt to Islamicize the society as a whole. The "morality police" wandering the streets of Teheran would coerce women into conforming to proper Islamic values. In Sudan, reforms instituted by the powerful National Islamic Front since it gained power in 1990 have similarly forced women to wear a veil, and urban women have replaced the traditional Sudanese dress with a full body wrap which Hale (1996:220) describes as "voluntary national dress." In Pakistan, a woman who steps outside her home without a veil is considered morally corrupt (Weiss 1997). In these contexts and elsewhere, reformist Islamic movements have clearly defined themselves, in some respect at least, as "anti-modernist" organizations, extending religiously sanctioned control over women's bodies as metonyms for control over society at large.

Although the Izala case bears undeniable similarities to the Iranian, Sudanese, or Pakistani contexts in these respects, it is important not to erase fundamental differences between these various Muslim societies or organizations. Regarding the education of women, for instance, Izala is anything but a conservative movement. Rather, it is an attempt to forge an alternative modernity for West African Muslims that is not rooted in Western concepts of power, morality, and accountability (Kane 1994). Recall, for instance, that a woman's primary obligation is to learn to read the Qur'an so that she can be a better and more responsible member of Muslim society.[33]

If the 'yan Izala's commitment to further women's education has resulted in the expansion of the Islamic school system in Dogondoutchi, it is not clear whether such strategies will lead to a more comprehensive integration of Muslim women in public affairs—as has been true in Nigeria where women, through their roles as political actors, have affected particular outcomes in the public realm. The lack of available funding, for one thing, has limited women's educational options: whereas in Niamey and Maradi, neighborhood Qur'anic schools have become popular places of female solidarity where women engage in income-generating activities in addition to attending literacy classes, in Dogondoutchi no classes are designed specifically for women (Alidou 2005).[34] Moreover, many local 'yan Izala stress that although women are theoretically allowed to go out as long as they are appropriately dressed, it is best to keep them partially or entirely secluded. This directly contradicts Sufism critic Sa'ad Zungu's teachings; the Nigerian nationalist associated seclusion with the corrupted values he wished to eradicate from Muslim life. The differing—and rarely consistent—positions that 'yan Izala have taken concerning women's mobility and visibility in Dogondoutchi reveal the heterogeneity of the Izala movement and the problem of drawing too rigid a boundary between what are conventionally defined as Sufism and Muslim reformism.

Izala's stance toward Mawri women must ultimately be assessed in the context of Islam's relatively short history in Arewa and of the limited religious training of local Izala leaders. In a region where, as the local imam put it, "before Islam, women went everywhere," members of Izala are especially eager to reaffirm their Muslim identity through distinctive practices—such as the gendered segregation of space—that "bridge the gap between religious discourse and practical realities" (Ask and Tjomsland 1998:2). Seclusion is now the preferred public expression of piety as well as a concrete means of re-Islamizing society. The models of pious, female erudition available to women in northern Nigeria (Boyd 1989; Mack and Boyd 2000) since the 1800s have had no impact in this region, where until a few decades ago women were virtually excluded from Qur'anic education. In contrast to northern Nigeria where women benefited from nineteenth-century *jihadist* Usman 'dan Fodio's promotion of female scholarship (Cooper 1998:35), there is no existing tradition in Dogondoutchi on which women can draw to secure power while at the same time asserting their commitment to the Qur'an. In Izala families, gendered roles are clearly defined: men are the providers and the source of authority, women the homemakers and the nurturers who instill proper values in the next generation (Bodman 1998). Except for a minority of educated women who hold jobs, Izala women in Dogondoutchi are excluded from visible political and economic activities.

Muslim women in Dogondoutchi have traditionally had little control over their religious identities. In contrast to northern Nigerian women who, by adhering to Izala, were able to emancipate themselves from their husbands because the latter were affiliated with a Sufi order and therefore did not practice "true" Islam, Mawri women did not join Izala of their own will; they necessarily followed a father or a husband. Although Izala everywhere shares with other Muslim reformist movements a wish to define itself in opposition to Western secular modernity, it has also been shaped by the culturally specific contexts in which it has evolved. The association in Dogondoutchi has developed its own distinct identity, even if it remains dependent on the reformist models of Islamic society circulating in northern Nigeria. Understanding the Izala vision of Islam and its role as defender of family integrity requires a recognition that Izala's positions are not codified. Despite the fractious rhetoric, that the Izala message leads to differing expressions of religiosity—resonating at times with anti-reformist values—highlights once more the problem of assuming the existence of a homogeneous Izala faction that uniformly and unambiguously opposes a sharply defined anti-Izala coalition.

Fertility, the Female Body, and Family

If Muslims, regardless of their religious affiliations, approve of the practice of seclusion in one form or another, they do not agree about whether human fertility should be regulated. In recent years, reformist Muslims have loudly proclaimed their distaste for birth control, even assaulting proponents of contraception to promote their pronatalist views. In 1993 the leaders of a family-planning campaign in Niamey were threatened by reformist Muslims for circulating information on how to regulate birth (Charlick 2004).[35] Izala preachers loudly advertise their anti-contraception stance in their sermons by insisting that birth control goes against God's wishes and is altogether un-Islamic. Niger has the highest fertility rate in the world, approximating eight children per woman. Although contraceptives are available to women at low cost, birth control remains a controversial practice, especially since the emergence of Izala and its widely publicized ban on the use of contraception. Public health officials euphemistically speak of birth spacing rather than birth control, to emphasize the benefits of this strategy and avoid bruising conservative sensibilities: when births are spaced out, babies are breast-fed longer and their chances of surviving are greater.[36]

Muslims traditionally questioned the justification for family planning on the grounds that it contradicted the Islamic belief of *tawakkul* (reliance on God) and *rizq* (provision by God). Countering claims that a rapidly expanding population impaired the country's chance of escaping poverty, they argued that controlling one's fertility by whatever means was an affront to God. God, they insisted, provides for His creatures; Muslims must trust in Him and not interfere with the divinely ordained plan.[37] In a country where so many still rely on agriculture for their economic survival, a numerous progeny easily translates into a much valued supply of labor during the farming season. Moreover, a large family is not just a conduit to wealth; it is wealth itself or, as Hausa speakers put it, *arzikin mutane* (wealth in people).

With the rise of Izala, the issue of family planning and contraceptive use has become politicized. Izala activists oppose the government's program of *espacement des naissances* (birth spacing) as a political move, invoking Islam in support of their position. Aside from occasionally suggesting that practices that prevent pregnancy are nothing but a form of infanticide (and are therefore prohibited by Islam), they claim that Muslims have the duty to produce a numerous progeny, thereby insuring that Muhammad will be surrounded by more disciples than any other prophet on Judgment Day. From this perspective, having a large family contributes to the empowerment of the Muslim community aside from demonstrating submission to God's will. It is also a means of countering Westerners' intrusion into national affairs, since family planning is seen as an imposition by Western powers. Several 'yan Izala told me that the Qur'an contained nothing about birth spacing; indeed, the Prophet himself was said to have told men to marry several wives and father many children to increase the size of his following.

Predictably Muslim opposition to family planning has considerable implications for women, who largely have no say in the size of the families they produce. That, despite the government's and external donors' efforts to regulate births,[38] Niger's population continues to rise by 3.3 percent a year is perhaps a sign of the relative popularity of a religious message that equates restrictions on the size of families with deviation from the rightful path. Only 5 percent of Nigériens currently use family planning and contraception, and one woman out of three has given birth to ten children or more (Institut National de la Statistique 2006). Whether by choice or because (as is the case for a great many women, especially in rural areas) they are uninformed about modern contraceptive methods and their availability, Nigériens remain largely pronatalist.

Even with conservative Muslims' loud objections to family planning, a small number of women in Dogondoutchi pay the equivalent of 20 cents each month to receive a monthly dose of contraceptives. French-educated couples, largely or exclusively dependent on wage income, are increasingly aware of the cost of raising children. They mention the price of uniforms and private school tuition in addition to the basic expenses incurred in providing for their progeny. Female high school students I spoke to in 2006 all insisted that, when married, they would take steps to limit the size of their progeny. For most of them, four or five children constituted the ideal family size. Aside from pointing out to me that having lots of children translates into a heavy financial burden, they also worried about the impact of numerous pregnancies on their health and their looks. In my experience, men are more likely to reject family planning because it challenges their exclusive rights to their wives' sexuality. As is true elsewhere (Ong 1995), they also fear that contraception might embolden women to disregard their husband's wishes and make decisions without previously consulting them. Although high school and university graduates generally described family planning as a crucial tool of development, a school leaver and father of three said that he was against contraception because it implied that he was not able to raise as many children as he wanted. Contraception was a threat to his masculinity because it challenged his ability to raise children. Despite the Nigérien government's sustained efforts to promote family planning, modern practices associated with sexuality and reproduction are met with suspicion by large segments of the population: they defy men's conjugal rights and their authority over women and are also perceived as a challenge to Islamic teachings.

Negotiations over the Family Code, domestic legislation that defines the legal relationship between husbands and wives and between children and parents, led to similarly contentious debates. Over the past decade and a half, implementation of the *Code des Personnes et de la Famille* (Code of Persons and the Family) has been opposed by reformist Muslims who claim that it is based on secular principles and therefore anti-Islamic. Shaykh Yousouf Hassan Diallo, a popular preacher who, between 1991 and 2000, preached some forty sermons in the context of activities sponsored by the Nigérien Association for Islamic Call and Solidarity (ANASI), proclaimed that the Family Code "promote[d] the destruction of the Muslim family" and was "written by people who do not believe in God and in Judgment Day" (in Hassane 2005).[39]

The controversy surrounding the Family Code project greatly contributed to the forging of an Islamist consciousness in Niger, as it mobilized those who wanted Islam to play a larger role in the nation's political life and also led to the creation of two female reformist associations (Niandou-Souley and Alzouma 1996). In 1999 protests by Islamic groups were so intense that the government, intending to ratify the UN Convention on Ending All Forms of Discrimination against Women, felt obliged to add reservations to its ratification—thereby effectively nullifying the ratification in the eyes of some Nigériens (Charlick 2004). A year later the second edition of the heavily publicized Festival International de la Mode Africaine, or FIMA, became the target of Muslim anger (see chapter 7). In Niamey businesses were vandalized, and scantily clad women were harassed. In Maradi, the nucleus of Izala activism in Niger, protests turned excessively violent and a number of businesses and compounds were destroyed (Cooper 2006). These incidents dramatically illustrate once again how local attempts to do away with Western values and normative constructs perceived as un-Islamic often center on definitions of virtuous womanhood based on a supposedly literal reading of the Qur'an.

Conclusion

The emergence of an overarching civic and political culture in Niger was promoted partly by the liberalization of Muslim discourse and the proliferation of distinct, often fiercely opposed, Muslim traditions whose competing visions of order, morality, and social control resulted in violent disputes over mosque ownership. Bowen notes that the control of a mosque has great political significance in Muslim society, adding that although a struggle over mosque control may have as its explicit object a relatively minor liturgical issue, it often catalyzes a much broader set of sociopolitical divisions (1993:309). Mosques, especially Friday mosques, are not simply places of prayer and education. They are crucial for the dissemination of religious and political ideas (Loimeier 1997b:216). Because they serve as meeting places, reformist mosques are often the headquarters of the Izala militancy (Sounaye 2006). The spread of Izala throughout northern Nigeria was largely concretized through the progressive control of important Friday mosques in major cities—a trend often accompanied by violence, leading authorities to require permits to preach at Friday mosques (Umar 2001). In the case I recounted, the societal divisions revealed by contests over control of the local Friday mosque are themselves part of wider transformations in Muslim lifestyles and thinking. As modes of reflection over, and criticism of, Muslim practice, they contribute to a public sphere of discourse substantially different from European formulations of civil society in which religion is markedly absent.

In Dogondoutchi recent critical debates over the nature of Islamic knowledge and worship have increasingly pressured religious practitioners to articulate their beliefs. These debates resemble religious disputes elsewhere, in that Mawri protagonists eschew culturally specific rationalizations for current practices to advocate religious action based on its degree of fit with the universal set of norms provided by the Qur'an and *hadith* (Bowen 1993:321). Concerned that the onslaught of Westernization and secularization threatens the Islamic order, members of Izala have implemented sweeping reforms, which, they insist, will establish religious, moral, and social practices more in keeping with Qur'anic injunctions. In so doing, they have also redirected the course of the ongoing debate on spirituality, knowledge, and piety that had long shaped 'yan bori and Muslim relations. Having successfully managed to rally certain discontents and declare war on a society that had long tolerated polytheistic and syncretistic practices, the current goal of Izala activists is to reform Nigérien society so that no aspect of social, familial, political, or economic life is outside Islam's purview.

109

In the 'yan Izala's vision of a Muslim civil society, religious truths are conceived as fixed and unchanging, which is precisely why one can aim to live one's life guided by the very words and deeds of the Prophet (as they are transcribed in the Qur'an and *hadith*). Eickelman and Piscatori (1990:2) note that "eternal religious truths [. . .] are perceived, understood and transmitted by persons historically situated in 'imagined' communities, who knowingly or inadvertently contribute to the reconfiguration or reinterpretation of those verities, even as their fixed and unchanging natures are affirmed." While this captures the essence of the reformist movement, it does not mean that Izala rejects "modernity" to return to a mythical past: that much is clear from their egalitarian vision of society, their stress on self-centered achievement, and their insistence that women be educated. As a particular expression of "tradition" based on a new scriptural interpretation of Islam (Asad 1986), Izala provides a framework for the growing individualism that has come to characterize postcolonial identities and increasingly monetized relations. In Dogondoutchi this reformed Islam actively engages with capitalist processes and a form of consumerism. As we have seen, its oppositional culture, while countering aspects of Euro-modernism, also counters long-standing local traditions of economic redistribution.

Through its contestation of a previously unquestioned orthodoxy and cultivation of an alternative socio-moral order comprised of entitled individuals and pious followers, Izala can be said to contribute to the emergence of civil society, a significant claim indeed. Granted, Izala's sustained efforts to reaffirm the centrality of Islam in both public and private life often promoted dissent rather than unity in the Muslim community. The reformist movement's struggle to establish a moral order accessible and useful to all through Qur'anic teaching often highlighted the clash of incompatible interests in Dogondoutchi. Moreover, despite its seemingly egalitarian ethos and valorization of women's educational roles, Izala is not all enlightenment and emancipation: it is contradictory, practical and at the same time hopelessly utopian, democratic yet also oppressive. Nonetheless, Izala in Niger clearly "sounds a warning to the widespread belief that African societies have tended to be ineffective counterweights to African states" (Watts 1996:184). By contributing an Islamic alternative to more secular models of nationhood, citizenship, family, and identity, the Izala discourse has actively shaped the emerging Nigérien public sphere. It has provided a religious framework for scrutinizing contemporary social arrangements and speculating on the forms that public and private life should take.[40]

Through its virulent claims that Islam is the answer to the problems plaguing Nigérien society, Izala opened the way for religious figures aiming to publicize their own version of Muslim authenticity. Prior to the country's political liberalization, the practice of preaching and the dissemination of knowledge obeyed strict rules. Preachers had to be authorized to preach before they were allowed to deliver a *wa'azi* (sermon) (Sounaye n.d.). With the emergence of multiple Islamic associations, rules have loosened, paving the way for preachers with diverse visions eager to capitalize on the *wa'azi's* potential as a tool of Islamization. Malam Awal is one of those preachers who entered the discursive arena shaped by his predecessors to mobilize ordinary Muslims around an alternative ethos that resonated with Izala values even as it disparaged them. It is to him that I turn my attention in the next chapter.

WHEN CHARISMA COMES TO TOWN: MALAM AWAL OR THE MAKING OF A MODERN SAINT

4

Before Malam Awal, we were in the dark, we were in ignorance.
—*Hawa, Dogondoutchi, 2004*

By making places out of spaces, Sufi saints have decentered and recentered the sacred topography of global Islam. New peripheries [. . .] converge ultimately on the epicenter of the Islamic universe—the sacred *ka'ba,* navel of the earth.
—*Pnina Werbner,* Pilgrims of Love

On the evening of March 27, 2000, a celebration was held in the Awaliyya mosque to commemorate Malam Mahamane Awal's arrival in Dogondoutchi some three years earlier. That morning, women and girls were busy sweeping the floor of the mosque with *tsintsiyoyi* (loose bundles of dried grass used as brooms) before the men covered it with a few dozen carpets. Metal chairs had been assembled to one side for important clerics and town dignitaries, and plush armchairs—to be offered to the preacher's close friends and associates—surrounded the throne-like seat reserved for the guest of honor. Separating this seating arrangement from the simple mats on the ground was a low table adorned with bright bouquets of artificial flowers and bowls filled with dates. Save for the fact that the building remained unfinished and roofless (despite Awal's best efforts to encourage further financial contributions from prosperous *'yan* Awaliyya), the scene bespoke the industriousness and commitment of the Awaliyya community.

The event had been scheduled to start around 9:00 PM. By 9:30 PM, a massive crowd was forming in front of the mosque, mostly young children and youths dressed in white. The girls all wore the *hirami*—a white head scarf tied under the chin and further secured by a length of cloth fastened around the head—signifying their affiliation with the Awaliyya, Malam Awal's recently founded Sufi order. Boys, each wearing a white *jaba* (a long-sleeved tunic worn over drawstring pants) and a white *hula* (cap), were singing *ishirinya,* devotional chants Malam Awal taught his students. Sung while rhythmically moving one's head and rotating one's body, they bring the individual performer to a euphoric state.

Soon the boys were walking in an orderly line toward the entrance of the mosque, followed by the young girls. One by one, they entered the building and stood silently in the aisles. Meanwhile, men were performing *zikiri* (protracted chanting repetitively intoning the names of God), a form of worship believed to purify the heart and produce a spiritual closeness with God. They bobbed their heads in unison as they muttered devotional formulas, producing a serene if slightly cacophonous murmur that filled the mosque. The women who had put away the food served to Malam Awal's out-of-town guests now assembled in a concealed section of the mosque, where they could listen to the sermon while remaining hidden from sight. Eventually the ecstatic humming subsided. Two men stood up to read a chapter of the Qur'an, as the video-cameraman recorded the scene for posterity.

Just as the reading of the Qur'an concluded, Malam Awal appeared. Resplendent in a white robe, sleeves adorned lavishly with ornamented purple cuffs, and a purple hooded cape richly embroidered with silver threads, he proceeded toward his "throne," a large wooden chair set above the ground, upholstered in dark fabric and equipped with a high back to make its occupant visually prominent. There was a ripple in the crowd of seated men as they turned toward him, and then each in turn stood up to greet him respectfully. Many had traveled from far away to attend the celebration. An old man, sitting in one of the plush armchairs, approached the preacher and embraced him at length while several others approached only to touch the hem of his garments and secure a blessing. Malam Awal shook hands with a number of men before sitting down. He grabbed a microphone and greeted the crowd of blissful 'yan Awaliyya with heartfelt appreciation. It had been three years, he loudly proclaimed, since he arrived in Dogondoutchi, and great things had been accomplished under his virtuous leadership. A *zawiya* (Sufi center) had been built, the membership of the order was increasing steadily, many young girls had married thanks to his injunction to lower the *sadaki* (bridewealth), and a growing number of youths were engaged in Qur'anic studies. God should be thanked, the preacher continued, for it was He who had sent Malam Awal to Dogondoutchi. Soon after, a preacher's assistant performed *zikiri* with calm and controlled gravity. The men around him responded by bowing in unison. As the young man concluded his recitation, a prominent friend of Malam Awal stood up to describe, emphatically, the numerous accomplishments of the Awaliyya since its creation three years earlier. He spoke of *'yan bori* who had converted to Islam and of *'yan* Izala who had become "true" Muslims,[1] and then recited the names of the many students who had committed the Qur'an to memory under Awal's guidance. At that point, five youths came forward each to recite a verse of the Qur'an and provide a *tafsiri* (exegesis) of it, a convincing demonstration that they had received an exceptional education at the hands of the preacher.

After these preliminaries Malam Awal launched into the *wa'azi,* which everyone had come to hear. Aimed to enhance the popular preacher's mythic appeal, the sermon dramatized the events that led to his appearance in town. Under the preacher's charismatic delivery, an otherwise banal visit was impressed with the stamp of the divine. Like other Sufi masters who enjoy high credibility, Malam Awal claimed that he had been appointed by God to lead the people of Dogondoutchi to reformation. Having originally gained recognition throughout Niger as a man of prodigious scholarship, he now sought to maintain his charisma by implementing a "ritual role" (Gaffney 1994:184) that would enhance his public visibility. By engaging in a colorful narration of his travels, he reminded audiences of the mission with which he had been invested and its divine character. Malam Awal understood the power of performance in the making of charisma. I argue in this chapter that the commemorative ceremony I have described (held every year) constituted the formula the preacher devised for extending his ritual role, asserted as a legitimate right, into the history of the actual community. Before examining how Awal came to Dogondoutchi, let us consider the preacher's public persona in light of the notion of charisma.

A Few Considerations on Charisma

Charisma, in Max Weber's classical formulation, is a highly personalized, passionate, and creative but ephemeral power that inevitably gives way to the highly routinized, calculating, rule-bound, and impersonal structures of bureaucratic authority. As an essentially volatile and revolutionary force, it constitutes a "'call' in the most emphatic sense of the word, a 'mission' or a 'spiritual duty'" (Weber 1978:244). Edward Shils, in an attempt to broaden Weber's definition, argued that charisma is a more pervasive quality that attaches itself to persons, actions, institutions, and material objects by virtue of their association or contact with a vital, order-determining force "located at the center of society" (1965:201; 1975). Building on Shils's reassessment of the Weberian formulation, Clifford Geertz, in an essay titled "Centers, Kings, and Charisma," located charismatic power at the very core of the social order. Charisma, he wrote, constitutes a "sign of involvement with the animating centers of society" (1983:124). Whether dressed up as redemptive virtue in the persona of Elizabeth Tudor, displayed mimetically as cosmic symmetry by a fourteenth-century Javanese ruler, or demonstrated through the mobility of the king in nineteenth-century Morocco, sovereign power, for Geertz, was the source of charismatic sacrality. Monarchs, ruling elites, and politicians alike drew from a repertoire of sacred symbols—crowns, coronations, processions, and progresses—to enhance their central role and formalize their aura of immanence. While recognizing that charisma's "most flamboyant expressions tend[ed] to appear among people at some distance from the center, indeed often enough at a rather enormous distance, who want[ed] very much to be closer" (1983:144), Geertz insisted that it was from the inherently sacred central authority that charismatic figures drew their power.

Even as they occasionally appropriate the sacred symbols of authority, however, those who present themselves as prophets, revolutionaries, and "corrective images of a lost order" (Geertz 1983:143) emerge as charismatic figures not because they emulate state powers but precisely because they oppose them, if only in appearance. Indeed, it is only their opposition to the state that gives them legitimacy and visibility. For the citizens of postcolonial societies, Pnina Werbner and Helene Basu (1998:15) note, the opposition between a morally grounded charisma and the state's rationalized authority is often a more accurate expression of social realities than equating charisma with state power and its routinized extensions. What is needed, they suggest, is a better understanding of the nature of charismatic opposition to the bureaucratic domination of the state. The history of Islam in West Africa offers compelling examples of the ways in which the call to abide by Islamic religious standards has regularly provided the moral framework for charismatic dissent and an oppositional discourse aimed at challenging colonial or state power. By contesting centralized powers and cultivating an alternative socio-moral order, Muslim leaders often filled a moral vacuum at the same time that they helped forge regional or national identities (Amselle 1985; Brenner 2001; Cruise O'Brien and Coulon 1988; Hiskett 1973; Last 1967; Robinson 1985; Soares 2005).

By spreading the faith among commoners in regions where Muslim practices were previously confined to urban elites, their movements for reform and state building "were instrumental in transforming West Africa into a part of the dar al-Islam"[2] (Robinson 2000:132). Fulani teacher Usman 'dan Fodio's declaration of war against the sultan of Gobir and neighboring Hausa rulers (which led to the creation, in 1804, of the Sokoto Caliphate, a loose confederation of some thirty emirates) is undoubtedly the best known of these reform movements (Hiskett 1973; Last 1967; Last and Al-Hajj 1987). As Robinson (2000:132) justifiably notes, the fundamental problem such movements faced was "the question of legitimation." To justify taking on the mantle of holy war and instituting an Islamic state, reformists such as Usman 'dan Fodio turned to the classical foundations of the faith and argued that only a religious authority modeled after the utopian picture of equality and justice that the early Caliphates provided could defeat the existing autocracy, political oppression, and social inequities. In the late nineteenth and early twentieth centuries, appeals to the classical Mohammedan concepts of *jihad* (struggle, warfare against apostates and non-Muslims) and *hijra* (withdrawal, flight) became for West African Muslims a crucial means of legitimizing resistance to European colonization or migration to territories not yet under colonial domination (Hanson 1996).

At the center of several of these reform movements were living saints who attracted followers partly through their *baraka* (*albarka* in Hausa), the wondrous blessings that they received from God and that singled them out as exceptionally venerable individuals. As the embodiment of virtue, piety, and devotion, Muslim saints strongly and distinctly personified religious authority often perceived to be directly opposed to the corruption, immorality, and abusive policies of state (or colonial) powers. The task of theorizing further about the nature of charismatic dissent in Muslim societies is beyond the purview of this book. Nevertheless I use Werbner and Basu's observations about charisma as a point of departure for discussing how Malam Awal came to personify Islamic authority in all its most flamboyant expressions as he set about calling Muslims back to the faith and claiming Dogondoutchi as a place of God. At a time when states all over the globe, restricted by the neoliberal reforms they are forced to implement, no longer contribute to their citizens' welfare, a disparate stock of charismatic figures have surfaced who, in return for unconditional allegiance, promise their followers the "truth" (Schulz 2003). Through the mobilization of various technologies for marketing themselves to their constituency, they provide their followers with alternative moral frameworks for rethinking their relationship to both their cultural heritage and the global community (Soares 2007a). Awal was just such a self-fashioned visionary: he pledged to instruct people on how to be "true" Muslims if they only put their trust in him. Like other Sufi figures of West African history, his understanding of moral community was often at odds with state-derived notions of citizenship, identity, and associational life.

Recall that Malam Awal's presence in Dogondoutchi had been requested by the traditionalist imam and prominent *malamai* who hoped that the potent denunciations of anti-Sufism for which the preacher was famous would convince recent Izala "converts" of the urgent need to return to the fold of "true" Islam. The preacher was expected to deliver a few sermons during which he would make clear that Izala was an improper path, leading to hell and not paradise. Much to everyone's consternation, however, he chose to protect local Muslims not only from the alleged ravages of an insidious anti-Sufi rhetoric but also from the errors of traditionalist Muslim teachers and preachers for whom he reserved his most bitter criticism. *Malamai* who collected *zaka* (a tithe) from local residents, Awal clamored in his daily sermons, were selfish and greedy, filling their pockets at the expense of the poor.[3] They also lacked discipline and failed to promote Qur'anic principles such as humility, asceticism, and sartorial modesty. Finally, they were ignorant and taught nothing of value to their Qur'anic students.

Malam Awal's denunciation of local Muslim elites generated enormous anger and turmoil in the Muslim community. Denied the use of the Friday mosque, he ignored repeated requests that he leave town and instead relocated to a nearby house (lent to him by a local Tidjani) and broadcast his sermons from there. Within a few weeks, however, the owner asked Malam Awal to vacate his lodgings. The preacher's verbal assaults on the very people who had hoped to channel his talent for oratory for their own purposes were becoming a liability and a source of growing embarrassment. Malam Awal soon found another venue for his sermons, and he continued to deliver scathing critiques of local Muslim religious specialists. A delegation appointed by the traditionalist imam was sent to pressure the undesirable guest to leave Dogondoutchi. But it was to no avail.

Ironically, Malam Awal's concerted attacks on both reformist Muslims and their critics had the unintended effect of momentarily bringing together the two adversaries. In their eagerness to stop the vicious harangues emanating from the preacher's daily broadcasts, *'yan* Izala and anti-Izala Muslims momentarily set aside their quarrels to jointly fight the preacher whom they saw as a threat to the stability of the Muslim community.[4] After unsuccessfully trying to dissuade him from preaching altogether, a coalition of Izala and traditionalist leaders, hoping to intimidate him, accused him of violating the law on a number of occasions.[5] The various charges against Malam Awal were later found to be unsubstantiated, and he was not convicted of any crime. Rumors circulated that Izala *commerçants* had offered him money to leave town. Malam Awal, however, with big plans to create a Sufi order, had no intention of leaving. Despite the virulent opposition he faced from leading members of both the Izala faction and the larger Muslim community, the crowds converging at the site of his sermons grew daily, testifying to the wide appeal of his message.

Initially the preacher presented himself as a venerable scholar who had been invited by local Muslim elites to preach the word of God. After he lost the support of the traditionalist imam and his followers, however, he could no longer rely on this claim to justify his presence in town. To garner validation for his doctrinal position, he created a public image of himself as a virtuous and selfless man invested with a holy mission. As he skillfully wove bits of autobiographical narratives in his sermons, a tale soon emerged that "mythologized" the preacher's visit to Dogondoutchi and captured the imagination of his audiences. A divine vision he had in Mecca predetermined his visit to town. He would leave Mecca, travel west, and found a Sufi order in a town with three hills. Since Dogondoutchi is known as the town with three hills, Awal's continued presence in town, the tale implied, had little to do with the imam's request that he speak out against Izala and much to do with the spiritual duty God had entrusted to him. As it was made clear to me during my conversations with Malam Awal's adepts, the imam had been an instrument of God's will. If he had originally invited the preacher to help him defeat Izala, the fact that so many of his own followers had left him to support Malam Awal was indubitable proof of divine intervention.

Although he claimed to depart substantially from the doctrinal orientation of the traditionalist preachers and teachers he so savagely criticized, closer attention to the basic principles enunciated in his sermons reveals no significant differences between his teachings and theirs, save for his insistence that *zaka* (tithe) be used to benefit the needy rather than the Muslim establishment's leading representatives; *sadaki* (bridewealth) and the wedding gifts a bride received should be minimal so that youth could afford to marry; and women should be more spatially and sartorially restricted. There was also the matter of the sixth prayer, which Awal urged his disciples to perform in the middle of the night, but since it apparently was not something he raised in his sermons, it did not become a subject of debate. Indeed, few people in Dogondoutchi had heard about the sixth prayer. Those with whom I spoke tended to label the sixth prayer "heresy"; others wondered if it was not simply another rumor intended to further discredit the preacher. That Malam Awal insisted on starting and ending *azumi* (the month of fasting) two days after the official sighting of the new moon was similarly perceived by his critics as an expression of the preacher's idiosyncrasies, just another attempt to separate himself from other Muslims.[6]

While Awal's pronouncements on *zaka,* marriage, and the scheduling of *azumi* aroused much controversy, surprisingly little was known of the preacher's Sufi training and of those who had initiated him into Sufism. Also unclear was how distinct Awaliyya was from the two most important Sufi orders in Niger, the Qadiriyya and the Tijaniyya. "Awal is not so different from those of the Qadiriyya. His disciples beat their chests like Qadiris," I was told by a university-educated *'dan* Izala who saw the Awaliyya leader as merely another Sufi.[7] Contradicting this statement, another resident assured me that Awal had been trained by a Tijani teacher before he was called by God to found his own order. In the opinion of a local Muslim scholar, the latter testimonies were both inaccurate, as Awal had not been initiated into either *darika* (Sufi order). What these contradictory views indicate, aside from the limited information available on the preacher's religious training, is that ordinary Muslims are hard-pressed to identify a Tijani from a Qadiri. In Dogondoutchi, Sufi orders are loosely institutionalized, and they play a limited role in community affairs. As elsewhere in Niger, most Muslims there are not affiliated with any Sufi order, although this does not mean that Sufi practices are unimportant. Indeed, the way that many Muslims understand Muslimhood is embodied in certain practices identified as "Sufi," particularly those involving the veneration of Muslim saints and the use of Islamic esoteric knowledge for healing, protective, and divinatory purposes.

Significantly, Malam Awal himself was reluctant to define his version of Sufism in opposition to other Sufi orders such as the Tijaniyya, the most prominent *darika* in Dogondoutchi. Rather than defining what set Awaliyya apart from other Sufi orders, the preacher distinguished practices that were Islamic from those that were not, and reminded his audiences that his role was primarily to prevent people from fighting and teach them how to get along. He made no claim to be a descendant of the Prophet Muhammad (as many Muslim saints do) but described himself as a great unifier, sent by God to eradicate conflicts and bring peace to Muslim communities across Niger. Malam Awal's intervention had a major impact on the local religious landscape, but rather than promoting harmony, it intensified existing discords and controversies among Muslims. Emerging in a context of intensified religious activism, Malam Awal's opposition to local ways of being Muslim should be seen less as a matter of doctrinal disagreement than as an expression of the struggle over the definition of truth and control over the institutions that produce it (Eickelman and Piscatori 1996; Schulz 2003). Like Izala reformists, Malam Awal couched his public interventions as a search for an alternative moral order with its source in the Qur'an. If *'yan* Izala and

Awal both favored a strict reliance on the power of the Scriptures when calling for a return to "authentic" Islam, they parted company on the role religious leaders should play. 'Yan Izala spoke of democratizing access to knowledge and challenging the authority of formally trained *malamai*. Malam Awal, on the other hand, intended to formalize his virtuous aura and retain authoritative control over the definition of Islamic tradition. To that end, the language of mythology would prove quite useful.

As he set about legitimizing his religious authority and, in the manner of Elizabeth I or Usman 'dan Fodio, enhance the messianic character of his mission, the Sufi preacher turned out to be an inspired *bricoleur*. By peddling a classic narrative of divine calling that not only suited the global aspirations of his Muslim audience but also closely paralleled a Mawri myth of origin, he enabled Dogondoutchi residents to establish a connection to Mecca, the Muslims' place of origin to which they yearn to return but that local believers generally experience as an absent, because distant, presence. With the saga of his travels from Mecca, the preacher conferred on a previously unremarkable town the distinction of being God's chosen place, destined to become the cradle of a revitalized, authentic Islam that would spread to the four corners of the world. In what follows I examine how Malam Awal's account of his divinely inspired journey from Mecca to Dogondoutchi not only established him as an esteemed luminary but also contributed to the fashioning of Dogondoutchi as a special town with a mystical link to Mecca. The town's transformation as a place of Allah and Awal's redefinition as an icon of blessedness presupposed one another. By mythologizing the events that led to his arrival in town, the preacher created a "fertile matrix" (Bilu and Ben-Ari 1992:675) for the creation of his new persona as a saintly Sufi and the enhancement of Dogondoutchi as a place of cosmic significance.

The Mission

At the opening of the sermon that he gave during the celebration of the third anniversary of his arrival in Dogondoutchi, Malam Awal recounted a personal story to the faithful crowd that had assembled in the still unfinished mosque. When living in Mecca, he told the crowd, he used to pray regularly in a particular mosque where there was always a pleasant smell and the air felt fresh, like the freshness one feels in the early morning during the rainy season. One day, as he was praying inside, policemen came to chase people out of the mosque. They made everyone leave except him. "Their eyes did not see me, I don't know if it was thanks to God." The doors of the mosque were closed and he was left inside, alone. It was dark and quiet, and he soon fell asleep.

Suddenly a light appeared, so bright, Awal said, that "one could have picked a needle off the ground." Four men appeared in front of Awal, dressed in white and beautiful. One of them had big eyes, and each time he blinked, the color of his iris changed: it turned to yellow, to green, and then to red. He also had very long, curly eyelashes, Awal recalled, and his nose was long and pointed upward. Thanks to the light, Awal could also see that the hairs on his chest were as long as fingers. Awal did not dare look at the men. He was so frightened, he said, that he almost urinated on himself. When called, he stood up, trembling, convinced that these were messengers of death, come to take him from this world.

"What are you doing here?" the men asked.

"I am here next to the tomb of the Prophet."

"What blessings did you seek?" they asked again, "You must go back."

Malam Awal was unable to move and stood there as if petrified. A cup appeared in front of him, so clean that he could see his reflection in it. It looked empty but when he put his fingers in it, it felt like icy cold milk. He was asked to open his mouth but, as frightened as he was, when the liquid was poured in his mouth, he could not even taste what it was. "All I remember," he told his listeners, "is that after that I was full and did not eat or drink for three days."

Soon after, one of the men said to Awal: "You must renounce the world. Do not become dependent on the powerful. Do not abandon the truth for lies." Another man told him something he told his audience he could not repeat, and the third one opened a small box, the size of a hand. Peering into the box, Malam Awal saw a man and a woman reading the Qur'an. Mustering his courage, he asked if he could have the box. "I will give it to you," said the man, "after you pray." As Awal was concluding his prayer, the box turned into water. He splashed the water on his face and his chest before sitting down again.

When he looked up, the men were gone. Confused, he tried to leave the mosque but could not find a door, so he just sat, waiting. Eventually the doors of the mosque opened to let people in for the dawn prayer. Then the assembled faithful dispersed, and the mosque was empty again. Exhausted by the previous day's events, Malam Awal fell asleep. It was not until the sun had risen and he was out of the mosque that he understood what had happened. The four men had entrusted him with a mission: he was to travel west, back to Africa, until he reached a town with three hills. There he would proclaim the glory of God and convert people to the "true" religion. After he left Mecca, Malam Awal journeyed westward. He preached in every town he visited until he was invited to come to Dogondoutchi, a dusty provincial town that owed its name to the *dogon doutchi*, the "long stone" whose imposing clay structure stood tall against the sun-parched Sahelian landscape. Beside the *dogon doutchi*, two rocky peaks tower over clusters of mud-walled compounds and sandy pathways. Thanks to the three rugged crests it is nestled under, Dogondoutchi is often referred to as the town with three hills. This allegedly was where God sent Malam Awal to bring people the "truth" and lead them on the virtuous path.

Like other aspects of Malam Awal's life culled from various sources, the incident the preacher described is filled with puzzles and inconsistencies. For instance, how do we account for the fact that he claimed to be standing next to the tomb of the Prophet (which is in Medina) when he was supposedly worshiping in Mecca? And admitting that the preacher was speaking loosely, should his statement be taken to mean that by worshiping at the tomb of the Prophet, he was actually praying to him? There is much controversy surrounding the practice of praying to Muhammad directly (and to dead saints, more generally), as it is perceived by many Muslims as a form of "idolatry." Like other practices assimilated to remnants of polytheistic traditions, pilgrimages to the graves of Muslim saints (or to the graves of the Prophet's wives and children in Medina) are condemned by Muslim reformists everywhere. In Medina, the behavior of pilgrims at the tomb of the Prophet is rigorously policed, and worshipers are routinely reminded that ostentatious displays of piety and emotion—praying, crying, and so on—are discouraged by Saudi religious officials.[8] All the same, against the backdrop of contentious debates about the authenticity of Sufi ways of being Muslim, the scene of Malam Awal worshiping at the tomb of the Prophet takes on added significance.

Manufacturing Charisma: The Making of Malam Awal

Thanks to Malam Awal's innovative and highly personalized leadership, and his artful sermon delivery and forceful condemnation of reformist Islam, local residents who had been confused or angered by Izala's caustic criticisms of their Muslim practices were reinvigorated. They admired the preacher's erudition and applauded his skillful performance of *zikiri*. Many greeted with enthusiasm his ruthless condemnation of the sober pietism of Izala. They also welcomed his tolerance of certain practices, such as the wearing of protective amulets that Izala preachers enjoined people to abandon. But, above all, they embraced the decisive style and panache with which he rebuked opponents on both sides of the reformist/anti-Izala divide by claiming to be working in the name of God. As Hassana, a devoted follower of Awal, explained to me in March 2000:

> The imam, and his people tried to have him arrested so he would stop preaching and reciting *zikiri*. Malam Awal told them: "I won't stop doing *zikiri* because I only call the name of God. In my sermons, I only speak of that which is in the Qur'an."

Until Ibrahim Bare Maïnassara's assassination on April 9, 1999, Awal, who was a close friend and confidant of the Nigérien president, enjoyed virtual immunity from the law. When his opponents succeeded in building a case against him—he was accused of poisoning, defamation, corruption, and embezzlement—the case file would mysteriously disappear before it reached the prosecutor's office and the charges would eventually be dropped.

In my presence, critics of Malam Awal often alluded to his political connections to explain his legal immunity. His followers, on the other hand, insisted that the protection he enjoyed was further proof of his blessedness. He was a vehicle of God's grace, and everything about him, including his immunity from persecution, both legal and physical, was an expression of this favored status. Several individuals pointed out how powerful and otherworldly he looked when they had first set eyes on him, and others spoke of being overtaken by a kind of awe mingled with fear in his presence. Most agreed that there was something exceptionally compelling about him. "Even if you don't agree with him, when you pass him in the street, you can't stop looking at him," one woman remarked to me. Another *'ya* ("female member of") Awaliyya once pointed out that what was so special about Malam Awal, aside from the fact that he knew and could talk about everything that happened in the world, was that he never insulted anyone: "He only invokes the name of God." Thus when the imam forbade him entrance to the Friday mosque and later tried to evict him from Dogondoutchi for allegedly disseminating lies, Awal had supposedly triumphed by calmly demonstrating how he spoke the truth: "Everything he said was in the Qur'an, so the imam could not make him leave."

Malam Awal's reputation as a man of God was further scripted and nurtured through a myriad of representational and discursive practices that extended his oratorical power. Every sermon, every event that Malam Awal attended, was systematically videotaped and the videos archived for further

Figure 4.1. A poster of
Malam Awal on the inside
wall of a home.

use. On the walls of numerous Awaliyya homes people hung a picture of
Malam Awal—a practice that the Sufi preacher encouraged by inviting disciples to photograph him during the theatrical ceremonies he held to reaffirm
his power.[9] Just as effective in propagating the preacher's charisma were the
songs his disciples had been taught and were instructed to perform publicly
during celebratory gatherings. Nearly everyone in town had heard the line
Malam Awali na Allah ne (Malam Awal is a man of God) from one of the
most frequently performed Awaliyya songs. An expression I heard often in
2004 aptly captures the reach of his formidable presence: *Gardama da Awali
a sara ce,* meaning "those who argue with Awal, they are done for," hints at
the perils facing those who would dare oppose him. Although Malam Awal
could not entirely control the production of narratives that helped spread (or
taint) his fame, he nonetheless actively participated in the circulation of numerous songs, stories, portraits, and mementos that not only expressed but
also concretized his virtuous authority.

The information that circulated about the preacher's personal history was scant. He was born in Goure, a Hausa town east of Zinder. When he was four years old, his parents left for Argungu, northern Nigeria, where his paternal grandfather, an accomplished Muslim scholar, was an adviser to the emir. Soon after, Awal's father relocated to Kano, where Awal began his Qur'anic studies and attended primary school for six years. After studying Islamic law in Argungu, he moved to Katsina to become a district chief for a year and a half. He then took a position as a judge, but because he was not interested in working with the law he pursued his Islamic studies and became a teacher.

While he claimed Nigérien citizenship, the preacher took pains to emphasize his Nigerian roots to enhance his charisma and respectability. For Nigériens, things, people, and places Nigerian exude a special aura. They are, by definition, sophisticated, smart, and cultured—in a word, superior. In the eyes of Dogondoutchi residents Awal was a foreigner,[10] which implied, for some, that he was polished and cultivated. His foreignness resonated with the image of the preacher as a cosmopolitan figure, who had traveled widely to Europe and the Middle East and was now sharing with local Dogon-doutchi residents the wisdom he had accumulated during his scholarly trips. For others, it confirmed that he was an impostor: Nigeria's mystique is often said to be compromised by the supposedly fraudulent practices of its inhabitants. On his actual intellectual genealogy, only blurry details are available. The preacher had not revealed who he studied with or how many years he attended a university. I suspect that he left those dimensions of his biography purposely vague. Too precise a life trajectory might have disclosed inconsistencies that the preacher was determined to conceal from the prying eye of his detractors. Furthermore, the mystery surrounding his prior life suited his objectives. As a result, most people in Dogondoutchi knew little about his background, only that he came from an illustrious Nigerian family, had received a distinguished education, and had traveled extensively.

In Dogondoutchi the charismatic preacher soon became widely known by virtue of two prominent social identities. One derived principally from his scholarly achievements and his cosmopolitan background.[11] He had attended prestigious Islamic universities, and his claim to having studied in Saudi Arabia for several years automatically established his scholarly superiority and challenged the authority of local Muslim leaders who could not boast similar achievements. He was often referred to as the most accomplished Muslim scholar in Niger. This claim, as far as I know, Malam Awal did not refute. The preacher was well aware that Islamic authority is mainly grounded in demonstrations of *ilimi* (knowledge) and that claims of competence based on the sustained and exhaustive study of Islamic sciences were central to the consolidation of his power.[12] During the interview he granted me, Awal carefully enumerated the various degrees he had successively earned from the Teacher's College Islamic Foundation [*sic*], the Usman 'dan Fodio Institute in Sokoto, Ahmadu Bello University in Zaria, and finally the Islamic University of Medina in Saudi Arabia. To attend each of these institutions of high learning, he had had to overcome great hurdles. He claimed to owe his success to God who had always been by his side to guide and protect him.

Aside from validating his authority as a leader and reformer, Awal's academic achievements became the stuff of widely reported stories that reinforced his reputation as a magnetic and mystically driven preacher. It was common knowledge in the Awaliyya community that, as a child, Malam Awal was already more accomplished than his teachers. A friend told me that his teacher had once exclaimed, referring to the young Awal, that he was already an eminent scholar who would "accomplish great things in this world." According to another man, when Awal was a child, a famed religious leader had told the preacher's father that his son was fortunate enough to have received God's blessings and that he would one day dispense his extraordinary knowledge of Islam to all those who sought it. Manifestations of stupendous erudition are a classic token of divine favor and an "overt demonstration of [a] Saint's sainthood" (O'Fahey 1990:13), that is, of the blessedness certain individuals (known as *waliyyai*, "friends of God") enjoy by virtue of their closeness to God. While reminding us that knowledge stands as "the first principle of Islam" (Rahman 1966:101), striking displays of *ilimi* also confirm that there are several sources of cognition, including divine illumination (Ewing 1997; Gaffney 1994; Hoffman 1995). Although Nigériens value literacy greatly, those among them who are Sufi will occasionally point out that the greatest Sufi masters received their knowledge not from books but directly from God. Like them, Malam Awal apparently displayed a remarkable breadth of knowledge that clearly exceeded what could be learned from books. The preacher claimed to have had seven teachers. The number 7 is a highly significant number in Hausa cosmology and symbolizes the union of male (3) and female (4) principles and is synonymous with life and reproduction.[13] This claim further "mythologized" Awal's past and singled him out as an extraordinary individual whose every action had cosmic significance.

The other dimension of Malam Awal's social identity that enhanced his charisma and endeared him to many Muslims derived from his prodigious abilities to tame the dangerous forces of the wild. The preacher was rumored to routinely engage in battles with mysterious assailants, evil spirits sent by his foes, and always emerge victorious. Whereas mystical insight and the ability to heal are powers commonly attributed to sainted Muslim figures in West Africa and elsewhere (Bilu and Ben-Ari 1992; Ewing 1997; O'Fahey 1990; Soares 2004a), battling evil spirits has traditionally been the prerogative of non-Muslim religious specialists, at least in this part of Niger (see Masquelier 2001b). Now that Islam has become an unquestionable dimension of daily life for most Dogondoutchi residents, spirit devotees have increasingly come to signify crude and embarrassing alterity. In their eagerness to present themselves as sophisticated urbanites, most Muslims avoid associations with "animists" and loudly claim they want nothing to do with *al-janu* (spirits).

Note that "animism," for contemporary Mawri, is not so much about believing in spirits as it is about worshiping them. The existence of *aljanu* is not questioned by local Muslims, many of whom purchase amulets and other Qur'anic medicines from *malamai* to ward off harmful spiritual influences. Even so, direct dealings with spirits are, publicly at least, denounced as sinful by the great majority of Muslims. In his study of Islam in Côte d'Ivoire, Launay notes that the problem for Muslims wishing to differentiate themselves from spirit worshipers is "essentially moral, not cosmological" (1992:105). The same can be said of Muslims in Dogondoutchi, whether or not they are devout. Muslim clerics occasionally claim to have the specialized knowledge that enables them, by making use of Quran-based techniques and formulas, to keep evil spirits at bay or perform exorcism, but doing so has invited reformists to speculate that they are drawing upon the powers of Satan rather than of God. Although they manufacture amulets and recite supplicatory prayers (*addu'a*) as protection against spirits, *malamai* say they do not confront spirits, work with them, or even notice their presence, relying instead on the power of *salla* (daily prayer) to invoke God's protection. They wish to avoid being identified as spirit worshipers or servants of Satan, which generally is viewed as the same thing.

That Malam Awal would willingly and publicly acknowledge having confrontations with spirits when he was not fighting human aggressors indicated not only that he possessed uncommon powers that enabled him to ward off nocturnal attacks at the hands of his enemies, but also that he was a conduit for divine grace. Only Malam Awal's closeness to the Supreme Being could explain such displays of magical powers which—his followers were quick to point out—were a far cry from the Satan-inspired techniques of *bori* devotees. Only God's blessings, some surmised, would enable the preacher to withstand both treacherous nightly raids by invisible creatures and potential accusations that he dabbled in *kafirai* (pagan) practices.[14] Aminatou, one of his disciples, described the attacks in this way:

> One day [Malam Awal's opponents] brought a powerful *malami* from Argungu to kill Malam Awal. They also asked ruthless thieves and criminals to go and attack him in his house. But when they went looking for his house, they could not find it. They left with guns to try to kill him, but his house was nowhere to be seen. Even in the night, there are people who try to hurt him. But he sees what they are doing, he is protected. . . . When they sent him the Doguwa [a native spirit known for her swift propensity to kill her human victims], nothing happened. She came back. Every night they sent her to attack Malam Awal. But she couldn't kill him. Doguwa told Malam Awal: "A *malami* sent me to kill you. But I cannot kill you. I am leaving."

Aminatou's account of Awal's victories over occult forces provides a measure of Malam Awal's vital inner power. Of particular interest in her testimony is the reference to the invisibility of the preacher's house. The disappearance of homes (and at time entire villages) from an enemy's sight is a classic scenario in pre-Islamic accounts of how, because they enjoyed the protection of powerful tutelary spirits, Mawri people neither had to fear assailants nor ever lost a battle (Masquelier 2001b). By spreading—or allowing others to spread—stories about how he could become invisible to his enemies thanks to God's divine gifts, Malam Awal mediated the past and the present in utterly novel ways. By demonstrating the superiority of his powers over occult forces, the preacher condensed in his persona both the powers of the pre-Islamic Mawri past and their encapsulation by Islam (see chapter 5).

Waliya: The Symbolic and Literal Cultivation of Sainthood

The preacher's powers were understood to derive from God, but his ability to overcome his enemies, human and spiritual, was spoken of in terms of specific superhuman abilities that distinguished him from ordinary Muslim preachers: he could predict the future (a sure sign of sainthood), see in the dark (he could see his enemies coming whether he was awake or asleep), change shape,[15] and hear whatever was said about him no matter how distant the speaker. He was allegedly able to see what people did in Mecca. A woman told me that, in Mecca, the preacher could touch the roof of the Ka'aba (building constructed next to the holy, black stone and Islam's holiest site) when he was sitting. Despite constant threats to his life, Awal acknowledged not even owning a gun, much less a knife. Words were said to be his only weapons. In any case, he had nothing to fear since he was under God's protection.

Against the backdrop of bitter religious dissent, a wondrous image of Malam Awal emerged, characterized by wisdom, sanctity, and virtue. He developed a mythical reputation as a fighter of demons and a champion of justice—like the Prophet, he became known as a defender of widows and orphans—and some of his followers compared him to the Madhi (the guided one of God), a saintly figure slated to appear at the end of time to "restore the supremacy of justice and Islam over ungodly forces" (Rahman 1966:133). People routinely referred to him as *shehu* (spiritual guide), but an acquaintance of mine insisted that he had a regal disposition: she had seen how one of his assistants shielded him from the sun with a large umbrella—as is traditionally done for high dignitaries—whenever he went anywhere. On another occasion she witnessed a young boy waving a large fan over him while he sat on his throne; this had impressed her greatly, for it was a treatment reserved for chiefs.

There was some debate as to whether Awal should be considered a saint (*waliyi*), that is, a person endowed with God's grace: whether or not they were affiliated with the Awaliyya, many Muslims acknowledged that aside from having amply demonstrated his spiritual powers, he had developed a reputation for piety and generosity, and seemed to be animated by some kind of transcendent insight. These must surely be proof of his saintly condition. Many who publicly acknowledged the preacher's sainthood emphasized his extraordinary piety and devotion. Others singled out his powers and good fortune as indisputable indexes of God's favor. "God is with Malam Awal," a 'dan Awaliyya explained, "this is why he has lasted so long in Dogondoutchi." Like other disciples, he believed that the preacher would have been chased out of town by local authorities had it not been for the divine protection he enjoyed. A woman claimed that when Malam Awal preached, people heard the sound of birds singing over his head, which was a sign that he was a *waliyi*, a saint. Another woman told me that the preacher's sainthood was recognized as far away as Mecca. This, she implied, was validation of the preacher's status, coming as it was from the place that provided the *umma* with the definitive model for Islam. Still others pointed out that saints rarely had children (and when they did, they never had more than one or two) and so Malam Awal's lack of progeny, despite his numerous marriages, was indicative of his blessed state. Others, on the other hand, denied that the preacher was a saint, insisting he was simply a very learned preacher. Some of his critics also pointed out that real saints never referred to themselves as such and that his saintly reputation was "made up." To these objections, Awal's devotees responded that the man had consistently denied being a *waliyi.* As one close disciple put it:

> People say, "he cannot be a *waliyin Allah* [a friend of God] since no one who is ever says so." His opponents only say that to criticize him. [They say], "he says he is a *waliyi.*" But Malam Awal has never said he was a saint. It's people around him who believe he is.

If anyone in Awaliyya ranks had doubts about Malam Awal's saintly status, the matter was surely put to rest after a student discovered a "miracle" in the *zawiya* (Sufi center). One morning in 2003, while sweeping the corner of the compound where Malam Awal made his ablutions, the young man found millet unexpectedly sprouting in an apparently random pattern. Upon taking a closer look at the swelling shoots, he noticed to his utter amazement that the pattern was far from random. The words "Malam Awal is a saint" written in Arabic script could supposedly be discerned among the densely growing millet sprouts. Word quickly spread that God had sent the people of Dogondoutchi a message to remind them of Malam Awal's holiness.

Although, for Awal's followers, the concreteness and immediacy of the message was indubitable proof of the preacher's closeness to God, others who had grown skeptical of his purported blessedness saw the writing on the ground as evidence of his fraudulent disposition. At a time when the preacher was vilified in the national press as a crook who preyed upon the naïveté of his disciples, this latest "buffoonery" further established the gullibility of the people of Dogondoutchi. Two outspoken critics of the preacher told me that the alleged miracle had conveniently occurred at a time of intense disaffection in Awaliyya ranks. This indicated that Malam Awal was willing to go to extremes to recruit new followers and consolidate his base among those who had begun to doubt the worthiness of his intentions.

The preacher, it is worth pointing out, had invited controversy from the start for his disregard for conventions, ostentatious personal style, and aggressive pursuit of power. Although he circulated in wealthy circles and boasted of his connections with people in high places, local officials saw him as a rabble-rouser come to disrupt order and test the credulity of the Dogondoutchi population. In the early 2000s rumors circulated that under the cover of bringing charitable contributions to recently widowed and impoverished women, he lured followers (married women, in particular) to distant villages where he encouraged sexual debauchery. Meanwhile, his diatribes against a society headed in the wrong direction and requiring reorientation toward a more religious ethos routinely provoked anger and consternation among the educated elite. On several occasions he denounced secular schools as dens of immorality, outraging followers who depended on these institutions for their children's education. When I spoke with him, he insisted that he had never discouraged parents from sending their children to school—he himself had attended secular schools—and that this was simply malicious gossip spread by his opponents.

Guided by his vision of a diseased society threatened by the government's secular orientation, he further urged his audiences to resist state policies as they only hastened the disappearance of moral values and the impoverishment of Nigérien communities. Recall that in 2003, on the eve of a National Vaccination Day aimed at inoculating young children against polio, Awal instructed followers not to have their children vaccinated: the government could not be trusted. These health campaigns, he claimed, were an attempt to sterilize children, part of a larger Western conspiracy to weaken Muslim populations worldwide.[16]

Awal's admonition that the polio vaccine was a contraceptive drug in disguise proved compelling. When the vaccinators arrived to administer doses of oral polio vaccine to children between nine months and five years of age, they were turned away by Awaliyya parents who would not be persuaded that the threat to their children was groundless (Masquelier n.d.). The vaccine was not safe, embattled residents reasoned, otherwise why weren't parents charged for it? It was widely known that with the retreat of the state from social services, the citizens of Niger should not expect health care to be handed out freely. In the eyes of 'yan Awaliyya, the only possible explanation for the state's eagerness to vaccinate children was that local officials were acting on behalf of impious Westerners, eager to undermine the country's Muslim resurgence.[17]

To stress the importance and safety of polio vaccination, Nigérien president Mamadou Tandja himself traveled to southern Niger in 2004, urging residents to cooperate with campaign volunteers and let their children be vaccinated (Donnelly 2004). Among 'yan Awaliyya, however, the president's message fell on deaf ears. When health workers visited local households to inoculate children against polio later that year, their efforts were once again thwarted by parents who remained fearful of the vaccine's effect on their progeny. By then Awal's prestige as a holy man had considerably eroded. Even so, protracted resistance against the polio vaccination campaign suggests that, for a dwindling minority, the preacher continued to embody virtue and personify religious authority.

Awal garnered widespread criticism for encouraging resistance to state-wide campaigns to eradicate polio and later measles. Local *malamai* described him as a dishonorable man who put the health of children at risk. A former 'ya Awaliyya whose grandchild died of measles in 2003 at the age of two bitterly denounced Awal's boycott of the vaccination campaigns. In her opinion, Malam Awal was a liar, a con artist who cared little about people's well-being. Aside from being castigated for his interventions in public health, Awal's alleged participation in a much publicized affair of embezzlement, his bitter quarrels with once trusted assistants, and his troubled marital history eventually tarnished the saintly reputation that he once enjoyed. Upon returning to Dogondoutchi in late 2004, after a four-year absence, I found that the number of 'yan Awaliyya had drastically shrunk. Many 'yan Awaliyya who had initially dismissed the accusations leveled against their spiritual guide were forced to recognize that they had been misled: Awal was not the pious and enlightened leader he claimed to be.

Returning briefly to Malam Awal's swift rise to saintly fame, most remarkable is the calculated manner in which he and his close disciples propagated his claims to charismatic virtue. Similar to the "mythologization" of two modern Jewish saints analyzed by Bilu and Ben-Ari (1992:673), Malam Awal's rapid sanctification was enabled by the careful and conscious framing of segments of his life into a mythical draft from which followers could selectively draw to generate their own version of how things had happened. Malam Moussa, a close disciple, summarized Malam Awal's vision and his subsequent mission as follows:

> Malam Awal was in Mecca. When he was in the mosque, he received a gift from God. He told us what he saw there and how he was given milk to drink. He was told he should go west, he would find a place where he would serve God by teaching the Qur'an to people. God gave him unlimited knowledge. This is what happened and how he came to this town. Now Malam Awal is loved by many people. They all want to work for him; hundreds come to harvest his fields. Neither kings nor chiefs receive this kind of support. [Theirs] is a gift to God. It's about serving God, not a worldly king.

By stressing the divine nature of Awal's mission, Malam Moussa justified the preacher using his disciples to labor on his land, which a wealthy individual had given him. Hoeing or harvesting the preacher's field, Malam Moussa implied, was not ordinary work. By serving Malam Awal, 'yan Awaliyya were serving God and therefore demonstrating their submission to Him. From this perspective, Malam Awal did not exploit his disciples when he invited them to cultivate his fields, as his detractors claimed. Instead, he gave them

132

an opportunity to express their devotion to God. Consider now how Zuera, a widow in her mid-fifties, related the events that led Malam Awal to initiate his journey to Dogondoutchi:

> When he went to Mecca, [Malam Awal] stayed in the mosque. When everyone left, he remained alone. No one could see him. When he came out of the mosque, the Arabs saw that he was more beautiful. The Arabs said: "This child, when he entered the mosque, his clothes were dirty, when he came out, his clothes were more beautiful than ours."

Congruent with the Weberian notion of prophetic revelation, this account of Malam Awal's visible transformation helps contribute to the "unified view of the world derived from a consciously integrated meaningful attitude toward life," which, for Weber (1978:450), provides a script for organizing practical life. In other versions I collected of the divine call, no mention is made of the preacher emerging from the mosque as if "cleansed" by the experience. The reference to his purification in this particular testimony must be assessed, I suggest, in light of Malam Awal's recommendation that his followers wear white from head to toe. By integrating mythical stories in addition to rituals, styles of dress, and comportment into his project of Islamic renewal, Malam Awal created for his disciples a coherent, underlying unity between social and cosmic events. By wearing white, Zuera's testimony implies, 'yan Awaliyya were not simply conforming to a universal Muslim preference for white garments that symbolized purity. They were also visibly demonstrating their affiliation with the Awaliyya by patterning mundane dimensions of their lives after Malam Awal's own life "in an integrally meaningful manner" (Weber 1978:450). Dressing in white was also said to increase one's chances of gaining access to paradise.

Another facet of the holy image Malam Awal carefully cultivated was his reputation for being generous toward the poor and the disadvantaged. The preacher repeatedly admonished followers against accepting alms from impoverished families in mourning and made highly publicized visits to the homes of poor, recently widowed women to whom he brought large bags of millet and gifts of money.[18] Devotees spoke at length of his kind and charitable nature. They eagerly shared stories depicting Malam Awal as an icon of virtue and a compassionate man genuinely concerned with the welfare of his fellow Muslims. A 'ya Awaliyya once proudly told me how her four-year-old son had allegedly demonstrated his veneration for Malam Awal. Upon returning with his mother from a sermon, the boy warned his father that if he did not pray he would burn in hell. Someone then tried to bribe the boy into retracting his words. He would receive 200 CFA francs if he denied any attachment to the preacher. The boy refused. When asked what Malam Awal had given him to "buy" his allegiance, he responded that the preacher had given him nothing. He just loved Awal for what he was. Flattering anecdotes that circulated in Dogondoutchi in 2000—intersecting at times, with other less generous accounts of the preacher's activities—exemplify the depth of people's veneration for Malam Awal. They attest to his success in crafting an image of himself as a benevolent and blessed leader at a time when the legitimacy of Sufism and Sufi practices was being seriously undermined by Izala religious reforms.[19]

Appropriating the Past

At the same time that Malam Awal was becoming a legendary personage (occasionally compared to the venerated Shaykh of Kiota, the leader of the Niass branch of the Tijaniyya in Niger), the town of Dogondoutchi was emerging as a mythical place of its own. The town was fated to become the center of the newly founded Awaliyya order, owing to the widely disseminated story of the preacher's divine calling. By skillfully weaving a mythical connection between Dogondoutchi and the holy city of Mecca, Malam Awal heightened local residents' awareness of their place within the transnational Muslim community, the *umma*.[20] Like other Muslim scholars before him, Malam Awal claimed that his mission was to preserve Qur'anic truth from the corrupting influence of practices of spirit veneration and spirit possession. The cultivation of ties to the spirit world, he insisted, had no place in Muslim life. Yet, unlike others who also spoke of the dangers of "animism" and urged followers to abandon *al'adai* (traditions) deemed un-Islamic, Malam Awal understood how the past could be salvaged and put to use to solidify his hold on the collective consciousness.

The preacher's divinely ordained mission bore an intriguing parallel with a well-known myth of origin that associated the founding of Lougou, the first human settlement of Arewa, with the arrival of Sarauniya, a queen-priestess who came from the East.[21] Sarauniya was possessed by the spirit Sarauniya. Like all the priestesses who had succeeded her, she had been described as a powerful but withdrawn figure spending much of her time crouched in prayer toward the East.[22] Free from mundane concerns, she rarely left her home and enjoyed restricted contact with outsiders. As the founder of the first village in Arewa, Sarauniya had exclusive control of the land, and anyone wishing to farm it first had to obtain permission from her.

Like the first Sarauniya, Malam Awal had come from the East. He also projected an image of piety and introversion, seldom leaving his home when he was in town, and he was vested with extraordinary powers, including the ability to communicate with spirits.

The analogy between Malam Awal's and Sarauniya's mythical personae should not be overemphasized, for the similarity of their respective life trajectories remained largely implicit in local discourses. Even so, the story of Sarauniya provided a compelling model for the "stranger from the East" scenario invoked by those who spoke of how Malam Awal's visit had been foretold.[23] In the prophecy, a stranger coming from the East—the direction of Mecca that Muslims in West Africa face five times a day during prayer—would appear one day to lead the people of Dogondoutchi much as the founder of Lougou was said to have guided the first generation of settlers. I was told by some 'yan Awaliyya that Malam Awal's arrival had been predicted more than a hundred years ago, although no one knew exactly when it would happen. According to some, Soumana Gao, a chef de canton (customary chief) known for his involvement in bori practices, had foretold before dying that a foreigner hailing from the East would settle in Dogondoutchi. Chief Soumana had urged the people of Dogondoutchi to welcome the foreign visitor. Others claimed that, before Soumana's time, a learned scholar had predicted that a foreigner would come and bring peace to dissenting Muslims. It is unclear how much Malam Awal knew about these predictions. What is certain is that the rumors that his arrival in town had been predicted further enhanced the preacher's charisma and facilitated his mission as he set out to convince local audiences that he had come to revitalize the practice of Islam in Dogondoutchi. Appearing as he did during a period marked by bitter disputes between 'yan Izala and 'yan darika, Malam Awal emerged as a heroic figure, destined to bring harmony and forge a sense of unity in a divided community. In the eyes of his followers, the preacher was making history, and they had no doubt that he would one day be remembered alongside other well-known figures of the Nigérien past.

The preacher was well aware that charisma is a precarious attribute requiring constant reinforcement if it is to have a lasting impact on those it is meant to impress. If the annual ceremony held to commemorate his arrival in town was any indication, Malam Awal worked steadily to preserve his mythic stature by fashioning a narrative of his life that resonated with local constructions of the past, especially the pre-Islamic past. Until recently, Muslims in Arewa generally felt uneasy about their "animist" past. In the Muslim ethos, the past was identified as jahiliyya (ignorance), a state of chaos, immorality, and permissiveness that typified the period preceding the arrival of Islam. Consequently Muslim residents saw no reason to celebrate the exploits of Sarauniya Mangu, the queen-priestess who, in 1899, had valiantly but unsuccessfully resisted the assault of the infamous Voulet-Chanoine column dispatched to claim southern Niger for France at the height of the "scramble" for Africa. They feared that acknowledging Sarauniya as a heroine would resurrect a religious past—replete with demonic spirits—that they would rather see buried. Rather than honoring historical figures such as Sarauniya Mangu, they wished to disown them. In their opinion, only by resolutely breaking with the age of *jahiliyya* would Dogondoutchi forfeit its reputation as a den of "animism."[24]

These efforts to relegate the pre-Islamic past to oblivion have been undermined, however, by cultural countercurrents directed toward the celebration of national heritage. Of late, Sarauniya Mangu has been reclaimed by intellectual elites as a tragic figure of the Nigérien past. For defying French guns with only a handful of archers, she has become a potent symbol of resistance to colonial penetration. In the eyes of many Nigériens, she is now a valued emblem of their cultural heritage, and she has even been featured in a historical novel that recounts the conquest of Niger. A high school and radio station in Niamey have been named after her, and she was recently immortalized in a film, a play, and several songs (one performed by a successful hip hop band). In 2005 five women in top government positions were honored in Lougou as "*dignes filles de Saraouniya*" (honorable daughters of Sarauniya) by the Nigérien minister in charge of the advancement of women. A year or so later, a request was made to the United Nations Educational, Scientific, and Cultural Organization (UNESCO) to include Lougou (where the queen-priestesses are buried and where Sarauniya Mangu battled against the French) as a World Heritage Site. In their search for authenticity, urban Nigérien elites have embraced Sarauniya Mangu and the ancestral values she embodies as a genuine part of their national history.

The 2000 Awaliyya celebration (as well as those preceding and following it), in which Malam Awal appeared sumptuously dressed and seated on a throne, invested the preacher's arrival in Dogondoutchi with historic, even mythical significance. To paraphrase Marshall Sahlins (1981:17), who analyzed the remarkable correlation between Captain Cook's historical itinerary around Hawaii and the Hawaiian God Lono's mythical itinerary in the heavens, it is perhaps not farfetched to say that Malam Awal turned himself into the "historical image of a mythical theory." Like the famous British navigator who was received by Hawaiians with all the pomp and circumstances befitting the ancestral spirit, Malam Awal became the incarnation of the mythic "stranger from the East" whose destiny had been patterned after that of the first Sarauniya, who fled the kingdom of Daura (in present-day Nigeria) to settle in Arewa. Like Cook's entrance into Kealakakua Bay, the preacher's appearance in Dogondoutchi entered history as "a perceived instance of a received category" (Sahlins 1981:7), the iteration of mythical events. Neither Cook nor Awal had originally measured the consequences of their first visit to Hawaii and Dogondoutchi, respectively. Awal, for one, only realized later that the resonance between his story and that of mythical predecessors could be exploited to solidify his hold on the popular imagination. Put differently, Malam Awal understood that he would strengthen his authority by convincing as many people as possible that the event of his arrival in the small Sahelian town represented "the working out of an established order" (Sahlins 1981:6). To that end, he held a yearly ritual that brought members of the Awaliyya order together in a euphoric reenactment of the "historic" event. At the same time that it marked the beginning of a new cycle in the Awaliyya calendar, the ceremony formalized the preacher's reputation as a saintly leader. It provided the spectacular scenery—complete with props, flourish, and drama—that Malam Awal needed to "stage-manag[e] the charismatic process" (Glassman, in Bilu and Ben-Ari 1992:683) and ultimately captivate his audience with the glorious enactment of his virtuous leadership.

The Centering of Dogondoutchi

Through the dispersal of his own life history, the preacher implied that the Sufi revival he was orchestrating had literally been envisioned in Mecca, thereby re-authenticating such practices as the performance of *zikiri* and the worship of Sufi saints which *'yan* Izala had condemned as syncretic and therefore un-Islamic. More important, perhaps, by weaving a narrative thread between Dogondoutchi and Mecca, he enabled local Muslims to imagine themselves in relation to the *umma*'s conceptual and spatial center. Muslims everywhere, as noted, bow and pray to Mecca five times a day. In Dogondoutchi Mecca is "the center out there" (Turner 1972:241), a place that is distant and foreign, yet also inescapably present in the moral imagination of local Muslims. As the birthplace of Muhammad and the site where he first heard God's call and later proclaimed His message, it is "the focal point that provides orientation in a world that is simultaneously physical and spiritual" (Delaney 1990:517).

By making the *haji* (pilgrimage to Mecca), Muslims not only fulfill one of the five pillars of Islam but also "touch the foundation of faith and drink of the wellspring that sustains and gives it meaning" (Delaney 1990:515). Because it requires a substantial financial investment, the pilgrimage remains closely associated with wealth and material success. Indeed, it is often taken as a measure of the pilgrims' commercial abilities and, indirectly, of God's benevolence to them. Wealth and Islamic piety, in the end, almost presuppose each other, which is why wealthy traders in Niger are addressed as *Alhaji* (Pilgrim) whether or not they have traveled to Mecca. Conversely, the *haji* is a mark of social distinction regardless of whether individuals owe their status as *alhazai* (pilgrims) to their own professional success or to that of a generous kin who financed their trip to the Hijaz. The prestige the *haji* confers on a pilgrim opens doors into the merchant community and can even be redeemed as material gains, for it is seen as an expression of good fortune. The pilgrimage, therefore, is a valued form of social and spiritual capital.

By peddling his account of a divinely inspired Islamic revival that would originate in Dogondoutchi, Malam Awal lifted the town from its isolation. The road to a revitalized *umma*, the preacher implied, would pass through Dogondoutchi. This would have momentous consequences for the inhabitants of this provincial town whose claim to fame had until recently more to do with its "animist" orientation than a purported Muslim identity. As a modest outpost on the Muslim frontier, Dogondoutchi has long been perceived as disengaged from the global forces (including Islamic revivalism) impacting larger urban centers. In the late 1990s the town still lacked communicative forms such as the telephone, access to the Internet, and so on, that were taken for granted elsewhere in the world. Thanks to the preacher's claim that Dogondoutchi would be the cradle of a worldwide religious revival, the town could boast a mythic, timeless connection to Mecca and present itself as an Islamic model for other, less distinguished West African Muslim communities.

As the birthplace of Islam, Mecca has long been a source of moral authority for scholars and religious leaders seeking to legitimize their position in a Muslim community. That historical fact is offered as justification for social and religious reforms initiated by pilgrims who returned home with ideas on how to transform local "traditions" so as to bring them in line with what Muslims did in Mecca (Launay 1990, 1992). Because these reforms, wherever they were instituted, have been largely shaped by local configurations of power and knowledge, they have not so much contributed to the homogenization of the Muslim world as they have created multiple, contrasting, yet also intersecting (and occasionally dissenting) Muslim communities. A notable instance of this process is provided by Ferme's (1994:28) discussion of how "Alhaji Airplane," the imam of a Mende village in Sierra Leone, set out to transform the religious practices of his home community based on what "he had seen in Mecca." In his attempts to Islamize the village, the ambitious imam introduced Muslim elements into the initiation ritual of Sande, the women's cult association, and disposed of the Sande spirit masks. Rather than abolishing the non-Muslim ritual altogether, he transformed it into a "Muslim" institution, thus exemplifying the extent to which, in implementing religious reforms, "much depends upon 'local' appropriations of 'global' discourses" (Shaw and Stewart 1994:12).

For Mawri Muslims seeking to appear modern and cosmopolitan as well as "proper" Muslims, Mecca similarly provides a model of Muslimhood that must be emulated on the basis that Saudis are more authentically Muslim: if a mode of dress, a religious observance, or a social practice has been seen in Mecca, one can then automatically claim it as Islamic. Conversely, the absence of a particular practice signals that it is un-Islamic and must therefore be abandoned. Because they see Mecca as an archetypical Muslim town— the ideal community that all other Muslim communities must model themselves after—many Dogondoutchi residents expect those who accomplish the *haji* to be transformed by what they have seen in the Hijaz. A devout *'dan* Izala who had not yet managed to go on the pilgrimage once explained to me that all those who had traveled to Mecca were *'yan* Izala. By this he meant not only that Izala members were more pious and therefore more likely to accomplish the *haji*, but also that the pilgrims who previously resisted the message of Izala became "better" Muslims upon their return from Saudi Arabia. From his vantage point, their newly found piety automatically cast them as members of Izala.

Because the holy city—and the Hijaz more generally—constitutes a vital reference point for local Muslims, appeals to the original source of the faith are not restricted to those who have gone on the *haji* or studied in Saudi Arabia. Ordinary Muslims in Dogondoutchi thus routinely refer to what Meccans allegedly do to justify their adoption (or rejection) of a particular ritual or sartorial practice. *'Yan* Awaliyya invariably responded to my questions about why they dressed in white by pointing out that, in Mecca, everyone wore white garments. Other Muslims similarly invoked Mecca to justify their performance of *zikiri* or their habit of ostentatiously displaying their prayer beads. Ironically, these were often the very practices that *'yan* Izala rejected on the ground that they did not exist in Mecca.[25]

When competing definitions of what is "proper" Islam appear to be evenly inspired by the same unique and seemingly unchanging model of Islamic tradition, we begin to appreciate how "the presumed constancy of dogma competes with the actual shift in meaning that dogma acquires in differing contexts and [how] the presumed universality of the Islamic community competes with the local communities in which Muslims actually live" (Eickelman and Piscatori 1990:xiii). In Dogondoutchi competing Muslim factions each claim to know what Muslims do in Mecca and struggle to invest their own beliefs and practices with the stamp of universality. On the assumption that there is only one correct way to practice Islam, members of one faction contrast their ways of being Muslim to their opponents' in terms of "knowledge" versus "ignorance," "truth" versus "lies" (Launay 1992). As they see it, the truth ultimately derives from gaining access to the Qur'an.

Because of his extensive schooling, as well as his visionary claims, Malam Awal was particularly well positioned to authorize his version of what it meant to be Muslim. Under his leadership, 'yan Awaliyya felt part of the *umma*, the worldwide community of Muslims, in ways they never had before. Thanks to the global connections the preacher forged through his words and deeds, Muslims in Dogondoutchi were shown how to conform to the ways of Meccans: prosperity presumably would soon follow. For ordinary Nigériens, the wealth and modernity of Saudi Arabia are contingent upon Saudi adherence to Muslim orthodoxy. Because modernity and Islamic orthodoxy were effectively "two facets of the same thing" (Bernal 1997:138), the expectation among 'yan Awaliyya was that by aligning local practices (prayer, dress, and forms of sociality) with their Meccan counterparts—as per Awal's instructions—the people of Dogondoutchi would soon enjoy the prosperity that Saudis boasted.

If the narrative of Malam Awal's vision highlights how Mecca, and to some extent Saudi Arabia as a whole, is a key source of authenticity for Nigérien Muslims, it also points to the limitations of conventional models that presume a straightforward distinction between center and periphery—with centers shaping culturally disparate peripheries into places of conformity. Awal, of course, claimed that he had brought Islamic orthodoxy to Dogondoutchi. Yet the content of his religious message discredits the notion that, as a globalizing force, the *haji* has promoted the homogenization of Muslim practices worldwide. On the contrary, it exemplifies how Islamic practices of supposed Saudi origin are indigenized by pilgrims on their return from Mecca (see Cooper 2001; Ferme 1994; O'Brien 1999).

In their critique of the notion of centers uniformly and unchangingly experienced as central by the periphery, Eickelman and Piscatori (1990; see also

Mandel 1990) suggest that the center should be conceptualized in the plural to fully account for the complex relations between unevenly positioned centers and the respective networks in which they are embedded. The concept of plural centers certainly captures more accurately the experience of West African Muslims for whom there exists differently valued hubs of Islamic activity in both the distant Middle East and in West or North Africa. Because they are more accessible than their Egyptian, Sudanese, or Saudi counterparts, West African Islamic centers often furnish more suitable models of religious identity for Nigérien Muslims. Granted, Mecca provides the central directionality that orients Dogondoutchi residents in time and space. But as already mentioned, it is an elusive place that most of them will never have a chance to visit. Libya or northern Nigeria, on the other hand, have become salient places of reference; they are less distant and therefore more affordable (and less daunting) destinations whether one is a Qur'anic scholar, a migrant laborer, or simply a youth in search of adventure and social advancement.

With the coming of Malam Awal, Dogondoutchi continued to feel the pull of Mecca, with which it could enjoy a newly privileged connection, but its relative position vis-à-vis other centers of Islamic scholarship, such as Sokoto and Kano in northern Nigeria, changed profoundly, at least in the eyes of 'yan Awaliyya. In the new spiritual geography etched by Malam Awal, the town had become a center of its own, with a visibility carefully maintained by crowd-pleasing commemorative rituals such as the one I have described. Muslims reportedly flock to the Awaliyya *zawiya* (Sufi center) from as far away as Nigeria and Mali during local celebrations. I was told that when Malam Awal was in town, a day did not pass without visitors showing up on his doorstep. Whether this was true, the overall perception among the Awaliyya community was that, under Awal's leadership, Dogondoutchi had become an important source of inspiration for Muslims throughout the region. 'Yan Awaliyya were fond of reminding me that Malam Awal had been invited to create his *zawiya* in half a dozen other more prominent towns, but he had chosen Dogondoutchi.[26] By making Dogondoutchi the physical and spiritual center of the Awaliyya order, the preacher had catapulted the town to prominence. For Abdou, a carpenter and staunch supporter of Awal, the town had managed to outshine neighboring Kiota, home to a well-known Sufi saint (and leader of the Tijaniyya) and a popular destination for West African Muslims in search of blessings. Testimonies such as Abdou's underscore the preacher's success in reshaping the religious profile of Dogondoutchi. In the view of Awal's constituency, the town had acquired such a glow under the preacher's blissful influence that it now eclipsed other distinguished centers of Islamic knowledge. Awal's followers felt touched, personally transformed by the preacher's charismatic energy. They believed that they were part of something important. Borrowing from Errington and Gewertz's (1995:108) characterization of the experiences of Christian missionaries and converts, one can say that they were endowed with "a sense of the portentous, a heroic sense of making history—of precipitating *events*."

As already pointed out, the town's sudden prominence was not seen as fortuitous by most 'yan Awaliyya. Indeed, many had come to believe that Dogondoutchi was actually predestined to become the focus of religious renewal. If it had lingered in the shadows of successive Islamic empires, there was currently nothing to prevent the small bustling community from acquiring its rightful place among other prominent Muslim metropolises. For many residents who had long struggled with the knowledge of their peripheral position in the Muslim world (and in the global economy), Dogondoutchi now exuded a powerful aura. As the center of the Awaliyya reform movement, it was uniquely positioned to reap the benefits of the new world order. Thanks to Malam Awal's timely intervention, the town was well on its way to becoming a new capital of Sufism that would no longer feel subordinate to established centers of Islamic knowledge such as Cairo and Khartoum or, closer to home, Kano and Sokoto.

Conclusion

In perfect Weberian fashion, the commemorative celebration of the preacher's arrival in town exemplified Malam Awal's strategy for reasserting his spiritual authority against the secular, routinized powers of the state. The preacher's rise to fame, I have suggested, had much to do with the calculated way in which he positioned himself as a disinterested leader who publicly denounced the secularizing policies of the government and identified the forces that threatened "authentic" Islamic values. Many of the preacher's public acts against local and national authorities can be analyzed as instantiations of the antithesis between charisma and bureaucratic domination. Consider the following incident that occurred during the visit President Mamadou Tandja made to Dogondoutchi in 2004 to take the pulse of the nation and publicize the accomplishments of his administration. As is routine for visits by heads of state, the entire community had been invited beforehand to attend the presidential address, and local dignitaries, state officials, and neighborhood and association leaders had worked actively to generate high levels of communal participation.

Malam Awal himself planned to attend Tandja's visit. To this end, he had enlisted the assistance of carpenters from among his loyal supporters to erect a scaffold on which he would sit comfortably—and in plain sight of the assembled crowd as befitted his purported rank—while the president delivered his speech. On the day of the presidential visit, the preacher, garbed in full regalia and surrounded by a large escort of more modestly dressed individuals, made a conspicuous appearance—he was carried by four disciples in what was described as a kind of hammock—minutes before the president was to address the people of Dogondoutchi. He sat under the protection of a large umbrella that shielded him from the sun but also signaled his rank. I did not witness the event but friends who did told me that during the time Malam Awal sat with leading Awaliyya members on the elevated stage he commissioned for the occasion, the president made no noticeable effort to acknowledge his presence—even though the preacher stood higher than the president. Malam Awal was said to be deeply offended by what he saw as flagrant disrespect to his illustriousness: among other things, Tandja also made no reference to the preacher in his speech. Consequently Awal decided to disrupt the proceedings by departing with his retinue before the president had concluded his address. Awal's noticeable exit—it looked, witnesses noted, as if half the attending crowd had left with him—was perceived by all remaining attendees as an affront to the authority of the head of state, which is exactly what Malam Awal intended.[27]

I mention this incident not simply to suggest that Malam Awal was an ambitious man whose public performances to broaden his charisma routinely invited controversy but also to highlight once again how the preacher's actions contributed to the re-centering of Islam in Dogondoutchi. By leaving the official gathering before Tandja finished his address, Malam Awal avenged himself for the humiliation he had suffered at the hands of the president. His walkout also demonstrated that his divinely sanctioned authority was not secondary to Tandja's strictly secular powers. Unlike the other assembled dignitaries and state officials who listened to the speech, Awal was not bound to submit to the president's authority; he could come and go as he pleased, even at the most solemn of moments. Indeed, his discourteous behavior was a measure of his prominence—and of the superiority of his divine mandate over the president's temporal (and necessarily ephemeral) powers.

The preacher's dismissal of secular authority further implied that Dogondoutchi was a center of its own not simply in relation to other spiritual centers such as Sokoto or Kiota but also compared to Niamey, the capital of Niger and the seat of Tandja's secular administration. The town's residents, specifically Awal's followers, were not subject to governmental policies. They had resisted the UN-sponsored campaigns to vaccinate children against polio because, in doing so, they were heeding Malam Awal's orders. 'Yan Awaliyya, armed with the knowledge given them by their clairvoyant leader that the vaccination campaigns were a government ploy to sterilize the next generation, protected those who would one day perpetuate the membership of their Sufi order and contribute to its expansion. By resisting the state-mandated vaccination of young children, 'yan Awaliyya not only proved that they were good Muslims, but they also reaffirmed their faith in their leader. By the same token, in defying the authority of the state, Awal consolidated his position as a legendary figure that transcended the bounds of worldly history. "Soon you will be gone, but I am here to stay," he allegedly declared to local officials who questioned his ascendency over the local populace or tried to have him arrested.

The construction of Malam Awal's public image during elaborate ceremonial performances occurred alongside a variety of dispersed, informal (but nevertheless highly publicized) means of capturing the Muslim imagination with instances of the preacher's transcendence. Malam Awal's rapid "mythologization," I have argued, depended on the redefinition of Dogondoutchi as an emerging Sufi center. By allowing his own personal history to resonate with the town's mythical past, Malam Awal revitalized the roots of Muslim identity and gave renewed relevance to a Sufi tradition that had been seriously undermined by Izala ideas about the self-sufficiency of scripture and the austerity of religious forms. For those who witnessed Awal's expanding fame and saw no limits to the impact of his religious revival, the fate of Dogondoutchi was intimately linked to that of the preacher. True, Malam Awal had established a vast network of devotional communities through voluntary loyalties that extended beyond regional and even national boundaries. He regularly visited these satellite communities to assist individual followers and maintain his charismatic hold on the masses. But the heart of his dominion and the seat of his authority remained Dogondoutchi, where, at least for a few years, he enjoyed unconditional support from a significant number of people; at the height of the preacher's popularity, there was a widely shared sense that the town's reputation as a place of religious significance could only be sustained through a direct connection with his virtuous aura.

I have suggested that Malam Awal's aura of holiness was inextricably linked to the notion that he was a foreigner. By emphasizing his foreignness—he cultivated a northern Nigerian accent to remind people he had spent much of his life abroad—and his Meccan connections, the Sufi master carved out a space of difference from which he could reassert his fundamental usefulness to the community. But that space was not so alienating that it could not be indigenized. In complex and fundamental ways, the opening of political debate, the liberalization of markets, and the development of new technologies of mediation have heightened Nigérien people's sense of connectedness to transnational communities, religious and otherwise. These transformations have strongly affected the definition of Muslimhood and led to a realignment of religious practices along more universal orientations. Yet, rather than demonstrating the universalization—or, in Appadurai's (1996) words, the de-territorialization—of religious practices, the case of Malam Awal compels us to consider instead how Islam becomes re-territorialized within the Muslim diaspora. As a divinely appointed messenger, the preacher helped revitalize previously devalued religious practices and institutions, transforming them into new expressions of collective belonging. For those who struggled over the meaning of Islamic tradition in an age of shifting values, the moral discourse, the expressions of religiosity, the cultural institutions, and the modes of sociality promoted by the Awaliyya resonated powerfully with local understandings of Muslimhood.

BUILDING A MOSQUE IN THE HOME OF A SPIRIT: CHANGING TOPOGRAPHIES OF POWER AND PIETY

5

All history is made of traces left behind. And though one knows that history is as much about forgetting as about remembering, it can be recovered only by reading traces left by others.
—*Mariane Ferme*, The Underneath of Things

Given the complex symbolic connotations which topographies of space and place are endowed with, it is to be expected that the conquest of space, its inscription with a new moral and cultural surface, will be regarded as an act of human empowerment.
—*Pnina Werbner*, Pilgrims of Love

In 1988 a close friend whom I shall call Bibata told me about the one time she dared disobey her husband. The day was May 10, 1981, and Bibata was pregnant with her fourth child. That morning she started feeling her first labor pains. Her husband told her to get ready for the trip to the nearby dispensary, where her previous children had been born. While Bibata was sorting through the items she would take in anticipation of her stay in the poorly stocked medical facility, a neighbor whispered across the mud wall separating their courtyards that Chief Soumana, who previously lay dying in a hospital bed in the Nigérien capital, had finally died. The neighbor heard it on the radio. Bibata greeted the news with alarm. She was hardly alone. Upon hearing of the chief's demise, everyone in town had promptly gone home. Shopkeepers closed up their boutiques, street vendors packed up their wares, mothers rounded up their children, and, within minutes of the radio announcement, the usually bustling streets of Dogondoutchi were deserted. Soumana Gao, also known as *Sarkin* Arewa (Chief of Arewa), had been the *chef de canton* of the local administrative district. Though he oversaw a district where, by then, Muslims overwhelmingly outnumbered *bori* devotees, he had never hidden his allegiance to the spirits. Nor had he denied his involvement in local *bori* practices of spirit possession. *Sarkin* (Chief) Soumana was said to communicate daily with the most powerful spirits—he even visited some of them in a nearby cave. The remaining members of the chiefly family were Muslim, however. Amadou Gao, who would ascend the chieftaincy and become the twentieth *Sarkin* Arewa at the death of his older brother, made a point of stressing his allegiance to the Qur'an. With a Muslim chief at the helm of the district, everyone assumed, there would be momentous changes.

But what had frightened local residents and sent them scurrying home upon hearing of Soumana's demise was neither the political transition itself nor the fact that Soumana's heir was a committed Muslim. Rather, they feared what the change in leadership implied for the mysterious but powerful creatures thought to inhabit the palace. Chief Soumana reputedly kept hundreds of *iskoki* (spirits) in the chiefly residence that he had occupied with his wives, children, and dependents.[1] Only he had the power to command these spirits, all fearful creatures who went by the generic name of Doguwa, "the long one." Although they can bestow power and prosperity on their worshipers, Doguwa spirits are just as often described as mean, quick-tempered, and vindictive. When angered or ignored, local residents attest, their ferocity is unequaled. Soumana was known to communicate with the spirits and periodically hold ceremonies to honor them, but, most important, he kept them satiated through regular sacrificial offerings. Thanks to the Doguwa spirits who guaranteed him wealth and political power, he had supposedly accomplished great things. Communities prospered, and children were healthy. Although he provided the sacrificial blood the spirits craved, Soumana, unlike his predecessors, did not feed his spirits human blood. Nor had he ever been overpowered by their insistent demands for human sacrifices—or so it was rumored.

People attributed this to Soumana's extraordinary knowledge of the occult, specifically his expert handling of potentially threatening Doguwa. In the *bori* community, the *chef de canton* had been uniformly perceived as a wise and experienced chief who knew how to access the resources of the spirit world while keeping his chiefdom out of harm's way. He was often referred to as the "owner of one thousand and forty Doguwa," an honorific title bestowed on him by local praise-singers. Muslims, however, expressed scorn for Soumana's polytheistic practices—and more generally for the traditional ways of their ancestors—even if they did not always deny their potency. A few acknowledged that Soumana had been a great chief, because he had not been afraid to surrender some measure of control to the spirits. Though they expressed contempt for *bori* practices, they nevertheless recognized what spirit devotees proclaimed, namely, that because he served the spirits, the *chef de canton* had learned to channel the power of Doguwa and control their destructive impulses. Baba, an old Hausa woman, explained to anthropologist Mary Smith in the 1950s that "all the rulers like the *bori*—if they didn't, would their work be any good?" (1955:222). From this perspective, the presence of the Doguwa spirits in the palace was more than an index of chiefly power; it was the very condition of that power. The French colonization had put an end to the synergistic relation the Arewa chieftaincy enjoyed with the Azna leadership, but the *iko* (power) of the *sarakuna* (chiefs) remained dependent on the spiritual forces hidden in the palace. To borrow the words of a *bori* musician who had performed for Chief Soumana for many years, "the house of the spirits [in the palace] was the cradle of the chieftaincy."[2]

Now that Chief Soumana was dead, however, there was no one to control the allegedly ferocious spirits living in the chiefly residence. With no one to command them, people feared that the Doguwa spirits would escape from the palace to look for blood and satisfy their needs for sustenance. Like other spirits who sought revenge for the neglect they endured, because people had abandoned them and turned to Islam, it was feared that they would likely target anyone who crossed their paths—with tragic consequences. Now that a Muslim, who avoided association with spirit devotees, had succeeded Soumana, what had been the *chef de canton*'s steady source of power would become Dogondoutchi's undoing: hence the debacle that followed the public announcement of Soumana's death.

Bibata had witnessed firsthand the pain a Doguwa could inflict on her victims, as several members of her family had been tormented by spirits. Fearing what could happen now that the Doguwa spirits had lost their master, she found the courage to defy her husband's orders. She would not walk across town to deliver her child at the dispensary. Doing so meant passing the *chef de canton*'s residence, a part of town she was now determined to avoid at all costs. In the face of her resolve, her husband eventually capitulated. The baby was born at home. Years later, in recounting the extraordinary events of that day, Bibata confessed that she had been far less afraid of her husband (and of giving birth unassisted) than of the Doguwa spirits that so many assumed were wandering through the streets in search of prey.

Fast forward to 1997, sixteen years after Chief Soumana's demise. Malam Awal, upon measuring the remarkable success of the sermons he delivered at the request of local Muslim leaders, decided to settle in Dogondoutchi. His inquiries about acquiring a home prompted a man to give him a parcel of land in the Maizari neighborhood.[3] Plans were drawn for a house, a mosque, and adjoining quarters—the *zawiya*[4] (Sufi center) where Friday prayers would be held, children would attend Qur'anic lessons, Muslim celebrations would take place, and out-of-town guests would be welcomed. Followers made contributions for the purchase of bricks and cement. Soon everyone was pitching in—bringing buckets of water, carrying sand bags, or providing meals for the workers. When the masons started constructing the walls of the mosque, however, they complained of being bitten so severely by ants that they could not work. Malam Awal, upon learning of the situation, was determined to do something about it. Standing at the opening of an anthill, as small black ants emerged, he "addressed" the ants, urging them to leave the workers in peace. Moments later, work resumed. The workers stopped complaining about ant bites, and the construction of the mosque proceeded without further interruptions. Witnesses grasped more from the incident, however, than simply the continuation of construction, for soon word spread that Malam Awal could communicate with spirits.

The land parcel that Awal had been offered, it turns out, was home to a Doguwa spirit. Malva, a widow aged sixty or so and a devout follower of Malam Awal, recounted various incidents that occurred on the construction site:

> Before someone tried to build a house there, but it fell apart. No one was able to stay on this spot, though some tried. A long time ago, *malamai* predicted that no one would be able to stay there but that one day a powerful *malami* would come. He would build a house without [encountering] problems. When ants came to torment the masons, Malam Awal came. He said, "*Uwata* [Mother], leave these men alone so that they can work for me." The ants were the Doguwa in disguise. . . . The ants started coming toward the house. But after he talked to them, *shi ke nan, ta tafiya ta* [that's it, she was gone].

Because they allegedly show no mercy to their victims when they intend to strike, Doguwa spirits, newcomers to Arewa quickly learn, are best avoided in most circumstances—especially when they have not been tamed through the forum of *bori* possession. Having lived in the Maizari neighborhood in the late 1980s, I knew, like everyone else, that a spirit supposedly lived on what was then a vacant lot—the place where a decade later Malam Awal would build a mosque. On the lot next to a termite hill grew a short, scrawny tree. It was there, I had been told, that the *iska* (spirit) had settled many years ago. Friends cautioned me not to go near the tree in the daytime and to avoid the area altogether past nightfall—bad things had supposedly happened there.[5] People reported having strange, scary encounters there. For a long

Figure 5.1. The tree that was cut to build the Awaliyya mosque.

time the plot had sat untouched, until one day a stranger from another region acquired it with the intention of building a house. Every time he started erecting the exterior walls, however, they would collapse. In desperation, the man eventually offered the parcel to Malam Awal who, at that precise time, was looking to build a permanent headquarters in town.

Apparently no one told Malam Awal about the presence of the spirit or what had happened to the previous owner's attempt to build a home—though it is not unreasonable to assume that the preacher may have been warned about the dangers of the place. In any case, once it became clear that the ants would not be chased away from the site and that they were seriously hindering the progress of the mosque construction, Malam Awal was informed of the problem. He was made aware of the cumbersome presence of Doguwa and of the fact that, since the erection of the mosque meant the destruction of her habitat ("her" tree had been cut off), she had tried to interfere with the project. It was she, people explained, who had sent a small army of warring ants against the masons.[6] Unlike the preceding owner of the land parcel who could do nothing to reclaim "his" land from the spirit, Malam Awal was better equipped. As he once told me, he knew how to talk to spirits, a power he claimed to have received from God. Upon confronting the angry Doguwa, he had soon placated her, demonstrating once more that even the fiercest spirit was no match against him. The testimonies I collected diverge regarding the spirit's fate following Awal's providential intervention,[7] but they all agree that his intervention led to the disappearance of the Doguwa. The preacher, many people agreed, had displaced the spirit from her home, effectively disempowering her by securing what amounted to her forced submission. The Doguwa would not return. In a matter of days, everyone in Dogondoutchi had heard of Malam Awal's confrontation with Doguwa and the fortunate outcome, a strong testament of the preacher's proficient mastery over occult forces.

Although the death of Chief Soumana and a spirit's interference with the construction of the Awaliyya mosque may seem unrelated, this chapter highlights their connection through an examination of the chronotope (Bakhtin 1981) into which Awal fortuitously stepped when he campaigned to abandon "un-Islamic" practices in a town reputed to harbor dangerous spirits.[8] In Arewa, the past routinely "irrupts in and confronts the present" (Lambek 2002:12) through its personification as fierce spirits seeking to hold people accountable for their neglect of *gado* (heritage). The land is peopled by resentful *iskoki* (spirits) who, because of the inattention shown them, avenge themselves by thwarting human projects and wreaking havoc and confusion in local communities. Although the preacher was apparently unaware of what had transpired between the prior owner of the land and the spirit—he was a foreigner after all, having only recently arrived in Dogondoutchi— what happened after the workers complained of the ferocious ant attack was not entirely fortuitous. Malam Awal saw a unique opportunity to impress his fledgling constituency by demonstrating his special powers. At the time he knew little, if anything, of Dogondoutchi's history except for what happened since the emergence of Izala, but he quickly understood that he could draw on the past to consolidate his hold on the town's residents, particularly those who lived in Maizari and knew that a Doguwa was in their midst.

The displacement of the Doguwa spirit and the ensuing events was yet another step in the progressive erasure of the "spirit memoryscape" (Shaw 2002:46) in which non-Muslim residents traditionally anchored their history and identity. Like other Muslim leaders in the community, Malam Awal was eager to erase the remaining signs of religious practices deemed un-Islamic and establish the supremacy of Islam. Unlike the other leaders, however, he was not afraid to fight *jahilci* (ignorance about Islam) by confronting the very forces that epitomized this ignorance, namely, the spirits around which un-Islamic practices were centered. His ultimate goal, of course, was to annihilate the forces—human or otherwise—standing in the way of bringing "true"

Islam to the people of Dogondoutchi. Undoubtedly, he also realized that a victorious confrontation with the Doguwa not only would enhance his reputation as a Sufi master but would consolidate his authority at the site of Doguwa's alienation, the very place that previously pulsed with the force of the spirit's invisible, ominous presence.

Many viewed Awal's willingness to confront spirits as a measure of his extraordinary might and proof of his divine calling. In contrast to local *mala-mai*, who asked their clients to trust in the efficacy of their amulets but forbade engagement with spirits, Malam Awal capitalized on the fact that even reluctant Muslim residents were occasionally drawn into the realm of the spirits by family crises demanding swift resolution. He knew that in the local imaginary not all *iskoki* had been relegated to oblivion. Despite sustained efforts by Muslims to erase the marks of their presence, spirits remained in intersticial or unclaimed spaces, saturating the landscape with the rage and sorrow they felt for having been abandoned by the descendants of long-dead devotees. By acknowledging the presence of the Doguwa who was hindering the progress of his mission, Awal showed that, far from being irrelevant, spirits had a role to play, if only as a foil against which he could reassert the superiority of his God-given powers. Much like Ewe spiritual powers whose presence was confirmed through their "translation" into the Christian image of the Devil in Ghanaian Pentecostalism (Meyer 1999), *iskoki* were a threatening reality that had to be squarely confronted, not treated as outdated superstition as 'yan Izala would do.

At a time when the relevance of Sufism was waning in the face of reformist Islam's growing popularity, Malam Awal's much publicized victory over the dreaded spirit demonstrates the continued prominence of religious authority in this corner of the Sahel. Save for some notable exceptions (Soares 2007a, 2005; Werbner 2003), Sufism has often been described as traditional, molded by parochial values in sharp contrast to the strands of reformist Islam that are energized by the ongoing desire to reform both society and the polity along a more standardized model of religion. Malam Awal identified himself as a Sufi but, as noted earlier, drew heavily from the reformist ethos in order to justify his condemnation of forms of reciprocity that, in their most ostentatious expressions, compelled individuals to spend more than they could afford. Although the devotional practices he taught his followers were patterned after Sufi rites, he never missed an opportunity to denounce what he saw as the corruption and laxity of local Sufi religious specialists. Like Izala, he had contempt for Western forms of socialization and governance deemed to threaten spiritual values, but he loudly condemned the reformist vision of an egalitarian society, where access to knowledge was democratized. By promoting a vision of Islam that owed to both reformist and traditionalist interpretations of the Qur'an while nominally rejecting them both, Awal helped redirect the discourse on sobriety and frugality while redefining the nature of charismatic authority. Note that Awal's message of moral renewal is not unique. The rise of charismatic Muslim preachers enabled by the recent democratization of national politics has been documented elsewhere (Schulz 2003; Soares 2005). As when the weakening of the state and the concurrent shift in religious authority promote the emergence of a new kind of religious leadership, Malam Awal appears to have uniquely benefited from the recently opened space of public debate and the decline of institutional Sufism. As such, his call for a return to "authentic" Islam illustrates the dynamic and innovative character of Sufi orders.

One caveat is appropriate here. I did not verify whether spiritual attacks have increased since the death of *Sarkin* Soumana—or what, if anything, *really* took place when people were reporting these attacks. Nor do I attempt to distinguish between what is conventionally called myth (a culturally significant account of "fictitious" events) and history (an account of empirically verifiable events). Instead, I seek to explore how stories of spirit attacks constitute a form of historical consciousness that reveals much about the ways that Dogondoutchi residents imagine their place in an emerging Muslim order cast against a "vanishing" non-Muslim tradition. An extensive body of anthropological literature has demonstrated that events need not be recorded through conventional discursive registers to become historical (James 1988; Lambek 2002; Shaw 2002; Stoller 1995). Through places and practices, dreams and divinations, rumors and revelations, past events are inscribed into a dense and intricate vortex of sedimented memories from where they can seep into ordinary life without ever becoming explicit narratives. We are familiar by now with the argument that the poetics of history lie "in mute meanings transacted through goods and practices, through icons and images dispersed in the landscape of the everyday" (Comaroff and Comaroff 1992:35). It is slivers of this elusive history that I wish to retrieve in an effort to understand how people are forced at times to remember the past in order to confront the present in all its contradictory and unsettling dimensions. Based on stories of people's encounters with spirits, this kind of "unofficial" history is both authorized and concretized by the "dubious evidence of personal experience" (Steedly 1993:75). Thus it is an important part of how people situate themselves in a constantly evolving religious landscape.

A Haunted Landscape

"It is difficult to maintain that there is a self-evident opposition between witchcraft and modernity," anthropologist Peter Geschiere notes in his ethnography of politics and the occult in postcolonial Cameroon. "On the contrary," he goes on,

> rumors and practices related to the occult forces abound in the more modern sectors of society. In Africa, the dynamism of these notions and images is especially striking: they are the subject of constant reformulations and re-creations, which often express a determined effort for signifying politico-economic changes or even gaining control over them. In many respects, then, one can speak of the "modernity" of witchcraft. (1997:3)

These remarks have since found echo in a burgeoning anthropological literature on the complex and varied ways in which modernity in the African postcolony has produced its own forms of "magic" that an impoverished majority struggles to understand and control in the face of the ever more mysterious and rapid means through which fortunes are amassed and power gained (Blunt 2004; Comaroff and Comaroff 1993, 1999; Englund 1996; Masquelier 1999, 2000, 2001b; Meyer and Pels 2003; Moore and Sanders 2001; Sanders 2003; D. Smith 2001; Soares 2004a). There is a widespread recognition that "far from slipping away with the resolute march of modernity" (Comaroff and Comaroff 1999:295), enchanted perceptions of the world play a central role in trajectories of modernization (Bastian 1993; Fisiy and Geschiere 2001; Masquelier 2002; Rowland and Warnier 1988; Sanders 2001; J. Smith 2004; West 2001). Remarkably, this recognition does not extend to Muslim modernity. Thus Islam and Muslim religious practices rarely feature in anthropological discussions of the occult in postcolonial Africa. Save for notable exceptions (Brenner 1984; Rasmussen 2001; Shaw 2002; Soares 2005), Muslim contexts have tended to be excluded from analyses of the occult. By focusing here on the magic of Malam Awal, and more precisely on the link between the occult and religious authority, I hope to contribute to an emerging anthropology of Islam in Africa that takes as its analytical object the relation between magic, power, and modernity.

Although the occult often characterizes new potentialities of the postcolonial epoch, it also underscores continuities everywhere by connecting the present with the past (Ferme 2001; Lambek 2002; Lan 1985; Steedly 1993) or providing ways to cope with the past (Honwana 2003; Rosenthal 1998; Shaw 2002; Taussig 1987). Recognizing the centrality of the occult in the making of history and memory has notable implications for an examination of Awal's iconoclastic treatment of local religious practices. Awal allowed spirits to gain a powerful hold on the Muslim imagination only so that he could chase them away and prove the superiority of his own powers. Yet, by invoking spirits, Awal paradoxically attributed power to them. Banishing them, as he did, to a past from which Islam tried to demarcate itself implied that they were potent forces not to be trifled with. Malam Awal's encounter with and victory over the Doguwa recapitulates the story of Islam in Arewa by reenacting the progressive erasure of the spiritscape. It also dramatizes a fundamental dimension of this iconoclasm, namely, that in the moment of their expulsion, spirits become *re-membered*. This remembering enables spirits to linger as stubborn traces of the past. Put differently, if Islam is often presented to local residents as a way to make "a complete break with the past" (Meyer 1998b), it rarely means that the past—and the spirits that animate it—can be effectively cast aside. The occult, as Nyamnjoh (2001:32) succinctly put it, "ha[s] no sacred spaces."

In Arewa, spirits are well entrenched in Muslim spaces despite attempts to cast spirit possession as evil and purge Islam from "animism." As iconic figures of the pre-Islamic past who stubbornly cling to the places over which they once had uncontested control, they are the ultimate mediators between the past and the present. The practice of *yanka* (sacrifice) and *hau bori* (possession) are the means through which people appease the past so as to confront the present made captive by that past. In Mawri country, the land was originally inhabited by spirits who dwelled in trees, caves, hills, or termite mounds (Masquelier 2001b). These spirits were instrumental in charting the spaces on which the first human occupants established their settlements. In exchange for the support and protection they received, people satisfied the spirits' need for nourishment by making periodic offerings of sacrificial blood: the sacrificial act re-inscribed the initial covenant established between human settlers and the spirits (the first occupants of the land).

Originally propitiated for their role in warfare and agriculture, the spirits generically known as Doguwa also went by the name *mutanen daji* (people of the bush), for they lived in the bush while their human counterparts settled in villages. Eventually the organization of the sacred evolved from communal propitiation of tutelary spirits to more individualized relationships between people and the *mutanen daji* (Masquelier 2001b; Piault 1970). Some spirits manifested themselves by riding "on the heads" of their priests and were placated on behalf of specific subgroups or lineages, and others were honored individually by villagers acting on their own behalf. Spirits in the latter category have almost all been incorporated into the *bori* pantheon, which, over the years, has expanded dramatically to incorporate spirits of various geographical and cultural origins. Today the Doguwa make up one of the largest families of *bori* spirits, and they often occupy center stage in local possession ceremonies.

Not all spirits have been domesticated through *bori*, however. Many have remained bound to the land by anchoring to physical sites, which makes both their mythical histories and their presence tangible to their human neighbors. Although land could not be possessed by individuals and had no intrinsic value unless it yielded a crop, sites known for sheltering *iskoki* were entrusted to the care of the groups responsible for sustaining these spirits. On the stone marking the location of a spirit at each site sacrificial blood was seasonally shed to placate the occupant and renew the bond that linked spirits and people since the beginning of time. In exchange for propitiatory offerings, the spirits insured familial or communal prosperity, guarded villages against drought and disease, and protected local residents from enemy raids. Landmarks—a tree or a rock formation, for example—were reminders of a spiritual presence and objectified the tenuous relations between people and their invisible protectors, transfiguring the landscape into a vibrant microcosm for those who understood the history of these relations (Masquelier 2001b; Nicolas 1975).

Following the French conquest of Niger at the turn of the nineteenth century, colonial engineers redesigned the topography of the Mawri landscape by cutting trees, erecting buildings, and creating roadways. Their plans to develop the colony by facilitating communication and commerce would have profound consequences for local communities (Masquelier 2002).[9] In making way for a new architecture based on secular, rational European values, road engineers destroyed numerous spirit sanctuaries, leaving homeless spirits who had established their abode in the trees and mounds dotting the landscape. Abandoned by the descendants of those who once offered them sacrifices, the spirits stubbornly hovered over the very structures that had dislodged them; occasionally they exacted a heavy tribute, in the form of blood, from helpless individuals who crossed their paths (Masquelier 2002).

French engineers had been cautioned against tempering with the local geography, as they would inevitably unleash the wrath of the displaced spirits. Ignoring these warnings, they proceeded with their plans to demolish whatever stood in the way of the roads they were building (Masquelier 2002). Their unwitting erasure of the local cosmography unlocked a Pandora's box in the popular imaginary. As longer and broader roads unfurled across the landscape, more spirits became unsettled. Rootless and restless, they now roam the roads of Niger in search of prey. As a result, no one is safe when traveling. People who are killed in automobile accidents are widely believed to have been the victims of revengeful "road" spirits against whom amulets and other protective medicines afford only limited immunity.

Not everyone, of course, gives credence to rumors of spirit-caused accidents or relates the rising number of transient spirits to the construction of colonial roads. Yet beyond the diffuse sense of menace that roads hold, it is widely, if implicitly, perceived that perhaps this invisible but threatening traffic would not have intensified to such an extent had people not disregarded their religious heritage. For some, the proliferation of spiteful spirits who inspire terror and provoke misery is also linked to the spread of Islam, the intensification of deforestation, and the development of marketing (Masquelier 1993). I have described elsewhere how the dwindling minority who have remained faithful to the spirits experience Islam's popularity and the adoption of *salla* (prayer) as a loss of tradition (Masquelier 2001b). Over the years, as growing numbers of residents gathered in prayer five times a day, they increasingly turned their backs on the spirits. Pre-Islamic communal rituals were forbidden, shrines were neglected (many of them ultimately destroyed), and the spirits were relegated to oblivion. Despite spirit devotees' efforts to resist the growing ascendency of Muslim practices, the spiritual geography in which the first settlers had anchored their history was progressively effaced. In the late 1980s a significant number of Dogondoutchi residents told me that the recent droughts and epidemics in the region were a direct consequence of the abandonment of *al'ada* (tradition). No longer protected by the spirits to whom they had once pledged devotion, human communities had become vulnerable to a host of destructive forces against which Muslim prayer and medicines were often powerless.[10]

For a number of Dogondoutchi residents, the problem is not simply that spirits have ceased to protect people from various calamities. Some have become dangerous, vindictive creatures eager to avenge themselves on those they blame for their unsettled existence. In June 1989 a road accident in which three passengers were killed was blamed on a Doguwa who had not received the sacrifice she was owed after a new marketplace opened. Angered by Muslim officials who had forbidden any propitiatory offerings to spirits, the spirit of the market became a great avenger (Masquelier 1993). In August 2003 rumors of a she-devil haunting the Nigérien city of Zinder provoked widespread panic among local residents (Masquelier 2008). Religious leaders later explained that the spirit was present because of the emergence of new neighborhoods in town. To accommodate the housing needs of its growing population, Zinder had progressively grown, incorporating rural lands into its urban fold. The urbanization of the *daji* (bush) caused the forcible dislocation of spirits from their habitat. These creatures now haunted the urban areas that had replaced the bush and, with it, their homes. The she-devil was perceived to be a displaced spirit who was reluctant to leave the site where she once lived and, with nowhere to go, roamed the streets of the city at night, frightening anyone she encountered.

Spirits are said to come and go. They are nothing but wind (*iska*), but they never totally disappear. Those who plague stretches of road or terrorize neighborhoods are simply displaced creatures compelled by circumstances to expose their transience to the people they hold responsible for their displacement. Whether it can be said that spirits "collect their dues" each time they shed blood, their proliferation is certainly widely linked in the Mawri imagination to the local history of land development and exploitation and to the growth of Islam.

The presence of the Doguwa spirit at the site of the projected Awaliyya mosque must be similarly read in the context of Islam's progressive encroachment over non-Muslim spaces. Like the she-devil of Zinder, the Doguwa spirit suffered the indignities of homelessness when the tree she called home—and which instantiated her rootedness in the local topography—was chopped down. By sending (or transforming herself into) a legion of biting ants, she sought to discourage the masons from doing their work and prevent the destruction of her environment. That the Doguwa's dwelling was eventually leveled to make space for a mosque, despite her aggressive intervention, speaks loudly of Muslims' successful eradication of a spiritual presence in Dogondoutchi.[11] Note that some ten years after the first brick was laid, the mosque still had no roof; the Awaliyya ran out of funds and never completed the building. Despite these shortcomings, the edifice nevertheless stood as a testament of Muslim enterprise. It was also a reminder of the day when Malam Awal had literally "stamped" a previously non-Muslim space "with the name of Allah" (Werbner 1996:167).

Although some places on the local landscape are dangerous because they bear traces of a violent past and resist containment by Islam (Masquelier 1993, 2002, 2008), the site of the Awaliyya mosque was no longer such a place. Following the inauguration of the mosque, there were, to Awal's credit, no signs of the displaced spirit (nor reports of bellicose ants) to indicate that she wished to retake her domain. "Even if the place is bad, as soon as Malam Awal prays, everyone is protected," a close assistant to the preacher assured me. "No one in his house has even had a nightmare. No one has been hurt or stumbled on a stone since he built his house. People are no longer scared. They flock to the mosque." I have heard numerous reports of *malamai* actively engaged in purging communities from the taint of "animism" by destroying spirit shrines. Friends have provided detailed accounts of zealous reformers injuring themselves severely in their attempts to rid their communities of the stones that served as shrines to the spirits. When they did not lose a hand or a foot to paralysis, these iconoclasts were allegedly overcome by blindness or succumbed to madness—all incontrovertible evidence that spirits actively resisted their forcible eviction. By documenting the *malamai's* failure to destroy "animist" shrines, the rumors suggested that Muslim clerics, no matter how skilled, were no match against the spirits.[12]

Unlike his predecessors, Malam Awal succeeded in banishing the Doguwa without sustaining injuries or causing harm to someone else. By demonstrating that he was more powerful than the spirit, Awal confirmed Islam's superiority over spirit-based practices. He also established the preeminence of God over other agencies and subsidiary spirits: by endowing the preacher with the power to defeat the enemies of Islam, God confirmed He was all powerful. Alhaji Boube described the circumstances leading to the building of the mosque in this way:

> Since the time of our ancestors, we've known from the people before that there was a termite hill and a *dirga* (short thorny tree) there. People were afraid. They thought that no one could live in that place. Someone saw fire coming out of the earth right next to the termite hill once. Then, there was a small market [there.] But it didn't take. All the people left, they couldn't get the market to attract people. [People from] the town hall measured the parcel a long time ago. The owner made a wall, but [couldn't build] a house. Then Malam Awal came.
>
> A long time ago, we heard from some people that there would be a *mai daukaki* [pious person] who would come and live there, to the west of the *dogon doutchi*. This is when Malam Awal came and built his house. We believe the prediction was realized. He is the saint that our ancestors predicted would come for us. The word of our ancestors, we take it seriously. The place he was given is a bad place. But ever since he came, nothing has happened. This must be a sign that God is with him.

In chapter 4 we saw that predictions of a stranger coming to Dogondoutchi to teach people the "true" message of the Qur'an are used by 'yan Awaliyya to imaginatively anchor themselves in a sacred Muslim geography. By taking possession of a land parcel that resisted human control, Malam Awal authorized local residents to confront the spectral presence of the past and "remember" an ancestral prediction about a stranger whose blessedness would subvert the powers that enlivened this past. That "nothing had happened" after these powers were subdued was a sign, Alhaji Boube pointed out, of both the veracity of ancestral predictions and Awal's closeness to God. The notion that Awal's mission to bring "true" Islam had been predicted long ago empowered local Muslims to believe in the sanctity of the mission without maligning their non-Muslim ancestors. Although they belonged to the world of ignorance—the world before Islam—ancestors were the bearers of the prediction. By making his ancestors part of a history that culminated in the age of Awaliyya, Alhaji Boube acknowledged the role his ancestors played in making Dogondoutchi a center of Muslim religiosity.

By summoning a world of spirits whose collapse made the powers of Islam more prominent, Awal's well-publicized handling of the Doguwa reasserted the presence of pre-Islamic cosmographies at the very site where their residual imprint had been erased. The construction of the mosque would remain associated in public memory with the spirit's attack on the masons and her subsequent expulsion from her home. Indeed, the spirit's aura lingered at the site, as people continued to speak of the incident several years after it happened. In spite of its persistent efforts to relegate "animism" to oblivion, Islam remains haunted by it, unable to completely disengage itself.

The Proliferation of Evil Spirits in the Age of Islam

Local Muslims, as we have seen, do not question the existence of spirits. The world as they know it is populated with spirits. Although they would rather shun casual contact with spirits for fear of reprisals, it is not always possible to avoid crossing the path of these creatures given their invisibility to humans. A typical scenario that people invoke to explain some sudden misfortune or an incurable ailment involves inadvertently stepping on a spirit while walking outside at night to urinate. The disturbed spirit may retaliate by causing harm to the "offender," if only to let that person know that an offense was committed that necessitates redress. It is to prevent such "bruising" encounters from happening (or to ward off spirit attacks altogether) that a number of Muslims routinely purchase amulets and other Qur'anic medicines such as *rubutu* (liquid Qur'anic verses that one drinks) from religious specialists (see Butler 2006).

If protecting oneself against spirits is deemed acceptable by some Muslims, communicating with them is not. In theory, at least, only non-Muslims have direct dealings with spirits—channeling their powers through the forum of *bori* for a variety of purposes (healing, divination, protection, enrichment, and so on). Because, from the perspective of *bori* devotees, spirits cannot be chased at will from the places or bodies they choose to inhabit, they must be placated with ritual offerings—and, in some cases, eventually domesticated in possession ceremonies. As noted earlier, these activities are denounced as sinful by most Muslims who believe that *bori* is inspired by Satan and that spirits are the servants of Satan. Preachers routinely admonish their Muslim audiences not to "shed blood" for the spirits, arguing that any action that enables communication with spiritual forces is, by definition, un-Islamic and expressly forbidden by the Qur'an. Those who sacrifice to the spirits, in their view, are guilty of "idolatry" (*shirka*), a sin that will lead them straight to hell. Good Muslims, the preachers insist, trust in the power of God alone and have nothing to do with spirits, even when threatened by them. Though precautionary measures—such as wearing amulets and drinking *rubutu*—can limit the impact of spiritual interference in human lives (unless, as noted, one is a reformist for whom even these practices are sinful innovations), reliance on the power of supplicatory prayer (*addu'a*) is the most effective remedy against malevolent spirits. This means that in the event of a spirit attack (or a suspected spirit-related misfortune), one must ignore the interfering spirit altogether and find licit means of alleviating one's symptoms or confronting adversity. As Alhaji Tankari, a sixty-year-old man, put it in 1994:

> The people of *bori* commit a grave sin because they ask for health not from God but from the spirits. They do not trust God. God created humans so that they would trust Him. Not to put your trust in God is a sin. [Through their invocation of the spirits,] they give God a co-wife.

Here Alhaji Tankari stressed the uniqueness of God. By summoning the help of spirits, *bori* devotees associated God with created beings, thereby violating God's wish that His creatures submit to Him in grateful obedience, and ultimately violated the oneness of God. By metaphorically equating the sin of "idolatry" to the institution of polygyny, Alhaji articulated the sinful implications of attempting to provide God with "helpers" who would contribute their share of labor as would a dutiful co-wife. God, he implied, needed no help. To suggest otherwise was to go against the vision of humanity He had created and engage in the gravest of offense.[13] Muslims generally agree with these pronouncements, but a few are quick to admit that the choice is not always theirs to make. Spirits can torment a person for years, and although it is technically wrong to seek the services of *bori* healers to try to appease them, victims who respond to the spirits' demands can hardly be blamed for wanting to regain their health. In the late 1980s Muslim healers, because of their superior powers, allegedly performed exorcisms to rid their patients of an unwanted spiritual presence, but those I spoke with consistently denied engaging in these practices or knowing anyone who did. To admit having dealings with spirits would threaten one's livelihood as well as one's standing in the Muslim community.

Partly because the spread of Islam is relatively recent in this region of Niger, Muslims are well aware of the danger of "improper" association with spirits. Save for youths and civil servants who wear Western-style clothes, every man wears Muslim attire—a *riga* (sleeveless robe) or a *jaba* (long-sleeved tunic) over drawstring pants and a turban or cap (Masquelier 2005; Nicolas 1975). Thus followers of the Prophet can no longer be distinguished from "animists." Muslims anxious to eschew the stigma attached to *bori* identity routinely denigrate spirit possession to redefine their own worthiness as members of the *umma*. Husbands forbid their wives from attending possession rituals, and, when questioned, they adamantly deny ever seeking the services of *bori* healers. In recent years the tendency to disparage spirit-centered practices that not so long ago were deemed essential to the well-being and prosperity of local communities has only intensified. Because spirits are Satan's creatures, local preachers say, they exist only in order to tempt people to commit that which God has forbidden. When they are ignored, however, the spirits supposedly grow tired of providing temptations and stop trying to lead people astray.[14] Among the younger generation, girls who might be tempted to attend possession ceremonies are discouraged from doing so by young Muslim men who flatly state that they will not marry women who do *bori*. Similarly, *malamai* who engage in the manufacture of amulets and other types of medicines aimed at preventing spirit attacks actively disavow any connection to spirit possession, insisting that the therapies they provide are based strictly on the Qur'an. Now that Islam is largely taken for granted for shaping life as it is lived, spirit devotees are increasingly perceived as crude and unprogressive by their Muslim fellow citizens, even if their powers to bring the rains or protect communities from epidemics are still recognized by many.

The recent disaffection with spirit-centered practices notwithstanding, it is precisely because everyone recognizes the existence of spiritual forces that rumors of the Doguwa's defeat at the hands of Malam Awal struck the local imagination so powerfully. Recall that Doguwa spirits are thought to have originally coexisted productively with those who settled in Arewa. In more recent times, however, people's increasing desire for wealth is said to have corrupted their relationship with the spiritual occupants of the land. Indeed, it is believed that the pressing need for cash combined with a rising inability to procure it (de Latour Dejean 1980; Raynaut 1976) has led some to strike Faustian bargains with Doguwa spirits in the hope of amassing money. Through these bargains, the Doguwa are made to do the bidding of their human masters if, in exchange for the wealth they produce, they are fed human victims. Rumors of *maita* (witchcraft) in which spirits become workers amassing wealth for their keepers attest to the rupture of the original alliance between spirits and people and also build on the widespread notion that accessing wealth is an increasingly risky business which requires that one tap into dark and dangerous powers. Because Muslims are often suspected of engaging in nefarious money-making schemes, these rumors complicate the view that Muslims have nothing to do with spirits and that the severing of ties with spirits underlies many problems local residents are currently facing in Dogondoutchi. They also help us understand why Awal's confrontation with a past that resisted containment was apparently greeted with great relief by Muslims with no ties to the Awaliyya community. As "enlightened" individuals who look down on what they consider the backward practices of their *bori* neighbors, Muslims cannot acknowledge any involvement with spirits. Yet they straddle the visible world of humans and the invisible world of spirits which local epistemology treats as compatible and complementary.

Finding a Doguwa to produce wealth for you, *bori* devotees will point out, is, at least initially, relatively painless. A person need only bring a calabash of milk to the foot of a tree known to shelter a spirit. Because any gift bears the expectation of a counter-gift, according to Mauss (1967), the Doguwa, upon accepting the milk, will generally ask the gift giver what he wishes in return.[15] At this point the individual should inform the Doguwa of his desire for wealth. Patience is essential in this process. By repeatedly offering milk and other foods, the person seeking wealth tames the wild creature and strengthens the bond initiated with the first gift. Eventually the Doguwa will agree to follow her self-appointed "master" home and produce wealth for him, in the form of cash or millet.

Once the spirit has entered her new master's home, however, there is no turning back. To sustain her, the wealth seeker must nourish the spirit with the blood she craves, and in exchange she will make him rich. Initially he will sacrifice chickens to keep her satiated. Soon, however, the Doguwa will tire of chicken blood and demand human blood—a requirement her keeper has no choice but to satisfy as best he can. At first she will prey on the individuals her master designates among strangers. Persons who are sucked dry of their blood by a spirit die quickly, however, and the keeper must continually look for new victims. Once he exhausts the supply of victims unrelated to him, the master is forced to select people from among his distant kin. Eventually the increasingly ravenous spirit requires the blood of his own progeny, thereby obliterating the very future that the individual was trying to secure through financial prosperity.

By all accounts, once the Doguwa has "tasted" a person, she becomes a fearful creature, ready to pounce on anyone she meets to satisfy her lust for human blood. Nevertheless, people widely acknowledge that spirits who attack humans to suck their blood did not originate as evil forces. They only become truly malevolent at the prompting of individuals who use them to serve their own selfish ends. Spirits, it is often said, are similar to children and will do everything they are asked to do. Like children who are taught wrongly, the Doguwa spirits learn from their unscrupulous masters how to perform immoral tasks. They become the unwitting instruments of human selfishness. Because their powers have been corrupted by their masters' greed, they can no longer be satisfied with the blood of domestic animals. Nor can they return to the peaceful tree they once inhabited. For this reason, individuals suspected of keeping a spirit to enrich themselves are called *mayyu* (witches). If sufficient evidence can be brought against them, they are forced to undergo a water ordeal that not only proves their guilt but renders them powerless, unable to profit from the vital force of others. During the ordeal administered by *'yan kasa* ("masters of the earth"), the harmful forces unleashed by greed are overcome.[16]

Making Use of the Past

In the 1980s Doguwa attacks allegedly rose in Dogondoutchi. People attributed this to *Sarkin* Soumana's death, because he was succeeded by his brother, Amadou, a fervent Muslim who did not believe that spirits could suck people dry of their blood. As one *bori* devotee expressed it: "It is because Soumana is dead that Doguwa are attacking so many people. [Chief Soumana] would slaughter the Doguwa to get rid of her if she refused to spare her victim. He knew how to deal with spirits." It was widely believed that chiefs, in precolonial times, had the ability to feed human blood to the spirits because they kept slaves, captured as "booty" during raids against enemy communities. Now that there were no longer slaves and Muslim chiefs discouraged the propitiation of spirits, bloodthirsty Doguwa had to fend for themselves, at times feeding on whomever they came upon. Another resident explained the increase in spirit attacks in this way:

Amadou, the *Sarkin* Arewa, is a *malami*. But Soumana had medicine to prevent Doguwa from killing the people they attacked. He had made a house for them. When you went to see him, you did not meet any Doguwa. He was not giving them people [to feed on]. He slaughtered animals for them. When he died, the Doguwa all left [the palace].

Not all Doguwa came from the *Sarkin* Arewa's palace, however. Some allegedly haunted ordinary homes where unfettered greed had authorized their transformation into vicious creatures that fed on human blood—sometimes long after the instigator of the Faustian pact had died. In 1988 I witnessed Chief Amadou's arbitration of a confrontation between a very sick woman claiming to be the victim of a bloodthirsty Doguwa and the man she accused of being the spirit's master. Amadou had to decide whether the suspected "witch" should undergo the water ordeal. Upon hearing the case, he peremptorily dismissed the accusations against the man, stating that the plaintiff suffered from acute epilepsy and that her ill health was not caused by a supernatural creature. The afflicted woman was promptly sent to the dispensary to receive treatment. Still, many people who witnessed the incident remained unconvinced by Amadou's declaration that no witchcraft was involved. Had Chief Soumana been alive, they surmised, he would have handled the whole incident very differently.

Those who lamented Amadou's dismissal of the old woman's claim saw Muslim elites' growing reluctance to recognize that Doguwa attacks required appropriate intervention as a loss of heritage. This fundamental loss was felt ever so forcefully not only because of the tampering with spirit homes and the destruction of sacrificial shrines but also because of the abandonment of rituals that people needed to negotiate the terms of their relationships with the "people of the bush." Soumana's death signaled the beginning of a new era characterized by the proliferation of angry, restless Doguwa who terrorized the local landscape. It also led to the disappearance of the very techniques through which people protected themselves against this terror. In the ensuing years I either witnessed or heard of several other cases of spirit attacks brought to Chief Amadou for arbitration. Occasionally the accused party had to undergo the water ordeal. However, the *Sarkin* Arewa made it increasingly clear that he did not favor bringing witchcraft accusations to their ritual conclusion. People who suspected they were victimized by a bloodthirsty Doguwa stopped coming to him, knowing that the Muslim chief would dismiss their case; instead, they enlisted the services of a *bori* healer to exorcize the Doguwa before it was too late.

Muslims throughout Dogondoutchi nonetheless participate fully in local efforts to ward off misfortune and keep dangerous forces at bay through the use of magic, amulets, and the practice of divination. Although anyone can purchase amulets or liquid verses from Muslim specialists, it is believed that *malamai* are more effectively protected against intrusive spirits because they have special secrets they use to manufacture powerful protective devices.[17] Whether people actually use amulets to protect their homes, millet fields, or personal health and fortune, their necessity is without question. Over time, many spirits have gradually been absorbed into the fabric of the past, but others remain and resurface when least expected. If Muslim prayer has successfully sidelined spirit-centered practices that once insured the continued vitality of local communities, it has not entirely done away with spirits—least of all spirits who were once controlled by powerful chiefs. For this reason, in addition to selling medicines against leprosy, theft, blows, divorce, or infertility, *malamai* derive a substantial income from the sale of amulets and prayers that insure protection against spiritual attacks.

With the spread of the Izala movement, these protective strategies have come under fire as reformist preachers enjoin everyone to dispose of their amulets and to trust in the power of prayer. *Layu* (amulets), Muslim reformists claim, have no place in Islam. Those who wear amulets or engage in their manufacture, reformists warn, will never taste the "sweetness of paradise" because on Judgment Day they will be found guilty of "idolatry."[18] Some even insist that wearing a *laya* (amulet) only makes one sicker, clearly an indubitable sign of God's wrath. While they wax eloquent about the sinfulness of amulet makers and wearers, Izala preachers have little to say about the spirits those devices are supposedly keeping at bay. The ideal world they paint for their audiences is of this earth, devoid of the *ruhanai* (the creatures that fall between spirits and angels) and the *aljanu* (spirits) that inhabit the edifying stories that non-Izala preachers recount in their sermons.

In the world 'yan Izala describe people must look to God for protection and dismiss altogether those who pretend they can provide magical safeguards against disease and misfortune. Predictably Izala preachers speak harshly of *malamai* who deceive clients by claiming they have the ability to access the powers of the spirits (Loimeier 1997b) or to protect people against their attacks by means of specific secrets (*asirai*).[19] Only God, they insist, has power over spirits. They urge Muslims to stop soliciting the assistance of "corrupt" *malamai* and rely instead on the services provided by the dispensary when prayer does not provide sufficient relief. Although the use of herbal medicines and the ingestion of honey are acceptable curative techniques (which, they say, the Prophet relied on when he was sick), they insist that, ultimately, only faith in God can ward off Satan's offensives. Amulets, *rubutu*, and other techniques for deflecting evil forces and insuring success only make people more vulnerable, as they create another focus of worship and further distance them from God.[20] The Qur'an is a source of inspiration, a practical guide for Muslims aiming to better themselves. It should not be used as a magical implement. Moreover, Izala preachers routinely point out, the Prophet never used amulets; wearing them because one's parents or grandparents wore them is to commit *bidi'a* (innovation).

The secularized vision of the world promoted by Izala preachers has been eagerly embraced by numerous Dogondoutchi residents, but most are hesitant to give up the security afforded by Qur'anic methods whose efficacy, in their view, no longer needs to be demonstrated. However, they also acknowledge that some *malamai* abuse their clients' trust by providing medicines of little or no use. As a preacher whose services had been extensively solicited, Malam Awal was well aware of this. Although he did not sell or make amulets himself, he cautiously recognized their effectiveness and defended their authenticity. Save for a few reformists who had broken rank with Izala members and joined Awal's following, the majority of 'yan Awaliyya had been critics of reformist Islam: like other Muslims, they resented 'yan Izala's denunciation of religious practices they had inherited from previous generations. They also did not approve of the heavy-handed manner in which *malamai* extracted resources from local Muslims by means of *sadaka* (alms) and *zaka* (a tithe), but still they could not reconcile their understanding of Muslim identity with the Izala vision of what being Muslim meant. By submitting to the authority of Malam Awal, they could continue to rely on the power of Qur'anic medicines while escaping the influence of Muslim religious leaders alleged to be covetous and controlling.

In contrast to the sober model of devotional practices championed by Izala reformists where Islam was disengaged from "superstition," the vision of religiosity promoted by Malam Awal built on local understandings of power, magic, and history. Rather than divesting Islam of what 'yan Izala defined as "improper" accretions, it capitalized on the popular belief that, as the "home of the spirits" (Steedly 1993:10), the memorialized past occasionally filtered into the present in the form of *iskoki* who spread terror wherever they appeared. It is safe to assume that Malam Awal never heard of the panic sparked by *Sarkin* Soumana's death. Nor, as noted, did he know about the Doguwa that lived on the site where he would build the Awaliyya mosque. Nonetheless, he quickly recognized the central role the local landscape played in the making of history and the possibilities this entailed for inscribing his own legacy.

Awal also implicitly understood that the development of Islam might be an erasure of past practices, but it never entirely effaced earlier values: traces stubbornly remained that enlivened places for those who noticed them. Wiping out the past in a more sweeping manner took a special effort that most Muslims were loathe to engage in, given the possible risks and repercussions. Never totally discarded, the past leaked, and occasionally leaped, into the present in the form of spiteful spirits reluctant to relinquish their hold on what once was theirs. Confronting the past, Awal knew, meant meeting these creatures head-on before they could further compromise the very process of erasure that was meant to finally exclude them from the present. Note that to permanently forget the Doguwa spirits—and the past they belong to—one first had to remember them. Only after their ominous proximity had been conceded and their powers acknowledged could they be driven into oblivion and the places they once occupied effectively cleared of their haunting presence.

As we have seen, Malam Awal did not intentionally set out to challenge a Doguwa spirit. That events unfolded as they did has more to do with how history is "read backwards" (Steedly 1993:146) from a revelatory conclusion routinely revised than with what could be called planned orchestration. The story of Awal's battle with the spirit took shape through the "prism" (Shaw 2002:246) of memories that worked to configure the present in terms of the (weighty and potent) past. In her ethnography of Karoland, Steedly (1993:145) remarks that, as inscriptions in the landscape, history is sometimes "emplotted less by chronology than by coincidence. Sympathetic encounters constellate across time, and inspire stories that trace in the pattern of coincidence and conjuncture a moment of encompassing origin which is itself a repetition." Still, however unexpected, there was something scripted about Awal's encounter with the Doguwa—as if the unexpected was *meant* to happen. Although the encounter was coincidental, it was also part of a larger pattern of events whose predictability could be retroactively established because of the way the past, alive and resonant, chronotopically provided a series of "places" from which to interpret the present.

Consider the notion—actively promoted by 'yan Awaliyya—that the coming of Malam Awal to Dogondoutchi was the realization of a prediction. Although most people claimed that long-gone ancestors—in some cases *malamai*—were the source of the prediction, Hajiya Salamatou, around sixty years of age, believed that *Sarkin* Soumana himself had predicted the coming of a formidable foreigner who would transform Dogondoutchi through his pious charisma and deliver people from a world of darkness. By insisting that

Soumana, known as the "owner of one thousand and forty Doguwa," predicted that after his death the Doguwa-filled world he lived in would end, Hajiya Salamatou invested Malam Awal's mission with the mantle of legitimacy at the same time that she positioned the preacher as a crucial figure of local history: he was a warring leader who stood to change the course of this history by purging the town of its demons and transforming it into a place of Allah.

The Masculinization of the Memoryscape

A year or so after the Doguwa was driven out by Malam Awal, a rumor surfaced that a small mosque (*masallaci*) had emerged overnight as if by magic a few hundred yards from the *zawiya*. In one version of the rumor, a young *'dan* Awaliyya noticed the new structure early one morning as he was walking behind the quarry on his way to a friend's house. Less than ten feet in length, the four-sided structure resembled many of the prayer grounds found in this part of the Sahel. It consisted of one single row of stones that symbolically delineated a walled space where men assembled at prayer time. Upon spotting the *masallaci*, the young man ran back to Malam Awal's home and told him of the wondrous discovery.[21] The preacher immediately took off with a small party of *'yan* Awaliyya to see for himself the mosque that had supposedly emerged from the earth. After verifying that the young man had spoken the truth, Awal concluded that the mosque was a sign not only that God approved of his mission to enlighten the Muslims of Dogondoutchi but that He also wanted *'yan* Awaliyya to pray on this very spot. In another version of the story, the Prophet himself appeared to Malam Awal and told him where he and his followers should pray. According to some *'yan* Awaliyya, the mosque had already been built by the time Awal received the Prophet's message. Contradicting this account, one man told me that Malam Awal had the mosque built after the Prophet spoke to him.[22] Regardless of the form these rumors took, what provoked widespread amazement among Awaliyya members was that the mosque stood on the flanks of the most potent reminder of the town's "animist" past, the *dogon doutchi* (long stone). Muslims had never tried to claim for Islam the rugged pillar of red clay that hovered over the sprawling neighborhoods of Dogondoutchi like a colossal termite mound.

Not everyone, of course, was inclined to believe the rumors centering around the appearance of a miraculous mosque.[23] All the same, except for passing tourists who climbed the picturesque rock for the spectacular view from the top, no one lingered in the vicinity. The clay monolith—part of a vast ensemble of cliffs bordering a fossilized valley—was home to Ungurnu, a spirit who traditionally warned the town's inhabitants of upcoming enemy raids by sending a swarm of bees to the home of the *mai gari* (town chief). Although Ungurnu had not manifested herself in a long time—the "pacification" that had followed colonial conquest relegated her to irrelevance—every year a black ox was still sacrificed to her. By climbing the steep flanks of the *doutchi* and shedding sacrificial blood on it, Ungurnu devotees periodically reclaimed Dogondoutchi as a place of and for the spirits; the annual sacrifice insured that part of the town would not be contained within the ever expansive fold of Muslim supremacy.

By building or claiming to have discovered a mosque just a few paces from the cave-like depression where Ungurnu resided, 'yan Awaliyya claimed the *dogon doutchi* as a place of Islam. In their determination to erase any trace of the spirits' lingering presence, they seized the significant landmark of the spiritual landscape. A few days after the alleged discovery, the mosque "sent by God" was inaugurated as a special prayer ground for the exclusive use of Malam Awal and his close disciples. 'Yan Awaliyya claimed that prayers made at the special site would be almost instantly answered by God. No one, except Awal's most trusted followers, was allowed at the site, however. Soon, Malam Awal forbade anyone outside his close entourage from even climbing the *dogon doutchi*. Those who—like myself—used the narrow paths on the flanks of the rocky peak as a short-cut when heading to another part of town were no longer authorized to do so. In 2003 a young Japanese woman, a founding member of a small nongovernmental organization who taught sewing to young girls, tried to hang a handmade banner on the western side of the *dogon doutchi* to celebrate her students' accomplishments. She was physically assaulted by club-wielding members of Malam Awal's private militia, and the banner was promptly destroyed. Later that year a group of French volunteers climbing the *dogon doutchi* was similarly terrorized by the *masu tsaro* (militia members) deputized by Malam Awal to patrol the site. Before they were chased off the mountain, those with cameras were compelled to erase all the digital pictures they had taken of the *dogon doutchi*—lest they capture on their photos the "aura" of the miraculous *masallaci*.

Significantly, by asserting control over certain landmarks that signaled the presence of a persistent spiritual presence, the preacher did not completely relegate the spirits to oblivion. As he seized the *dogon doutchi* to incorporate it into the mythic history of the Awaliyya, he implicitly redefined the place of spirits in the order of things, even when they were perceived as an absent presence. Consider the following conversation I had with Harouna, a *'dan* Awaliyya:

> HAROUNA: There are many mountains in Doutchi. God could have chosen another mountain [as a place to erect a mosque] but he chose this one—the *dogon doutchi*—and it is near Malam Awal's *zawiya*.
> A.M.: But that mountain, that's where a spirit lives.
> HAROUNA: Even spirits know Islam. They have Sufi orders. And there are spirits who pray. Even in Mecca, there is a place where you throw stones at Satan.[24]

Spirits, Harouna implied, had to be fought even in Mecca. As creatures of Satan, they lurked everywhere to tempt Muslims into sin (even if, paradoxically, they also performed pious acts and seemingly conducted themselves as proper Muslims). Harouna's testimony highlights once again the centrality of the non-Muslim other in local definitions of Muslimhood. Far from becoming irrelevant to the moral imagination, spirits symbolize the age of *jahiliyya* against which Muslims articulate their identity. They are both the dreaded symbols of a past Muslims are trying to suppress and a useful foil against which to assert the superiority of Islam. In stressing the cosmological significance of the *dogon doutchi* as a place both of spirits and Islamic worship, Harouna hinted at Islam's dependency on pre-Islamic cosmologies as well as the constantly renegotiated terms of Muslims' relationships to the spirits.

Like the spirit's home that was destroyed to make way for a mosque, the *dogon doutchi* was appropriated to make way for Malam Awal's vision of an overwhelmingly Muslim landscape, where even the most enduring sites of pre-Islamic history would, once freed of demons and imprinted with the mark of God, become part of the Sufi master's territory. This was a territory whose boundaries he protected with the assistance of dozens of uniformed men, who, clubs in tow, policed the town on his behalf and buttressed his authority. Those who (unwittingly) violated the rule of no trespassing by treading on the site that recapitulated Islam's victory over the world of spirits were treated harshly. A young boy who was walking by the *zawiya* during the Friday prayer had been beaten so severely by *masu tsaro* that he had to be hospitalized. Local residents were regularly chased by militia men if they walked by the mosque when Malam Awal was delivering a sermon.

Significant in this process is the way these non-Islamic spaces, home to female spirits, have been masculinized through Awal's intervention. Although in practice many avoided walking by the tree that, before Malam Awal's arrival, supposedly sheltered a Doguwa, anyone, at least theoretically, could have approached the spirit to request her assistance. Now that the mosque had been erected, however, the site was Malam Awal's property. It was where the preacher built his own home and where he dispensed advice on the proper way to follow the Qur'an. Though women were allowed to attend gatherings at the mosque, they had to remain hidden behind the walled partitions separating the central prayer grounds from the more secluded aisles.

As far as I know, Ungurnu did not protest the invasion of her territory by Muslims determined to eradicate every vestige of the pre-Islamic past. Nor was there any reported attempt by Awal to dislodge the spirit in order to further strengthen his identity as a fighter of spirits and of the *jahiliyya* they represented. Nonetheless, the message was clear: God, in erecting the mosque overnight on the flanks of the most visible reminder of the spirits' presence in town, had signaled His wish that the *dogon doutchi* become a place of and for Islam. The monolith that was home to Ungurnu and that spirit devotees—most of them women—ascended annually to propitiate the spirit was claimed as a Muslim space—and as a symbol of the patriarchal order whose rigid boundaries the preacher took pains to define in great detail during his sermons (see chapter 8). This was a space from which all women were rigorously excluded. By "taking hold of the land" (Ranger 1987) and, in accordance with God's wishes, requisitioning the *dogon doutchi* as a "house of prayer," Awal invested a site of female power with the stamp of the male-centered world of value he was busy fashioning for the residents of Dogondoutchi.

Sacralizing Space, Militarizing Experience

The vision of Muslims ridding the land of spirits and building mosques on the very sites where spirit shrines once stood is not exclusive to the Awaliyya. Indeed, it is a recurring motif in West African history. Some ten centuries ago Muslim iconoclasm in the Nigerian city of Kano followed a similar scenario. According to the *Kano Chronicle*,[25] the founding clans of Kano were once warned by their priestly leader, Barbushe, that a stranger would come to town. This stranger, their leader predicted, would cut down the sacred tree (a spirit shrine) and build a mosque (Paden 1973). Eventually the people of Kano—known as Maguzawa by Muslim Hausa speakers—would embrace Islam: "If he comes not in your time, assuredly he will come in the time of your children, and will conquer all in this country" (Palmer 1928, 3:98). Indeed, a man named Bagauda arrived in AD 999, wrested the country from the Maguzawa, and became the first king of Kano (Palmer 1928, 3:97–100).

Later, during the reign of Muhammad Rumfa (1463–99), a central mosque was built in Kano, local Muslim elites established linkages to the Sharifai, and the sacred tree was destroyed (Paden 1973). According to Paden (1973:48), another mosque, known as the Madabo mosque, was built "on the site where the pre-Islamic sacred tree once grew." After the tree was cut, Maisinberbere, the spirit of the tree, was thought by *malamai* to have relocated to a nearby area. Thus, in Dogondoutchi and in Kano, the spiritual conquest of "pagan" lands was comparable.

In inscribing spirit-populated places with the name of Allah, Malam Awal strengthened his image as a divinely inspired warrior summoned to combat the supernatural forces allegedly arrayed against him. Banishing evil spirits has traditionally been part of the inventory of "miracles" that Muslim saints perform, in part to demonstrate their sainthood. Yet, I contend that more than simply replicating the performances of previous Sufi masters who, through God's grace, could do things no ordinary Muslim could accomplish, the preacher was also militarizing the religious experience of local residents. By using military concepts to concretize the struggle against evil that characterized not only his own divinely motivated conquest over alien spaces but the daily life of his followers, he framed his campaign to bring "true" Islam to Dogondoutchi within the Manichean terms that have come to order the world of many Nigériens since the tragic events of 9/11.[26]

Consider the following comments by Aminatou, a close disciple of Malam Awal: "Even in the time of the Prophet, there were people who did not listen to [the Prophet.] This is what's happening here as well with Malam Awal. Some people refuse to listen to what he has to say even though he only tells the truth." By comparing his situation to that of the Prophet who fought ignorance and alienation as he spread his monotheistic message across the Arabian peninsula, Aminatou casts Awal as a formidable figure with a formidable mission that could only succeed if he cast out demons, in addition to combating ignorance and aggressively mobilizing support for societal reforms. Aminatou was not the only one to draw parallels between Malam Awal and Muhammad. In fact, the preacher himself routinely invited this comparison by referring to the Prophet in his own description of the mission he had been vested with.

In his war against Satan's creatures—human and otherwise—Malam Awal himself did not use conventional weaponry. Whether describing his battles against fierce spirits sent by enemies or his combat against the more diffuse forces of ignorance, he emphatically stressed that he carried no knives and that divine protection alone shielded him from deadly threats. For many of his followers, his lack of fear in the face of imminent danger was further proof of God's favor, for fearlessness arises precisely from the "conviction of being in God's hands" (O'Fahey 1990:12). Words, Awal insisted, were his only weapons in his fight against evil in all its guises. "Preaching is like making war: it is about fighting pagans," Aminatou told me, to emphasize the militant nature of Awal's leadership.

But if the preacher curtailed his warfare to the spiritual plane, members of his militia did not. Armed with swords and sustained by the assurance that they were accomplishing God's will, they chased intruders from the *dogon doutchi* and other places, leaving terror in their wake. In December 2004 I was trying to photograph a sign a couple of hundred yards from the *zawiya* advertising the Awaliyya mission when two women standing at the entrance of their compound motioned for me to stop immediately. When I approached them for an explanation, they said that I should be careful because members of Awal's militia were always on the lookout for anyone taking pictures, and "they beat people up." A number of times, women who lingered too long in front of the *zawiya* were pursued by militia members wielding clubs. Soldiers had surfaced quickly and spared no blows to rid the place of "trespassers." The Doguwa spirit was no longer a threat to passers-by, but now they had to guard against Malam Awal's own army as it zealously protected the mosque's integrity from alien contamination.

Associated with Sufi orders, Werbner (2003:57) notes, is an "ideology of supra-human spatial and earthly transformative power" that both constitutes and expresses the Sufi leader's charisma. By cleansing sites of spirits and imprinting upon them the stamp of the divine, Malam Awal made them less threatening to local residents while colonizing them for the Awaliyya, thereby demonstrating to all his charismatic authenticity. At the same time, he endowed these sites with a sanctity that now required constant redefinition. Acts of ritual sacralization such as congregating at these spaces at prayer time or chanting *zikiri* were not enough. These newly "Islamicized" spaces also had to be purged of an intrusive, contaminating presence and their boundaries policed—by physical force, if necessary. While ostensibly freeing the people of Dogondoutchi from the "weight of the past" (Lambek 2002) through his territorial claims over spirit-occupied territory, Malam Awal ultimately excluded many from the moral spaces he had helped create through his victories over the so-called forces of Satan.

HOW IS A GIRL TO MARRY WITHOUT A BED? WEDDINGS, WEALTH, AND WOMEN'S VALUE

6

If her family can afford it, [a Hausa woman] will have a four-poster bed piled high with mattresses, covered with a satin spread adorned with many pillows. This bed is the central decorative piece in the room and she neither sleeps nor sits on it.
—*Barbara Callaway*, Muslim Hausa Women in Nigeria

Mothers, they have nothing. They work and they spent everything they earn on their daughters. Their daughters' room are filled with things and their [own] rooms are empty.
—*Nafissa, Dogondoutchi, 2000*

A [Mawri] mother must [. . .] contribute to the dowry of the young bride who should arrive at her husband's with her calabashes, ladles, basins, mats, water pots, furniture, etc., which will be exhibited for all to see. Fashions change. Today, a mother will burst with pride if, on her wedding day, her daughter can display a metal bed with a mattress in addition to all the conventional utensils.
—*Éliane de Latour*, Les temps du pouvoir

"Fathers, they have nothing to say about marriage. It is our business," a woman interjected as I was discussing bridewealth (*sadaki*) with my neighbor in March 2000. "If the daughter wants a man for a husband and her mother agrees, *shi ke nan* [that's it]! They 'tie' the marriage," she concluded. By insisting that marriage was women's business, this senior resident was resolutely challenging patriarchal authority and defining wedding prestations as a female arena of power from which men should be excluded, at least theoretically. She further implied that women should systematically resist Islamic ideologies that undermined forms of accumulation through which women traditionally created value and generated status for themselves. Her testimony echoed the beliefs of numerous Mawri women similarly anxious to secure some measure of autonomy and preserve their power bases at a time when economic forces and religious reforms are increasingly working against women's interests and agendas. In this chapter I discuss how female residents of Dogondoutchi have been challenging patriarchal notions of social order that have emerged under the banner of reformist Islam.

Whenever people discussed bridewealth and marriage in Dogondoutchi in 1994 and 2000, women grumbled about the ridiculously limited quantity of household items they could buy with the small *sadaki* payments many families received now that both the government and Muslim reformists had put a cap on bridewealth transfers. Men, in contrast, often complained bitterly that bridewealth had become such an extravagant expense that no one could afford to marry anymore. In the last two decades or so, weddings and the complex and multidirectional gift transactions they entail have become a frequent source of controversy among Dogondoutchi residents who struggle to meet their social obligations in an era of dwindling resources and opportunities. Amid competing visions of how to solve the problem of marriage in contemporary Niger, Mawri women feel increasingly compelled to articulate their own perceptions of what weddings entail and what their own rights and responsibilities are when a daughter marries.

Throughout the African continent, bridewealth practices are frequently debated, as many people have been forced to reconsider these complex transactions in the face of collapsing national or regional economies and the emergence of new markets and new forms of production. In defiance of Uganda's tradition of bridewealth paid by the bridegroom to the bride's family, a twenty-five-year-old scooter taxi driver recently invited older women to vie for his hand in marriage and present what they thought would be an acceptable "dowry" (Fisher 2000). In the KwaZulu Natal Province of South Africa, where the traditional use of cattle in bridewealth exchange has long been replaced by money that migrant workers earned, a man decided to adorn his only daughter with cash and clothes to concretize her value as a future wife and mother (Stengs et al. 2000). In southern Sudan a Nuer brother and his full sister began living together as husband and wife; they were cattleless orphans with no marriage prospects—she had no extended family that her in-laws could call upon in times of need and he had no cattle—and so they had nothing to lose if they were later killed for committing incest (Hutchinson 1996). Each of these three incidents constitutes, in its own way, fairly unique modes of creatively circumventing increasingly contentious practices, but they must still be seen as part of a larger debate through which ideologies of gender, marriage, and family are brought under heightened scrutiny at a time when sources and perceptions of prosperity quickly shift with the flow of money and markets.

In Niger, women's grievances about the changing rules regulating bride-wealth (and gift giving) and their creative efforts to defy the limitations imposed by a collapsing economy similarly underscore wider concerns about changing definitions of gendered roles and realities. In this chapter I describe how women in Dogondoutchi are shaping the debate on bridewealth just as the recent emergence of anti-Sufism has sparked intense questioning over the management of wealth, the status of women, and, more generally, the relevance of Islam in the lives of ordinary Muslims. By defending what they consider to be their daughters' interests and expectations, senior women often end up contesting newly emerging standards of Muslim piety, virtue, and civility. While most mothers in Dogondoutchi do not necessarily agree that fathers "have nothing to say about marriage," and they sometimes even challenge one another as they confront husbands, Muslim elites, and the Nigérien authorities, they have definite ideas about the purpose of bridewealth exchange and they make their voices heard whenever they can. Meanwhile, even as they feel pressured to indulge their daughters' dreams of bourgeois domesticity, they are also mindful that respectability has increasingly been defined through the language of Islam.

When 'yan Izala (and later 'yan Awaliyya) started implementing measures to revitalize the Muslim community, they insisted that flaunting wealth during wedding celebrations violated an Islamic moral order. As one Izala member put it: "For the wedding, one should simply buy a mattress, a cooking pot, and a few bowls. That's enough."[1] For Muslim women who devoted their resources and energies to fill their daughters' marital homes with furniture, hand-woven blankets, mats, and bowls, however, Izala's condemnation of ostentatious consumption made little sense. Far from being inimical to the concepts of morality, piousness, and frugality promoted by Muslim reformists, the consumption practices of Mawri mothers were the instrument through which these values were objectified at a time when the fabric of society and the moral basis of identity were increasingly scrutinized. Amid the controversies generated by Muslim reformists' denunciation of conspicuous consumption, women's discourse on bridewealth and wedding gift exchange provides a useful commentary on gender relations and the manifold anxieties of consumer culture. It also highlights how contested Muslim visions of gender, power, and domesticity have given rise to, as Bernal (1997:148) described it in the case of Sudan, "both new mechanisms for controlling women and new opportunities for women to renegotiate their positions in gender relations."

Through an analysis of women's creative efforts to redefine their roles and responsibilities in the matrimonial economy, I hope to contribute to the anthropological debate on globalization. By focusing on the cultural dynamics of global processes, this debate has made it increasingly clear that globalization can no longer be equated with cultural imperialism and described as a process of homogenization promoting the convergence of cultural style and resulting in a world of sameness (Friedman 1994; Inda and Rosaldo 2002; Meyer and Geschiere 1999). Far from gradually making the world over in the image of the West on the problematic assumption that globalization is synonymous with Westernization, global flows have turned out to presuppose and even promote local fixity. Rather than eroding boundaries, the seeming intensification of change appears to reaffirm borders and redefine categories. Thus globalization is about uprooting as much as it is about rootedness. Making sense of this "paradoxical articulation of flow and closure" (Meyer and Geschiere 1999:3) means attending to the sometimes highly variable ways in which people everywhere use global capital (consumer goods, foreign logos, information technology, etc.) to reassert local values and reinscribe cultural identities. For my own purposes, the recognition that global consumption and local transformation are two sides of the same coin can be used to understand the creative strategies through which Muslim women customize imported goods to redefine themselves in resolutely local terms. By embracing emblems of the foreign to reaffirm cultural distinctions, women in Dogondoutchi actively resist the tide of Islamization at the same time that they participate in local redefinitions of Muslim identity. If they are neither the passive recipients of global cultural imports nor the silent victims of male-centered hegemonic designs, they are nonetheless struggling to respond to the challenges and limitations imposed by social transformations currently affecting their world. Out of this struggle emerge new expressions and understandings of Muslim identity. Following Butler (1997), and by considering women's preoccupation with bridewealth and wedding gifts, I demonstrate how the processes and means that have secured Mawri women's subordination are also the conditions through which these women have become aware of their marginalization; marriage transactions, I argue, are central to the strategic redefinition of women's social worth

Aside from their impact on local religious debates, Dogondoutchi women's resistance to appeals from conservative Islam along with their dynamic engagement in an ever widening global consumer market underscores the difficulty of trying to predict, first, how commodities—beds, beads, or bicycles, for example—will be used by local actors and, second, what understandings of modernity will emerge out of these experiences (Graeber 1996; Hunt 1999; Renne and Usman 1999; Straight 2002; Weiss 1996). Theorists' assumptions about modernity and globalization notwithstanding, the interface of global and local processes has produced multiple ways of being modern and of understanding both the material and moral impacts of modernization. And although there is widespread agreement that globalization "is itself a deeply historical, uneven and even *localizing* process" (Appadurai 1996:17), we cannot ignore the central role of people's agency in creatively engaging this process. In contexts where people increasingly consume resources that were neither produced in their own societies nor produced for purposes they are now used for, it becomes crucial to trace the complex ways in which the appropriation of foreignness becomes not simply a strategy of self-production but occasionally also a means of empowerment and self-defense against the perceived forces of change. For Dogondoutchi women who struggle to reinvent themselves in light of both the temptations of the consumer market and newly emerging discourses on marriage and morality, the creative appropriation of globally circulating emblems of domesticity highlights the resiliency of time-honored local forms of productivity and sociality. It also reminds us that in Niger, as elsewhere in the Muslim world, modernity does not solely or necessarily come from the West.[2] Abu-Lughod (1998b), Bernal (1997), and Cooper (2001) have already shown for urban Egypt, northern Sudan, and Hausaphone Niger, respectively, that Islam has become a crucial source of modernity for members of the Muslim diaspora. By proudly reasserting their rootedness in a resilient economy of female-centered practices, Mawri mothers and daughters thus learn to juggle selectively with two competing paradigms of modernity—one Western, the other Islamic—and to profit from, and not fall prey to, their powers.

Although women's grievances have focused largely on the *sadaki*, bridewealth payment is only one of several transactions that take place before the bride actually enters her husband's home, and these gifts and counter-gifts also have been subject to inflation and cost reform. Note also that mothers do not directly receive the *sadaki* money, which is transferred from one of the groom's senior male agnates to one of the bride's senior male agnates. The resources they can count on to acquire *kayan 'daki* (things for the room) for their daughters are therefore based on the numerous and multidirectional marriage transactions that occur, one of which is centered on the *sadaki*. This means that although current struggles over the term of marriage transactions may ostensibly focus on the size of the *sadaki*, one should recognize that other transactions that are part of the marriage process have been similarly affected by local and wider efforts to limit (or expand) wedding expenditures. It could be said that references to *sadaki* in local discourse (especially in Izala sermons) function as a shorthand for an array of marriage transactions, from the *kyauta* (gift) that initiates the marriage process to the concluding *valise* (a set of tailored outfits together with shoes, lotions, perfume, and jewelry that the groom gives to the bride). When women complain of low *sadaki*, they are implicitly alluding to a wider set of gift prestations, the value of which goes up and down in tandem with the bridewealth.

The Contest over *Sadaki* in Islamic Discourse

Although debates about increasing bridewealth and wedding expenses have lately acquired unprecedented prominence, the concerns they betray are far from new. The high cost of weddings, in fact, was already a matter of intense interest in the colonial period. Later, the first postcolonial regime attempted unsuccessfully to regulate the matrimonial economy but with little success. In 1975 President Seyni Kountché, troubled by the moral climate resulting from the spiraling inflation of bridewealth, made the following remarks to the women of Niamey:

> Faced with this social and moral chaos, the CMS (Conseil Militaire de Sécurité) has decided—I am confirming it—that, from now on, we will not tolerate any wedding celebrated with ostentation and extravagance. Wedding expenses cannot exceed 50,000 CFA francs; noisy bridal processions spilling out of the town hall with fake veils and a nouveau-riche look are strictly forbidden. Equally forbidden—I am declaring today—are the one hundred roasts that have surfaced out of who knows which gluttonous tradition. [Forbidden] as well are the collections of outfits for the bride conspicuously exhibited throughout the city's streets and the loud and pretentious baptisms.[3]

In an attempt to curb the moral and material excesses of the previous government, Kountché actively promoted discipline, restraint, and frugality at work, at home, and in public. He did not mention religion in his speech to Nigérien women. Nevertheless, Islam would become a building block of this new order, where ostentatious displays and consumption of wealth ideally had no place. Most remarkable about the formal presidential announcement is that it was addressed exclusively to women. Women, Niger's head of state implied, controlled the means and modes of wealth expenditure associated with wedding celebrations and were therefore responsible for their excesses. Women must therefore be the targets of campaigns aimed at ridding Nigérien society of "gluttonous traditions" and "moral chaos." As has been convincingly demonstrated in a growing body of literature on gender in Africa (Allman 2001; Hodgson and McCurdy 2001; Hunt 1991; Vaughan 1991), often women ultimately are identified as the "problem" when far-reaching changes in economic relations are translated as moral crises and described in terms of chaos, degeneration, and disease. Apparently Nigérien society is no exception in this respect.

Some twenty years after Kountché's denunciatory speech, in a strikingly similar fashion 'yan Izala generated considerable interest as well as resentment among Nigériens for loudly condemning the ostentatious redistributive practices that integrated local communities through complex and enduring socioeconomic networks. Among other demands, Izala reformists insisted that bridewealth payments should be limited to a token sum that most men would be able to accrue fairly rapidly. They also encouraged women to spend wisely and conservatively when acquiring the *kayan 'daki* that mothers traditionally invested in to ensure their daughters' prestige and well-being (see Cooper 1997a; Nicolas 1986; Pittin 1979). As noted earlier, 'yan Izala's condemnation of excessive materialism and pleas for frugality were perceived by many Dogondoutchi residents as intrusive attacks against legitimate and long-standing local traditions through which individuals continually affirmed their social worth. While the assertive individualism of Izala angered those who perceived it as a threat to society and family, it nevertheless provided many youths with a publicly sanctioned way to avoid the costly social obligations (bridewealth, gifts to patrons or clerics, birth celebration expenses, etc.) that often exceeded their meager incomes.

Taking advantage of the moral panic sparked by Westernization, the development of public education, the flood of commodities onto local markets, and the dispersal of family and community through migrancy, Izala preachers boldly challenged the authority of the state and of Muslim elites. This challenge attracted a great number of people frustrated by the failure of the government and local authorities to deal with their problems. At a time of intense parental preoccupation with the slackening of social control, the disintegration of family ties, and the spread of "immorality" among unmarried youths, the Izala message about reducing bridewealth payments resonated with earlier visions of a pristine moral order unsoiled by modernity and secularization. By insisting that bridewealth should be paid with 10,000 CFA francs ($20) rather than the customary 200,000 CFA francs, Izala leaders technically enabled young men to marry quickly. More important, perhaps, low bridewealth enhanced the ability of *budurwoyi* (unmarried girls) to marry, thereby preventing the dreaded possibility that they could "spoil" before acquiring a husband.[4]

Some mothers complied with the reformists' recommendation and re-duced the expenses they incurred to acquire their daughters' *kayan 'daki*. The large majority, however, responded to the Izala campaign for a more frugal and moral society by ever more openly flaunting their daughters' wealth at wedding ceremonies. Although senior women's preoccupation with young girls' sexuality betrays a growing concern with the loose moral standards Izala reformers so aggressively criticize, few mothers are prepared to give up the money and gifts they feel entitled to receive from marriage transactions, which they use to purchase *kayan 'daki*, for the sake of their daughters' virtue. Respectability, then, to some women, means reducing one's expenses, whereas to others it means flaunting one's wealth. Mothers' divergent attitudes to-ward the *sadaki* controversy thus reveals a substantial division within the fe-male community at a time when religious identity has become ever more central to the ways in which Mawri women constitute themselves as "respect-able" persons.

The Changing Content and Value of Bridewealth

C. Piault (1963), M. Piault (1978), and Cooper (1997a) have noted how the terms and content of marriage prestations in Hausa-speaking communi-ties have changed dramatically in the last century and, with it, the meaning of marriage, as new kinds of material goods and new modes of producing wealth emerged in tandem with the commoditization of services, land, and labor. In precolonial times, bridewealth payments amounted to more than 1,500 cowries (Piault 1978:422). The *kyauta* (gift), which initiated the period of betrothal and enabled the *sai hita wuri* (wait until the harvest)—when beans would be sold to pay the *sadaki*—was a negligible sum. By the 1930s in Dogondoutchi the *sadaki* varied according to the wealth and status of the groom's family, but it generally consisted of two heifers, an ox, and 115 francs[5] (République du Niger 1936). In the mid-1970s the *kyauta arme* (wed-ding gift) had risen to 2,500 CFA ($10) francs in Dogondoutchi and, despite the cap of 20,000 CFA ($80) francs instituted by the government, bride-wealth usually amounted to a considerable sum (Piault 1978:422). Piault re-calls that a young office clerk who could not rely on his kin for support was asked to pay 75,000 CFA francs as *sadaki*: this was an extravagant sum in those days, all the more so given that neither he nor his future in-laws could boast wealth or claim membership in a chiefly lineage (ibid.:422). In the early 1980s it was not unusual for families to pay a bridewealth of 60,000 or 70,000 CFA francs, and the *kyauta* itself could reach 45,000 CFA francs. In the 1990s the *sadaki* was officially set at 120,000 CFA francs if the bride had never married before and technically was a virgin (*budurwa*). Childless women who were married once before commanded a *sadaki* of 50,000 CFA francs, and those who married for a second time and had given birth expected their future husbands to pay 30,000 CFA francs. At a time when unskilled laborers could rarely hope to make more than 30,000 CFA francs a month, earning the cash necessary to pay bridewealth for a *budurwa* (unmarried girl) was quite challenging, especially when Dogondoutchi mothers, mindless of the Izala message, decided the marriage would not be "tied" unless their financial expectations were met.

In addition to paying *sadaki*, the groom has to provide an array of gifts for the bride's family. In the past, these gifts were part of an elaborate and complex exchange that was crucial to solidifying the couple's marriage, which was defined less in terms of husband-wife relations and more by the linkages established between their respective kin through marriage transactions. Successful marriage transactions still hinge primarily on the groom's ability to secure the support and patronage of numerous kin and friends who, through their *gudummawa* (assistance in the form of gifts), help meet the demands of the bride's family. However, the mobilization of these social networks has become harder to achieve. Young men can no longer routinely call upon their families to meet the many demands of their future in-laws. They are often expected to leave their father's compound and set up their own households when they marry—an impossibility for many of them given the rising price of land parcels in Dogondoutchi in the past decade.

Thanks to generational divisions, increasing individuation, and economic privatization, Mawri men are now free to choose their own brides, but they are less able to depend on shared family resources for procuring the cash and goods they need to fulfill their numerous and onerous obligations (de Latour Dejean 1980). The problem with marriage, as young men see it, is therefore not simply that financial obligations have multiplied and grown more burdensome, thus slowing down the processes culminating in the "tying" ceremony. It also hinges on the erosion of the complex web of relationships—traditionally forged through reciprocal wedding gifts—that enabled a marriage to occur in the first place. Amid dwindling economic opportunities, increasing land shortages, and the loosening of social ties, Islamic campaigns against immorality and profligacy have found eager support among a number of residents for whom reforms in wealth management provide a welcome solution to the exigencies of modern life.

Kayan Aiki: Female Images of Industriousness and Fertility

As men struggle to meet their financial obligations at marriage, women scramble to assemble the *kayan 'daki* (things for the room) their daughters will use to carefully decorate their new homes. They invest considerable time, labor, and resources to acquire impressive arrays of household goods that will ensure the stable beginnings of married life for young couples.[6] Not so long ago, a mother's steady labor—spinning cotton or growing groundnuts—allowed her to accumulate the cash needed to acquire the gifts her daughter would one day proudly exhibit in her home. A significant portion of the goods were further obtained through social networks she carefully nurtured by attending and contributing to other wedding and birth celebrations. Reciprocal gift giving was key to the way that women built wealth for their soon-to-be-married daughters. Old women I interviewed recalled that once the marriage had been "tied" and the wedding celebration was over, the bride would then leave her parent's compound with her *kayan 'daki.*

Piault (1978:427), in his account of marriage in Mawri society, similarly notes that when the young woman departed for the marital compound, she would take with her "all the necessary cooking utensils" that her mother gave her. Malka, a sixty-some-year-old widow described the wedding gifts she received:

> When I married, 2,000 francs were paid for *ku'din arme* [bridewealth] and 1,500 francs were paid for the *kyauta* [gift]. Cloth was brought; there can't be a wedding without cloth, you see. Calabashes and cooking pots were brought, as well as a *talla* [leather bags to draw water from the well]. How can you bring a bride to her husband without her *kayan aiki* [work things]? It is the mother of the bride who buys everything she [her daughter] needs. I did not get a bed, but I brought a *kujera mata* [women's low wooden stool]. I also brought a pestle, and my husband brought the mortar.

Most striking in Malka's description of the gifts she received in the early 1950s is the emphasis on "work things." In contrast to the *kayan 'daki* which brides receive today primarily to adorn their rooms, Malka stressed that a bride entered her marital home with not so much decorative but practical items—utensils she would use daily to perform the requisite household chores: pounding the grain, cooking millet flour, preparing sauces, drawing water from the well, and so on. From this perspective, the little stool she mentions was not merely furniture designed to "look good" and be admired by visitors. Instead, it was a functional item that she could sit on as she cooked food or braided another woman's hair.

"Work things" evoked images of industrious domesticity but, like the ubiquitous mortar and pestle, some had further symbolic resonances. Together they represented the fruitful unity of and complementarity between male and female principles, providing the basis for local conceptions of the universe and its reproduction (Last 1979; Nicolas 1975). In Malka's youth Mawri brides brought the pestle, and their new spouses provided the mortar. The vision of the pestle and the mortar had potent sexual implications during the wedding, but thereafter, in the daily act of pounding, the woman symbolically reenacted the fecund union of complementary elements (mortar/womb; pestle/penis) so crucial to the viability of marriages and the vitality of society because of what it produced (food/child). Today the mortar and pestle are purchased together at the market, which has only faintly weakened their association with sex and reproduction.[7] Calabashes, too, evoke fertility and the life cycle. Grown, collected, and carved by women, they were treated in the past not only as utensils but also as objects of decoration which housewives proudly exhibited in carefully assembled rows. Because they visually resembled the ridges on a farm and the multiple rows of harvested grains—both images of agricultural fecundity—the high columns of stacked calabashes "bespoke," Cooper suggests, "of future fertility and wealth earned through the work of creating and nurturing social ties" (1997a:95).

At another level, calabashes call to mind images of fecundity and reproduction through their common association with the womb. Unadorned calabashes often feature in ceremonies to promote the fertility of afflicted individuals. Thus, before twin sisters can marry, they must break a calabash into two pieces to liberate the fertile potential that was locked in their problematic "oneness." Only by breaking the womb of twinship can they be reborn as single and separate beings, each with her own womb (Masquelier 2001a). As womb-like products of the land and through their various stages of growth and decay, calabashes graphically reproduce critical stages of the human life cycle—in this case, processes of production and reproduction.

The colorful hand-woven cotton blankets women received during their weddings also evoked fertility and reproduction. They were, and still are in some households, displayed prominently on the walls of the women's rooms at the birth of a new child to celebrate a mother's fertility. The very manufacture of these *sakala* (blankets) metaphorically reenacted the process through which the social fabric is woven. The basket and the spindle, both used to spin cotton, symbolized, respectively, the male and female genitals in their productive coupling (Darrah 1980:125). In Mawri society, women spun and men wove (and also dyed cotton thread) (Masquelier 1996). Husbands provided women with the raw material for spinning cotton after which the thread would be sold or brought to a weaver and then a dyer before being worn. Thus the cloth she wore concretely "tied" a wife to her husband. The rise of the market economy, which made imported cloth readily available during the colonial period, progressively led to the demise of local cotton production (Cooper 1997a), but the act of tying clothing still bears conjugal associations. The verb *'darme* (to tie), which describes the action of putting one's clothes on, also refers to the process of contracting a marriage (*'darmen arme*, "tying of the marriage"). This is why, as Malka put it, "there can't be a wedding without cloth." When the bride was sent to her new husband's home with her *kayan aiki*, the display of these images of fertility and reproduction in the streets of Dogondoutchi further underscored the sexual symbolism of the wedding ceremony.

Mothers' Work: Reconfiguring Wealth and Worth

In their respective descriptions of the marriage ceremony in Mawri society, neither C. Piault nor M. Piault mentioned the festive and colorful parades through which brides publicly display their *kayan 'daki* as they are ushered to their new homes. This silence over what I found in the late 1980s to be a conspicuous part of the wedding celebration suggests that, prior to the late 1960s or 1970s, bringing the *kayan 'daki* to the bride's marital compound was not so elaborate as it has now become. Although brides obviously derived significant prestige from the pots, bowls, and calabashes that promoted their productive and reproductive capacities and effectively launched them into the world of marriage and motherhood, the public act of bearing *kaya* (things) was unremarkable enough to escape two anthropologists' scrutiny in the early 1960s. In contrast, contemporary public displays of *kayan 'daki* are one of the most visually stunning dimensions of the marriage process through which women actively contribute to their self-actualization. Once the "tying" ceremony and the *semaine* (three-day wedding celebration sponsored by the groom's friends) are over, the bride's mother assembles in her compound all the *kayan 'daki* she has acquired, including the bed, mattress, and other furnishings.

After a close and drawn-out inspection that allows everyone in the neighborhood to check the quality and quantity of the goods, female kin and friends each hoist a bundle of gifts on their heads and proceed in a loud and boisterous column toward the bride's marital compound. Known as *kan kaya* (carrying the things), the joyful procession of ululating women bearing cala-

Figure 6.1. Women participating in a *kan kaya* (carrying the things) during a marriage celebration.

bashes, cloth, and cooking implements convey an image of "head-borne wealth" that is essential to the prestige women earn as brides, as Cooper (1997a:94) points out. Meanwhile, the bride hides under a heavy woven blanket and—together with a similarly veiled friend acting as a "decoy"—reaches her husband's house inconspicuously protected from the potentially deadly glare of jealous onlookers. Her own invisibility during the *kan kaya*, however, enhances the importance of her "things," while these, in turn, promote her and her mother's worth by providing a concrete measure of their productive abilities and social network. Once they have been paraded in the streets all the way to their final destination, the goods belong to the bride and, as movable property, are hers to keep should the union end in divorce.[8]

The *kan kaya* has gained increasing prominence partly because the content and value of the gifts themselves have shifted in the last half-century with the changing economy, the weakening of social ties, and the impact of mobility, migration, and consumer goods. As imported goods flooded local markets and wealth became increasingly derived from access to cash rather than land, the calabashes women decorated have been largely replaced by enameled metal pots of varying sizes and shapes. Mass-produced wall hangings with images of Mecca or of horses or kittens playing with their mothers outnumber the locally woven *sakala* (blankets),[9] and wooden utensils have given way to metal spoons, porcelain teapots, and Pyrex cups made in China. Brides are still sent to their new homes with peanut oil, grain, onions, and salt—a reminder, perhaps, of the organic basis of traditional forms of wealth in a region still dominated by farming—but the prominent gifts a young woman receives today are neither handmade nor produced locally. Wealth and prestige are increasingly articulated in the language of money, modernity, and cosmopolitanism. The fashionable outfits migrant laborers bring back from Abidjan or Cotonou, the video cassette recorders (and, more recently, the DVD players) that pilgrims buy in Mecca, and the shoes or watches that traders smuggle from Nigeria have firmly inserted Mawri people in the global economy. The best and priciest wax cloth is referred to as "Java," a term that enhances the appeal of the fabric by designating it as "foreign." Similarly, I suggest, it is no coincidence that the elaborate metal beds so prized by housewives in the 1980s and 1990s were known as *gadon Kano* (bed from Kano). Rather than evoking fertility, actualizing ties to the land, or reflecting their makers' skills as they once did, wedding gifts now display a different kind of value, linked to the complex translocal circuits of migrancy, marketing, and smuggling through which Mawri people acquire, exchange, and consume mass-produced goods of all sorts.

Because they can no longer count on the support of extensive social networks, groundnuts, or spun cotton to generate the resources needed for their daughters' *kayan 'daki,* women have responded to this economic challenge by actively reforming the use to which the *sadaki* and other marriage payments are put. In the past a large portion of the money was redistributed among the bride's kin—in compensation for their contribution to the collection of *kayan 'daki*—as well as the various individuals who assisted the two families through the various stages of marriage transactions. Today the *uban arme* (literally, "father of the marriage"; a senior agnate who oversees the marriage transactions), the two women who wash the bride with henna, and the siblings of the bride's parents receive a small gift of money from the groom, but the bulk of the marriage payment automatically becomes the property of the bride's mother, who, in turn, is solely responsible for equipping her daughter with the latest indispensable commodity—a bed made of pressed wood covered with laminate (a *pernika*) with adjoining shelves and drawers for displaying knick-knacks and storing clothes. In addition to the mattress, sheets, pillows, and coverlet that she must purchase to set her daughter up, the bride's

Figure 6.2. Wall hangings, posters, and metal trays hanging in a woman's room.

mother is sometimes pressured by her daughter to buy a matching laminated armoire and vanity chest for storing the young woman's ample collection of metal bowls, plastic containers, and Pyrex dishes in neat vertical rows. Two decades or so ago, a must for any self-respecting bride was the *mai rumfa* bed, a canopy metal bed with innumerable mirrors and alarm clocks. It was so indispensable to the wedding, Fala Habi Aboubacar (1988) notes, that its absence could mean postponing the ceremony.

Like the bowls, blankets, and calabashes that are conspicuously paraded through town to convey prosperity and confer value, the imposing bed acquired nowadays by the bride's mother will be carried through the streets for all to see. When beds were simple wooden structures (or consisted of assembled metal parts), a maternal cousin of the bride was traditionally assigned to haul the bulky wooden structure or metal headboard and footboard to the bride's new home. If the bed had been purchased by the father instead of the mother, a paternal cousin of the bride would carry it on his head. The sheet or hand-woven blanket he used to cushion his head during transport was his to keep after the wedding. Today women noisily parade with head-borne calabashes

Figure 6.3. Armoire and bed in a woman's room.

overflowing with grain or with bundles of enamel bowls tied in checkered cloth, but because the bed is massive and heavy, it arrives on a truck or, more rarely, by donkey cart. Before returning home, each participant in the *kan kaya* is rewarded by the groom with a *tukuici* (token of appreciation to the bearer of a gift) of 1,000 or 1,500 CFA francs ($4 or $6).

Because it so visibly exhibits a mother's wealth as well as her capacity to produce that wealth, the *kan kaya* must dazzle onlookers with the sheer quantity of items displayed, and so the more items, the better. As Cooper (1997a:95; see also M. F. Smith 1955) notes, profusion and repetition, not the originality of each piece, are key in that they create an image of *arziki*, prosperity. Failure to express satisfactorily one's (and one's daughter's) worth is worse than no *kayan 'daki* at all, because it lodges permanently in the social memory to mark a woman's reputation. It is not uncommon, therefore, for mothers with no available cash and limited means of raising funds at the time

Figure 6.4. Decorative objects
in a woman's glass-front
armoire.

of their daughter's wedding to postpone the *kan kaya* altogether for two or
three years until they can adequately impress the community with a belated
but still sufficient display of wealth.

So crucial is this ceremony that publicly demonstrates a mother's productivity and value that when a father negotiates a "marriage of alms" (*armen
sadaka*) for his daughter,[10] it is understood in Dogondoutchi that he must re-
imburse his own wife for the loss of *sadaki*. Women do not generally oppose
their husbands' plans to give their daughters "for nothing" provided that they
receive from their husbands the cash they need to acquire the bride's bed and
mattress. In addition, a father should give his wife a *kyauta arme* of 40,000 or
50,000 CFA francs so that, as one woman explained, "she can start the work
of acquiring bowls for her daughter." It is good to display piety, in one woman's view, because it might ensure entry into paradise. But even *lada* (divine

191

Figure 6.5. Laminated bed with shelves and compartments filled with bowls, cups, and other items.

reward) should not come at the expense of one's earthly honor. For the majority of local women who cannot count on a salaried kin or a profitable business to provide easy access to cash, a large portion of the *sadaki* they now receive when a daughter marries has become an inalienable right that they are unwilling to sacrifice even for the assurance of eternal salvation. For some, this further translates as a right to dispose of the money for whatever use they see fit. As a mother of eight bluntly put it: "You know, the wife of that prophet Boubacar [*sic*] who returned the *sadaki* to her husband, she was a fool. Me, I would have kept the money and started a trading business." In this mother's eyes, bridewealth, once it was paid, became a woman's property regardless of the circumstances, even in extreme cases when it did not ultimately serve to purchase items for the bride's room.

A Bed for Hadiza

I noted at the start of this chapter that Mawri women's struggles to be valued are played out in the controversial arena of marriage, where their understanding of wealth, prestige, and social capital often clashes with more

Figure 6.6. Glass-front
armoire filled with bowls.

conservative ideologies of gender, family, and society. The following conversation between a young migrant and a senior woman illustrates how women
carve out spaces of self-determination in a society that militates increasingly
against them despite the recent liberalization of national politics and the
concomitant proliferation of religious discourses.

"So, where is the bridewealth you are going to bring so I can buy Hadiza
the fine bed she wants for her wedding?" Bebe asked Boubacar in a provocative tone. Tired of finding Boubacar hanging around her daughter, my friend
Bebe was demanding that he start seriously thinking about *sadaki*. It was
April 2000, and everyone in town was hoping that the coming rainy season
would offset the catastrophic losses of the previous year. Upon returning to
Dogondoutchi after a three-year absence, Boubacar had learned that his wife
had divorced him because he hadn't sent her money from abroad. He was
now courting Bebe's oldest daughter, Hadiza, hoping that she would consider

193

Figure 6.7. Armoire and vanity filled with bowls and other decorative objects.

marrying him. Hadiza had recently divorced her husband because he could not provide for her and their young daughter.[11]

"Women, that's all you think about, things you can show off to your friends," Boubacar responded warily.

"But you know Hadiza will not consider you otherwise. She already has a suitor," Bebe teased, "a rich *commerçant,* who brings her gifts every Friday [market day in Dogondoutchi]."

"Even if she got a bed worth one million CFA francs, would it ensure that she is happy with her husband and that the marriage will last?" an exasperated Boubacar retorted.

"No, of course not," Bebe said.

"Well, there," Boubacar countered. "So why always think about the bed? There are more important things in marriage."

"Yes," Bebe responded. "But Boubacar, listen! What is going to happen if your wife comes to your house with a *karaga* [wooden bed]? Aren't all her friends going to make fun of her? You, yourself, will feel shame for your wife."[12]

"Of course," Boubacar reluctantly agreed. "I wouldn't let her come home with a wooden bed. But there's a difference between a *gadon kara* [bed made of millet stalk] and a 100,000 CFA franc bed! One must be reasonable and not live above one's means."

Burdened by the need to take care of her daughter as any respectable mother would, Bebe refused to entertain Boubacar's plea for moderation on the matter of wedding expenses. Despite the financial difficulties she faced since her husband had gone "mad" and been unable to earn a regular income in the early 1990s, she felt that her reputation would suffer if she did not send her daughter off with an impressive array of *kayan 'daki* when the young woman remarried.

Bebe's attitude toward wedding gifts illustrates a widespread female concern with changing definitions of marriage, sexuality, and respectability. On several occasions my friend had confided her worries about her daughters' dissipated lifestyles and her frustrations at not being able to curtail their freedom. She was anxious to marry them off. She knew that times had changed and that modern girls now freely hung out with their boyfriends before settling into married life. Yet, like other Nigérien mothers forced to acknowledge the rise of premarital sexual encounters and the proliferation of unwed mothers, Bebe lent a deaf ear to the exhortations of Izala preachers promoting the virtues of low bridewealth. While she grappled with the sexuality of her unwed daughters and concurred with her peers that illegitimate pregnancies brought nothing but shame upon families, she was not ready to concede that doing away with customary bridewealth arrangements and ostentatious *kan kaya* would solve the "problem" of marriage and help young girls achieve matrimonial respectability. It was precisely the transfer of *sadaki* and the performance of *kan kaya* that conferred value on the bride and her mother, which, in Bebe's view, was essential to the production of female respectability.

Boubacar's belief that Bebe was far too interested in Hadiza's material comfort and was obsessed with beds and other pricey items may have stemmed from a bad experience in his previous marriage. After paying the *sadaki*, sponsoring the *semaine* (three-day wedding celebration), and giving his new wife an impressive *valise* (a supplemental gift of clothes, shoes, soap, perfume, and jewelry) to demonstrate his generous intentions, his in-laws had insisted that he bring additional gifts of cash to several individuals not traditionally designated as recipients of the groom's largesse. Hoping to generate goodwill, he had acquiesced to their demands. Despite his efforts to satisfy his in-laws' expectations and provide, at least initially, for his young bride, he was now without a wife. He wanted to remarry and was attracted to Hadiza, but he had no intention of handing over to his future mother-in-law the equivalent of several months' wages so she could buy a bed too bulky even to fit into what would be his new wife's quarters in the family compound. In the end, while everyone speculated whether she would marry the young Izala trader who brought her gifts every week, Hadiza married a bush taxi driver. A couple of months after my departure, Bebe wrote me a letter expressing her disappointment at her daughter's choice of husband. Even though the Izala merchant already had a wife, she had approved of him because he was kind and patient, worked hard, and had honorable intentions. He was an active member of the Izala association but displayed none of its followers' proverbial parsimony: he regularly brought gifts to all Bebe's children and showered Hadiza with expensive clothes and jewelry for nine months in an effort to win her heart.

After Hadiza announced her imminent wedding, Bebe worked feverishly to earn the money needed to purchase the wedding gifts. For almost a year she participated in an *adashi* (rotating credit association) to save enough money for Hadiza's mattress. In addition to the salary she earned by assisting me with my research, she was slowly earning money through petty trade. As a secluded wife, she relied on her younger daughters to buy condiments and vegetables in rural markets that she would later resell at a profit in Dogondoutchi. Despite her multiple income-earning strategies, she could not save money fast enough. With her husband out of work and the family field in the hands of an unscrupulous brother-in-law, her regular resources were already stretched to the limit. On good days Bebe earned enough cash by braiding women's hair or having her daughters hawk food door to door to buy a new ladle or a pair of flip-flops for one of her eight children. On other days, however, she had to scrimp to feed her large family. Only weeks before, some of this hard-earned cash had gone to fix the family's crumbling thatched house that threatened to fall apart even further with the coming rains. Despite these obstacles, Hadiza eventually left her parents' home with the assortment of bowls, the new laminated bed, and the mattress her mother managed to purchase. In her frenzied *neman ku'di* (search for money), Bebe tapped into all her cash reserves and exhausted every available resource. Hadiza even took the family's only pair of sheets, which I had given her mother as a parting gift. Bebe's honor was safe.

The Bed of Marriage and the Mother-Daughter Bond

Originally mother and daughter had disagreed on the kind of bed they would purchase: Bebe felt that 50,000 CFA francs would buy a very nice bed, but Hadiza had her sights set on a bed twice as expensive. Despite their differences, both knew long before Hadiza had chosen a husband that the young woman would eventually own a fine looking *gado* (bed) designed to elicit the admiration of her female visitors. Bebe, like many of her peers, was determined not to let her own poverty limit the reputation she was carving out for herself as mother of the bride. Senior women's preoccupation with *kan kaya* tells us much about Mawri mothers' attempts to define themselves as creators of value and about the bonds they form with their daughters. Women's worth, as already noted, is inscribed publicly through the performance of *kan kaya* which testifies to their capacity to assemble wealth (see Cooper 1997a). By amassing items that their daughters will then store in their own room, women forge intergenerational female bonds that compensate for their transient status in a society where marriage is virilocal. Moreover, the wealth a young wife stores in her room in the form of beds and bowls may one day be used to acquire the items for the room her own daughter will expect to bring to her marital home. Thus, despite changing tastes and fashions, *kayan 'daki* may literally and figuratively tie generations together. When members of Izala started forbidding high bridewealth and the ostentatious display of *kayan 'daki,* they effectively prevented women from symbolically expressing the bride's wealth and the mother's productive capacities, thereby negating senior women's social contributions and revoking their status as providers.

By discouraging traditional forms of *kan kaya, 'yan* Izala are also disrupting the mother-daughter bond that women work so assiduously to create through gift giving. The *kan kaya* loudly and colorfully concretizes the lasting connection between a mother and her daughter through the physical link that the long parade of head-borne *kaya* (things) creates between the bride's parental compound and her new marital home. In articulating, through a graphic trail of moving things, both the departure of the transient daughter and her attachment to her mother, the *kan kaya* weaves together two places through what de Certeau (1984:99) terms "pedestrian enunciation." When they complain that Izala marriage reforms are foolish and absurd, women who decry the ban on costly weddings are also indirectly lamenting the erasure of the mother-daughter connection so vividly inscribed through the "rhetoric of walking" (de Certeau 1984:100) implicit in the *kan kaya*.[13] 'Yan Izala are notorious for rushing events and insisting that the bride be brought to the groom's home five days after the marriage has been "tied." Such a short interval leaves little time for the bride's mother to acquire the *kayan 'daki* once the bridewealth has been paid. "What kind of work can a mother do in five days?" Maimouna, a savvy trader and mother of six, once asked rhetorically to underscore the lengthy and painstaking labor of women who, I was often told, traditionally started "working" for their daughters long before the latter reached the age of marriage. Aside from cheating her of the wealth and the time she requires to properly fulfill her responsibilities as provider, Izala marriage practices also render the bride's mother invisible, literally: in Izala households the *kan kaya* typically occurs at night, when no one can watch and assess how many gifts the bride has received. Ostentation then becomes irrelevant, because one's worth is expressed through frugality and piety rather than through images of *arziki*. It is precisely this invisibility that women are resisting when, in total defiance of Izala rules, they loudly parade through the streets of Dogondoutchi at midday bearing *kayan 'daki* on their heads.

Of Beds and Other Modern Things: Making Value and Marking Difference

To my question about the wedding gifts a young girl would receive upon marrying an Izala devotee, my neighbor Rakiya answered succinctly, "What can you buy with 30,000 CFA francs? Not even a good mattress." Rakiya's response, like other complaints I heard about "unaffordable" wedding gifts, must be understood in terms of both the material and symbolic losses senior women experience when they can no longer be publicly honored for their wealth-producing capacities. It is as much the absence of social capital as the lack of material wealth that women decry when they criticize the stinginess of 'yan Izala and complain about the transformations affecting marriage. While many of them agree implicitly with reformist Muslims that an early marriage is the most effective prevention against the shame of single motherhood, they still actively resist Izala's calls to facilitate weddings by doing away with burdensome expenditures. Besides openly manifesting their disapproval by simply declining low bridewealth offers, women further resist their gradual exclusion from the matrimonial economy by feverishly working to equip their daughters with *kayan 'daki* whose value resides not in their practical utility or in their evocations of fertility—as they once did—so much as in their association with national and transnational circuits of wealth and information.

When wealth in the form of possessions is held as the last bastion against the marginalizing impact of an increasingly male-centered economy, ensuring a daughter's well-being means acquiring household furnishings whose comfort and characteristics owe more to Western ideas of a bourgeois lifestyle than to an Islamic vision of frugal domesticity.[14] Besides the fact that beds, armoires, night tables, and vanity chests remain items of prestige in households where, until a few decades ago, mats and women's stools were the essential furnishings, their value further resides in their exchangeability; for example, during hard times a woman may sell some of her furnishings to obtain cash for food or medicine (Schildkrout 1982). As shameful as it might be, selling one's *kayan 'daki* is sometimes the only option for women whose access to scarce resources is becoming increasingly challenged by the worsening of the Nigérien economy and the normalization of Islamic values. Bebe herself was forced to sell her bed when her husband fell sick and lost his job at the car park. Her insistence that Hadiza be provided with a costly bed before settling into a new marriage must perhaps be seen against the backdrop of her own history of poverty and deprivation. From this perspective, that Hadiza's bed was worth at least 50,000 CFA francs was not simply a form of insurance against hard times. It also served to actualize Bebe's personal victory against adversity: having lost her own bed in a desperate struggle for economic survival, she could now buy it back, so to speak, and use her daughter's *kan kaya* to ensure that many people would witness her triumphant display of *arziki* (prosperity). Hadiza's marriage thus afforded her a unique opportunity to transcend the crippling limitations of poverty and dependency: it enabled her to re-create herself in the image of a young prosperous bride—her daughter—and polish her own image as an industrious and resourceful mother who could afford to marry off her daughter in lavish style.

In demonstrating how women have fought Islam and the state's efforts "to 'moralize' the matrimonial economy" (de Latour 1992:71), thus far I have focused on the roles, activities, and preoccupations of senior women. Even if they do not speak with a unified voice, many senior women agree that women should control the terms of marriage, especially the management of wealth, because, in so doing, they preserve a space for self-determination. Young women who contemplate marriage and dream of prosperous homes have their own concerns and aspirations that do not always accord with those of their elders. An examination of the frustrations and ambitions of this group of women reveals another dimension of the complex value-making process associated with the current consumption of laminated beds. During my visit to Dogondoutchi in 2000 and 2004, the perceived shortage of still unmarried, educated civil servants was a routine subject of conversation among schoolgirls and young school leavers eager to escape their mother's rustic lifestyle and embrace bourgeois values. Mindful that many of them "offered" themselves to professional men in the hope of securing marriage,[15] Muslim preachers regularly admonished parents to keep their daughters "at home" and advised young women to lower their matrimonial expectations and marry hardworking and honorable farmers.

Although very few young women married educated men whose salaries allowed them to fully indulge in the comforts of bourgeois domesticity, owning a modern bed covered with laminate (or wood adorned with hand-painted floral designs) was on the mind of many future brides. Besides coming with their own display shelves, these new beds are coveted precisely because they differ so starkly from the metal canopy beds women brought to their marital homes a generation ago. By insisting on laminated or hand-painted plywood beds, young women are distinguishing themselves from their mothers and creating the generational differences that enable them to establish their own spaces of agency as they settle into matrimony. In contemporary Mawri society, wedding beds are not simply emblematic of consumer culture and bourgeois values. Through their imposing presence, first in the *kan kaya* and then in the marital home, they become objects of female pride and central repositories of value.

Aesthetics and Interiority

In his work on modernity and mass consumption in Trinidad, Miller (1994) describes how hanging curtains, trimming cakes, and doing other decorative tasks associated with Christmas celebrations reassert the physical interiority of the home itself for family members in a manner that changes their relationship to it. In this festive reawakening and celebration of domesticity, Miller suggests, "the physical environment is inseparable from the social values to which it is host" (1994:89). Whether Trinidadians decorate their windows or their cakes, most significant, Miller argues, is that these aesthetic tasks highlight the centrality of the experience of enclosure. Celebrating Christmas, in this context, becomes a means of focusing on what is "inside" from an aesthetic, social, and spatial perspective. Creating (or reasserting) interiority by focusing on physical enclosure is equally important for Mawri women, and it is precisely in the context of birth and wedding celebrations that this concern can be appreciated.

Just as the Trinidadian family "strives towards a sense of quiet solidity" (Miller 1994:101) once new or newly cleaned curtains have been hung days before Christmas, so new Mawri mothers aim to transform their rooms into womb-like enclosures for the naming ceremony of their newborns. By hanging hand-woven, colorful wedding blankets (or mass-produced wall hangings with animal or religious themes) in the room so that all the walls, even the doors and windows, are covered, they create a warm, dark, and comfortable environment where their child can be "reborn" as a named, and therefore fully human, individual, a person. In contrast to the traditional birth of a baby in their mother's natal compound, birth in a hospital, with its impersonal white-walled and brightly lit "public" space (from which mother and baby depart a few days later to return home) has altered the significance of these aesthetic preparations. Despite these transformations, "interiorization" (Miller 1994:217) remains a central concern for mothers who welcome their kin and friends into their homes on the day of the *biki* (birth celebration). By literally reinforcing the boundaries of her room with heavy blankets or wall hangings that prevent dust, breeze, and even light from entering, the new mother constructs an "ideal of intensive sociality" (Miller 1994:216) as well as a space of rootedness in which all, including the newborn child, can belong.

If naming ceremonies provide a compelling example of enclosing practice, they are hardly exceptional. Taking cues from Miller once again, I suggest that the labor-intensive and now increasingly controversial task of "filling up" a home with beds, wall hangings, armoires, and additional *kaya* must be viewed similarly as part of the "centripetal aesthetic" (Miller 1994:144) through which women in Dogondoutchi anchor their sense of family and morality. By working, at times feverishly, to equip their daughters with cumbersome furniture, some barely fitting into the small spaces they are destined to embellish, mothers effectively reassert the dichotomy between "inside" and "outside." Once the bride's room is furnished, it is a potent expression of beauty and prosperity, not simply because of the sheer quantity of *kayan 'daki* but also because, by literally filling up the place until, in some cases, there is hardly room to stand, much less walk around, the conspicuous wedding gifts (and the room itself) reaffirm the sense of interiority so central to women's moral and sexual identities. Because their bodies are perceived as containers, women must strive to preserve their personal integrity and prevent external forces from contaminating them despite their inherent openness (see Masquelier 2001b). Accumulating stuff in one's marital room is thus a step in the process of progressive incorporation through which, as Miller puts it in the Trinidadian context, "the domestic becomes not merely an enclosed space but a kind of centripetal force striving to incorporate as much of the outside world as possible into itself" (1994:101).

Far from being antithetical to the moral values preached by conservative Islam (and enforced through practices such as veiling and seclusion), *kan kaya* and the congested rooms it produces reinforces the notion of enclosure so vital to female productivity and respectability, thereby becoming the very means through which these qualities are given form. Moreover, although the beds that young girls and prospective brides yearn for may be coming from

Figure 6.8. Blankets hanging in a woman's room during her newborn's naming ceremony.

Kano or an equally distant place, in the end they are more than mere symbols of the modern and the foreign. Through their incorporation into the cramped rooms they adorn, they not only bring in the outside world but also become transformed by the context. By saturating the inside space with their solidity and beauty after having been prominently displayed through town, they enable the kind of enclosing and incorporative aesthetic that ultimately reaffirms local ideals of female domesticity. From this perspective, *kan kaya* is not a morally reprehensible practice that should be banned, as *'yan* Izala insist. On the contrary, it acts to visibly insert new brides into the space from which they will derive their identity and respectability as wives, mothers, and mistresses of their homes.

Conclusion: Marriage, Identity, and Agency in Dogondoutchi

Even if the multiple and antagonistic expressions of Islam increasingly focus on women as the instruments of its reforms, Muslim women in Dogondoutchi are not powerless pawns in the ideological battles in which dissenting Muslim factions advance competing visions of gender, domesticity, and social control. Despite the erosion of income-generating strategies that wives traditionally used to secure autonomy and enhance their visibility, women largely appear to be gaining greater control over the terms of marriage and the sources of prestige derived from conspicuous wedding ceremonies. Their efforts to resist marginalization in an increasingly male-centered economy have taken on a more aggressive form since many of them started openly denouncing marriage reforms that threatened to undermine their own networks of wealth and value. Hence, when they criticize the stinginess of Izala grooms, point to the defective quality of certain wedding gifts,[16] or, directly contradicting reformist norms, stage ever more impressive *kan kaya*, mothers and daughters are striving to preserve control over both material wealth and their capacity to generate social capital, affective bonds, and self-identity. More generally, women's active engagement in redefining marriage as a traditional, female-centered process highlights the complex ways in which globalization and belonging work to simultaneously encompass and reject imported forms as they transform them. Put differently, women's participation in the matrimonial economy and their selective appropriation of foreignness is a striking illustration of how globalization, far from simply leading to an erasure of local traditions, is directly implicated in the "production of locality" (Appadurai 1996:178).

When Malam Awal presented himself as a Sufi liberator who could end both the corrupt exactions of Muslim elites who opposed reformist Islam and the egalitarian excesses of Izala leaders, local residents listened attentively to his sermons. Predictably, *sadaki* was one of the contentious issues initially raised by the charismatic leader in his campaign against greed and immorality. Arguing that few girls would marry if their parents persisted in requiring bridewealth payments that no one could afford, Malam Awal convinced many that a small *sadaki* payment was better than none. To implement his matrimonial reforms, he routinely berated women for their acquisitive dispositions and urged them to give up the quest for *kayan 'daki*. Women's materialism, he argued, threatened to contaminate the moral fabric of society and should be severely curbed. In the preacher's view, women's attachment to material possessions was not simply responsible for delayed marriages and the subsequent surge in immorality but also contributed to a loss of spirituality. In a January 1998 sermon in the neighboring village of Bagalou, Awal made it clear that the accoutrements with which women adorned their rooms were dangerous to the spiritual health of society, as they directly interfered with the performance of religious duties:

> Instead of staying home, women go to the market to sell peanut oil. And they
> say to each other on the way to the market: "In this house, there is a bed more
> beautiful than mine; in that house, there are far more beautiful bowls than
> mine." These women, they keep thinking they don't have enough bowls or beds
> and that's why they don't pray, they don't recite *salati* [Sufi prayer] with their
> prayer beads, they don't do *zikiri* [repetitive chanting of God's names].

So convincing was his rhetoric that in just months the Sufi preacher had
supposedly facilitated the marriage of some three hundred young women
from Dogondoutchi and the surrounding region by negotiating for each a
bridewealth payment of 30,000 CFA francs. Urged by their parents to be
"good" Muslims, young girls dutifully complied with Awal's dictate that they
marry early and remain frugal in their domestic acquisitions. Their marriages
became known as an example of *"armen Awal"* (Awal's marriage) in recognition of the preacher's role in the newly configured matrimonial economy.

At first Malam Awal's "progressive" policies seemed to have broken new
ground by convincing a number of senior women that they could require the
groom to pay for the bed and mattress or, alternatively, that the *kayan 'daki*
could be brought after the marriage had been celebrated and the bride sent to
her new home. A few years later, however, it became abundantly clear that
the initial enthusiasm for the preacher's campaign for purity and piety was
fading as women were coming to terms with the social implications of these
marriage reforms. Those who originally had not dared to speak up to their
husbands were finding the courage to resist Malam Awal's marriage initiatives and defend their own interests.[17] I was told that some young women had
threatened to spoil their own wedding ceremonies by refusing to enter their
marital homes if they received a *karaga,* the traditional wooden bed their
grandmothers slept on and which Izala preachers had been promoting as an
alternative to the pricier laminated models. Lately Izala rules governing wedding procedures appear to have progressively relaxed, and marriage celebrations in some Izala households have become more ostentatious. In 2006 I
met several brides whose recent marriages to 'yan Izala had by all accounts
involved extravagant, conspicuous spending in direct violation of the original
Izala directive that wedding expenses be kept to a minimum. Thus, if marriage in Hausaphone communities "has served as a central institutional and
discursive locus for the mediation of change," as Cooper (1997a:xlviii) rightfully notes, it has also provided a fertile terrain for women's self-actualization
as modern brides and respectable mothers.

In considering the growing popularity of laminated beds among Mawri
brides, I have suggested that we reevaluate the conventional assumption

made by anthropologists and reformist leaders that, when women buy wedding gifts for their daughters, they tend to channel their resources into unproductive and impractical investments.[18] Far from being burdensome or useless property, the beds that future brides admire in their friends' homes before eventually acquiring their own have become vital means of creating material wealth, moral capital, and generational identity for women whose social aspirations have been thwarted by the combined effects of economic collapse and religious intolerance. In challenging Muslim reformists' efforts to limit wedding expenditures and the visibility of wedding celebrations, women rarely refer to Islam and the Muslim world. I argue, nonetheless, that their stance against those who wish to curtail their role in the matrimonial economy must be understood as part of a larger debate on Muslim identity and community.

Through their participation in local debates on bridewealth and wedding gift exchanges, Dogondoutchi women have come to understand how the Izala (and later the Awaliyya) vision of moral order has influenced their power and visibility in society. The restrictions they experienced as they struggled to retain respectability and fulfill their social obligations as wives and mothers have compelled many to resist Izala reforms on marriage and assert their roles as contributors to the matrimonial economy. Thus we see that by successfully limiting women's powers of autonomy and self-expression, reformist Islam has also fueled women's discontent with these limitations. Through what Butler (1997) calls the paradox of *subjectivation,* the very structures Izala established for securing women's subordination have become the means through which women can regain control over their lives. In their attempts to reclaim control, women are also actively shaping what it means to be both modern and grounded in the secure interiority of their domestic world.

FASHIONING MUSLIMHOOD: DRESS, MODESTY, AND THE CONSTRUCTION OF THE VIRTUOUS WOMAN

7

The big difference between Izala and *darika* has to do with the protection of women. Izala women must cover their heads with a veil—hide their bodies—so that men cannot see them.
   —*Malam Salissou, Dogondoutchi, 1994*

Those women who wear no headscarves, they will be cursed by angels on Judgment Day.
   —*Aminatou, Dogondoutchi, 1994*

In November 1999 the Second International Festival of African Fashion (FIMA) that was to be held in Niger's capital was the target of unprecedented reformist anger. Weeks earlier, Izala leaders condemned the festival on local radio stations, insisting that the public display of scantily clad women was contrary to Muslim norms of modesty and would "only call down the wrath of God" on Nigérien people. They pressured the government to cancel a show whose purely "Satanic" nature, in their eyes, "further undermined public morality," but local officials ignored their request (Mayer 2000a). On the eve of the festival some fifteen hundred Muslim reformists demonstrated in front of the National Assembly to protest the event. Calling it "a debauchery" and an "incitement to fornication," they threatened to take just and effective steps against FIMA. This then led to violent clashes between protesters and the police who were called on to contain the angry crowd. Protesters soon rioted, destroying any "Satanic" work they encountered. Cars were burned and shops looted (Arji 2000). On the opening day of the festival, an angry crowd of Muslim clerics and students standing outside Niamey's *Grande Mosquée* demanded that the festival not be held. According to one protester, the show was "contrary to Islam, because there are naked women, wearing indecent clothes, parading before invited guests."[1]

Despite the widely publicized threats, FIMA, a creation of Niger-born designer Alphadi, took place.[2] The event by all accounts was a huge success, bringing together some thirty fashion designers from countries ranging from Senegal to Bangladesh to Russia and attracting a large number of tourists from Europe. The designers' stunning sartorial creations were witnessed by more than two thousand people gathered in a tented village protected by a contingent of security forces. Protesters failed to disrupt the fashion show, but riots soon broke out throughout the capital. City streets were blocked with barricades, national lottery kiosks and nightclubs were attacked, and women in short skirts were harassed. The next day the protest spread to Maradi, the country's economic capital and the nucleus of Muslim reformist activity. There clashes between angry crowds and the police turned more violent as hundreds of rioters took to the streets, destroying or looting sites representing sinfulness and moral degradation. The compound of a Protestant mission was ransacked and burned. Betting kiosks, bars, and the homes of prostitutes were set on fire and their occupants severely beaten (Cooper 2006).

Numerous arrests were made in the following days, and seven Islamic associations were eventually banned by the government for "disturb[ing] public order" (Mayer 2000b). For so colorfully exemplifying Samuel Huntington's (1996) "clash of civilizations"—with fashion designers, models, and FIMA organizers standing in for the West and reformist activists symbolizing all that was wrong with "the rest"—Niger briefly garnered international attention. As the "disturbances" surrounding FIMA made the headlines of several European newspapers, protesters were widely denounced as "fundamentalists" who stopped at nothing to insure women's continued subordination. Meanwhile, Prime Minister Hama Amadou was quoted as saying that the peaceful conditions in which FIMA had taken place effectively demonstrated "the government's determination to fight obscurantism."[3]

At some level the incident poignantly illustrates how local efforts to carve out a moral order have routinely focused on the creation of the virtuous woman in contrast to Western models of womanhood perceived as morally degenerate. However, it should not be seen as an indication that reformist Muslims are unconditionally and uniformly against fashion. It is true, of course, that at a time when women's bodies are ever more critical sites of ideological struggles about Islamic morality, the Izala movement has been remarkably successful in enforcing forms of female encompassment and sartorial control deemed essential to the preservation of moral boundaries and chaste selves. In many Mawri households tight-fitting, form-enhancing garments have been abandoned in favor of more modest attires. However, close attention to the specific situations in which modest attire is worn, the various forms this modesty takes, and the diverse meanings attached to it reveals a complex picture of Muslim sartorial trends in which piety is not necessarily antithetical to fashion and modest clothes can have decidedly "chic" implications, especially in contexts where notions of purity and cosmopolitanism are the object of ongoing, at times personalized, redefinitions.

If women's dress has been impacted by the redefinition of modesty in Muslim reformist discourses, it is nonetheless problematic to assume that the concept itself had no prior currency in the region. I argue in this chapter that women's understanding of modesty and their experience of veiling actually antedates the current debates over whether to wear *hijabi* (veil). Partly because they were more embodied than discursive, the practices through which women traditionally displayed Muslimhood have been eclipsed by the more visible presence of the *hijabi*. Although the new head coverings have become important markers of both personal faith and communal affirmation of piety, one must not overlook women's prior efforts to fashion their bodies as "Muslim." Aside from complicating the picture of veiled female bodies as signifiers of the wider moral order, a focus on the diversity of women's sartorial traditions and trends helps trace continuities between past and present practices.

Whether in the colonial imagination, in feminist discourses of various origins, or in the writings of Islamic studies specialists, the veil has borne a heavy semantic load as an icon of Muslim identity. To some, it evokes restriction, patriarchal domination, and, inevitably, "backwardness" (El Saadawi 1980; Mernissi 1987). For others eager to recuperate women's agency from its previous invisibility, it is an expression of female resistance and emancipation (El Guindi 1999; Zuhur 1992) or a form of "accommodating protest" (MacLeod 1991). Whether they vilify or glorify the practice of veiling, these perspectives are based on the problematic assumption that Islam is the main determinant of women's status, operating rigidly to set both limits and opportunities in the lives of women (Abu-Lughod 1998a; Bernal 1997; Cooper 1998). By constructing Islam as a monolithic entity that exists independently of the socio-historical context within which it develops, these approaches constrain our understanding of how women selectively make use of Islamic tenets in their struggle to reconcile what at times are competing societal and religious requirements. By focusing on the veil strictly in terms of identity politics, these views overlook women's lived experience as well as the ways in which *hijabai* (veils) and other modest garments circulate as objects of consumption and desire, subject to the dynamics of a constantly evolving fashion market.

The salience of the veil in contemporary debates about Muslim women's rights, Ahmed (1992) points out, can be traced to colonial efforts to portray Muslim societies as backward—and therefore in need of civilizing reforms. In the British campaign to conquer the hearts and minds of Egyptian subjects, veiling was a key signifier of women's oppression and, by implication, of the backwardness of the religion promoting these oppressive customs. Much was done, therefore, to insure its elimination. Western preoccupation with the veil spawned debates among Egyptian elites, who in turn mobilized to eradicate the symbol of the "quintessential otherness and inferiority of Islam" (Ahmed 1992:149; Fanon 1965). Through its capacity to condense a history of struggles over the definition of Muslim womanhood, the veil acquired a much broader significance over time, becoming, in the way it both constituted and challenged power, a prime example of dress as "political language" (Allman 2004:1).[4] The problem with this legacy, Ahmed (1992) contends, is that regardless of whether it is perceived as empowering or repressive, the veil—and the ideological battles surrounding it—has ultimately little to do with Muslim women's efforts to define their place in society. As an item of clothing, Ahmed notes, "the veil itself and whether it is worn are about as relevant to substantive matters of women's rights as the social prescription of one or another item of clothing is to Western women's struggles over substantive issues" (1992:166).

Without denying that the historical co-optation of feminism by colonial and patriarchal institutions has clouded the debates surrounding the veil, I still maintain that focusing on women's articulation of how these issues bear on their everyday realities is crucial to any analysis of Muslim womanhood. This is all the more so in the present case given that, unlike Qur'anic preachers who urge women to cover their bodies as a form of resistance to Western imperialism, women in Dogondoutchi focus instead on notions of piety, morality, and interiority when prompted to explain why they veil. With the intensification of reformist appeals for a common Muslim identity in the early 1990s, these notions were granted a more universal significance and the *hijabi* itself became iconic of reformist identity. Nonetheless, these ideas remain actively informed by local social realities, acquiring slippery and contradictory valences in certain contexts, such as when the *hijabi* is used as an instrument of disguise by women only wishing to appear virtuous.

Mindful of Lazreg's (1994:14) observation that, "while the veil plays an inordinate role in representations of women [. . .], it is seldom studied in

terms of the reality that lies behind it," I examine the highly diverse and personalized strategies[5] through which Dogondoutchi women balance the sometimes conflicting demands of trend-setting fashions and Islamic norms, and
how, in the process, they reformulate both the "fashionable" and the "moral."
By centering not on the general significance of head coverings but on the particular meanings they acquire for specific actors in specific circumstances, I
address three interrelated issues. First, I discuss women's lived experience of
the *hijabi*, as well as other head coverings, in light of traditional notions of
modesty and emerging conceptions of female bodies as repositories of a newly
prescribed Islamic morality. Second, I examine Mawri women's contextual
responses to the heightened moral concerns of Islam by charting attempts to
fashion pious personas—focusing specifically on the situational use of the
hijabi. Finally, to highlight the diversity of cultural models that inspire the
vision of modesty currently peddled on the streets of Dogondoutchi, I consider the role that foreign soap operas play in lending "cinematic authority"
(Appadurai and Breckenridge 1995:35) to local fashions. While casting doubt
on claims that local *hijabi* styles are "authentic" Islamic dress, the selective appropriation of foreignness that televised drama appears to authorize among
youthful audiences further instantiates the creative and contextually specific
ways that women influenced by moralizing discourses on female piety and
propriety fashion themselves as moral persons.

By addressing women's experience of Islamic dress, I hope to show that
if women rarely control the terms of debates about Muslim womanhood,
they are nonetheless afforded various opportunities to articulate their own
perceptions of what femininity, modesty, and elegance entail. Mawri wom-
en's sartorial efforts to conform to emerging ideals of female piety while accommodating changing fashion requirements illustrates how Islam provides
a moral scaffold for dealing with the challenges posed by local communities'
growing social integration into the world system. The dilemma, particularly
from the perspective of young women, is that Muslim dress must reflect both
the wearer's fashionability and her virtue. In the process of authorizing access
to sartorial modernity, emerging notions of Islamic modesty ultimately expand the repertoire of representations that Mawri women draw upon to fashion Muslim identities.

Embodying Virtue, Reasserting Interiority

Since the early 1990s Izala women in Dogondoutchi have been wearing
the *hijabi*, a tailored veil, allegedly modeled after Meccan sartorial creations,

that often encompasses the body from the head to the ankles and functions as a kind of "mobile" seclusion—theoretically allowing women to move in previously inaccessible public spaces. The professed intent of the *hijabi* is to hide women from the public eye and protect their virtue. In Izala households, women and girls as young as four may be seen donning unicolored veils signifying their pious intentions. Over the years, the *hijabi* has undergone significant alterations. In the 1990s the bright shades of women's ankle-length veils enhanced the wearer's visibility, and yet the generic designs of this early attire insured uniformity. Today the veils young women wear are often shorter and duller in color, but they have become substantially ornamented. Though they have lost in vividness, they have gained in stylishness and individuality; in fact, even non-Izala girls are wearing these statements of sartorial modesty in their effort to publicly fashion themselves as pious Muslims. They may even be encouraged to do so by mothers who only a decade ago virulently condemned their *hijabi*-clad neighbors for their sartorial excesses. Meanwhile, other styles of head covering have surfaced, informed and inflected by Izala modalities of piety, to create new solidarities and, inevitably, new distinctions as well.

Given the salience of the *hijabi* in religious discourse, one might easily forget that most adult women, before the emergence of Izala, already wore some type of head covering variously referred to as *lullu'bi, mayafi,* or *zane.* A simple rectangle of cloth that covered (*li'ke*) the upper body, the *lullu'bi* signified respectability. In the 1980s prepubescent girls could appear bare-headed in public, but grown women who did not wear a *lullu'bi,* as well as the smaller headscarf (*diko*) that was conventionally part of a woman's attire, would inevitably be identified as loose women, their lack of virtue matched by their sartorial laxity. Ordinary yet practical, the *lullu'bi,* long a marker of Muslimhood, can be used for myriad purposes from tying an infant on one's back to providing insulation from the cold. Despite, or perhaps because of, its ordinariness, it was eclipsed by the *hijabi* when 'yan Izala began making sartorial corrections to local female garb. In their attempts to fashion a more compelling expression of moral womanhood, Muslim reformists invested the *hijabi* with religious significance, an issue explored further below.

Lullu'bi-wearing women do not understand modesty as a strategic expression of religious identification. These women have been socialized into a world of Muslim values rooted in social practices that are experienced not as identity fashioning so much as embodied praxis. For those who learned to cover their heads and stay home long before Izala preachers enjoined every woman to do so, wearing a head covering and living in partial or total seclusion con-

Figure 7.1. Woman wearing headscarf and *lullu'bi*.

tributes to an ethics of embodiment that bears only tenuous relations to the politics of religious identity that have emerged in recent years. Yet, the veil they wear (silently) participates in the constitution of pious subjectivity. One can say that the *lullu'bai* that women put on when stepping out of their homes function not as a symbol of their religious sensibilities so much as a "social skin" (Turner 1980)—at once part of their intimate selves and of that which mediates their relationship to the wider world. These head coverings thus contribute to shaping women's sense of who they are as social actors on the Muslim scene.

Clothes, of course, have materiality and texture, which we often forget as we narrowly set our sights on what the veil *stands for*. Among anthropologists and cultural studies scholars, the analytical focus has largely been on the way that "cloth is turned into clothing," a focus that betrays how interest in the materiality of clothing has given way to an interest in "the sociality of clothing" (Norris 2005:83). Miller (2005:2), in his introduction to *Clothing as Material Culture*, notes that this attention to the social significance of clothes—a legacy of the Barthesian emphasis on semiotic decoding—reduces clothing to "its ability to signify something that seems more real—society or social relations—as though these things exist above or prior to their own materiality." As a result, the clothing that ostensibly is the subject of the analysis "remains a ghostly presence, coming to appear immaterial by the very lack of engagement with the physicality of clothing" (Woodward 2005:21). Concentrating on the materiality of clothing, I suggest, is central to developing an understanding of women's experience of veiling. It implies, among other things, paying attention to how head coverings affect bodiliness, how they alter women's sense of self and their sense of space, and how they function as a protective cover.

When asked why they wear a head covering, women in Dogondoutchi rarely elaborate beyond the usual response: "We veil to cover [*li'ke*] our bodies." As stereotypical as it may seem, this response provides clues as to what the veil *does* to women's bodies. *Li'ke*, which means "to cover," also means "to close." By covering their heads and shoulders (and, in some cases, much of their upper bodies) behind the folds of their head coverings, women seal themselves off to the outside world, creating a pious interiority that is integral to their moral selfhood. In short, the veil does more than hide the body; it also "protects, reassures, [and] isolates" it (Fanon 1965:59). In so doing, it plays an essential role in the constitution of agency, autonomy, and subjectivity.

In his vivid description of the profound physical trauma that recently unveiled Algerian women experienced during the War of Independence, Fanon (1965:59) offers hints of the protective physicality of the head covering and of the way it helps a woman inhabit space and develop self-determination:

> Without the veil she has an impression of her body being cut up into bits, put adrift; the limbs seem to lengthen infinitely. When the Algerian woman has to cross the street, for a long time she commits errors of judgment as to the exact distance to be negotiated. The unveiled body seems to escape, to dissolve. She has an impression of being improperly dressed, even of being naked. She experiences a sense of incompleteness with great intensity. She has the anxious feeling that something is unfinished, and along with it a frightful sensation of disintegrating. The absence of veil distorts the Algerian woman's corporeal pattern. She quickly has to invent new dimensions for her body, new means of muscular control. She has to create for herself an attitude of unveiled-woman-outside.

By reporting on how the unveiled women must relearn her body, its outline, the way it moves in space as well as its relation to surrounding space, Fanon shows how the veil, as a "technique of the body" (Mauss 1973), participates in the *incorporation* of Algerian womanhood, helping, literally, to define the contours of women's physical and moral selves. Pious femininity, here, hinges not on a verbal articulation of what it means to be a Muslim woman but on a corporeal sense of self-defined interiority, one that is experiential rather than verbalized, actualized as it is through the layering of cloth around one's body and the sense of agentive autonomy this layering produces. Following Bourdieu (1977, 1990), one could say that this interiority is part of the *habitus*, the generative principle through which social rules are inscribed in the bodies and dispositions of persons. The *habitus*, Bourdieu argues, is learned through "practical mimesis"—a process through which rules become naturalized without ever becoming the subject of explicit reflection. From this perspective, "'what is learned by the body' is not something that one has, like knowledge that can be brandished, but something that one is" (Bourdieu 1990:73).

Izala preachers implicitly understood the extent to which the success of their mission to cover women's bodies depended on the formation of a *habitus* through which head coverings would be mimetically learned to eventually become a "social skin"—an intimate part of women's social persona—as well as the basis for "naturalizing" moral rules. Girls, they admonished Izala parents in their sermons, should start wearing a *hijabi* as early as four or five years of age. Veiling girls at an early age insured proper training in the habituation of wearing *hijabi*.[6] "Girls who have worn a *hijabi* since they were little have grown used to them," Alhaji Omar explained, "they are comfortable with them," so comfortable that, without them, one might surmise that customarily *hijabi*-clad Mawri women would feel as "poorly dressed, even naked" as their unveiled Algerian counterparts. The notion of comfort to which Alhaji Omar alluded is key, for it suggests that rather than being experienced as restrictive, the practice of covering her upper body (or her entire body) enhances a woman's self-definition. Thus it indicates that this practice is not simply expressive but also *constitutive* of the pious integrity it is often assumed to represent (Mahmood 2005; also see Friedman 2002). In other words, being "comfortable with the *hijabi*" entails both a confident sense of mobile agency and a "naturalization" of the moral distinctions the vestmental item helps outline in the first place.

That head coverings (and seclusion) have traditionally contributed to a moral interiority that, for some women, is largely embodied was clarified for me one evening in 1994 as I walked with my friend Bebe through the *tasha*, a former car park converted into a permanent market. Bebe, an assertive woman in her late thirties, married at fifteen and has lived in partial seclusion

Figure 7.2. Sisters from an Izala household wearing *hijabai.*

ever since. Although she could visit kin and neighbors after nightfall, she was technically restricted to the marital compound during the day. Occasionally she twisted the rules a bit to attend a naming ceremony in a nearby compound, believing it was her duty to help a new mother with a gift of cash. Despite her seclusion, Bebe knew everyone in the vicinity; she was apprised of every birth, wedding, divorce, and death that occurred in her neighborhood and could always be relied on to provide the latest gossip. She spoke candidly about the problems of Nigérien women, who, like her, were expected to defer to their husbands in all things. And she had an opinion on just about everything. Ever since our first encounter—when she boldly called out to me from the entrance of her compound one January morning in 1988— I thought of her as a self-assured, assertive woman. That resilient confidence, I came to realize that evening, was deeply rooted in the secure interiority afforded by her seclusion.

As we made our way across the stalls of the marketplace—a shortcut on our way to visit Bebe's recently widowed kin—my friend told me that she had not been at the marketplace since she was fifteen years old. Instead of experiencing a thrilling sense of new-found freedom, however, she seemed ill at ease, continually readjusting her *mayafi* as if trying to tighten its protective grip around her shoulders. Later, on our way home, she told me that walking in the marketplace in the presence of so many men had made her feel deeply ashamed. The men had looked at her, and she had literally felt the weight of their stares on her body:

> When I was young, I liked going to the *tasha*. I went all the time. But now, I feel such *kumya* [shame]. I know these men, I cannot be around them. I have been in seclusion too long. It felt so heavy in there, I could barely walk. It is *kumya* that prevents me from entering the *tasha*.

Rather than enjoying a sense of liberation by walking in a public space,[7] Bebe felt paralyzed; the awareness of her immodesty had produced a crippling feeling of inadequacy and shame. It was dark, she kept repeating afterward, as if to convince herself that her exposure to the world was minimal. But that had not helped: she was unable to shake the sense of degradation that had engulfed her in the marketplace.

"Praxis," Moore (1994:78) points out following Bourdieu, "is not simply about learning cultural roles by rote, it is about coming to an understanding of social distinctions through your body, and recognizing that your orientation in the world, your intellectual rationalizations, will always be based on that incorporated knowledge." In the *tasha*, Bebe's incorporated knowledge of her secluded status resurfaced through her intense feelings of vulnerability upon being exposed to the outside world, an environment lacking the boundaries within which women in *kubli* safely anchor their selfhood. Even with darkness concealing her from potential onlookers, Bebe felt the impropriety of her presence in the marketplace through her body. She was so accustomed to the comforting presence of her courtyard's mud walls that her *mayafi* was of little use against the penetrating gazes of male traders and passers-by. Similar to Algerian women's account of how they felt without the protection of the *haïk* (veil), Bebe's testimony reveals the trauma she experienced on being exposed to the glares of men who knew her, both in the sense of knowing who she was and being able to see her.[8] By walking through the *tasha* instead of avoiding it as she had done on previous occasions, my friend had not so much invaded that space as she herself had been invaded. It was *she* who felt violated, an experience she described as intensely distressing. The heaviness, anguish, and paralyzing fear she experienced in the crowded marketplace were symptomatic of her overwhelming *kumya*. Bebe *knew* she was committing an impropriety, even if she pretended not to know at the time: this knowledge had surfaced and translated into a deeply somatic experience of shame.

In Hausa, *kumya* means "shame," as well as "modesty" and "propriety." Whether it is understood as inhibition or appropriate conduct, the concept is central to local understandings of moral discipline and social order. Mothers are said to feel *kumya* toward their first born, a sentiment that connotes avoidance. *Kumya* prevents a mother from calling her oldest child by his or her name and also demands that she not publicly demonstrate her affection for that child. *Kumya* also translates into the deference that affines feel toward each other and that a person feels toward his or her parents. The feeling can also be aroused by one's sense of having violated a social rule. Thieves (or disrespectful children) are said to feel no shame, and a young woman who gives birth to a child out of wedlock is said to inflict shame on her family. *Kumya* can be a matter of embarrassment: deep shame (*kumya*) surrounds the discourse of sexuality, and youth avoid any reference to sex and intimacy when in the presence of elders, and vice versa. Grown men who have no wives to keep house for them and thus depend on another household for sustenance are said to feel *kumya*, or social inadequacy. Beik (1991), in her study of Hausa theater, similarly reports the feeling of *kumya* experienced by young women who were asked to perform as actresses before an audience. The shame and inhibition that overtook them on stage was so intense that much time was spent training them to "speak up, to hold their heads up without hiding their faces in their headscarves, a modest gesture common to Hausa women outside their homes" (ibid.:235).

Aside from helping us understand how customarily secluded women may experience public places as a contraction, rather than an expansion, of subjective space, Bebe's uncomfortable ordeal reminds us that "to take on the *higab* is a very different thing from having always worn some sort of head covering, having always thought of yourself as religious and moral, or having never left the bounds of family control" (Abu-Lughod 1997:511). Although current controversies about Nigérien women's sexuality, space, and status may well be about nationwide struggles over the definition of moral community, for women like Bebe pious self-determination did not take the form of a distinctly articulated statement. It was neither a kind of political action nor a declaration of difference. Rather, it took shape within the naturalizing grounds of the physical self, a profoundly wordless yet meaningful experience. As both learned and naturalized, bodiliness, Durham (1999:392) notes, is "an important modality for inarticulate mutual recognition between people." Thus

Bebe's shameful experience alerts us to the urgency of focusing our analyses of Islamic dress on forms of embodied praxis that have received scant attention since the emergence of the veil as a symbol of religious militancy in many parts of the Muslim world.

Emerging Definitions of Modesty

When Muslim reformists started making vestmental corrections to local garb in the early 1990s, they enjoined both men and women to wear modest, locally made, inexpensive attire that reflected the moral values they were championing. New Izala recruits thus abandoned the cumbersome and prohibitively costly *babban riga* (an ample robe worn over a matching long-sleeve shirt and drawstring pants that had become the outfit de rigueur for Muslims long before Izala emerged) because of its association with the tainted religious practices they aimed to eradicate. They began wearing the less eye-catching *jaba* (a shorter, long-sleeved tunic worn over shin-length pants) to promote frugality and resource conservation. Though Izala men, too, were concerned about the modesty of their appearance—sleeves buttoned up to hide wrists, heads turbaned to cover hair—their efforts to redefine the boundaries of respectability centered primarily on women's dress and deportment. For Izala wives and daughters, acknowledging membership in the reformist movement thus translated into wearing the *hijabi*.

Although the practice of veiling predates the advent of Islam, 'yan Izala insisted that the order to veil came directly from the Scriptures. From this perspective, men who did not order their wives and daughters to wear *hijabai* demonstrated their unfamiliarity with the content of the Qur'an. The Prophet told his wives to cover their bodies, Izala preachers tirelessly proclaimed, and therefore pious women should emulate these archetypical figures of Islamic virtue and wear a veil, especially if, despite the admonition to stay home and serve God through marriage and reproduction, they had to leave their compound. Aside from promoting piety and frugality, these modest attires also minimized class differences, which were seen as a threat to Muslim unity.

Though, as noted, the avowed purpose of the *hijabi* was to cover women's bodies and shroud them in respectability, the luminous yellow, bright green, or vivid turquoise shades of the *hijabi* cloth insured that they would be noticed wherever they went, certainly more than their "heathen" counterparts wearing mostly polychromatic wrappers and matching blouses and headscarves. According to Moussa Boubacar, a 'dan Izala who made a living as a butcher,

Figure 7.3. Man wearing the attire of devout Muslims—long-sleeved tunic, shin-length pants, and embroidered *hula* (hat).

In the Muslim religion, the woman must hide her body and be dressed modestly. She cannot just walk wherever she wants. My wife remains at home; we have another woman who comes to bring us water from the pump, and I pay someone to bring us firewood. My wife is free to leave [the house] and visit her mother or go to the dispensary during the day as long as she asks my permission. All Muslims should keep their wives at home.

Echoing the now widespread notion that wearing the *hijabi* is the duty of *all* Muslim women, Moussa Boubacar's testimony also reveals that if the veil was meant to hide female bodies from undesirable stares, it still did not replace seclusion.[9] A survey I conducted in 2000 of forty-one Muslim households in two Dogondoutchi neighborhoods revealed that, except for the strictly secluded wives of traditionalist Muslim clerics, women who lived under some form of seclusion were overwhelmingly members of Izala.[10]

Rather than enabling them to move with reasonable freedom in public areas, the *hijabi*, by casting women as devout Muslims, reinforces the image of piety that their status as secluded wives already communicates to the world.

This partly explains why, although both Izala men and women routinely insist that *hijabi*-clad women are not barred access to the Friday mosque (*masallaci juma'a*), in my experience only postmenopausal women, who are no longer a source of seductive distraction, ever attended the Friday prayer.

Whether made of stiff brocade or lighter fabric, the *hijabi* is meant to cover a woman's hair and hang in such a way as to hide the contours of her upper (and sometimes lower) body, making it nearly impossible to assess her shape or even her size. Ideally it should conceal curves and flatten out shoulders, breasts, and buttocks to produce a generic body shape. It is sewn so that the opening for the head fits snugly around the wearer's face (an elastic band helps young girls keep it in place), making pins or knots unnecessary and allowing the woman to retain the use of her hands. As such, it differs strikingly from the clingy prayer shawls that started appearing in local markets in the early 1990s. These mass-produced items whose shapes, designs, and ornamentation are subject to evolving trends often feature embroideries, sequins, or silky fringes. They are popular in Muslim circles where Izala fashion is unpopular: their slippery folds must be continually adjusted by their wearers, an "inconvenience" that young women have learned to exploit when they want to make use of the garments' seductive potential. Although these veils ostensibly hide the figure underneath, allowing for a semblance of propriety, they can become a "provocative shape-revealing item of apparel" when maneuvered by expert hands (Rugh 1986:109). Because they are often made of gauzy, semi-transparent fabrics of loose weave, they ultimately reveal as much as they conceal.[11]

It is precisely to remove the seductive potential of head coverings and highlight the distinctiveness of Izala's sartorial emblem of female piety that reformist husbands and fathers were instructed on the characteristics that the *hijabai* of their womenfolk should bear. Only the face and hands should be seen emerging from the tent-like cloak draped around a woman's body. If a woman carries an infant on her back, the child's body should be wrapped tightly against its mother's with a sash before the veil covers their bodies—although even infant girls tied on their mother's back could technically be fitted with their own tiny *hijabai*.[12] To guarantee that no body parts other than the face and hands show, Izala women were originally attired in long-sleeved tunics and drawstring pants whose color matched the *hijabi*. The pants and long sleeves insured that the wearer's limbs were covered without hindering mobility or preventing the performance of household chores. Women could thus carry water buckets on their heads, bend to sweep the floor of their compounds, or simply sit while in the presence of visitors with-

Figure 7.4. Woman wearing lightweight *lullu'bi.*

out having to incur shameful exposure. The preservation of modesty, it was widely recognized, should not come at the expense of domestic productivity. Nor should the veil (and the garments accompanying it) be restricted to members of prosperous households. If it was to serve as widespread proof of women's pious dispositions, it had to be not only practical and dependable but also affordable.

Alhaji Boubacar, a tailor and member of Izala who once told me that "it was God who said that women should hide their bodies," began making veils for his wives after returning from the *haji* in 1990. After seeing what the Muslim women were wearing in Mecca, he copied their models of *hijabi:*

> Any color can be used [for a woman's garment] as long as the fabric doesn't shine: red, green, black. But shiny material [*mai walkiya*] is no good because it attracts men's attention.[13] Some veils are very long [shrouding the ankles], other are shorter. But for grown women as well as little girls, the veil should normally fall to the ground. Women can wear beautiful outfits made of *bazin* [brocade] but only to wear at home. They can't wear them in the street, in town.

Figure 7.5. Women wearing plain *hijabai.*

Besides exemplifying allegiance to God, Alhaji Boubacar concluded, wearing the *hijabi* was an expression of positive virtue: like other pious acts such as praying or giving alms, it would increase a believer's chances of being justly rewarded on Judgment Day. Alhaji Boubacar's statement of sartorial modesty was quickly imitated by other Izala men, who requested that the tailor reproduce his design for their own wives. Foreign practices were thus reinterpreted by individuals eager to answer local concerns. Soon every Izala woman in Dogondoutchi was wearing an outfit tailored by Alhaji Boubacar or his assistants, declaring their family's purifying intentions.

That Izala women can make themselves attractive but only at home in order to please their husbands highlights the distinction between public and private spaces that is at the heart of numerous debates on the "woman question" (Abu-Lughod 1998b:243). For Fatima, a twenty-five-year-old mother of two who had grown up in an Izala household and started veiling at the age of eleven, there was no question that Muslim women could enhance their

Figure 7.6. Girls wearing Awaliyya dress.

natural beauty with whatever means available so long as they did so within the confines of their home:

> When it is almost evening and my husband is about to come home, that's when I wash. I wear a nice outfit. I put on eyeliner and perfume to be beautiful for my husband. If I wear *kwali* (eyeliner) in the street, men will look at me, that is not good.

In the world of Izala women there is a place for jewelry, makeup, and the like, but the use of these glamorous items is restricted to the nurturing of spousal relations. Women can thus beautify themselves but solely to enhance their husband's pleasure.

In his eagerness to fashion a new identity for Muslims, Malam Awal urged his followers to wear white clothes.[14] He devised the *hirami,* a white headcloth that knotted under the chin and was further secured with a small bandana-like scarf tied around the head, for his female adepts. Wearing the *hirami* insured that the latter would be distinguishable from the *hijabi*-wearing women of the Izala association and the large majority of women clad in their *lullu'bai*. Aside from creating a distinct Awaliyya look, Awal told his audiences during sermons, wearing *hirami* increased one's chances of entering paradise. In the dry, sandy Sahel where wind, dirt, and dust conspire to rapidly cover every surface with grime, regularly wearing white clothes takes real dedication. As part of one's Muslim identity, it automatically signals the depth of one's religious commitment—and even more so when one comes from a poor household where soap and water allocations are minimal.

In the late 1990s women in Dogondoutchi could be identified at a glance depending on whether they wore a *hijabi*, a *hirami*, or a *lullu'bi*. As one Muslim leader and severe critic of Izala explained in 2000,

> A woman must wear a long dress that covers her body entirely from her neck to her ankles. She must wear long sleeves to hide her wrist and then a *lullu'bi*. If you see a woman wearing a *hijabi*, you know she is a *'ya* Izala. If you see a young girl who wears a scarf across her forehead to hold her veil, you know she is a *'ya* Awaliyya. The [Awaliyya] men wear their prayer beads around the neck. And the women, they wear white clothes. We just have girls and women wear a *lullu'bi* and that's it. There are three kinds of veils; even if you are not from Dogondoutchi, you can tell, looking at a woman, whether she belongs to the *darika* [Sufi order], to Izala, or to Awaliyya. It is the arrival of Awal that started [the trend of] women wearing *hiramai*. Before, there were differences only between us and the *'yan* Izala.

Muslim women who wear *lullu'bai* often insist that, although they are meant to cover a women's head, these head coverings are about fashion, not religion. Faith and fashion need not be mutually exclusive, however. Indeed, the emergence of these various forms of Islamic consumption suggests that the relationship between fashion, morality, and modernity is more complicated than is conventionally recognized. The proliferation and diversification of head coverings of both Izala and non-Izala inspiration are evidence of wider efforts to recast women's image in a society increasingly concerned with correct Islamic conduct yet reluctant to sacrifice women's desire to "move with fashion" (Hansen 2004:387). Over the last decade, as the *hijabi* itself became redesigned to suit emerging fashion sensibilities, it lost its exclusive association with Izala militancy to signify piety in a more encompassing sense. Muslim leaders who once objected to Izala's fervent bid to cover women's bodies, arguing that the *hijabi* was un-Islamic, have stopped denouncing women who adopted this type of head covering. Many now share the reformists' vision of the veil as a divinely ordained means of promoting moral order in Muslim communities. "The *hijabi* is *tuffafi na addini*—the dress of Islam," one preacher who never lost an opportunity to excoriate Izala explained to me. "One cannot reject it. Every woman, whether she is black or white, must wear the *hijabi*." With the partial unmooring of the *hijabi* from its radical associations, growing numbers of non-Izala women have incorporated the modest item in their wardrobe. "We wear the veil *sabo da addini*—because Islam demands it," young girls invariably respond when asked why they wear a *hijabi*. "*Sabo da addini*" has become a litany of sorts for young Mawri women seeking to align themselves with increasingly normative expressions of sartorial propriety.

Given that the *hijabi* does not conceal a woman so much as it marks her as a moral person, the distinctive Izala dress was initially an effective way for Izala men looking for wives to narrow the field of eligible candidates at a glance.[15] In recent years not only have *hijabai* been progressively adopted by non-reformist young women eager to carve out newly configured expressions of morality, but Izala men's choice of wives has also reflected increasing flexibility. It is not unheard of today for reformists to marry young women from non-Izala households when they trust that the latter have received the proper moral education. As noted in chapter 6, most young girls who have grown up in non-reformist households remain suspicious of the Izala agenda, which they see as threatening the forms of domesticity to which they aspire in their quest for comfortable middle-class life. With the recent relaxation of rules based on the Izala ethos of consumer restraint, however, a few have nonetheless accepted marriage proposals from reformist suitors—wealthy traders, mostly. In 2000 Binta, a young, recently divorced woman, was contemplating marrying the young *'dan* Izala who was courting her. He had a prosperous business, and she would be well taken care of. Though Binta had been raised in a household where Izala values were disparaged, she now felt that putting on a *hijabi* (to follow her husband's wishes) was a small price to pay for the material comforts she would enjoy in her new marital home. Not only did many of her friends (none of whom belonged to Izala) own a *hijabi*, but by then veiling was well on its way to becoming a generic marker of Islamic re-spectability for young women hoping to attract a husband.

The Commodification of the Pious Look

When *hijabai* first appeared on female bodies, they generally fell to the knee or the ankle and matched the rest of the monochromatic outfit—marking their wearers as pious, enlightened Muslims. A few years later these vestmental items were shorter, in some cases considerably so, and the draw-string pants (too masculine, I was told) were jettisoned altogether. The long-sleeved and rigorously plain tunics remained as a sign of devotion to Prophetic ideals. This seemed to be a satisfying compromise—but not for long. Even the tunic was eventually abandoned in favor of more flattering and fashion-sensitive garments. By 2004 most Izala women I knew had gone back to wearing traditional wrappers made of multicolored, factory-printed textiles and matching blouses—locally tailored and adorned with a profusion of flounces, buttons, and contrasting trims. On market day, when people don their finest attire to go anywhere, or when attending a naming ceremony, they could be seen wearing expensively tailored outfits made of rich *bazin* (uni-colored cotton brocade) or *wax* (pricy wax-print textile with vivid designs) underneath their *hijabai*.

Thus, in less than a decade, the strict and sober simplicity of the original Izala dress gave way to the sartorial excesses that the reformists, hoping to diminish expressions of class difference, had originally condemned as a sign of impiety. In the process, the role of the *hijabi* in local vestmental practices was radically reconfigured. Originally fashioned as a class-leveling device signaling loyalty to a radical concept of piety, the *hijabi* today has become a way to convey difference (Bourdieu 1984). *Hijabi* styles now proliferate, enabling women, through the choices they make, to distinguish themselves as they negotiate the interface between fashion and morality. Some *hijabai* connote trendiness, others less so. Prices vary, depending on the fabric, the cut, and the amount of ornamentation—proof that the notion of frugality so central (initially) to the configuration of Izala identity has had to compete with other practices of identity-making indexed through conspicuous consumption. Increasingly young girls wear the *hijabi* not so much to blend with their devout counterparts but to demonstrate their sartorial savoir faire. For others, the *hijabi* is a convenient way to satisfy both aesthetic and religious requirements. In short, although it remains a central element of pious identities, the *hijabi* has also become a "fashion statement."

Among young girls especially, *hijabai* now often fall just below the shoulder and their colors have either faded or become very dark. No longer manufactured locally to the wearer's specifications, they are often mass-produced in Nigeria. The bright yellows, deep purples, or intense blues of earlier days have been replaced by more somber tones: dark green, blue, black, white, or brown, with an occasional light pink, orange, or pale blue. Today *hijabai* are rarely color-coordinated with the rest of the wearer's outfit. Sometimes they are made of lighter, more flexible fabric—often a synthetic blend rather than

Figure 7.7. Girl wearing ornate *hijabi*.   Figure 7.8. Girl wearing ornate *hijabi*.

the heavier cloth of the previous decade. As if to make up for their more somber color, *hijabai* are now often prettified with stylish decorative touches. A recent, popular *hijabi* ornamentation is a lace trim of a contrasting shade sewn to the hem of the veil. In another pattern, the lace fringe adorns the opening surrounding the wearer's face, and the hem of the veil falls asymmetrically on the shoulders. In 2004 these fancy veils were prized by young girls from non-Izala households striving to keep up with the latest styles. That year, yet another modification of the standard head covering included a *hijabi* with an upper section made of rich, lacy material and a color-coordinated lower section of plainer fabric, both fringed with four inches of cream lace. Originally meant to conceal a woman's attractiveness, the *hijabi* has become part of the attraction.

A number of girls told me that they had purchased a *hijabi* (or asked their mothers to purchase one), because it was fashionable and because they liked the way these head coverings looked. If their fathers may have objected to the idea a decade ago, they no longer do. *Hijabai* are now standard gifts that suitors bring to the girls they court—together with heeled slippers, hair extensions, and perfumed lotion. As was demonstrated to me by a group of unmarried girls who wore *hijabai* to go to the market and later donned more revealing head coverings (coordinated to their richly embroidered *boubous*—full-length gowns) to attend a social event, the *hijabi* is not necessarily worn all the time—or everywhere—but only when the occasion demands. As an example of the way dress functions as "public display" (LeBlanc 2000:448), the *hijabi* is worn when going out—whether on top of one's "good clothes" or over one's everyday faded clothes. One would not wear a *hijabi* to attend a wedding celebration, but the *hijabi* constitutes appropriate attire for running errands or attending a public event.

A young girl who told me that when she wore the *hijabi* it was both to look modern and gather approval. Aside from symbolizing piety, the *hijabi* provides a way to distance oneself from the "'ignorance' of tradition" as well as from the "'evils' of modernity" (LeBlanc 2000:445). As such, it has become particularly popular among non-Izala girls who wear it as an accessory to achieve a particular effect. Instead of erasing a young woman's singularity, it helps her achieve a distinctively pious look that she may find most suitable to the public space of the market, where a woman's presence is often read as a sign that she has too much freedom for her own good.

Rather than encouraging uniformity in dress, as was originally intended, the spreading popularity of the *hijabi* has opened up new possibilities for young, fashion-conscious girls wanting respectability but not invisibility. Paradoxically, the *hijabi*'s popularity has contributed to the erasure of Izala women. Now that anyone can wear a *hijabi* regardless of one's commitment to Islam, the veil has ceased to be the defining element of female Izala identity. A young girl's religious affiliation can no longer be determined simply by whether she wears a *hijabi*, especially now that the growing success of the pious look has spurred the appearance of copycats: head coverings modeled after Izala veils—with a tailored opening for the face—are not, their wearers insist, *hijabai*. Because they are made of locally printed cloth with vivid designs, they belie the message of austerity that Izala head coverings should ideally convey.

Note that the insertion of modest garments in the realm of fashion is not an exclusively Nigérien phenomenon. In Egypt, Armbrust (1999:128) points out, the "ascetic, class leveling, and radically pious" head covering of the early days of the reformist movement has become tangled up in complex webs of commercialism. Today Egyptian women are likely to wear the *hijab* with bright accessories and blue jeans, and not the severe gowns of militant Islam. In Yemen the late 1990s witnessed a prolific production of pious dress (head coverings adorned with fancy buttons, embroidered motifs, and rhinestones), much of it intended for wealthy elites eager to differentiate themselves from the pious masses (Meneley 2007). In Turkey the adoption of *tesettür* (religiously appropriate modest dressing) by middle-class, educated urban Muslim women has spawned a growing industry of Islamic dress that is highly sensitive to the demands of taste and fashion (Sandickci and Ger 2005). Women everywhere are experimenting with what it means to be modern and Muslim through the endless reconfiguration of Islamic chic.

Staging Piety: The Dynamics of Concealment and Revelation

Although the presence of *hijabi*-clad young women in the streets of Dogondoutchi is as much a sign of fashion consciousness as an index of piety, still it would be a mistake to minimize the impact that moralizing discourses on female dress have had on local understandings of piety and propriety. At a time of heightened Muslim anxiety about the capacity of the clothed female body to signify various levels of purity, young women have become increasingly aware of the importance of appropriate body coverage in certain contexts. Consider Rabi, a nineteen-year-old single mother for whom dressing up to attend a *vin d'honneur* (dance party to honor a bride and groom) generally meant wearing boldly revealing outfits of Western inspiration such as *pantalons patte* (bell bottom jeans) or *mini-jupes* (knee-length skirts) and clingy, curve-enhancing tops generically known as *tufafi serré* (literally, tight clothing). As I was sitting in her mother's compound admiring the various goods a young neighbor was hawking door to door in a large enamel bowl, Rabi asked to see the girl's merchandise. After longingly inspecting the small purses that are now a must-have for any fashionable young woman, she turned her attention to the Nigerian-made *hijabai* at the bottom of the bowl. "I want a black one," she told the girl. Before anyone could object, she added quickly that most of her friends owned at least one *hijabi*. The young peddler had no black *hijabai* left in her bowl. Rabi told her to come back when she had a new assortment of merchandise for sale. "I want people to show me *daraja* [respect]," she blurted out by way of explanation when her mother, a steadfast critic of Izala, had expressed skepticism about her daughter's intentions.

I never found out whether Rabi ultimately bought a *hijabi* from her neighbor, but I argue that her gesture exemplifies a growing need among young women to create themselves as respectable Muslims as they start thinking about marriage. Recall that Muslim clerics who, only a decade ago, bitterly criticized Izala women's headdress have recently recognized that the *hijabi* should be part of every pious woman's attire.[16] A number of clerics are now urging Mawri women to veil so they look more like the women of Mecca.[17] Rabi did not pray or fast, a situation her mother lamented: How would she find a husband? The nineteen-year-old had no intention of giving up her tight, revealing outfits, at least for the time being, yet she understood how she could capitalize on the *hijabi*'s moral value to project an image of piety when circumstances required it.

The cloak of piety Rabi planned to purchase would not only cover her body, it would also conceal her impious self. Bauer (2005) has shown that, during the revolution, women in Iran used the veil to disguise themselves and deflect attention from their actual intentions, when necessary. These tactics of concealment succeeded because the women inscribed themselves in a context of expectations about the performance of purity. By *appearing* to follow rules of propriety, women were able to deceive those who associated modest dress with pure intentions. In Dogondoutchi as well, young women like Rabi have learned that purity lies in the eye of the beholder, that it is not simply about following rules but also involves the strategic capacity to project a virtuous public image. By wearing *hijabai* when they want others to perceive them as pious, they deploy an image of modesty that matches local expectations of what proper women look like while simultaneously hiding their impiety behind a virtuous facade.[18]

Mass-produced *hijabai,* which come neatly folded in protective plastic bags, are now widely available through young girls who peddle various fashionable goods from women's purses to hair extensions to brassieres, illustrating how piety can be suitably packaged and commercialized to appeal to youthful sensibilities. In her pursuit of the latest fashion, a young woman may well decide that instead of a new brassiere or a pair of fancy *babouches* (open-heeled shoes with a narrow heel generally reserved for dressy occasions), she needs a lace-trimmed *hijabi* to complement her wardrobe, an unthinkable gesture a decade earlier when *hijabai* were an undisputable expression of the frugal piety of reformist Islam. The Nigerian origins of these items further enhance their appeal. Despite its growing woes, northern Nigeria remains a bountiful source of fashionable trends as well as a highly respected destination for Qur'anic students seeking further enlightenment. Women who strive to define their identities in light of both the temptations of consumer culture and the newly emerging discourse on piety have latched onto Nigerian goods that can satisfy their fashion sensibilities as well as their religious inclinations. Because they bear the stamp of the foreign while also meeting current modesty requirements, *hijabai* made in Nigeria have become particularly popular among young, unmarried women who, like Rabi, are mindful of the growing need to present themselves as pious Muslims in public but are unwilling to sacrifice elegance for the sake of virtue. Cases such as Rabi's ultimately remind us that dress is both "the outcome of collective thinking and a flexible medium people manipulate to project the kind of public image they want others to know them by" (Rugh 1986:3).

That the *hijabi* can be used as a means of disguising the self has occasionally prompted some Muslim women to question the motives of their Izala peers.[19] I was occasionally told that the *hijabi* was no guarantee of the purity of a woman's character. In 2000 three of my neighbors, all wives of the same Izala man, were suspected of sneaking out of their compound in broad daylight to engage in activities no "reputable" women engaged in. The *hijabi*, a friend once argued, was for hypocrites, for those who had something to hide. Another friend recounted the misadventures of a secluded Izala wife who had gone to sell cooked food at the weekly market while her husband was away. The young woman had been hoping to avoid detection but acquaintances of her husband reported seeing her in public—her purple *hijabi* had stood out. She was severely punished. The cloak of respectability provided by the *hijabi*, my friend implied, was no protection against the power of gossip.

The story further suggests that it is problematic to assume that women who "veil" are automatically afforded additional autonomy simply because the layers of cloth they wrap themselves in shroud them in respectability. Although the *hijabi* technically enables its wearer to enter spaces that would otherwise be prohibited in what remains a highly gender-segregated society, Izala husbands, in my experience, were often reluctant to expand their wives' freedom outside the home. Recall that, except for some notable exceptions, seclusion is more systematically enforced among Izala households. Other Muslim women, many of whom initially perceived their Izala counterparts to be victims of overzealous husbands, would probably chuckle at the notion that the *hijabi* is an emancipatory device: Izala wives remain mostly in the marital compound while their husbands spend a great deal of time engaging in professional activities, preaching, or attending meetings—to such a degree, in fact, that they are rarely home to grant their wives permission to go out.

That Izala wives occasionally get caught when they try to circumvent the rules of proper conduct suggests that the *hijabi* does not invariably function as a form of "portable seclusion" (Papanek 1973:295) that enables women to move in and out of enclosed living spaces, as has previously been assumed. Although public places such as the mosque have theoretically become accessible to *hijabi*-clad women, most remain off-limits, at least to married women of child-bearing age.[20] On the other hand, that the *hijabi* has been adopted by non-Izala girls aiming for a modest look indicates that veiling does give some women space in which to maneuver without breaching the boundaries of proper behavior. Regardless of a woman's degree of piety, the veil she wears marks her as inherently virtuous—and therefore desirable to potential husbands. Indeed, it is precisely because it signifies that a woman is unavailable that the *hijabi* heightens her appeal. By designating her as "clean," chaste, and virtuous, it neutralizes her sexuality while enhancing her moral qualities—something Rabi, in her wish to purchase a head covering, evidently understood.

The notion that women use the anonymity afforded by the *hijabi* to conceal disreputable facets of their lives is, I argue, largely without basis. Nevertheless it has generated a lively debate about the complicated relations between fashion and morality, as rumors of a veiled she-devil searching for seductive encounters in the streets of the city of Zinder attest. As noted in chapter 5, in August 2003 reports that a veiled female spirit was haunting certain neighborhoods of Zinder provoked a moral panic among local residents. The mysterious creature was said to be as beautiful as she was dangerous. Aside from giving shape to Zinder residents' emergent fear of moral disorder, the spirit uncovered the deception behind wearing a *hijabi:* by hiding not only her bodily charms but also her harmful intentions, the veil enabled a "pagan" creature to look like a pious Muslim woman (Masquelier 2008). Accounts of the veiled spirit propositioning men echo reports of *gabdi* (high-class prostitutes) using the *hijabi* to appear as respectable, pious women to the Izala traders they wish to marry (Alidou 2005). The *hijabi* highlights a woman's moral character by downplaying her sexual attributes, but as the veiled she-devil and the former *gabdi*-turned-respectable-housewife make clear, it can just as easily become a screen cloaking women's impious nature. The debate on female morality and modesty set in motion by the alleged presence of a veiled she-devil in Zinder also underscores wider concerns about the place of women in Muslim society and their role in the objectification of Muslim identity. Yet, beyond a growing consensus that women should wear modest attire that signifies their pious intentions, women do not cover their heads in the same manner. Nor do they agree on what modesty means. How the *hijabi*, for instance, figures in Muslim women's articulation of virtuous femininity varies enormously. The diverse, at times contradictory, uses of the *hijabi* ultimately compel us to turn our attention away from reified models of veiling and attend closely to the ways that women negotiate their moral identities as wives, mothers, and daughters by adopting modest clothing.

Contested Understandings of Modesty

Though Izala's (and Awaliyya's) focus on women as upholders of purity has intensified debates about the proper ways of expressing modesty, the various concerns these discussions expose are not new. Norms of modesty—and the extent to which these should be indicative of female virtue—were controversial long before Izala activists arrived on the local religious scene. Consider, for instance, the disagreements that *bori* practitioners and Muslims have had over the sartorial parameters of female respectability. Spirit devotees, it is widely acknowledged in Muslim circles, are often inappropriately dressed and show little concern for preserving acceptable norms of body coverage during possession ceremonies (Masquelier 2005). Their demeanor and dress have long offended Muslim sensibilities for their apparent lack of restraint, especially given the public nature of *bori* performances. Young women who show up in short-sleeved, curve-enhancing clothing at these events and who attract attention through their dancing are often assumed to be prostitutes.[21] Given the powerful message that wrongful exposure conveys about improper sexuality, it is not surprising that *bori* performances have long been identified as sites of spoiled femininity and moral decadence.

Although, in the 1980s, Muslim women did not veil in the stipulated Izala or Awaliyya manner, they did cover their heads. The rectangle of cloth known as *zane* or *lullu'bi* (worn with a matching wrapper and *marinière*—a hip-length tunic with wide, often multi-tiered sleeves) that women draped over their headscarves when leaving the marital compound was further proof of their virtue. When it was not loosely folded around the neck and shoulders or simply placed over the head—with the ends trailing gracefully at the wearer's side—the cloth would be wrapped tightly around her hips or over the torso if there was a baby to be carried on the back. Around the hips it enhanced the curves of a slender figure, revealing the shape it was meant to conceal. As a head covering, it marked social distinctions as well; for example, its slipperiness interfered with farm work and housework. By never taking their head coverings off, women hinted at their freedom from physical work, thereby further signaling family affluence or seniority.

As we trace the shifting regulations of the gendered body and their attendant implications for the aesthetic, social, and moral distinctions they help produce, stylistic continuities emerge that shape the context in which women have been operating as they variously fashion Muslim identities all their own. Stated otherwise, the moral sensibilities which Izala leaders cultivated in Muslim women through the injunction that they adopt more modest forms of dress did not develop in a social vacuum. The seeds of sartorial propriety had already been sown by earlier efforts to redefine norms of modesty and, through them, some of the more visible parameters of Muslim identities.[22] Thus, when Muslim women criticized the *hijabi* as un-Islamic, inappropriate, or even ridiculous, they were not protesting the emergence of the veil so much as they were expressing resentment at Izala's unwarranted intrusion into the world of feminine fashion. After all, they, too, covered their heads in accordance with local norms of modesty. By insisting that the *hijabi*, despite its kinship with local head coverings, was foreign not only to Dogondoutchi women's sartorial repertoire but to Islamic dress, they ultimately challenged Izala's right to interfere with local definitions of Islamic propriety.

When Malam Awal requested that his female followers cover their heads, women in Dogondoutchi had long been doing so regardless of their specific religious identities. His injunction that Awaliyya women wear a head covering of his own design did not reform local definitions of modesty so much as it complicated the local field of identity politics. Among other things, Awal also insisted that women wear pants at a time when Izala women were just abandoning theirs. Aside from signifying the purity of its wearer's intentions, the white *hirami* identified its wearers as a member of Awaliyya; other women might wear white *hijabai*[23] but they did not secure their veils with scarves tied across their foreheads. Adopting this style of head covering, Awal informed his female disciples, would bring them additional blessings, for it conformed more closely to the Prophet's recommendations for women. As the preacher told me:

> The *hijabi* is not good. It is just hypocrisy. There was a follower of the Prophet. His name was Sidi Omar. One day a woman in a *hijabi* approached him. She had a hidden weapon to kill Sidi. His friends had paid no attention to her. But when they saw the weapon, they realized that the woman wearing a *hijabi* had carried it. This is when the Prophet said not to wear *hijabai*. *Hirami* is proper. You can also dress like an Arab [wear a veil that must be held in place with one hand]. But the *hijabi* is a dress of hypocrisy.

By construing the *hijabi* as a symbol of deceit, a cloak behind which women could hide even the most criminal intentions, Malam Awal capitalized on Muslim women's suspicion of the *hijabi*.[24] Although the head covering he promoted entailed only a minimal shift in body coverage, that shift spoke loudly of the wearer's transparent intentions. By leaving the two sides of the veil open in front (rather than having them sewn together as on the *hijabi* where the only opening is for the head), the *hirami* of Awaliyya members signified honesty, integrity, and compliance with the Prophet's wishes. Because it hid women's hands and what they could be holding, the *hijabi* hid too much. The symbol of the reformists' deviant practices—and of their alleged departure from the original model Muhammad handed out—must therefore be replaced by a head covering unambiguously signaling 'yan Awaliyya's devotion to the Prophet's vision of moral order.

Mass-Mediated Models of Islamic Fashion

Whether Dogondoutchi women cover their heads as part of naturalized pious dispositions or to align themselves with emerging norms of sartorial propriety or to express their commitment to a particular vision of Islam, most significant is that the intended meanings of Islamic dress are reconfigured in the process. Neither pure expressions of local sartorial sensibilities nor straightforward imitations of Middle Eastern fashions (after which local styles are supposedly modeled), the varied, changing, and often contested forms that modest dress has taken in Dogondoutchi in recent years point to the lack of consensus over the definition of "Islamic attire" (Masquelier 2007). They also highlight the difficulty of predicting what will become fashionable, for whom, and in what context. At the dawn of the millennium some girls had taken to wearing Nike caps under their *hijabai*, and others accessorized their head coverings with winter caps or headbands bearing the names of Colorado ski resorts or the inscription "2000." Although they allowed only a sliver of the headband or cap to be visible under the *hijabi* cloth, they still made sure that the foreign logo could be seen. These logo-centric fashion trends exemplify how local lives are "shaped by any number of imaginative links to 'elsewheres' near and far" (Weiss 2002:101).[25]

If these accessories of Western provenance are meant to enhance the cosmopolitan nature of the wearers' outfits—Nike ski caps alone are considered sufficiently fashionable to be worn at an infant's naming ceremony—they also highlight their modest appearance by further containing hair and scalp in a tight restraint and acting as an additional layer of protection. "I started wearing a *hijabi*," eighteen-year-old Aminatou told me, "so that my father would let me go out. Before, my father did not let me go anywhere. Islam orders women to veil. Women must wear the veil *don a li'ke jikinsu* [to cover their bodies]." By sporting a black Nike headband under her *hijabi*, Aminatou made her body impermeable to intrusive gazes—the headband fit snugly around her forehead, keeping both hair and ears out of sight. Of course, paradoxically, the famous logo, a symbol of the foreign and the fashionable,

Figure 7.9. Unmarried young women dressed up to attend a wedding party. Note the Nike cap worn by the girl on the left.

was eye-catching and would insure that the young woman was perceived as a sophisticated dresser. Although women, young and old, who scrutinized her outfit knew neither the provenance of the logo nor the name of the company it publicized, they nevertheless recognized it as foreign.

Not all forms of cosmopolitan identity have their source in the West, however. Increasingly Nigériens have begun to "imagine the 'possible lives'" (Weiss 2002:102) available elsewhere such as in India or Latin America. For young girls seeking a modest look that also spells worldliness, Latin American television serials and Indian films have become valuable sources of inspiration. That the characters portrayed in these productions are not Muslims makes little difference. As Larkin (1997:406) notes in the Nigerian context, "Indian films have entered into the dialogic construction of Hausa popular culture by offering Hausa men and women an alternative world, similar to their own, from which they may imagine other forms of fashion, beauty, love, and romance, coloniality and postcoloniality." In Dogondoutchi, fashion-conscious *budurwoyi* (unmarried girls) are shaving their eyebrows and highlighting their contours with black pencil in imitation of the pretty heroines of Hindi films that are flooding the local video and DVD rental market. Under

Figure 7.10. Girl wearing *hijabi* over a headband marked "2000."

their *hijabai,* a few don the single wrap dress known as *a sari*—a fashion some preachers encourage on the basis that women in Mecca allegedly wear these. Some women apply a spot of red nail polish between their eyebrows to achieve what is locally known as the "Hindu" look. They have learned to imitate to perfection the graceful arm motions of dancing Indian heroines, and although they have no understanding of Hindi, they routinely intone the melodies and mimic the sounds of the Hindi songs featured in popular Indian films.[26]

Through their indigenization of Hindi fashions and aesthetics, young Dogondoutchi women routinely demonstrate the extent to which the models of consumption provided by Indian cinema have become central to Nigérien public culture. "Modern fashion," Hollander (1993:304–305) notes in the context of Euro-American sartorial practices,

> is confirmed and enhanced by the glamour of screen and television stars, under the guise of being ordinary clothes. For modern clothing, certain commonly accepted coiffures, ways of opening the collar, choices and combinations of common garments, when worn by the superstars confirm the acutely contemporary

"rightness" of the particular mode and the sense of glamour. The audience achieves a sense of glamour by association, even in wearing the very common mode.

Just as the baggy pants, oversized T-shirts, ankle-high athletic shoes, and baseball caps of rap performers are now part of the outfit de rigueur for young Nigérien men wishing to appear fashionable, so the Hindi look, inspired by Indian cinema, has become popular among their female counterparts. In this regard, I suspect that sheer scarves imported from South Asia and adorned with subtle blue, yellow, or green impressions became the rage in the mid-1990s—when Indian cinema became available for local consumption—partly because they resembled the flowing head veils sometimes worn by female characters in Indian films.

Latin American telenovelas, widely described by conservative Muslim leaders as a threat to the moral order because of their explicit depictions of romantic love and sexuality, provide another precious source of inspiration for fashion-conscious young women. Many of the style tips—skin-tight pants, curve-enhancing tops, and straightened hair—that can be gleaned from these television programs are worn by secular, French-schooled Muslims for whom clothing is a means of signaling their cosmopolitanism rather than a mark of religious identity. Yet even *hijabi*-clad young women occasionally find confirmation in their favorite television series that their (or someone else's) looks can be modest and glamorous at the same time. In a conversation with Fatima on how women should demonstrate piety in their personal appearance, the young woman instructed me on how to wear the *hijabi*. It is important that both hair and ears are hidden, she pointed out. As she was tying my head scarf—a simple square of cloth—around my head to demonstrate precisely how it was done, her younger sister pointed out excitedly that my newly configured head covering looked just like the headscarf worn by Laura—one of the main protagonists of *La Rue des Mariés*, a popular Brazilian soap opera airing in Niger in 2004. "It is very pretty," she had exclaimed, referring to my head scarf, "as pretty as Laura's." What intrigued me, aside from the young girl's assumption that "Laura" was so famous as to need no introduction, was how Brazilian urban fashions could serve as a model of Islamic propriety for West African girls (as well as Western visitors seeking to adopt a modest look).

That a foreign television star wore a headscarf not only enhanced the glamour of the item but also confirmed its contemporary "rightness" in the eyes of a young Izala follower looking for validation. Now that it was associated with the sophisticated fashions of *La Rue des Mariés*, the headscarf her sister had tied around my head was no longer an ordinary item. It had acquired a particular aura, which, rather than clashing with Muslim rules of pious deportment, affirmed their appropriateness.[27] Besides confirming Nigérien youth's participation in a global order of cultural practices, the recent infatuation with certain Hindi or Latin American styles demonstrates how local emblems of sartorial modesty are caught up in various "webs of signification, some contradictory, some complimentary—providing both ambiguity and flexibility" (Durham 1999:395). It also shows that the Middle East is but one of many places of sartorial inspiration, "one node of a complex transnational construction of imaginary landscapes" (Appadurai 1996:30). Whereas Meccan fashions authorize the creation of various sartorial expressions of purity and piety, the local images of modesty these fashions inspire occasionally resonate with, but just as often are contradicted or even undermined by, other images from other places that young Mawri girls selectively appropriate in their efforts to claim membership in a worldwide community of seemingly empowered consumers.

Conclusion

The *hijabi* that was originally emblematic of the austere and uncompromising values of Izala—as well as a concrete expression of divisiveness—is now part of a wider moral aesthetics through which young girls, even when they are constrained by fatherly expectations, can engage in more masterful and fashion-conscious acts of self-definition. Not unlike the Egyptian veil that is now worn with "bright accessories and blue jeans" (Armbrust 1999:128) rather than as the severe, loose-fitting uniform of reformist Islam, the *hijabi* has "migrated" across different bodies, markets, and moral arenas as local expressions of what is deemed "Islamic" shifted, pushed along by the transnational tides of fashion and religiosity. Along the way it has acquired diverse meanings, has been caught up in different frames of moral references, and has been used to formulate changing modes of religiosity.

Partly because the *hijabi* in Dogondoutchi, in addition to undergoing stylistic changes, has moved along the local spectrum of fashionability and expanded the range of religious affiliations it represents, it is problematic to describe it exclusively as an undifferentiated sign of piety, an expression of subordination (El Saadawi 1980; Mernissi 1987), an unambiguous vehicle of emancipation (MacLeod 1991; Zuhur 1992), or, conversely, a symbol of resistance (Fanon 1965; Kandiyoti 1991). To do so would imply a consensual intentionality among *hijabi* wearers that is lacking in the current context. If anything, the flexible signifying capacity of the *hijabi* (and other head coverings) sheds light on the slipperiness of religious identities and the "shifting positionality of persons caught in the web of group-affiliations" (Durham 1999:390–391). It is that elusiveness and the "shifting positionality" the veil enables that I have tried to illuminate by examining the different contexts that inform and inspire, and in some cases naturalize, the wearing of head coverings. Through this focus I have shown that the meaning of the veil is not "exhausted by its significance as a sign" (Mahmood 2005:56). Occasionally, what the veil does, how it feels, and how its texture and shape speak to the wearer and to those who see her emerges in the context of particular practices—such as watching Brazilian telenovelas—that are neither religious nor approved by the local Muslim leadership.

That young women seeking to fashion Muslim identities look to Brazil or India for inspiration complicates conventional equations of globalization as cultural homogenization. It also suggests that the West is hardly the only source of cultural capital for those seeking access to things modern and to symbols of the "modern." At the same time women's growing tendency to wear *hijabai* (if only occasionally) nonetheless suggests an intensified concern for appearing to order one's life according to what are perceived as uniformly defined Islamic standards of piety and propriety.

In stark contrast to the articulate exegeses produced by Egyptian women who assemble in the mosque to debate the meaning of the veil and the practice of veiling (Mahmood 2005), women in Dogondoutchi rarely, if ever, feel the need to explain why they veil beyond the customary "I veil *sabo da Allah*—because God demands it." When asked directly why they wear a *hijabi*, some invoke *kumya* (shame, modesty), others mention the benefits of receiving *daraja* (respect), but most simply say that it is a means of "covering the body." I contend that women's lack of satisfying explanations for wearing *hijabi*, *hirami*, and *lullu'bi* is itself indicative of the ways that head coverings, regardless of the religious identities they are meant to emblematize, silently participate in the constitution of virtuous subjectivities. Because the meaning of veils, for some women, encompasses an entire mode of being-in-the-world that is acquired mimetically, the modesty expressed and cultivated through veiling obeys a logic that seems vested more in embodied experience than in conceptual categories. From this perspective, saying that the *hijabi* "covers the body" is considered an adequate response to the question about why women need to veil. One could say, paraphrasing Bourdieu's (1977:167) famous *bon mot:* "It goes without saying because it comes without saying."

Although the debate over whether women should veil, and, if so, at what age and in what circumstances and the very practice of wearing *hijabai* (and, in many cases, *hiramai*) are mostly controlled by men and driven by husbandly desires, it would be wrong to assume that women have relinquished all control over matters of modesty. Indeed, women have found many ways to gain influence over the terms of dress and morality. The selective appropriation of foreignness that televised drama appears to authorize among youthful audiences is but one instance of the creative and contextually specific ways that women caught in polemics about religious authenticity redefine their identities as moral persons. Thus Fatima, who insisted that a woman could wear makeup and shiny clothes but only to please her husband—and in the privacy of her own home, routinely instructed her own husband on the specific type of veil she wanted him to bring back for her from his trips to Nigeria. She was accustomed to getting what she wanted. As a child growing up in a prosperous Izala household, she always wore fashionable shoes that the neighborhood girls all envied. She was an excellent student, and her father happily rewarded her for her scholarly successes by buying her the shoes she had set her eyes on, no matter the cost. Even when not particularly loquacious about the subject of veiling, women nevertheless participate in struggles over the terms in which virtuous modesty is inscribed onto their bodies, struggles that are "at once political, moral, and aesthetic" (Comaroff and Comaroff 1997:222). Because they are often silent, these struggles signal the need for a "politics of presence" (Moors 2006:120) that would allow women's nonverbal forms of engagement in the public sphere to be recognized as a suitable mode of communication.[28]

"THE FART DOES NOT LIGHT THE FIRE": "BAD" WOMEN, "TRUE" BELIEVERS, AND THE RECONFIGURATION OF MORAL DOMESTICITY

8

The paradise of woman lies under the foot of her husband.
—*Mawri proverb*

Women must stay home and when the *mai gida* [head of the household, husband] comes back from his studies, they must be ready to wash his clothes and his prayer beads. If you do the work, women, you will enter paradise. If you don't, you will burn in hell.
—*Malam Awal, sermon of November 1999*

If a woman does not speak kindly to her husband, on the day of resurrection, God is going to pull her tongue till it reaches seventy meters and wrap it around her body to shut her up. She will go to hell forever and her tongue will be tied like a rope around her body.
—*Malam Awal, sermon of April 22, 1999*

"You women, do you hear me? Keep on going to the market after you have put on your makeup. If you are alive today, tomorrow you will die!" Malam Awal bellowed during one of his sermons in March 2000. Ever since his arrival in Dogondoutchi, the Sufi preacher had latched onto women as the most patent site of "wickedness" that had to be thoroughly eradicated if society was to survive the looming threats to its already compromised moral integrity. Wicked women, in Malam Awal's view, challenged the standard expectations of piety, modesty, and respectability that "good" Muslim wives, mothers, and daughters ideally exemplified. They not only violated established norms of gendered behavior but also threatened the moral foundation of society. As noted earlier, much of the debate over what constitutes pious behavior in contemporary Niger has centered on women's activities and deportment, as their moral constitution is perceived as a symbol of the broader social order. It is widely acknowledged among conservative Muslims that the growing number of ills—from unemployment to AIDS to corruption and prostitution—currently plaguing Nigérien society are caused by moral decadence and a loss of spiritual values. In their selfish pursuits, people have forgotten their religious duties and have fallen prey to foreign ideologies. 'Yan Izala blame this situation on the government's failure to model its constitution and legal apparatus after the Qur'an. Only by implementing and enforcing *shari'a* (Islamic law) will the government succeed in solving the problems afflicting the country. Their view is a reminder that, for many Nigériens, the notion of a constitutionally secular but overwhelmingly Muslim society is inherently problematic.

For those who believe that imported visions of society only encourage immorality while yielding few social improvements, Islam provides an ideology that is "divinely sanctioned and hence far superior to those of mere human provenance" (Gaffney 1994:114). From this perspective, it is only by returning to a pure and "authentic" Islam, highly concerned with women as repositories of morality, that Nigérien society can hope to survive the corrupting influence of the West. Despite their distinct orientations, the various Muslim traditions that have proliferated since the recent emergence of democracy in Niger appear to share a preoccupation with female agency and female spaces. Because their role as emblems (as well as promoters) of piety and purity is so critical to the definition of moral boundaries, women have become the object of increasingly regulatory practices ultimately aimed at restoring order in a society that for some is on the verge of moral bankruptcy. In this chapter I examine some of these practices by focusing on the rhetorical strategies through which Malam Awal routinely threatened women into behaving as pious believers. I also discuss local women's responses to the stigmatization of their identities as wives, mothers, and Muslims.

Recall that Malam Awal, when he first started preaching, attracted a sizable audience among Dogondoutchi residents who had come to resent the exactions of *malamai* suspected of siphoning alms intended for the poor and the remonstrances of reformist Muslims denouncing people's ignorance and impiety. Women especially were drawn to the preacher. They believed that his vision of Islamic society provided a welcome alternative to the current moral order by letting them adopt newly configured signs of piety, such as "proper" head coverings, without sacrificing to certain deeply entrenched Sufi traditions (such as the veneration of Sufi masters) which Izala activists denounced as un-Islamic. More important, perhaps, Malam Awal routinely addressed women's concerns (about marriage and domesticity, for instance), providing concrete, illuminating discussions of the relevant issues and supplying corroborating evidence from the Qur'an and *sunna* (code of conduct modeled on the Prophet as told in the *hadith*). Because the large majority of his disciples were women, Awal earned the sobriquet of *malamin mata*, "teacher of women," from sarcastic 'yan Izala wishing to ridicule him.

Despite his constant efforts to expand his following and solidify his power base, Malam Awal's popularity was short-lived. Those who had heartily supported him when he first disseminated his message of reform began to doubt his integrity. Rumors circulated in 2001 that he did not live by the values he so aggressively championed: he missed prayers, engaged in promiscuous behavior, and lied about his miracles. Furthermore, he relentlessly pressured his followers for additional funds, even after it had become clear that not all the money contributed toward the construction of the mosque had been used for that purpose—which is why, perhaps, the structure still lacked a roof several years after the first brick was laid. Feeling used and disillusioned, the prosperous merchants who had financed much of the project gradually deserted him, dragging women, children, and other dependents with them. Prominent town officials, among them the mayor and the town chief, similarly withdrew their support. Their move in turn precipitated additional desertions in their entourage.[1] Two former disciples told me that they had pulled their children out of Awal's school because the preacher no longer taught the children anything but songs.[2] Many people suspected that he encouraged dancing and singing (at the expense of Qur'anic studies) to attract young girls so that he could select new potential mates from among the prettiest ones. They felt that Awal's personal agenda increasingly clashed with their expectations of how a religious leader should act. Instead of promoting the cultivation of discipline, devotion, and virtue among his students by presenting himself as a model of ethical improvement, Awal took advantage of his disciples' trust to satisfy his own yearnings.

As rumors of his alleged impiety spread, people's devotion to the preacher increasingly gave way to skepticism and resentment. Attendance at Awal's sermons felt. In late 2004, some four years after the lavish celebration to commemorate Malam Awal's arrival in town, which I described earlier, the membership of the Awaliyya had dwindled to a few households. Of those who remained members, most lived in Maizari, Awal's own neighborhood; their continued commitment to the order was presumably facilitated by their proximity to the Awaliyya mosque. That year the preacher's considerable loss of prestige was most effectively conveyed by a neighbor who jokingly pointed out that Malam Awal was "the only man" at the *zawiya*. Everyone knew, he later explained, that the membership of the Awaliyya had shrunk considerably and that most men had abandoned the preacher. Aside from the two dozen households heads and their dependents who still professed allegiance to Awal, there remained a compact nucleus of elder women—mostly widows who no longer had to submit to a husband's authority. A few young men on the brink of adulthood also remained loyal to Awal. Some were members of the militia that the preacher had created. It was widely believed that they continued to support the preacher because they lacked maturity and therefore could not see the preacher's flaws. Anyone with any *wayo* ("sense") had grown tired of the preacher's antics and ended their association with the Awaliyya. The handful of white-clad female elders who, in 2004, passed by my house every morning on their way to the Awaliyya mosque confirmed the widespread perception that, as one former disciple tersely put it, "only old women now follow Malam Awal."[3]

Women of childbearing age had severed their ties with the Awaliyya under the dictates of disillusioned husbands eager to dissociate themselves from the preacher's project of spiritual reform. Most senior women, on the other hand, left of their own accord. Many were widows or divorced women who could do as they pleased without incurring opprobrium and who did not fear divorce as was true for their junior counterparts. Of the senior women who were married, large numbers had originally defied husbandly authority to follow Malam Awal. Eventually they felt compelled to reject (or at least ignore) Malam Awal's message rather than be subjected to the preacher's unrelenting criticism and mercenary designs. They had much to say about the climate of "spiritual insecurity" (Ashforth 1998) cultivated by the preacher, which no longer corresponded to the religious sensibilities they once hoped to develop under his guidance. According to Ashforth (1998), the epistemic anxiety fueled by a conceptualization of socioeconomic struggles in religious terms is a form of spiritual insecurity, which develops in contexts where an overabundance of interpretive authorities claiming to speak the truth about what ails society prevents any from achieving dominance. It often manifests itself in an ongoing apprehension about the parameters of religious life. In this chapter I explore how Malam Awal targeted local women's alleged lack of virtue as a symptom of society's moral ills and how the economy of anxiety his preaching generated affected women's religious sensibilities. To understand how women came to reject the religious authority they had originally embraced, I analyze the "sinful" wife and other moralizing terminologies employed by Malam Awal in the context of his own experience of women and marriage, and as part of a wider discourse of masculine power that seeks to contain women within continuously renegotiated socio-moral norms.

For some of Awaliyya's most fervent disciples, it was the preacher's repeated insistence on the impious nature of his listeners and on the inevitability of their hellish fate that drove them away. Disillusioned by Awal's obstinate focus on the punishment awaiting sinners, they, too, progressively withdrew their support. Among them were many of the senior women who had flocked to the preacher's electrifying sermons in the heyday of his popularity and who, through their labor and resources, had contributed to the vitality of the Awaliyya. The testimonies of some of these former disciples suggest that contrary to the idealized portrait that has been painted of some Muslim saints (Roberts and Roberts 2003), the allegiance that binds a Muslim leader to his disciples is neither permanent nor necessarily stable. By focusing on women's capacity to evaluate the preacher's mission, I explore some of the ways in which, despite their limited involvement in matters of religion, women in Dogondoutchi "participate in their own ways in Islam, manipulating it and accommodating it to their needs" (Coulon 1988:115).

In examining female resistance to Muslim authority, I am mindful of Abu-Lughod's observation that, in giving women credit for defying the power of those who control much of their lives, we must be cautious not to attribute to them forms of consciousness that "are not part of their experience" (1990:47). Routinely Mawri women defy some of the restrictive practices (such as seclusion and modest behavior) to which they are subjected by covering up for one another in front of their husbands, by sneaking out to visit a friend, or by resisting marriage, but these acts of defiance do not threaten the status quo. Although subversive, their stance is not easily encompassed by such notions as counter-hegemony. Nor can it be said to be motivated by a feminist consciousness. Indeed, the problem I faced when considering female agency was often that women appeared to both resist and embrace the rules that defined their place in society.

By looking at the ways in which former Awaliyya women I spoke with justified their progressive disaffection with Awal's vision of Islam, I trace the particular forms that female resistance takes when it is articulated around what Foucault (1980:83) calls "subjugated knowledge," that is, knowledge that has been categorized as low-ranked because it is insufficiently elaborated, lacks cohesion, and is therefore inadequate to the task. In Dogondoutchi, women are seen by men (but also by women themselves) as irreligious and bound by tradition. Although they do not engage in public acts of piety (such as attending prayer at a local mosque), they rely heavily on *malamai* for advice, to procure medicines for various ailments, and to seek protection from spiritual forces or jealous co-wives, practices their husbands often de-

246

plore. They are perceived as gullible and lacking in judgment, and therefore less likely to differentiate "truth" from "quackery." In the late 1980s a popular northern Nigerian song that made fun of women who fell prey to charlatans described in much detail how the victims lost their savings, and at times their virtue, to unscrupulous *malamai* in whose care they foolishly entrusted themselves.

But these gendered views of knowledge and religiosity should not blind us to the multiple ways that women claim space and status in the emerging moral order. Though it is largely true that women enjoy limited access to Qur'anic education, rarely attend mosque activities, and do not officiate at religious festivals, they are nonetheless helping to shape religious discourse as well as the conditions of their collective existence as Muslims. When senior women became disenchanted with the Awaliyya, they voted with their feet and abandoned their religious leader. Rather than openly voicing their discontent, they simply stopped attending Malam Awal's sermons. They also stopped contributing domestic help and logistical support—a move that would profoundly impact the preacher's livelihood and the functioning of the Awaliyya. Aside from reminding us that women are "neither passive objects nor merely symbols given meaning by men" (Bernal 1994:56), women's rejection of Awaliyya values highlights the gendered dimension of religious experience: many *yan* Awaliyya turned their backs on Awal's preaching precisely because they felt devalued as women and wives.

My examination of women's response to Awal's punitive rhetoric is guided by the recognition that the conditions securing women's subordination occasionally also provide them with the means to resist that subordination (Butler 1997; Foucault 1980). A number of women I spoke with continued to adhere to Awal's model of Islamic virtue, its principles, and its modalities, even after they rejected the preacher. A brief examination of three senior women who challenged the preacher's authority even as they continued to live in accordance with the vision of Islam articulated by Awal illustrates that women's capacity to critically assess the Sufi master's message was enabled by the very content of that message. First, however, contextualizing the local practice of listening to sermons is in order.

Attending Sermons

Traditionally Dogondoutchi women did not attend *wa'azai* (sermons). Aside from the fact that their presence at local mosques violated strict rules of gender segregation,[4] their domestic duties would generally have kept them busy during much of the day. Although women are expected to be knowledgeable about the Qur'an, seeking an education outside the marital home was largely impractical, until recently. Once a woman is married, it is her husband's responsibility to see that she is exposed to the salvatory effects of the Qur'an so that she in turn can educate her children.[5] In the late 1980s I met few Muslim wives who claimed to have been tutored at home and fewer still who had completed the *sabka Alkur'ani* ("putting down the Qur'an," the ceremony held after students have memorized the entire Qur'an). Most women, however, could recite the first few verses of the Qur'an. In the early 1990s Muslim reformists, in their attempt to eradicate *jahilci* (ignorance about Islam), held bi-weekly night sermons that housewives could attend after their daily domestic chores were accomplished. They encouraged their wives and daughters to congregate in the part of the mosque specifically designated for women and from which one could hear the sermon delivery in relative privacy, away from men's presence. Women complied eagerly.

In addition to providing exegetic elucidation of the Qur'an and clarifications on basic religious duties, these weekly meetings were valued for the social possibilities they afforded women who were otherwise rarely allowed to step outside the marital compound. By creating a context in which women could meet female neighbors and friends, Thursday and Sunday night sermons provided a kind of "alibi" for women's social gatherings, as the following incident illustrates. One Thursday evening in 1994, while attending an Izala sermon with a friend, I noticed that the women around me were engaged in animated conversations, seemingly oblivious to the words of the preacher. The latter was addressing issues of education (*tarbiyya*) and of parental responsibility, but, despite my best efforts, I could not understand him. Frustrated as much by the women's lively chatter as by my inability to make out the preacher's words, distorted as they were by the substandard sound system, I asked the young woman sitting next to me whether she could tell me what the last bundle of crackly sentences escaping from the amplifier had been about. The preacher, the young woman told me, shrugging her shoulders and tilting her head, was from Nigeria. She, too, was having difficulty understanding his Hausa, as it was inflected with a Kano accent. After asking in vain for another woman's assistance, I realized that none of the women present was actually listening to the preacher. The shrill sound distortions produced by the loudspeakers, the preacher's heavily accented speech, and his repeated use of Qur'anic excerpts in Arabic discouraged their attempts to grasp the content of the sermon. Actively engaged in their own private conversations, the assembled women paid no attention to the preacher's words.

None of them understood Arabic, and yet they were clearly enjoying the moment.

By muddling the message, poor sound transmission, noise, and foreign accents ironically reproduce the very conditions that Izala reformists have been trying to eradicate in their move to facilitate women's access to religious education. These conditions exonerate women for their ignorance of Islam and their lack of engagement with Muslim life, thereby reaffirming the status quo. Because some Izala sermons are largely unintelligible to women, their didactic impact on female audiences is limited.[6] If Thursday and Sunday night sermons appear to provide minimal, or at least uneven, opportunities for women's religious enlightenment, they nonetheless offer a welcome respite from seclusion. Like the female-based Qur'anic literacy classes in Niamey that have become gathering places for female activities such as trading in women's products (Alidou 2005), sermons are productive spaces of interaction for women who seek to escape the confines of the household without violating norms of propriety and privacy. Because of the religious content of these lectures, Alidou notes (2005:18), "most Muslim men who would normally object to their wives and daughters attending female gatherings end up granting them permission" to go to the schools. Similarly, rather than objecting to their womenfolk going out at night, 'yan Izala in Dogondoutchi encourage these activities because they are motivated by the pursuit of greater insight into ways of being a "proper" Muslim.

When Malam Awal started preaching nightly, women in my neighborhood regularly left their homes once darkness had set in to congregate at the site of the sermon. To secure company and garner emotional support (against a disapproving husband, for instance), they often arranged to meet neighbors before making their way to the zawiya, the Sufi center, at the other end of town. Predictably only senior women who could no longer be seen as potential objects of seduction dared leave the family compound on their own to attend Awaliyya sermons. Even if their actions were interpreted as defiance against husbandly will,[7] they could claim a higher moral ground as God's dutiful servants: after all, wasn't seeking enlightenment one of the primary duties of a Muslim woman?

Religious enlightenment can assume a variety of forms. In this respect, the notable fact that women attending a sermon may only partly understand its content should not lead us to assume that sermon attendance is purely a social act, devoid of religious significance. Piety, for local women "listening" to an admonition peppered with Qur'anic verses they do not understand and filtered by a defective broadcast system, may reside not so much in the reflexive space opened up by the preacher's words as in the motions, emotions, and sensations that constitute the experience of attending a sermon. Besides providing a discursive message to audiences, sermons also shape the sensibilities, habits, and affects of their listeners by contributing to the "acoustic architecture of a distinct moral vision" (Hirschkind 2006:8). If sermon oratory can be said to "recruit the body of the listener in multiple ways" (Hirschkind 2006:98), in Dogondoutchi women's capacities to hear (not only with their ears but with their hearts) were nevertheless severely constrained by their limited linguistic comprehension of Izala admonitions.

By contrast, Awal's charismatic sermon delivery was compelling. His flamboyant style and eloquence, the vividness of his narratives, and the gravity of his admonitory lessons brought sermon listening to a heightened level of experience—and, given the interactive format of his sermons and the clarity of his exposition, to a sharper understanding as well. In the opinion of his female disciples, his oratorical prowess was unmatched. Unlike his Izala foes who often "mystified the listeners with Arabic phrases" (Kaba 2000:203), Awal spoke in plain language. Whether he listed a woman's many duties to her husband or explained how the meat of a slaughtered ram should be apportioned among kin, friends, and neighbors, he provided straightforward responses to people's questions and illustrated his argument with concrete, illuminating examples. Sermons, he explained to me, should provide practical information in a manner similar to the way traffic signs guide drivers on the road.

In the "aurally saturated environment" (Hirschkind 2006:10) of Dogondoutchi's central neighborhoods, the forceful sound of Malam Awal's voice, amplified through the many loudspeakers hanging from trees or rooftops, cuts through the background noise rising from the streets to urge listeners to live as devout Muslims and reject the devil's temptations. During my two-month stay in 2000, a day rarely went by without a local broadcast of his strident, often angry voice blaring through amplifiers strategically positioned throughout Dogondoutchi's central district so as to maximize transmission across neighborhoods. Recordings of his sermons could also be heard from within tailor shops, market stalls, and compound walls at any time of the day and night. Inasmuch as the democratization of sermon distribution ushered by the proliferation of mass media can be said to have "transform[ed] popular perceptions of what constitutes a religious genre" (Schulz 2003:157; Eickelman and Anderson 1999; Meyer and Moors 2006), Malam Awal's performances effectively blurred the boundaries between worldly and religious matters by infiltrating secular settings. For those who listened regularly to

250

the preacher's sermons, sermon consumption was first and foremost a matter of spiritual enlightenment. Yet it could also be experienced as an exciting event, a form of "infotainment" that captured the imagination of its audiences. Malam Awal understood well how to use the media to add flair to his revivalist message and expand his following. The preacher was known for telling "very good" stories. Ironically, if Awal's reliance on broadcast technologies enhanced his audience's spiritual experience, as we shall see, the economy of images and sounds it spawned ultimately contributed to the preacher's downfall.

Throughout all his public performances, Malam Awal presented himself as a religious expert uniquely qualified to define the terms of pious living and lead his followers on the path to virtue. As the rightly guided *shehu* (leader) who, by defeating ignorance and immorality, would rescue the town's residents from the hellish fate that previously awaited them, Malam Awal originally enjoyed wide approval among those who felt that he "spoke the truth." That he occasionally formatted part of his sermons as question-and-answer sessions on doctrinal, ritual, and moral issues highlighted for many the breadth of the preacher's erudition. Only a scholar armed with vast stores of knowledge would, people surmised, consent to be interrogated on a wide variety of issues on the spot. When the preacher was away, videotaped versions of his admonitions would be routinely aired in front of the Awaliyya mosque. Although, by 2002, he had largely become invisible (in keeping with his reputation as a holy man and also because he occasionally fled to Nigeria to dodge arrest), Malam Awal remained, owing to his daily vocal presence, the most ubiquitous figure of what, admittedly, was a contested sonic landscape.

The Sufi scholar was a gifted raconteur who could narrate the life story of a prophet or discuss a well-known allegory with all the necessary contextual details before delivering a dramatic but edifying conclusion. He was also an accomplished singer, much admired for his artful performance of *ishirinya*, devotional songs that he taught to the young, unmarried members of his order as part of their religious training. These songs had a joyful dimension that soon made them an essential feature of local Awaliyya wedding celebrations and naming ceremonies. In the evening, live or recorded *ishirinya* performances would regularly take over the local soundscape, at times clashing with the preaching voices of Izala clerics berating the faithful for sinfully indulging in the sensuous pleasures of dancing or listening to music. The birth of a child or the Prophet's birthday, the preacher insisted, should be celebrated in expansive style. Drumming, singing, and dancing were excellent conduits for the expression of joy and delight.[8] In one of his sermons, the preacher explained it to his audience:

> During the time of the Prophet, the people were celebrating Idi [celebration in commemoration of the sacrifice of Abraham]. At a feast, a woman came to play the *dunduha* [long narrow drum]. Someone asked, "How come there are drums in front of the house of the Prophet?" The Prophet answered, "Leave her. Everyone has a way of celebrating Idi. It is not harmful to be joyful and play music." It is acceptable to prepare food, to engage in pleasing activities, and to meet with friends.

Like other Sufi leaders, Awal believed that the life of a Muslim should be filled with emotionally and aesthetically pleasing acts that expressed one's devotion to God. Because he enjoined his disciples to sing and dance when honoring God, Izala preachers derogatorily referred to him as *"mai wa'ke wa'ke"* (the one who sings night and day). Yet it was precisely the cheerful and heartwarming dimension of these devotional practices that had attracted local residents to Awaliyya in the first place. Though they were inclined to adopt an ethic of frugal commensality similar to Izala's, they were unwilling to abandon Sufi-inspired practices such as chanting, which they saw as central to the cultivation of a closeness with God.[9]

Cultivating a Fear of Death

In his elegant and persuasive account of the Islamic revival in Cairo, Hirschkind illuminates how cassette-recorded sermons effectively move listeners to scrutinize their moral conduct and ultimately bring them closer to God; listening to sermons, he claims, is a way of "'remortifying' life within the larger reality of death and the hereafter" (2006:176). In Niger, the extent to which the forceful reality of the afterlife "imprints itself on mundane existence" (ibid.:174) is routinely demonstrated by the profusion of sermons on the torments and misery awaiting "unbelievers" in hell and the many acts of piety that Muslims perform to ward off this dreaded potentiality. Muslim preachers commonly evoke the hellish pains that await impious Muslims to cultivate in their listeners a fear of God. True believers, they proclaim, should fear God; *tsoron Allah*, which means literally "fear of God," is the expression Hausa speakers use to refer to faith. Those who fear God, the term implies, are faithful to God at the same time that they fear His punishment. Fear of divine retribution moves Muslims to lead a virtuous life in accordance with the precepts of the Qur'an. In the words of one Izala preacher, "God told

Muslims, 'You, Muslims, work diligently and fear me. If you have not worked hard, if you do not fear me, even if you have the Qur'an in your hands, I will send you to hell, to the hottest hell.'" Describing hell as a place with varying degrees of pain is a frequent rhetorical device preachers use to motivate their audiences into abandoning their sinful ways.[10] I once heard an Izala preacher describe in great detail the four levels of hell where one could be sent depending on the severity of one's wrongdoing. Each level of hell was extremely hot, but the hottest was reserved for those who did not fear God—and who did not take the threat of divine retribution seriously.

Ideally, Hirschkind (2006:177) notes, an emphasis on death shapes an ethical sensibility and gives "direction and purpose" to life while helping to avoid misconduct. People tend to err, I was often told, when they are not thinking about God. They become distracted about *abubuwa duniya* (the things of this world) and forget that they should only be thinking about pleasing God. When they are routinely reminded of God's possible retribution, they are less likely to commit faults. In Dogondoutchi, however, the awareness of mortality and its consequences has a more ominous potential for those who take literally the admonition that they will suffer the worst imaginable pains if they are ultimately found to be undeserving of eternal felicity. In the popular imagination, each failure to observe Qur'anic proscriptions, each lapse in the performance of religious duties, automatically translates into a misdeed, the sum of which eventually determines whether one ends up in *lahira* (paradise) or in *wuta* (hell) on *ranar hisabi* (the day of accounting). Because they widely believe that offenses (*alhuka*), even if largely unintentional, will be weighed against the rewards (*lada*) one accrues through the performance of pious acts, Muslims live in fear that their bad deeds will tip the scale in their disfavor on Judgment Day.

One can never know, of course, the overall weight of one's bad deeds, especially since preachers occasionally engage in complex arithmetic—certain misdeeds are so serious that they cancel out any *lada* one has accumulated—to impress upon their audiences the gravity of a particular offense.[11] The added possibility that the deeds of someone whom one has hurt or mistreated will be heaped onto one's own scale—or that one's own bad deeds will affect one's kin's chances of eternal bliss—further complicate the picture many Dogondoutchi residents have of their possible fate.[12] To minimize the possibility of an eternal life in hell, some engage in additional acts of piety (for example, extra prayers, alms giving, or sending parents or spouses on the pilgrimage to Mecca) that together with routine commitment to Qur'anic principles will outweigh bad deeds. For instance, a young man I knew followed a rigorous disciplinary regimen that included sleeping on a narrow bench with his limbs twisted and tangled in such a way that he supposedly reproduced with his body the name of Allah in Arabic script. Too poor to imagine ever being able to wash out his wrong actions by going on the pilgrimage to Mecca, he had devised this particularly Spartan means of shaping his body into a vessel of piety in order to accumulate rewards. Aside from pointing to the far-reaching, intimate ways in which some "adjust [their lives] to accord with death" (Hirschkind 2006:184), adopting such an ascetic and exacting lifestyle also demonstrates the extent to which the notion that one must forego worldly pleasures to taste the sweetness of paradise is ingrained in local understandings of the hereafter.

Dread and Felicity in Awaliyya Sermons

As part of a widespread effort to cultivate *tsoron Allah* (faith) in their audience, Muslim preachers depict in graphic detail the dreadful suffering awaiting those who do not heed the lessons of the Qur'an. In this respect, Malam Awal was no exception. Although the hellish punishments he described defied even the most vivid imagination, they almost always fit the deed. Recall his admonition to women (cited at the opening of the chapter) that if one of them spoke unkindly—read, disrespectfully—to her husband, God would ultimately "pull her tongue till it reache[d] seventy meters and wrap it around her body to shut her up" before sending her to hell. By evoking torments of the most unlikely kind, the preacher aimed to capture his listeners' moral imagination, stretched to accommodate the wide diversity of calamities awaiting those found guilty of an offense. Rather than helping cultivate a pious self, however, the images of stretched tongues and scorched bodies that vividly imprinted themselves on the mind appeared to foster deep insecurity about the narrow parameters of Islamic morality and inevitable damnation on Judgment Day.

At a sermon I attended, Malam Awal explained that if the site where one dug a tomb for a dead person was very hard, that meant the deceased was a wrongdoer who would not enter paradise. A friend who had accompanied me told me afterward that she was sometimes afraid to listen to Awal's speeches because doing so reminded her of her many deficiencies: "It's always about hell. There is no place where you can go to have your misdeeds erased." Because she worried so much about her fate in the hereafter, my friend preferred sermons that were balanced with references to God's benevolence and His capacity to forgive. A good preacher, she insisted, would not simply allude to the horrors of the grave. He would also mention the "good things" awaiting pious believers in the hereafter. In her opinion, people needed to be jolted into submission, but they must also be encouraged by regularly being told that their efforts to follow the righteous path were not futile.

To his credit, Malam Awal did combine the rhetoric of fear with that of hope in his admonitions in an effort to revitalize a community that, in his eyes, sorely needed moral reform. Yet he delivered such dire warnings to his listeners that he gave them few assurances that the fiery tortures of hell could be avoided. Aspiring to develop in his audience an ability to scrutinize everyday conduct, he implacably went over every scenario that would inevitably condemn the perpetrator to an afterlife of pain and anguish. Women, he insisted, were especially at risk. Consider the following excerpt from a sermon the preacher delivered in June 1999:

> Whatever the worthiness of a woman, regardless of who she is married to, if she is not caring and patient with her husband, she won't see heaven. [. . .] If she has refused to help her husband when he needed money to buy firewood and feed the family, on the day of resurrection, her face will turn all black and she will go to hell. I am informing you women that nothing can save you on Judgment Day except God. You may be married to a king or an important man, it won't make any difference. God is going to bring the angels of hell to prevent those who tempt you into behaving in a sinful manner. The power of God will win over anything. But he will not forgive you if you have not served your husband well. The Prophet told his daughter Fatima that regardless of a woman's social worth, she should not criticize her husband for his failings. If she did, she would never even smell heaven. Even if you are 500 years away from heaven, you can still smell it. But a woman who berates her husband, she will not even get a whiff of it. Even if she prays, God will not accept her prayers.
>
> If you steal from your husband, [the same fate awaits you]. Say a husband gives his wife 500 CFA francs, and she hides 250 CFA francs, or he gives her a kilogram of rice, and she hides half of it to sell later. All the prayer that she performs all her life, God will not accept them. He will not accept any of her fasts for as long as she lives because she has stolen her husband's wealth. Even if she gives the money she has stolen as alms, it won't do any good. She will burn in hell. It is her husband who will receive the *lada* [reward received for the performance of a pious act] from her alms and he will also receive as alms a sum matching that which his wife stole from him.
>
> But I am going to give you good news. If a woman welcomes her husband back home with a bowl of water or some *fura* [millet porridge] and if she holds the *faifai* [round mat used by woman to cover calabashes] until he finishes his drinking, God will reward her like he rewarded Rahamatou, the wife of the prophet Ayouba. She will receive many rewards, as many as was given Rahamatou. As well as Mariama, the mother of Issa [Jesus]. And all the women who behave in such a manner toward their husbands, God will make sure that they meet in heaven. Where are you, women who want to go to heaven? This is a good path for those who want to reach heaven.

> The Prophet also said to Fatima, "All the women who try to prepare a bed for their tired husband, who are concerned about their comfort, God will send seventy angels who will serve them in their tombs and their tombs shall be filled with light." This is the good path to follow if you want to reach heaven, women.

In this sermon, Malam Awal zeroed in on some of the unforgivable misdeeds a woman should abstain from committing if she wished to attain eternal felicity in the life to come. Aside from being unsupportive in times of need (by refusing to purchase firewood with her own income, for instance), criticizing her husband and stealing from him were two such offenses. What particularly alarmed Awal's female listeners was that the advice the preacher provided focused not on obvious faults (such as failure to pray or complete the fast) but rather on what, in the experience of many women, were inevitable responses to the deficiencies and disillusions of marital life. A wife is ideally expected to behave demurely in the presence of her husband and to follow his command—an ideal that emerging Islamic ideologies have only reinforced. Aside from the daily performance of time-consuming household duties, she is "always at the beck and call of her husband for other small services such as spreading mats for his guests and bringing them water" (Saunders 1978:248). She must carry water to her husband for his daily bath, and she must serve his dinner before she can feed anyone else in the household.[13] I was often told by both men and women that modesty and submission to one's husband were the most desirable traits for a wife, especially if she was young. Since women are strongly enjoined to maintain their image of reserve and deference to their husbands, they often have no other options than to leave in earnest to express dissatisfaction with the marriage (Cooper 1997a).[14]

The women with whom I discussed these matters did not dispute that they should ideally avoid confronting their husbands, yet they took issue with Malam Awal's claims that failing to do so was enough to condemn them to a hellish eternity. Many women are unhappy with the terms of their marriage or with the man they are married to—especially if they are not sufficiently provided for or suffer physical abuse. They expect to be fed, housed, and clothed, as it is a husband's duty to do so. Marriage is above all "a civil contract" (Callaway 1987:35), and any breach of contract—including failure to provide sufficient food or an adequate wardrobe—can be used by a woman to obtain a divorce. If some women choose to endure marriage for the sake of their children,[15] that does not mean that the sources of marital conflicts have been eliminated; indeed, this situation only increases the possibility of angry confrontations. Over the course of my research I witnessed several bitter fights between husbands and wives that were often provoked by the presence of a new co-wife or by competition over the control of monetary resources.

This brings us to the issue of stealing. My female friends were incensed that Malam Awal declared stealing to be a grave offense, when, to them, it was a well-known strategy for economic survival. But still they worried about their fate. It was common knowledge that women surreptitiously saved some of the money their husbands allocated for the purchase of daily food supplies. Women did not view this as stealing from their husbands but rather as cleverly engaging in a redistribution of cash resources enabling them to contribute to their own upkeep and that of their children (which, as noted, is technically a husband's responsibility). It was a lie, one of my friends remarked after hearing Malam Awal's admonitory address, to claim that wives stowed away half the food money for their own needs. They generally took minute amounts, which, she insisted, they were usually entitled to since it was money they had managed to hold on to as much through clever bargaining as through skimping on spices or meat. Besides, another woman added, the meager sums she managed to save in this way occasionally went right back into the household "pot" when her husband could not come up with the cash needed for clothing or medicine for one of his children. In sum, whether Malam Awal's sermons focused on women's alleged immorality, their rebellious nature, or their excessive attachment to material things, they were, in the view of many female listeners, intolerably harsh and punitive.

Knowledge and the Definition of the Pious Woman

As Patrick Gaffney (1994) reminds us, the messages and ideas conveyed through mosque preaching cannot be isolated from other local, national, and even international spheres of experience and their corresponding systems of value without sacrificing a large measure of the sermons' significance for those who hear them. Malam Awal preached at length about women's frailties and faults. His denunciations of women's impiety in all its diverse and dangerous forms must be seen in the context of ongoing efforts by Muslim activists to redefine female virtue in direct contrast to Western models of womanhood believed to be a major source of moral degeneracy worldwide. As noted earlier, women have become ever more central to Nigérien Muslims' visions of the moral order. They play a crucial role as guardians of civic virtue. It is precisely because women figure so prominently in the moral imagination that the issues of domesticity, marriage, and family, so critical to the definition of Muslim womanhood, are the subject of virulent national debates (Masquelier 2008).

By extending religiously sanctioned control over women's bodies as a metonym for control over society at large, Malam Awal was able to promote his vision of Islam as a corrective to what he saw as un-Islamic practices. Implementing this vision naturally required that women were informed about the proper ways to conduct themselves as "good" wives, mothers, and daughters. To that effect, the preacher routinely embedded the moral lessons he wanted to teach women within narratives of incidents said to have occurred during the life of the Prophet. In a sermon whose taped version was widely available in town in 2000, he told the following story:

> A father once asked his daughter, "Do you like this man?" She answered yes. So he said, "I give him to you." As soon as the man left, the young girl came to the Prophet and said: "My father gave me a husband but I don't know the law of marriage. I am afraid everyone will burn in hell [if I don't conduct myself properly]. Help me to learn what I must do to be a good wife." You see, she knew nothing about how to treat her husband. She did not want to make mistakes and risk going to hell. The Prophet laughed and said: "God bless you!" And then the Prophet told her, "You must always be ready to answer him. Don't answer with a loud cry. Answer softly, respectfully. If you respond with a scream, you can spend sixty years praying and fasting, but God won't accept your prayers." "Is that all?" the young girl asked again. "That is not all," answered the Prophet. "If you go out [of the house] without first asking for permission, every time you take a step, you bring your feet closer to hell. The angels will take away your blessings." "There are women," the Prophet continued, "who take their veil and step out the door as soon as their husbands leave. Some don't even veil. Men will see them and say, 'Look, this man's wives are outside without a veil. He is not a Muslim. He left God, he left the Prophet. He follows his wives. God will leave him.' God will impoverish him and close all the doors of happiness. Because he has let his wives go out naked without saying anything. He follows his wives more than he follows God." The young girl asked again, "Is there something else?" "Yes," the Prophet responded, "if your husband wants to touch you and you refuse to lay with him, God will not look at you until Judgment Day. And you will not receive *rahama Allah* [God's glory]." The young girl asked again, "What else?" The Prophet answered, "If a wife prays, but she has not prayed for her husband so that God may protect him and give him health and prosperity, God will not accept her prayer." The young girl then said, "There are too many things I must do, this is too much, I will not marry." This is what you, men and women, must know to follow God's laws. If you want kindness from God, these are the rules you must follow.

Implicit in this description of the proper Muslim marriage is a criticism of marital relationships based on companionship that are the primary focus of Latin American telenovelas available for consumption on Nigérien television. In recent years, foreign televised drama have profoundly affected youthful understandings of love and marriage, an issue I return to. For our present purposes it is enough to note that what made this an arresting story, aside from Malam Awal's riveting delivery style, is that the rules of conduct a good wife should observe came directly from the Prophet's mouth. There could be no mistake, therefore, about these rules. That the narrative involved the Prophet—and not some lesser known figure of Islamic history—also enhanced its appeal, and perhaps the ease with which listeners would remember it at opportune times. Basira, a pious widow who had attended many of Malam Awal's sermons before eventually deciding that doing so only heightened her dread and confusion, told me that preachers who referred to obscure religious figures she did not know only frustrated her attempts to learn. It made it difficult to understand the context of the story ("they never tell you when it happened") as well as its significance. In delivering the above sermon, Malam Awal kept his listeners attentive by enabling them to empathize with the young girl's situation so they, too, would wonder if "there was something else" that they needed to know in order to become obedient, submissive wives who would earn God's favor.

Also implicit in many of Malam Awal's admonitions was the notion that knowledge of Islamic principles was paramount to becoming a good Muslim. Recall that since the successful reformist campaign to promote Muslim awareness and demystify Qur'anic literacy, Islamic knowledge has assumed a new relevance and urgency. Many see it as directly helping to establish a moral alternative to secular models of citizenship, family, and identity. With the democratization of access to religious knowledge ushered in by a wide range of media-savvy actors intent upon "staging virtue" (Salvatore 1998), religion has become, in the words of a 'dan Awaliyya, "serious business." Those who engaged in morally tainted practices (such as going to market wearing makeup) because they did not know it was wrong to do so could no longer be exonerated. On the other hand, Malam Awal was fond of saying, those who taught others about the precept of Islam would be rewarded. In one of his sermons he pointed out that Qur'anic scholars who taught women how to conduct themselves in their marriage would receive 6 percent of the *lada* (divine reward) destined to these women. Women, in turn, would be rewarded if they reared their children well.

As noted, mothers play an important part in the transmission of knowledge to the younger generation. Because the future of the community is in their hands, it is essential that they are given the education (*tarbiyya*) they need to carry out their task successfully. Husbands thus routinely buy taped sermons for their wives to listen to. Today the simple possession of a few

259

sermon recordings is a sign of piety. Unlike activities such as reading the Qur'an that require concentration—and presuppose literacy—or that, like prayer, are useless unless the worshiper has performed ablutions, listening to a taped sermon can be accomplished anywhere and requires no preliminary preparation. One need not interrupt one's activities while the tape is playing. Aside from providing a distraction from tedious daily tasks, listening to cassette sermons is a safe and economical way to accumulate rewards from God.[16]

Reconfiguring Moral Domesticity

Given the widespread circulation of taped sermons that teach about Qur'anic principles, ignorance is no excuse, even for secluded wives who cannot attend public wa'azai (sermons). Women who are confined at home by their husbands or lack the confidence to attend public sermons occasionally listen to Malam Awal's recorded sermons in the privacy of their compounds. When I entered my neighbor Bilkisa's compound one afternoon, I found her sitting in the shade, sifting cornmeal in preparation for the evening meal. Beside her, three young girls were engaged in a joyful hand-clapping and singing game, and a fourth—Bilkisa's daughter—energetically scrubbed a pile of dirty dishes. A tape of one of Malam Awal's sermons was playing. As I sat down, I heard the preacher list the kinds of behaviors wives should ideally avoid if they wanted to elude the threat of hellish fire. "These are the women who will not go to heaven," the preacher hollered before enumerating the reasons why:

> The wife whose husband cannot trust her because she steals, she lies, she hides things from him. Women, if you act like that, go ask your husband for forgiveness.
> The wife who tells her husband's secrets and betrays his trust. She will go to hell.
> The wife who does not lend money to her husband so that he can give alms or make a gift and who accuses her husband of squandering her wealth, she will go to hell. All the work they have done for forty years with Islam [prayer, fasting, alms, etc.] will be erased. They will receive no reward for this work.

Bilkisa's ten-month-old son, who previously lay sleeping on a mat, started wailing. Bilkisa put down the calabash of corn meal to pick up the infant. She nestled him in her lap and offered him a breast before returning to her sifting task. By then a handful of young female visitors—all neighbors—had entered the compound. After greeting Bilkisa, they sat down at her feet and proceeded to show her the various items they had just bought at the market. The tape continued playing, but, by then, I was the only one listening. I strained my ears to hear Awal's taped words. "Believing in God," the preacher went on, "is not about praying and fasting. It involves avoiding that which God does not want." Women, he implied, should refrain from performing sinful actions if they wished to please God and avoid divine retribution. The wife who "refuses her husband at night" or who "walks around complaining about her husband, telling everyone what he does wrong," she would not enjoy the "smell of paradise," he continued implacably. Further, if a woman went out without a head covering and showed her hair to everyone, God would "make a special fire for her." In his conclusion, Malam Awal targeted wives who "cannot ask for their husbands' forgiveness because they are too proud to say they are sorry after having disputes with their husbands." These women, too, he insisted, would pay dearly for their lack of humility.

In this particular sermon the preacher provided a list of unacceptable wifely dispositions but without the supporting narrative that often lent focus and concreteness to his admonitions. These faulty dispositions were presented as offenses so serious that they automatically canceled out any rewards from God that women might have accumulated in the performance of prayer, fasting, and other religious obligations.

Although the preacher's rhetoric was meant to encourage women's submissive attitude toward their husbands—which young brides are routinely admonished to cultivate if they want to make their husbands happy—it also touched on some of the sorest nodes of spousal tensions. Aside from promptly attending to the needs of her husband when he is hungry, thirsty, or in need of a bath, a wife should ideally refrain from complaining about her husband, betraying his confidence, or adopting a proud attitude. Indeed, submission, loyalty, and humility are qualities on which men place a high premium when they look for a wife. Paradoxically, women are often stereotyped as disobedient, untrustworthy, and quarrelsome.[17] In Hausa folk tales, wives are routinely portrayed as chatty, disloyal, and undependable creatures from whose scheming dispositions men must learn to protect themselves. I have occasionally heard husbands comment that women are by nature gossipy and deceitful. Although some women do seem to conform to the image of the ideal wife, the common perception is that very often they do not, which is why marriages are fraught with tension.

If spousal conflicts are widely perceived as an inevitable dimension of married life, for Malam Awal they were also a sign of women's moral degeneracy. Pious women, he liked to say, submitted to the desires of their husband, could be relied on at all times, and were supportive wives. Those who could not abide by those rules would suffer the pains of hell, for in doing so they went against God's wishes.[18] Though Awal occasionally admonished husbands to be kind to their wives, treat them fairly, and satisfy them sexually, he focused far more often on the numerous duties and obligations that wives were expected to perform. In this respect, women felt unfairly singled out, especially given the harsh penalty supposedly awaiting wrongdoers.

Especially frightening for women who listened to the preacher's caustic admonitions was not the allegation that women who disobeyed their husbands were "bad" wives (after all, obedience to one's husband was the primary duty of every Muslim woman). Rather, it was the implication that "bad" wives automatically faced a life in hell with no way to retrace their steps and avoid this dreaded fate. In Malam Awal's vision of a new moral order, the previously "secular" realm of domesticity became the new terrain on which the battle against sin and wickedness should be fought. Women who were traditionally selective of those practices they identified as regulated by Islam (and therefore a potential source of corrupt conduct) now had to constantly guard against disobedience or worse as they went about their daily occupations. In the new order outlined by Malam Awal, working steadily toward the preservation of virtue in one's daily life was critical: the most minor transgression to the code of marital conduct was enough to seal a woman's fate irremediably. For those who aspired to become more virtuous Muslims, the close scrutiny of routine actions (and mainly womanly conduct while in the presence of husbands or in the company of kin, friends, or co-wives) had become a source of considerable anxiety.

Piety, Agency, and the Struggle for Self-Expression

This anxiety, a former Awaliyya member told me as we were discussing the preacher's vision of Islamic piety, stemmed from the recognition that if Malam Awal's message were true, not a single woman in Dogondoutchi would be worthy of paradise. For who among them had not, at least once, complained to a friend of her husband's failings or stubbornly stood up to her spouse when she felt wronged? According to Salamatou, a former disciple of Awal,

> He is always threatening everyone with hell. Especially women. It's women who are accused of getting in trouble. Why does it have to be about scaring people? Even if you have studied and learned how to behave, you are bound to forget some things. You will forget to pray before you urinate. So are you going

to hell for each of these offenses? Everyone forgets one prayer, one thing, every once in a while. Does that mean we are *all* going to hell?

Salamatou initially attended every one of Malam Awal's sermons, but each time she felt sick afterward. She was deeply bothered by the preacher's harsh criticisms of women and his insistence that they be entirely subservient to their husbands. Amina, a fifty-year-old widow, once confessed to me that she had left Malam Awal's teachings precisely because she was tired of being constantly threatened with the fires of hell. She did not want "to live in constant fear." Although she no longer had to worry about how to remain submissive to her husband—he had died some three months before—she had had her share of disagreements with him during their thirty-four-year marriage. Feeling that she was being unfairly threatened with divine retribution for trying to be a better Muslim, she had eventually decided to ignore the preacher's admonitions. Though she remained plagued by doubts as to her eternal fate, she no longer was so concerned about every transgression she might have knowingly—or unknowingly—committed.

Ironically, rather than helping her observe stricter Muslim conduct in her daily life, Amina's disillusion with the Awaliyya order led her to experiment with Pentecostalism. For almost half a year she attended weekly services and revivals at a local Pentecostal church, attracted by the rhetoric of salvation and the emphasis on God's compassionate nature. Though she saw no contradiction between Pentecostalism and the teachings of Islam (among other things, she felt that they both taught her how to become a morally responsible person), she eventually stopped going to church. Warnings by local *malamai* that she could not remain a virtuous Muslim if she prayed with Christians had convinced her to confine herself to the performance of Islamic duties. She now performed the five daily prayers without fail. Although she yearned to resume her association with the Pentecostal community, she feared the criticisms that this would surely elicit from her brother-in-law, a staunch Muslim who lived in the compound adjacent to hers and whose counsel she must follow now that her husband was dead. Like a number of other women I met, she was torn between the desire to seek further religious knowledge and the worry that she would be ostracized by the Muslim community if she dared to assert herself religiously. Some of the neighbors in whose company she had attended Malam Awal's sermons had also deserted the *zawiya* after measuring the social cost of being associated with Awaliyya at a time when a growing number of residents accused the preacher of being a fraud and an opportunist. Biliya, who lived across the street from

Amina and had been one of Malam Awal's earliest followers, had stopped attending the preacher's sermons after her husband pressured her to do so. A prominent member of the Muslim community and a close associate of the traditionalist imam, he could ill-afford to have his wife be a source of public embarrassment.

Not all the women I met, however, left Malam Awal because they feared public opprobrium or their husband's authority. A'i, a former disciple of Malam Awal who had striven to minimize religious discord in her household ever since one of her sons had embraced Izala against his father's wishes, reached the decision on her own. After arriving at a better understanding through Malam Awal's teaching of what God desired of her, she realized that she could no longer rely on the preacher to show her the "correct" way to practice Islam. She thought that the preacher's insistence on the hellish fate awaiting those who failed to secure God's pleasure was simply unwarranted:

> Malam Awal tells people that those who don't follow the right path, they are going to burn in hell, even the *malamai* who don't follow the righteous path, they are going to hell. But nobody knows whether one goes to hell or to heaven, only God knows who is going where.

If the preacher's inflammatory style of delivery had occasionally shaken her, it had not frightened her. She remained confident that she had earned her place in paradise. Muslims should not be discouraged by the preacher's harsh words, she told me. They should simply learn how to serve God. Among a Muslim's duties, prayer was paramount, of course, but so were acts of kindness and charity:

> One receives rewards from God for giving alms to the poor. Those who take care of their parents, who feed them and provide for them, will also accumulate rewards. My parents did not pray [i.e., were not Muslim] but I loved them. All those who love and care for their parents, they are going to go to heaven. My husband and I, we pray. And my children, too, pray.

A'i was not afraid to acknowledge that her parents were not Muslims and that she herself had started praying only after she married her husband. She spoke with the quiet assurance of a person who knew that, despite Malam Awal's threatening advice to the wives of Dogondoutchi, she had become a pious person by performing those acts of submission and benevolence that God required of Muslims.

Most notable is how A'i articulated her own definition of piety based on a personal interpretation of the injunction to give alms—a duty whose performance Malam Awal routinely encouraged. While recognizing that generosity toward the poor was a cardinal virtue, she singled out loving and caring for one's parents as a central obligation that Muslims must accomplish if they wished to avoid the tortures of hell. Significantly, her insistence that Muslims must care for their elders regardless of whether the latter are Muslims—or even pray the "proper" way—directly contradicted the reformists' injunction to avoid eating, socializing, and praying with "impious" Muslims. Thus A'i assertively redefined some of the moral principles Muslims must follow by placing them outside the ethical framework articulated by both Awaliyya and Izala reformists. Her testimony illustrates that women relate to doctrine in practical ways and make selective use of Islam at a time when Islamic knowledge has become central to the ways in which Dogondoutchi residents constitute themselves as respectable and pious persons.

A'i's initial decision to follow the preacher's teaching had been difficult for her. As was true for Amina, it meant directly disobeying her husband's wishes that she remain home. Forced to choose between submitting to God's will (assuming that Malam Awal was sent by God to instruct local residents) and yielding to her husband's authority, she chose to seek religious instruction and ignore her husband's objections. Malam Awal's repeated insistence that a married woman's primary obligation was to her husband placed contradictory demands on her. There was no easy way for her to reconcile the conflicting requirements of commitment to God and loyalty to her husband. Obeying her husband automatically meant abandoning Malam Awal's teachings and the search for a pious life—an action that would, in the preacher's view, inevitably unleash the wrath of God upon her. She had chosen to submit to God.

A'i, Biliya, and Amina eventually stopped going to the *zawiya* once they became aware of the abuses they were subjected to, but they did so under different circumstances, illustrating women's divergent responses to the dilemma they face in their pursuit of knowledge and virtue. Amina, who lived in seclusion, had been forced by the circumstances of her husband's prolonged illness to violate the norms of wifely isolation in order to feed her large family. She rationalized her frequent excursions outside the marital compound by invoking her children's constant need for food, clothing, and school supplies and her responsibility as the major income earner (upon her husband's death, however, she had complied with the strict rules of seclusion and avoidance that apply to recently widowed women).[19] Precisely because it was she who provided for the family—her eldest son, twenty-three years old and only sporadically employed, no longer helped with the harvest—she believed that no man should have jurisdiction over her religious education. She felt no compunction about leaving the family compound to attend Awal's sermons. After all, she was only trying to become a better Muslim. Moreover, since neither her husband nor her son was religiously observant, she felt they had no grounds for dismissing her sermon attendance as inappropriate. Eventually she decided that the intense scrutiny she was required to apply to her everyday actions to conform to Malam Awal's model of pious behavior was unsuitable. Rather than help her cultivate a pious self, the preacher's sermons produced paralyzing doubt. This realization prompted her to sever her ties with the Awaliyya.

Biliya, as noted, stopped attending Awaliyya sermons after her husband grew increasingly uncomfortable with both her absence from the marital home and her dedication to Malam Awal's cause, which he had originally also espoused before concluding that the preacher's vision of moral order did not accord with his own. Like numerous other women in town, until then Biliya had never considered engaging in religious activities antithetical to her husband's. Whether they grow up in reformist, anti-Izala, or Awaliyya households, women in Dogondoutchi take on the religious orientation of their husbands.[20] Because husbands are accountable for their wives' virtuous conduct,[21] it is they who make decisions regarding religious orientation, activities, and education. In this respect, by following her husband's wishes that she stop following Malam Awal's teachings, Biliya was behaving in a socially approved way. Since, by all accounts, she had no choice, no one could accuse her of impiety. Women in Dogondoutchi know well the risks they take by pursuing religious paths that their husbands disapprove of.[22] Besides wanting to minimize conflict with her husband, Biliya came to resent Malam Awal's characterization of women as inherently "bad" Muslims destined to an afterlife of fiery suffering. No doubt she, like other former 'yan Awaliyya I met, also felt a sense of embattled isolation in relation to other women in her neighborhood, most of whom wanted nothing to do with Awal.

A'i, on the other hand, had learned to deal with the tensions inherent to a household in which members held divergent religious views. This helped her break away from her normative role as a dutiful wife and become more assertive in challenging her husband's potential objections to her association with the Awaliyya. But after listening to Malam Awal explain God's commands, especially as they pertained to women's role and responsibility in the family, she grew increasingly frustrated with his negative characterization of women. In her view, one should strive to lead a pious life, but because no one was faultless, virtues inevitably coexisted with faults even in people who deserved the rewards of paradise.[23] A'i had thus stopped attending sermons at the *zawiya*, preparing cooked food for the preacher's guests, and going door to door to secure financial contributions to help pay for Awal's water and electricity bill. All three women variously became aware of themselves and of their rights from the very conditions that limited their autonomy and awareness in the first place. Their ability to reject the preacher was not "the residue of an undominated self that existed prior to the operations of power" (Mahmoud 2005:17). Rather, it was born as a result of those operations. By teaching Dogondoutchi women to think critically about themselves, Malam Awal provided a reflexive space in which his female audience could ponder the import of his message—and ultimately discard it.

Contesting Authority

Aside from women deploring Malam Awal's accusatory focus on women's faulty dispositions, there was also the matter of the preacher's own marital instability. Malam Awal, it was commonly acknowledged, had wed an estimated thirty young girls between May 1997 and December 2006, but few of the marriages lasted more than a few months.[24] None of the brides, on being divorced and sent back to their fathers' home, had anything good to say about their short union to the notoriously inflexible man. At first, the brief duration of these marriages was blamed on the young women's immaturity and on their not being able to endure the preacher's rigid rules governing seclusion, most notably his injunction that they not leave the marital compound, not even at night to visit kin, and that they receive no visits.[25] In late 1999, however, the preacher's reputation as a pious man and an exemplary Sufi teacher began to crumble after one of his ex-wives revealed that he routinely "forgot" to pray and that when he claimed to be "going to Mecca" to attend the Friday prayer there (one of the miracles some claimed he routinely performed), he simply locked himself in his room to nap. Other rumors began to circulate about his fancy for fifteen-year-old girls with fair complexions, his sexual habits, and his surprising lack of progeny despite repeated marriages.

His personal life soon became the object of intense scrutiny. While his disciples argued vehemently that the rumors about his dishonorable conduct were simply lies his enemies were spreading to discredit him—who would be so stupid as to believe that Malam Awal could fly to Mecca like a bird, for instance?—detractors insisted that regardless of whether the stories were true, there was something suspicious about the preacher's repeated marriages that did not last. In 2004 I learned from a couple of women that after chasing one of his wives out of his home, Malam Awal had presumably given the clothes she left behind in her precipitated departure to the new bride he wed a few weeks later. Like other women who had heard the story, they were incensed by the pettiness of the act. Recall that wedding transactions were the focus of intense controversy in the 1990s, when reformists tried to put a cap on bridewealth payments to enable struggling families to marry off their children. Anxious to preserve their power base, women have challenged the new Islamic ideologies that have undermined forms of accumulation through which they traditionally created value. On a par with the reformists' injunction that resources be spent conservatively, Malam Awal encouraged parents to accept low bridewealth payments in an effort to facilitate marriages. In accordance with his own philosophy that wealth should never determine one's ability to marry, the young women he married supposedly brought nothing to the marital home except for the clothes they wore—another departure from the conventional pattern. If it was honorable for a groom to discharge his mother-in-law of the burden of equipping her daughter with the requisite clothes, furniture, and cooking equipment and take on the burden himself, everyone agreed that it was altogether disgraceful of him to steal from one departing wife in order to supply a new unsuspecting bride with the clothes her new marital status required.

Perhaps most disappointing to many of the preacher's once ardent supporters was that he apparently did not live by the principles he preached. Given his role in the sustenance of the moral order, a religious master's personal behavior should "be seen to accord with the purity of knowledge he invokes" (Lambek 1990:30). Recall, for instance, that Malam Awal tirelessly advocated that young girls should marry early to insure that their virtue be protected. Finding a husband for one's daughter, he often pointed out, was one of the most important duties of a pious mother. To make his point, the preacher would explicitly describe the dire fate met by those who failed to marry their daughters before they became sexually active. Consider the following excerpt from a sermon he delivered in 1998:

> You must educate your daughter well. You must find her a husband when she is ten or eleven. You should not wait until puberty. If you wait until your daughter ends up sleeping with a man, God will write you a hundred sins. It is not because she committed adultery, it's because you left her unmarried until she was attracted to a man. All the prayers her parents will make for forty days will not be accepted. And seventy people in her family will go to hell. They will be actually stuck in between [hell and heaven.] If [your daughter] does it again, her kin will come closer to hell. The third time she commits adultery, they will go

to hell, all because you have let your daughter go through puberty without giving her a husband.

At first, Malam Awal's own marital trajectory appeared to exemplify the very
principles he was advocating—his wives married young, they remained in
seclusion—to minimize the moral threats that women's sexuality posed to
the Muslim community. Yet, as women often pointed out to me, once his
wives were sent back to their parents' home, their chances of making a good
marriage were considerably lessened. They were divorcées and therefore less
appealing to potential grooms than their unwed counterparts. A'i, whose
niece had almost wed Malam Awal before the girl's uncles had intervened,
blamed this state of affairs on men's search for respectability and spiritual
capital. She thought that fathers (and, at times, mothers) impulsively offered
their young daughters to the preacher without questioning whether this was
in their daughter's best interest. Other senior women faulted Malam Awal for
taking advantage of his position to prey on innocent girls[26] and for increasing
the chances that, once divorced, these young women would remain unmarried—in direct contradiction with the Sufi preacher's injunction that girls'
sexuality be safely contained within the bounds of marriage.

If people widely assumed that, as religious leaders, public figures like
Awal were bound to exemplify the moral principles they routinely invoked,
there was also a sense that their very position exempted them from having to
live by their own words. Malam Awal's presumed saintliness, in other words,
was demonstration enough of the man's inherent piety. From this perspective, if the fulfillment of religious obligations confirmed his moral superiority, so did the license he enjoyed in the performance of moral duties.[27] Indeed, that Awal produced no progeny despite marrying so many women was
originally taken by some as an indication of his saintly status. It was well
known, I was frequently told, that Muslim saints have few children—if any
at all—despite marrying numerous times.

Eventually Awal's numerous, short-lived marriages stopped being re-
dundant signs of sainthood. His matrimonial instability attracted suspicion
of darker, more pedestrian motives, and his lack of progeny came to be seen
as problematic. But as to what prompted Awal's religious license no longer to
be seen as the privileges of office but rather as impious and fraudulent, there
is no straightforward answer, especially since the question of tolerance is
relative. I suspect that *excess* was at the root of local audiences' disenchantment with the preacher's antics. The question, in other words, was one of
scale, not content. The sheer magnitude of Awal's deviations from the norm,

and not the deviations themselves, made his actions objectionable to those who had previously praised his conduct as exemplary. Thus, although a religious leader is allowed some latitude in his search for appropriate marriage partners, the number of women the preacher had wed and then "discarded" in a nine-year span was simply excessive—and therefore intolerable. By late 2004 Malam Awal had clearly discredited himself in the community of Dogondoutchi.

Marriage, Fire, and Domesticity

Malam Awal's focus on the proper rules of marital conduct must, as noted, be set against the backdrop of newly emerging representations of marriage as companionship promoted by an ever widening array of Latin American televised dramas as well as *soyayya* films, which are videotaped romances of northern Nigerian provenance (Larkin 1997; Whitsitt 2003). Because they explore the exciting intimacy of romantic love in all its complexity, telenovelas have become especially popular among school-educated youths in the throes of courtship who see them as educational tools partly, viewers told me, because they depict not just moments of bliss and intimacy but also the painful ordeals faced by courting lovers and married couples. For young people who feel that relationships are private and personal matters—rather than subject to collective regulation as was traditionally the case—televised dramas and videos that provide narratives of romance and intimacy are valuable sources of insight on who and how to love. In some instances, they are perceived as a vehicle of development by youth looking for moral instruction as well as training in the language of love.

In the context of public debates about the contentious issues of polygyny, marriages of coercion, and the marriage of young girls, foreign televised dramas have also become forums for exploring the forms that marriage should ideally take. To defenders of religious authenticity such as Malam Awal, however, these foreign representations of courtship and marital life are doubly controversial: first, they prompt moral decay by encouraging inter-gender gatherings in the compounds where the televised dramas are shown and by circulating "indecent" images of gendered behavior; second, they promote youthful disobedience by providing scripts for inappropriate relationships based on "dangerous" notions of shared intimacy and companionship. The consequences are disastrous: young wives become insubordinate, young men are attracted to the "wrong" kind of women, and ill-matched lovers marry without parental consent.

Although Malam Awal was not alone in condemning teledramas and romance videos for their corrupting impact on youthful sensibilities, he was one of the video industry's most adamant critics. At a time when many youths spoke of having relationships, building long-lasting romances based on shared visions and mutually enjoyed pastimes, and connecting deeply with the objects of their affection, the preacher's relentless focus on wifely submission, modesty, and labor was aimed at reconfiguring marriage within the narrower parameters of Islamic tradition: this was a tradition the younger generation of women would do well to remember, he argued, if they wanted to be saved from impending depravity and destruction. As we have seen, Malam Awal's strategy to remind women at risk of looming threats to their moral constitution included the use of vivid stories of approaching doom, stark descriptions of hellish fires, and lengthy lists of condemnable actions that led one straight into the fiery pit. On occasion, the preacher was not averse to quoting proverbs that could illuminate for his audiences the points he wanted to drive home. Proverbs are useful mnemonic devices. Through linguistic synergy and the mental pictures they evoke, they help concretize deeper truths in condensed form. Hausa speakers routinely draw on the vast stock of available proverbs to translate abstract notions into the language of the concrete and the familiar. Take for instance, "the fart does not light the fire," the adage that provides the title of this chapter. As he addressed the Awaliyya community one evening in March 2000, Awal concluded his admonition with the following words:

> When I arrived in Doutchi, many people started saying: "Who is this man? He does not even wear his prayer beads! He is a pagan, he is ignorant!" Despite all the things that they said about me, many people converted to Islam. Many learned to pray, many pagans abandoned their traditions. They may call me ignorant and pagan, but I have helped many people follow the righteous path. I call on you people to keep doing good things that will keep you on the righteous path. *The fart does not light the fire* [my emphasis].

'Yan Awaliyya's confidence in their future should not dissolve into complacency, Malam Awal warned, for the process of establishing an enlightened mode of religiosity for all was ongoing. Although conversion to Islam and the dutiful performance of pious acts were important steps toward achieving virtue, the quest for piety did not end there. Muslims must remain vigilant, ever attentive to potential sources and signs of unvirtuous conduct, for as many would ultimately learn to their detriment, the righteous path was narrow. To those who complacently assumed that since they dutifully engaged in the "correct" religious practices, they need not do more, Malam Awal wished to impart one additional lesson. It was pithily stated: the fart does not light the fire. In this particular context, the proverb, well known among Hausa speakers, means that pursuing a life of piety requires intense, heartfelt commitment to the teachings of the Qur'an (and by implication, unquestioned devotion to one's teacher) just as making a fire demands sustained and forceful blowing on the part of the fire-maker. In other words, an accidental gust of "wind" will not do.

By comparing the earnestness of a religious person's pursuit of piety to the zealousness of the fire-maker blowing intently—and intentionally—to ignite sparks, I like to think that Malam Awal was addressing Dogondoutchi women (who, three times a day, light cooking fires during meal preparation) and reminding them that cooking for one's husband is a central duty of Muslim wives. In a society where marital relationships are defined, to a large extent, through the preparation and consumption of food, women who regularly purchase cooked food to avoid having to cook for their families are considered lazy and indulgent. For good wives, on the other hand, the moral ethos of domesticity revolves around the careful and efficient preparation of meals for the household. By tending the fires of domesticity, Malam Awal implied, Muslim wives lived in closer accordance with Qur'anic principles and were more likely to escape the scorching fires of hell.

The Power of Knowledge and the Virtues of Seniority

If Islam is about submission,[28] Malam Awal's vision of moral domesticity, replete as it was with images of female subordination to husbandly power, turned out to be aptly iconic of Qur'anic tradition. Women, the preacher tirelessly argued, should never forget the rules governing the constitution of pious selfhood, especially those pertaining to marriage and domesticity. On women's careful observance of Islamic practice hinged not only the preservation of their virtue but the future of society: as wives and mothers, Muslim women bore the burden of insuring the moral purity and spiritual enlightenment of the next generation. Awal's emphatic message, with its focus on knowledge, piety, and submission, resonated powerfully with Muslim women's experiences and aspirations. Paradoxically, it also contained the seeds of its own undoing. By routinely encouraging women to search for sources and signs of impurity, the preacher taught them to be discerning listeners and enlightened participants, well positioned to identify immorality wherever it could be found—including in his own failure to abide by the moral principles he routinely invoked. In part because the knowledge he bestowed upon his disciples insured that, by taking the practice of Islam seriously, they would ultimately come to reject him as an inadequate, because insufficiently pious teacher, Awal's mission was doomed from the start.

Note that the emergence of knowing subjects whom we can call, following Gramsci (1971), "organic intellectuals," occurred exclusively among senior women. This, I would argue, is no coincidence. By virtue of their structural position in society, elder women typically demonstrate a boldness—in words and deeds—that their junior counterparts have yet to develop, as they are constrained by social expectations of obedient, demure submission to husbandly authority. Because they are past their childbearing years, senior women are not constrained by rules of wifely seclusion and can claim more autonomy—in principle, at least. Thanks to their seniority—and the relative independence from household chores and child rearing it implied—female elders were able to contribute substantially to the growth of the Awaliyya. When they described the construction of the Awaliyya mosque, a number of residents recalled watching with a mixture of shame and astonishment the laborious progression of *tsohuwai* (old women) carrying heavy cement bags on their heads. The scene of female elders struggling under the weight of their loads—and at times, falling—epitomized for many the abuse which Awaliyya members were subjected to. To 'yan Awaliyya, the scene signaled the disciples' loyalty and dedication toward their saintly master, but to outsiders it was a perfect example of how Awal routinely and ruthlessly exploited Dogondoutchi residents' good-will and gullibility. Mawri women are traditionally called upon to perform a variety of physically demanding tasks—cutting firewood, fetching water at the pump, and pounding grain, for instance—but they do not participate in the construction of houses or mosques. That is the responsibility of men.

That neither gender nor seniority precluded elder women from engaging in such strenuous activities provides a good measure of their initial devotion to the Sufi preacher—and of their disillusion once awareness set in that they were being abused, or at the very least, misled. Seniority played a role, too. Recall the anger and disbelief with which some women received the news of Awal's controversial appropriation of a departing wife's wardrobe to equip a new bride. After initially approving the Sufi preacher's implementation of marriage reforms that would benefit all by facilitating wedding transactions, senior women came to resent his meddlesome involvement in the marriage economy, over whose terms they fought to regain control. Given the centrality of wedding gifts to the creation of women's social capital, there was something wrong about weddings in which the girl's mother contributed no *kayan 'daki* to furnish her daughter's marital abode. That Awal's own marriages—in which the brides received no gift—would become so controversial in some quarters is therefore not surprising. The preacher allegedly conned young girls into believing that because they had the big eyes of a *waliya* (female saint), they were destined to marry him. Young women, flattered by the preacher's attention, rarely resisted his offers of marriage, but many of their senior counterparts, wary of witnessing the disenchantment of his former brides, became fervent critics of his matrimonial *modus operandi*. The unions, it was obvious to them, produced nothing but resentment among the young women's kin. It was high time, I once overheard a former disciple exclaim, that Malam Awal stop preying on the pretty girls of Dogondoutchi. It is tempting to add, it was also high time that he learn that "the fart does not light the fire."

CLOSING REMARKS

"You know, back then, I told Rakya not to listen to the preachers. She had already given birth to eight children. I told her, 'that's enough. You must start taking the medicine so that you have no more children.' But she wouldn't, she said that contraception was *haram*—forbidden," Mariama exclaimed. I was sitting in my mud-walled home, listening to the three women who had come to visit on a particularly dusty December afternoon. The *harmattan*, the dry wind of the cold season, had been blowing hard all day, raising clouds of dust and making people and animals irritable. I had used the lack of visibility outside as an excuse to stay home and catch up on my work. I was engaged in the tedious task of transcribing a recently taped conversation when my neighbor, Mariama, appeared on my doorstep, followed a few minutes later by two neighborhood women. Seeking relief from the dust we sat inside, they on the mat I had spread on the sandy ground and I on the edge of my mattress. It had been a lonely day, and I was grateful for the company. Our conversation, as often happened when women got together, drifted to the topic of domesticity and motherhood. "So there she is now, with ten children," one of the women lamented of Rakya, "and she is not done." With a disapproving click of the tongue, her listeners signaled that they shared her assessment of Rakya's predicament.

Recall that although contraceptives are available to women at low cost, birth control remains a contested practice, especially after Izala leaders publicly condemned any form of family planning as essentially un-Islamic and encouraged women to have many children. Large families, they implied, were a sign of God's blessing as well as a demonstration of religious commitment. Malam Awal similarly opposed family-planning programs on the grounds that, together with polio vaccination campaigns allegedly aimed at sterilizing children, these practices were rooted in a Western conspiracy to undermine Muslim society. By reducing the number of Muslims, the West ultimately sought to destroy Islam, he warned his adepts. In his view, those who used contraception (and who allowed health workers to vaccinate their children against polio) were already sliding down the slippery slope of moral degradation, "contaminated" by the anti-Muslim rhetoric of unscrupulous Westerners. Thus good Muslim women had the duty to produce large families not just to express submission to God but also to contain the threat of Western intrusion. In this regard Rakya was no exception. During my successive research trips, I met a number of women, young and old, who loudly affirmed that family planning was prohibited by Islam. Unlike women who approved of birth control, these women tended to be less educated, younger at first marital cohabitation, and more likely to be in polygynous marriages.

This fragment of conversation about Rakya and her rejection of contraception not only points to the impact of conservative Muslim ideologies on the reproductive lives of women but, more important, suggests the extent of women's participation in debates about reproduction, contraception, and women's health at a time when the moral import of women's traditions, their knowledge, and their modes of socialization and empowerment have come under increased scrutiny. Although knowledge of contraceptive methods varies with education, urbanization, age at first marriage, and access to television (Peterson 1999), it would be mistake to assume that women are not interested in controlling their fertility. Even though a significant number admit to wanting numerous progeny, women nevertheless observe one another's reproductive lives closely: they know how many children each of their female acquaintances has had, how far apart the children were born, and whether the mother practices birth control—a sign, perhaps, that the silence that has traditionally surrounded matters of sexuality and reproduction is giving way to more informed discussions of these issues. I have heard friends speak scornfully of other women whose babies were born in too close succession. Implied in their comments was a sense that such women were "bad" mothers for failing to control their fertility and thus putting their babies at risk.[1]

Despite the spread of moralizing arguments that identify contraception as part of a Western plot to weaken Islam, growing numbers of women—especially those who have access to education—are beginning to see large families as burdensome. They do not see themselves as anything but practicing Muslims and have come to resent religious leaders, who, under the guise of dispensing advice on how to practice religion properly, lecture women at length about their "pagan" traditions or, worse perhaps, about their "Western" ways. Mariama, who had given birth to eleven children, seven of whom made it past infancy, felt that she had suffered greatly to raise her children. The suffering she alluded to was not simply the pain, discomfort, and exhaustion of numerous pregnancies; it was also the hardship that poor mothers went through to feed their children in times of food scarcity—an ever recurring threat in drought-ridden Niger.

Mariama was fifteen and attending secondary school when the man who would become her husband noticed her—she had passed his house on her way to class—and decided to make her his second wife. Overnight her parents pulled her out of school and told her she would soon be married. After the marriage was "tied" and bridewealth exchanged, Mariama was brought to her marital home where she had to endure the bitter jealousy of her co-wife. Her first two babies, both boys, died in early infancy. When I first met her in February 1988, Mariama had recently given birth to a baby girl, her ninth child. At that time she made several inquiries about procuring birth control, and I offered to take her to the dispensary for a consultation. For some reason she decided against it. Perhaps she was afraid her husband would find out. By the time I left Dogondoutchi in June 1989, Mariama was pregnant with her tenth child, though I did not know it. I only found out several months later when she sent me a letter announcing the birth of her son. She had been too embarrassed to share the news of her pregnancy before my departure. Deep shame surrounds pregnancy—it is a sign of sexual activity, which is a "shameful" act, and pregnant women take great pains to conceal their condition for as long as possible. When I returned to Niger in 1994, another child had been born. This is when Mariama, who was thirty-seven years old at the time, decided that she would not go through another pregnancy. Unbeknownst to her husband,[2] she started taking contraceptives and later insisted her grown daughters do the same. "I don't want them to suffer like I did. I tell them you *have* to take the *magani* [medicine] against pregnancy. Even if your husband doesn't want you to. You just do it."

This admission from a former staunch supporter of Malam Awal suggests that despite intensified concerns over the forms that proper womanhood should take, pragmatism sometimes prevails. Although it ostensibly contradicts the language of piety promoted by conservative Muslims, this pragmatism is rooted in understandings of agency, power, and personhood that, for women like Mariama, are not at odds with the teachings of Islam. Prominent religious leaders may condemn family planning as a sinful practice that must be rejected if the Muslim community is to thrive, but for mothers who struggle to raise children in the most adverse circumstances, these conservative ideas make little sense.[3] Ultimately women may be spurred to articulate their personal vision of motherhood against the reformists' own, although, when they do, it is mostly in private.

In this book I have tried to highlight women's strategic efforts to defend their interests and agendas when these are threatened by emergent ideologies and conventions centered on the redefinition of Islamic orthodoxy. Whether these efforts encompass sartorial practices, the production of domestic value, or the quest for spiritual capital, they must be seen as an agentive capacity through which women assert their participation in society, however uneven, dispersed, and informal. This capacity for action, I have suggested, is enabled by historically and culturally specific relations of subordination. As demonstrated by women's rejection of Izala and Awaliyya leaders' moralizing rhetoric, agency here emerges out of the realization of "one's own interest against the weight of customs, tradition, transcendental will, or other obstacles (whether individual or collective)" (Mahmood 2005:206). It can lead at times to strikingly personal forms of morality and piety.

Whether they are embraced, tolerated, or resisted, reform projects aimed at normalizing public expressions of piety and bringing local forms of religiosity in alignment with a supposedly orthodox tradition have affected Mawri women's lives profoundly. My aim in this book has been to trace some of the distinctive ways in which Islam in Dogondoutchi has come to figure as a central dimension of women's world at a time when women have themselves become the focal point of anxieties over the moral community, its boundaries, and its relations to the wider world. Because Islam there has become the idiom to express moral purity—an idiom whose signs and symbols are most prominently displayed on female forms and in female spaces—the burden of truth has weighed particularly heavily on women. Gender, the anthropological literature has amply demonstrated, is a central axis of difference through which ideas of pollution and immodesty—or, conversely, purity and reform—have been widely and frequently instantiated. The recent history of Islamic reforms in Dogondoutchi vividly exemplifies how women's bodies provide a fertile terrain for imagining, reasserting, or contesting the porous boundaries of moral worlds. The diverse struggles to cover—or uncover—women's bodies documented in this book testify to the creative ways that bodies are used as sites of individual agency and instruments of social control.

If women are increasingly pressured to deploy through dress and deportment, frugality and fertility, knowledge and prayer the marks of their newly configured Muslim selves, this hardly implies that Islam operates "from above" to constrain women by uniformly defining the contours of their identities and the limits of their autonomy. Save for some notable exceptions, the study of women in Muslim societies has been guided by the paradigmatic assumption that religion is "at once the cause of and the solution to gender inequality" (Lazreg 1990:756). Because women in such studies are presented as "bearers of unexplained categories," they appear to have "no existence outside these categories" (Lazreg 1988:94). In documenting Mawri women's lived experiences, I have tried to uncover the principles governing women's world, their (at times, contradictory) definitions of value and agentive personhood, and their sense of what it means to be Muslim. My focus on dress, domesticity, and religious education was dictated by women's own interests and concerns—that is, by their sense of what *mattered*. Their particular concerns and motivations pushed me to critically examine concepts usually taken for granted such as "the veil" and ponder what "modesty" or "religious piety" might mean not to Western social theorists but to local actors who experience, or comment on, these states. By attending to some of the ways—symbolic and material, discursive and embodied—in which women situate themselves in the local religious economy, this book has highlighted the profoundly gendered dimension of Islam. The new religious sensibilities and conventions that have emerged in the wake of the Islamic revival in this corner of West Africa have heightened the distinction between women's and men's understandings of Islam and Muslim practice, complicating the notion of an increasingly uniform, homogenized Muslim tradition.

In the debate opened up by the momentum of democratization—a debate in which urban elite women have increasingly participated thanks in part to a number of initiatives in education, politics, and the performing arts—rural and mostly uneducated women struggle to reinvent themselves in light of the encroachment of global forces in their world and the legacies of time-honored traditions. The Islamic revival, many of these women would agree, has brought them advantages: greater access to divorce and education, a better understanding of their rights, a deeper appreciation of what being Muslim might mean, and a sharper sense of their participation in the global Muslim community. Even seclusion, which by constraining women's mobility significantly impacts their ability to engage in income-producing activities, is seen by many as a sign of social advancement and, ultimately, a good practice: it releases them from certain domestic burdens such as carrying water from the neighborhood pump and presupposes the financial ability to hire domestic help or install plumbing.

Yet, the revival has also brought changes that women perceive as detrimental to their interests and aspirations partly because, as elsewhere in the Muslim world, the much debated woman question is dictated by men's concerns, not women's. These changes have elicited resentment for—and resistance against—emergent forms of knowledge and power that curtail women's ability to produce value, earn social capital, and secure some measure of control over their own lives and persons. In the end, the processes that have secured Mawri women's subordination have also provided the conditions for a *prise de conscience* of their victimization. It remains to be seen to what extent emergent Muslim traditions will continue to regulate women's mobility, their (re)productive capacities, and their economic options while, paradoxically, conditioning their self-awareness and their ability to question the way things have become in light of the way things were.

Glossary

addini	religion, Islam
addu'a	supplicatory prayer
albarka	blessings, prosperity
aljani	spirit; pl., *aljanu* (also *iska*; pl., *iskoki*)
arme	marriage (known as *aure* in other Hausa-speaking regions)
Awaliyya	Sufi order founded by Mahamane Awal in Niger
Azna	non-Muslim person who venerates tutelary spirits
bidi'a	unwarranted innovation for which there was no precedent at the time of the Prophet, heresy
budurwa	literally "virgin"; unmarried girl of marriageable age
darika	Sufi "path" or order
'darmen arme	literally "tying of the marriage"; public ceremony in which bridewealth is transferred from the groom's kin to the bride's kin
faifai	round woven mat used to cover calabashes
fura	millet porridge
gado	bed, property inherited, heritage
hadaya	gift; refers here to the giving of gifts to Muslim religious leaders
hadith	preserved records of the Prophet's words and deeds
hajiya	woman who has accomplished the pilgrimage to Mecca
haji	pilgrimage to Mecca
halak	that which is permissible and legal; that which is part of Islam
haram	that which is forbidden and unlawful; that which is not part of Islam
hijabi	veil; more specifically, the local version of the headscarf worn by female members of the Izala association; pl., *hijabai*
hirami	veil one ties under the chin; worn by female members of the Awaliyya
ibada	serving God by praying, leading a good life, and performing religious duties
ilimi	knowledge, education, learning
Izala	shortened designation of the Jama'atu Izalat al-Bid'a wa Iqamat al-Sunna, Society for the Removal of Innovation and the Restoration of Tradition
jahilci	ignorance, ignorance about Islam

Glossary

jahiliyya	period preceding the coming of Islam
kan kaya	literally, "carrying the things"; public celebration during which wedding gifts are brought to the bride's marital home
kayan 'daki	literally, "things for the room"; wedding gifts a bride receives for her room
kubli	locked (as in "he locked the door"), seclusion (known as *kulle* in other Hausa-speaking regions)
kumya	shame, embarrassment, respect, avoidance
lada	reward, merits accrued with God
lahira	paradise, the Next World
laya	amulet (also *korfo*); pl., *layu*
lullu'bi	woman's head covering, veil; pl., *lullu'bai*
malami	teacher, scholar, Muslim religious specialist; pl., *malamai*
marabout	Muslim religious specialist, Qur'anic scholar, teacher
masallaci	mosque
maulidi	date marking the birth of the Prophet Mohammed
mayafi	woman's head covering, veil; pl., *mayafai*
Qadiriyya	Sufi order founded by 'Abd al-Qadir al-Jilani (d. twelfth century)
rubutu	literally "writing, written matter"; liquid Qur'anic verses that one drinks as protection or remedy
sadaka	alms, charity
sadaki	bridewealth payment from the groom to the bride's family upon marriage
salati	prayers members of a Sufi order recite with the help of prayer beads
salla	Islamic prayer ritual that Muslims have a duty to accomplish five times a day
sarauniya	chieftainess, queen
sarki	customary ruler, chief, emir
sharia	Islamic law; in Niger, *sharia* follows the Maliki school of law
shaykh	honorific term applied to a highly esteemed Muslim religious leader
shehu	leader, scholar (Hausa for *shaykh*)
shirka	idolatry, associationism
soyayya	love, desire, affection
Tijaniyya	Sufi order founded by Ahmad al-Tijani (d. 1815) in North Africa
ulama	Muslim religious scholars
wa'azi	sermon, admonition; pl., *wa'azai*
Wahhabi	reformist Muslims who follow the teachings of Muhammad b. Abd al-Wahhab from Arabia; sometimes applied uncritically in referring to reformist Muslims in West Africa
waliyi	Muslim saint, "friend of God"
wazifa	prayers of the Sufi order, usually prescribed by a Muslim saint and repeated a prescribed number of times
wuta	fire, hell
zaka	obligatory alms, a tithe

zawiya   Sufi center, place where members of a Sufi order gather for praying, instruction, and socializing

zikiri   protracted chanting in which the names of God are repetitively intoned; remembrance

Notes

All translations from foreign texts are the author's.

Preface

1. Dogondoutchi is often shortened as "Doutchi" by Nigériens.

2. "Hausa" is a term Mawri people use when referring to Hausa-speaking people from northern Nigeria—not to themselves.

3. A significant number of people who identify as Hausa also live in scattered communities throughout West Africa from Ghana to Chad and as far south as Cameroon (see Cohen 1969; Pellow 1977; and Works 1976).

1. Gender and Islam in Dogondoutchi

1. See Brenner 1984; Coulon 1981; Copans 1980; Cruise O'Brien 1971; Cruise O'Brien and Coulon 1988; Paden 1973; and Roberts and Roberts 2003.

2. *'Yan* literally means "sons of" ("*'dan*" is the singular form) but usually refers to membership in a group or organization. Hence *'yan bori* is translated as "members of the *bori*" and *'yan* Izala means "followers, or members, of Izala."

3. The Wangarawa, merchants originating from what is now Mali, played a central role in the dissemination of Islam in Hausaland and also belonged to the Qadiriyya.

4. Common to all reformist movements, Roy (2004:11) and others have noted, is the "quest to define pure religion beyond time and space."

5. In the eyes of many who lamented the spread of Izala values and the perceived insubordination of youth toward elders, Malam Awal brought order and civility back to the community. As one elder man put it,

> Since Malam Awal's arrival, young men and women pray, greet their parents respectfully, and wear veils, and do everything else a good Muslim should do. Now they all go to school. Some have finished memorizing the Qur'an, others haven't done so yet. But none are *voyous* [louts] anymore.

6. Awal's instructions regarding prayer beads contradicted reformist and traditionalist principles, no doubt to enhance the visibility of his followers and set them apart. Whereas Muslims who are not part of Izala generally wrap their prayer beads around their wrists in a discreet show of piety, members of Izala decry this tendency as ostentatious, arguing that piety is not something one displays "on the outside" for public consumption. Prayer beads, they say, should remain in one's pocket, hidden from sight. In

2004 I heard Muslims with no discernible religious allegiances insist that prayer beads should be kept in one's pocket, a sign perhaps that they wished to differentiate themselves from 'yan Awaliyya and align themselves more closely with Izala identities.

7. As one local official put it, "Awal, he eats off people's backs" (*ya ci bisa ban mutane*).

8. In Maradi, the commercial capital of Niger, residents refer to a church as a *makaranta*—a place for reading and learning (Cooper 2006:254). Notably *makaranta* is also the word Hausa speakers everywhere use for "school," an indication, perhaps, that the vast majority of Muslims perceive Christians primarily as "literate" people.

9. Although *bori* has lost much ground to Islam on the visible terrain of religious practice in the past decades, it would be hasty to assume that almost everyone has turned their backs on the spirits. Recall that the interaction between Muslim and non-Muslim worldviews has been far-reaching and complex, and a significant number of Mawri, even if they identify as Muslims, continue to discreetly invoke the assistance of spirituals forces when confronted with the problems of contemporary life.

10. Muslims elsewhere in West Africa, however, do call themselves Wahhabi (Soares 2005).

11. In 1984, in northern Nigeria, some members of Izala opted to diverge from the defining Izala doctrine and declared that adherents of Tijaniyya and Qaridiyya were "true" Muslims. They split from the core Izala faction, severing all ties with those who remained faithful to their original hard-line position (Umar 2001).

12. Note that Malam Awal is not the only Muslim leader who has outraged secular Muslim intellectuals with his claims that the polio eradication program is part of a Western conspiracy to undermine the Muslim community. In Maradi, an infamous Muslim cleric known for his inflammatory radio sermons, claimed that vaccination campaigns were the disguised means for Western nations to perform genocide in Africa by "deliberately killing children with bad vaccine" (Cooper 2006:46). I was told of another preacher south of Dogondoutchi who similarly engaged in anti-Western diatribes. This Muslim cleric had provoked controversy by accusing government officials of aiding whites to curtail fertility in Muslim communities by sterilizing children they pretended to vaccinate against polio.

13. In this respect, Hodgkin (1998:198) perceptively notes that the obsession of the West with so-called Islamic fundamentalism has clouded people's perceptions of the Muslim world, often reducing diverse expressions of Islamic revival to a single movement. In popular as well as academic thought (Westerlund and Rosander 1997), the tendency is to see everything in terms of "fundamentalism" and "anti-fundamentalism."

14. The so-called decline of Sufism in the face of secular modernity has been further explored in the works of Eickelman (1976), Gilsenan (1973), and Trimingham (1971).

15. Niger is currently part of an ambitious program aimed at training and equipping certain West African countries in the "war against terror." Known as the Trans-Saharan Counterterrorism Initiative, this program, which began in 2005 on the heels of the more modest Pan Sahel Initiative, provides weapons and training to the Nigérien military in its fight against groups supposedly linked to al-Qaeda (Ellis 2004).

16. Because *addini* (literally, "religion") and Islam are understood to be the same thing, people often refer to Islam as "*addini*."

17. "Les influences méditerranéennes en Afrique Noire" (1950): 4. AFF POL 2158. Aix-en-Provence: Archives d'Outre-Mer.

18. The holy wars of the eighteenth and nineteenth centuries, for instance, have generated a voluminous literature. On the *jihad* movement of Usman 'dan Fodio, see Adeleye 1971; Hiskett 1973; Hogben and Kirk-Greene 1966; and Last 1967.

19. On women's participation in Sufism in West Africa, see Coulon 1988; Hutson 1999; and Sule and Starratt 1991.

20. Dunbar (1991) notes that, in contrast to Nigeria, there is no trace in Niger of the *'yan taru*, the movement for the education of women founded by Usman 'dan Fodio's daughter, Nana Asma'u.

21. On Islamic education in Niger, see Alidou 2005; and Meunier 1997. On French-based secular education, see Miles 1994.

22. Women themselves occasionally participated in the disparagement of fellow Muslims. I heard a woman belittle her female neighbor who recently returned from the *haji* because the trip had been financed by the neighbor's son. Rather than enhance the pious reputation of the woman, her new status as a *hajiya* elicited contempt and criticism: she had not paid her way, and therefore her *haji* was neither proof of religious commitment nor evidence of God's blessing (in the form of prosperity).

23. I often had to listen to accusations and counter-accusations across factions and on occasions heard radically different versions of the same event. I was very careful not to disseminate information from one person or group to another so that trust could be preserved. Although I made it clear that I condemned violence, I was not always able to steer clear of local politics and often found myself agreeing (or disagreeing) with informants even as I claimed to take no positions in internecine rivalries.

24. Though his taped sermons punctuated the daily life of Dogondoutchi residents, reminding them to follow the demands of Muslim piety and resist worldly temptations, Malam Awal, paradoxically, was rarely seen. To his followers, his limited visibility was an expression of his humility and confirmed his piety. To his detractors, however, it indicated his culpability. On many occasions, Awal fled to Nigeria to escape the law. I was told that he usually reappeared after tempers had cooled and he no longer faced imprisonment. Regardless of what actually happened, the preacher's apparent seclusion enhanced his reputation as a holy man (see Eickelman 1976).

2. "Those Who Pray"

1. Lieutenant-Colonel Noël sur la situation politique du 3eme territoire militaire. 1er trimestre 1903. A74. Niamey: Archives Nationales du Niger.

2. Mahant, Capitaine. Monographie du secteur de Dosso. 1913. Document 5.1.5. Niamey: Archives Nationales du Niger.

3. I am not suggesting that all administrators developed distaste for the colony. True, a number of French officials appointed to Niger mostly waited for the next mutation that would end their forced "exile" (Fuglestad 1983), but others grew fond of Niger, at times developing romanticized views of the place and its people. As was occurring elsewhere in West Africa, French colonials appointed to districts with so-called nomadic populations spoke reverently at times of the "noble bandits" who systematically resisted military domination (Bernus et al. 1993). Certain sedentary populations also elicited the esteem of local colonial officials. Jean Sermaye, who served as a young administrator in Dogondoutchi and wrote two novels based on his experience among Mawri populations, is an example. His first book, *Barga: Maître de la brousse* (1937), is

a detailed and vivid, if idealized, account of precolonial life in Arewa. Although largely unknown, *Barga* won the Grand Prix de la Littérature Coloniale in 1937.

4. At Independence, for instance, Niger only had eight miles of paved road (Charlick 1991:39).

5. Between 1918 and 1928 in the *cercle* (or district) of Dosso, not only did the per capita tax soar from 1.25 to 7 francs but new items became subject to taxation, notably the small stock owned by farmers (Fuglestad 1983:127).

6. In his account of his travels from St Louis (Senegal) to Tripoli, Louis-Parfait Monteil (1894), for instance, described the stunning contrast he perceived between the "barbaric" regions occupied by "fetishist" populations and the more "civilized" Islamized territories.

7. The lack of consistent policies toward Muslim populations in West Africa led some scholars to assert that a Muslim policy proper never existed (Fuglestad 1983; Gouilly 1952; Oloruntemehin 1972; Triaud 1974). Instead, the colonial period witnessed adaptations to internal and external circumstances in which individual prejudice as well as collective obsessions played an important part.

8. Far from being military combatants who fought against the French, however, most members of the Sanusiyya were merchants who adapted to the colonial occupation (Vikør 2000).

9. French authorities loosely labeled "marabouts" Muslim religious specialists who engaged in activities ranging from leading prayer, preaching, and teaching to divination and amulet making. Before the advent of colonization, most of them were typically members of Muslim lineages. Those who could claim to have descended from the Prophet Muhammad enjoyed significant powers (Soares 2005).

10. No local religious leader wielded influence comparable to that of Sufi masters in Senegal, except perhaps Shaykh Aboubacar Assoumi of Kiota. The Shaykh of Kiota visited Kaolack (Senegal) and became a close disciple of the charismatic leader Ibrahim Niass. As noted earlier, he was largely responsible for the development of the Niass branch of the Tijaniyya in Niger.

11. Rapport politique, 4eme trimestre. 1912. Niger VII dossier 1. Aix-en-Provence: Archives d'Outre-Mer.

12. In the village of Matankari, some twenty-five kilometers north of Dogondoutchi, an itinerant preacher, Malam Kaboye, was arrested in July 1910 by French authorities on suspicion of engaging in anti-French propaganda. See Subdivision de Doutchi. Correspondance. 1910. Document 6.7.1. Niamey: Archives Nationales du Niger.

13. The policy of arresting Muslim religious leaders suspected of subverting French interests has a long history in colonial West Africa and is not specific to the World War I period. At the turn of the nineteenth century Amadou Bamba, founder of the Mouride order in Senegal, was exiled by French authorities before eventually being released in 1910. In 1941 Shaykh Hamallah, founder of the Hamawiyya in Mali, was exiled and sent to France where he died (Soares 2005). Far from weakening their influence, however, these measures only strengthened the unity of their respective movements (Brenner 2001).

14. E. Roume. Le Gouverneur Général de l'AOF à M. Robert Arnaud. AOF 1906. II Dossier 3. Aix-en-Provence: Archives Nationales d'Outre-Mer.

15. The colonial record in West Africa reveals how reflections inspired by the Muslim question throughout the colonial period can be roughly classified in two opposite schools of thought: one saw in Islam the cradle of all subversions and a fundamental threat to colonial domination; the other conceived of Islam as a monotheist religion, analogous, if not preferable, to Christianity (Triaud 1974). In practice, however, these two perspectives did not give rise to separate policies. Policies were often taken in response to given circumstances and varied with changing personnel (Cruise O'Brien 1967).

16. Fifteen members of the Gao family, rulers of Arewa, enlisted in the French army (Fuglestad 1983).

17. In reality, however, no Muslim teacher ever applied for the subsidy to teach French (Cruise O'Brien 1967).

18. The Hamawiyya spread to western Niger around 1935, and despite the active counter-propaganda the French deployed, its expansion was swift. Members of the Hamawiyya, many of them recruited from among former slaves, contributed to the politicization of the western region. According to Fuglestad (1983), the Hamawiyya presence as an anti-colonial movement paved the way for the emergence of the *Parti Progressiste Nigérien,* Niger's first political party.

19. In the mid-twentieth century, French colonials thus identified "Wahhabism" as the "new Muslim threat" (Brenner 2001:62) in West Africa. In their annual political reports, local administrators described Wahhabism as a radical, but corrupted, form of Islam that had been brought by Muslim pilgrims from Mecca. Because of their violent opposition to Sufi orders, Wahhabis were perceived to be dangerous individuals requiring close surveillance.

20. Clozel à M. le Commissaire du Government Général du Territoire Militaire du Niger. Enquête sur l'Islam. 18 Août 1915. Microfilm 14 MI 861. Aix-en-Provence: Archives d'Outre-Mer.

21. In 1806 the *Sarkin* (chief of) Arewa was vanquished by the Fulani chief of Binji (northern Nigeria) and was forced to recognize the latter's sovereignty. Though tribute was thereafter paid in the amount of one hundred cowries per family, the Mawri population was not pressured to convert to Islam (Périé and Sellier 1946).

22. Belle. Monographie du secteur de Dogondoutchi. 1913. Document 6.1.2. Aix-en-Provence: Archives d'Outre-Mer..

23. Mahant, Capitaine. Monographie du secteur de Dosso. 1913. Document 5.1.5. Niamey: Archives Nationales du Niger.

24. Belle. Monographie du secteur de Dogondoutchi. 1913. Document 6.1.2. Aix-en-Provence: Archives d'Outre-Mer.

25. Rapport sur l'Islam. Secteur de Dogondoutchi. 1914. Microfilm 14MI861. Aix-en-Provence: Archives d'Outre-Mer.

26. Rapport sur l'Islam. Secteur de Dogondoutchi. 1914. Microfilm 14MI861. Aix-en-Provence: Archives d'Outre-Mer.

27. Conclusions du rapport sur l'Islam. 1914. Cercle de Mainé-Soroa par le commandant de cercle en tournée. Aix-en-Provence: Archives d'Outre-Mer.

28. République du Niger 1912:13. Niamey: Archives Nationales du Niger.

29. Notes sur la question musulmane. 1912. Microfilm 14Mi 861. Aix-en-Provence: Archives d'Outre-Mer.

30. As Brevié (1923:168) poetically put it,

Like foreign plants that are transplanted to another climate and terrain and therein require attentive care, Islam could only develop in the Sudan with the support of a secular structure. But when this structure was missing, it was destined to die, choked by the luxuriant vegetation of naturism; because of its inherently rustic and vibrant nature, naturism, on the other hand, could put out new shoots as soon as the normal conditions of life were reestablished.

31. From this perspective, Christianity was just as unsuitable if not more so. In his treatise on Mawri society, Abadie (1927:226) wrote that Christian religions are

totally inaccessible to the minds of blacks. Indeed, given the principles of absolute equality they advertize, they might lead blacks to believe themselves to be the equals of whites and thus to undermine the positive influence and authority which the latter derive from the unquestionable superiority of their race and civilization.

For an insightful analysis of Christianity in Niger, see Cooper 2006.

32. Rapport sur l'Islam. Secteur de Dogondoutchi. 1914. Microfilm 14MI861. Aix-en-Provence: Archives d'Outre-Mer.

33. The Voulet-Chanoine Mission was a military expedition sent out from Senegal in 1898 to conquer the Lake Chad region and unify the territories of French West Africa. The mission was directed by Captain Paul Voulet and Lieutenant Julien Chanoine. In western Niger it encountered drought, severe shortages of supplies, and strong resistance to its attempts to conscript porters. Voulet and Chanoine resorted to massacring villagers, seizing food supplies, and burning down villages as they led their troops eastward. In Arewa the "infernal column" left a trail of destruction in its wake.

34. Despite the stiff resistance put up by the archers of the Sarauniya, the village of Lougou—seat of Azna power—was burned to the ground by the forces of Voulet and Chanoine.

35. Notes sur la question musulmane. 1912. Microfilm 14Mi 861. Aix-en-Provence: Archives d'Outre-Mer.

36. Lettre à M. le Gouverneur-Général de l'Afrique Occidentale. 1914. Microfilm 14Mi 861. Aix-en-Provence: Archives d'Outre-Mer.

37. Circulaire du Gouverneur-Général au Lieutenant Colonel Thierry de Maugras, Commissaire du Government Général du Territoire Militaire du Niger. Août 1, 1913. Aix-en-Provence: Archives d'Outre-Mer.

38. Rapport de la subdivision de Dosso. 15 Mai 1914. Microfilm 14MI861. Aix-en-Provence: Archives d'Outre-Mer.

39. Lettre à M. le Gouverneur Général de l'Afrique Occidentale. May 12, 1914. Microfilm 14MI861. Aix-en-Provence: Archives d'Outre-Mer.

40. Rapport sur l'Islam. Secteur de Dogondoutchi. 1914. Microfilm 14MI861. Aix-en-Provence: Archives d'Outre-Mer.

41. Mawri people, regardless of whether they were Muslims, recognize the power of the 'yan 'kasa (masters of the earth), heads of the priestly lineages associated with the foundation of the first villages in Arewa. See République du Niger. Monographie de la subdivision de Doutchi. c. 1936–1940. Document 6.1.6. Niamey: Archives Nationales du Niger.

42. Rapport de la subdivision de Dosso. 15 Mai 1914. Microfilm 14MI861. Aix-en-Provence: Archives d'Outre-Mer.

43. Compte-rendu des tournées effectuées du 8 au 19 avril 1947. Chef de subdivision de Doutchi. Document 6.1.8. Niamey: Archives Nationales du Niger.

44. Compte-rendu des tournées effectuées du 6 au 4 février 1947. Chef de subdivision de Doutchi. Document 6.3.42. Niamey: Archives Nationales du Niger.

45. Revue trimestrielle du 1er trimestre. Subdivision de Dogondoutchi. 1947. Document 6.4.4. Niamey: Archives Nationales du Niger.

46. Revue des évènements du 2eme trimestre. Cercle de Dosso. 1947. Document 5.5.7. Niamey: Archives Nationales du Niger.

47. The Islamic Conference is an organization of forty-two member states dedicated to the renaissance of the Muslim world, support for the Palestinian cause and the liberation of Jerusalem, and cooperation among member states. In addition to Niger, the Islamic Conference counts fifteen Sub-Saharan African countries (Nicolas 1981).

48. When a title holder is installed, a turban is ceremoniously tied around his head while praise-singers sing his praises and members of the audience make offerings of money.

49. Muslim burial is a simple affair. After the corpse is washed and laid out in a white shroud, it is carried to the local cemetery and interred facing east. Women do not attend the burial. Except in cases when the deceased was officially identified as a member of *bori* and surviving kin explicitly rejected the participation of *malamai*, the presence of Muslim religious specialists was (and still is) essential to a properly conducted Muslim burial in Dogondoutchi.

50. In recent years the spread of Izala has further heightened the centrality of funerary rites in local processes of identity politics (Masquelier 1994). Although a focus on funerals is beyond the purview of this analysis, it is worth noting that, in Dogondoutchi, the control of bodies at death is implicated in the contested definition of Muslim identity. Burials and the practices observed by mourning households currently serve to reaffirm religious distinctions.

51. On the influence of Nigeria as a source of religious knowledge and proselytism in Niger, see Grégoire 1992.

52. Note that although Muslim proselytizing has not been ostensibly targeted at Christians (recognized as one of the "people of the book"), Christians nonetheless have had to occasionally endure the scorn and disapproval of Muslim neighbors. Some have felt compelled to conform to what has become religious orthodoxy. I met several individuals who left the Catholic Church because they could not bear the constant teasing of their peers and the pressure from their kin to return to Islam.

53. This means that Muslims should avoid consuming the meat of animals that have not been ritually slaughtered by a Muslim man and abstain from impure meats such as pork (originally raised at the Catholic mission where they fed on kitchen garbage) and bush meat (porcupine, chameleon, boar, and so on). Traditionally Muslim food proscriptions were a frequent source of teasing on the part of *bori* devotees, who noted that Muslims avoided *haram* (forbidden) meats only as long as they had something else to eat. In times of famine, 'yan bori often pointed out to me, few people claimed to be Muslim. Significantly, dog consumption (which features prominently in the possession performances of Nigérien immigrants in the Gold Coast famously portrayed in Jean Rouch's film *Les Maîtres Fous*) is not a hallmark of *bori* identity. Although I was told that the Mossi spirits (hailing from Burkina Fasso) who were part of the *bori* pantheon ate dogs,

I never witnessed it. I suspect that dog consumption by Mossi spirits rarely, if ever, happens.

54. Among other things, Fulani men were accused of having sex with their mothers (de Latour 1992).

55. In principle, Fulani herders should not let cows graze on a cultivated field before the millet has been collected. Only after the harvest is completed can cows feed on the remaining stalks.

3. Debating Muslims, Disputed Practices

1. I first heard about the incident at the mosque in an informal chat with a town official following my arrival in town in 1994. Although he deplored the violent outcome of the dispute and criticized Izala activities, the man had no qualms telling me what supposedly had happened. But when I visited the local police station hoping to gain access to police records, several individuals told me that no such records existed and that, to their knowledge, no fight had ever taken place.

2. Following the Maitatsine riots, the Sufi order tried to discredit Izala by accusing its leaders of associating with the 'yan Tatsine. To counter these accusations, 'yan Izala were compelled to adopt more peaceful strategies for promoting their message of reform (Loimeier 1997b).

3. Habermas (1989) saw the emergence of the public sphere and the decline of religion as an intrinsic dimension of "modern" society. Though such modernist narratives have been criticized from various perspectives (Asad 2003; Casanova 1994; Comaroff and Comaroff 1999; Meyer and Moors 2006), the waning of "the sacred" is still largely assumed to be an inevitable consequence of modernization in the public sphere.

4. That Niger's financial survival hinges on external support is demonstrated by the fact that about 45 percent of the government's budget for 2002 was derived from donor resources.

5. Ironically economic factors may prove more decisive than any political decision as the cost of paper and printing, both imported from neighboring Nigeria, continues to rise. With the creation of websites, many papers have managed to increase their circulation, if only virtually. Even the cost of operating a website is occasionally too high, however, and not all newspapers are able to maintain their presence on the global scene.

6. In 1991 Tuareg militia, claiming that the Niamey-based government had discriminated against them, initiated a war against the Nigérien state to win autonomy. Although many of their demands have yet to be met, Tuareg groups signed peace accords in April 1995 after the Nigérien government agreed to absorb some former rebels into the military and, with French assistance, help others reintegrate into civilian life. In early 2007 military attacks resumed, but the Nigérien government has responded forcefully in an effort to crush incipient revolts.

7. In Maradi, a hotbed of Izala activism in Niger, the Izala movement has a longer history. By 1990 tensions between Izala members and their critics had intensified to the point that local authorities had to intervene "to promote understanding and calm tempers" (Grégoire 1993:11).

8. Iran, no doubt because of its Islamic revolution, is often said to provide the model for the 'yan Izala's utopian dream of an Islamic civil society, even if, paradoxically, Shi'ite doctrines are thought to be just as un-Islamic as the views advocated by Sufi orders.

9. At the same time, as is attested in neighboring Nigeria, where the Maitatsine uprisings resulted in hundreds of deaths (Barkindo 1993; Isichei 1987; Lubeck 1987) and where 'yan Izala's aggressive preaching has often led to violent physical confrontations (Umar 1993), the mobilizing potential of the movement cannot be ignored. A cursory examination of the mosque incident described earlier in this chapter—and the riots that erupted in protest of a 2000 fashion festival (see chapter 7)—makes clear that Izala also has this potential in the Nigérien context.

10. 'Yan Izala insist that the traditional prayer schedule adopted by local Muslims is incorrect. They have created a prayer schedule of their own, in which daily prayers take place half an hour after the 'yan darika prayers. Arguing that the Prophet allegedly remarked that "praying on time" was the most important obligation of a pious Muslim, they warn their followers and foes alike that exactitude in prayer is a good way to ensure one's place in heaven (see Masquelier, in press).

11. 'Yan Izala were not the first to make concessions to allow the use of certain media in the promotion and practice of Islam. Indeed, the issue of what is an acceptable innovation has been the object of considerable debate in the last half-century. Tijaniyya leader Ibrahim Niass's eloquent defense of the radio as a "necessary" innovation that, together with airplanes and printing presses, would "strengthen the law of Islam" because it facilitated communication and the spread of knowledge, was welcomed by those who used such technologies in the service of religion (Paden 1973:133).

12. The word for co-wife is *kishiya*, "jealous one." While co-wives frequently compete for the attention and resources of their husband, they just as often benefit from the division of labor that takes place in polygamous households.

13. A '*dan* Tijaniyya, with whom I discussed doctrinal and ritual differences between Izala members and 'yan darika, noted philosophically that "prayers are more efficacious than *layu* [amulets], but for those who know nothing, who cannot read the Qur'an, amulets work. One cannot tell them 'Go read this *sourate* [verse of the Qur'an], it will protect you.'" Although he did not encourage people to wear amulets, he disagreed with 'yan Izala for whom the practice of wearing *layu* was sinful in all contexts, regardless of one's educational and social standing.

14. I was told by a '*dan darika* that many prominent Muslim scholars had convincingly shown which verses of the Qur'an could be taken as proof that *laya* (amulets) and *rubutu* (medicine made with the washed-out ink used to write a Qur'anic verse) were acceptable Muslim practices. Only because of their ignorance did 'yan Izala reject these practices as unacceptable innovations.

15. Idris, who was born in Katagum, Nigeria, started his religious career by working for Jama'at Nasir Islam, a powerful educational organization headquartered in Kaduna (Isichei 1987:203). In 1974, after his views led to trouble within the organization, he left to become an imam in the army. There, too, his religious opinions eventually contributed to his discharge.

16. Radio Kaduna, which broadcasts over much of Nigeria, Niger, and many surrounding countries, has the largest radio audience in West Africa (Larkin 1996).

17. Few studies have been done on the Izala movement in Niger. In addition to Charlick's (2004) and Miles's (2003) general retrospectives of Islam in Niger, see Grégoire's (1992, 1993) study of Muslim identity among the merchant class of Maradi, Sounaye's (2005) analysis of reformist Islam in the context of national politics, Glew's

(1996) discussion of Islamic associations, and Niandou-Souley and Alzouma's (1996) perceptive account of religious pluralism in neoliberal Niger.

18. Ultimately much of the financing for the erection of the mosque supposedly originated from Maradi. Kuwait was rumored to have initially expressed an interest in funding the construction of the mosque, but disagreements arose regarding the design of the edifice—Izala reformists wanted to hire a local architect—and so Kuwaiti financiers eventually retrieved their offer.

19. The local Izala association boasts a president, a vice president, a secretary general, and a treasurer. It is the official organ through which local members of Izala relate to the state, receive funding from donors for local projects (such as mosque construction), and communicate with other members to organize national preachings known as *wa'azin 'kasa* (during which prominent scholars of Islam preach on various topics ranging from *ibada*—worship—to the life of the Prophet to how to raise Muslim children).

20. Muslims who disapproved of the Izala ethos often referred to one another as "true Muslims" (*musulmi kwarai*) to emphasize that, in their views, *'yan* Izala were impostors.

21. It seems only fair to point out that according to Shaykh Gumi himself, violence was perpetrated by members of the Muslim orders on Izala followers rather than the other way around. Gumi (1992:158) described what happened in his memoirs:

> At first the *darika* leaders and their followers did not take any particular notice of the preachers, but soon it became apparent that Izala was spreading fast and the people were questioning their past mistakes. That was when organized violence began against the association.
>
> The first victim, I think, was Malam Ali, a Nupe man living in Kawo, a Kaduna suburb. . . . One day, he went to . . . preach as usual. He had hardly begun when many *darika* followers surrounded him and demanded that he should stop. He stopped immediately, but as he was getting ready to go away a few of them shouted that he should be killed. A scuffle ensued and in the process someone brought out a knife and stabbed him to death.
>
> Also, not long afterwards, an Izala public meeting was attacked by irate *darika* followers in Lafia, Plateau State. Many were wounded and their vehicles were shattered or burnt . . .
>
> Then also the *darika* leaders resorted to other tactics, like threats and intimidation against the law enforcement agencies in order to force them to ban Izala meetings.

22. These debates over the length of pants remind us of the centrality of dress in the fashioning of religious identity. Whereas in the eyes of *'yan* Izala, long pants signaled disrespect for God at prayer time, for their opponents they were intrinsic to the construction of moral personae and Muslim tradition. By covering their legs, Muslims distinguished themselves from their "animist" counterparts who, in the past, wore a simple loin cloth made of goat skin.

23. If Nigériens keep reproducing at the current rate, the country's population is expected to more than quadruple by 2050 (Institut National de la Statistique 2006), imposing unmanageable demands on the economy, the environment, and social services such as health care and education, according to foreign analysts.

24. According to one Izala member,

prayer beads are just pretense. They don't mean that you are a learned scholar. They don't mean that you fear God. Everywhere you see 'yan darika with prayer beads around their wrists as if they were learned *malamai*. I remember this imam I met in a village, who held large prayer beads in his hands but could not recite the second verse of the Qur'an.

25. Significantly the notion of *bidi'a* (innovation) was key to Usman 'dan Fodio's definition of what constituted an unbeliever. In his attempts to define a Muslim in nineteenth-century Hausaland, 'dan Fodio distinguished between merely sinful practices such as numerology and the observation of lucky and unlucky days from those that contradicted the oneness of God and therefore constituted unbelief, for example, the veneration of trees and rocks where sacrifices were performed (Last and al-Hajj 1987).

26. In Nigeria as well, many costly social and religious practices were abandoned or curtailed to minimize the financial burden on the poor.

27. Truthfulness is a crucial characteristic of a good person (*mutum kirki*) in Hausa-speaking communities. Those who spread lies about others in order to stain their reputation are just as guilty as those who avoid the truth—about Islam, for instance—because of their ignorance and immorality. Those who can claim to have *gaskiya* (truth) are morally superior, which is why truth is such a central concept of the Islamic revival.

28. Abubakar Gumi developed strong relations with Saudi Arabia at a time when Saudi leaders especially wanted to curtail the influence of the Iranian revolution and Shi'a Islam abroad. According to Alidou (2005), the leaders of Izala in Niger are connected to Nigerien merchants with business partners in northern Nigeria. These businessmen in turn have established linkages with reformist traders in, for example, Saudi Arabia, Iran, Malaysia, and Pakistan. For a detailed account of Izala's connections to the Middle East, see Kane 2003.

29. As Doutté (in Goody 1968:227) explains,

since the graphic sign which represented the words are much easier to handle than the sounds and are capable of enduring, as they have a material form, it is inevitable that magical force is seen as encapsulated in them; in other words, writing itself is reputed to have magical powers.

30. The Izala dissemination of religious education through radio sermons and the circulation of cassettes was also instrumental in reconceptualizing the role of Muslim scholars, because orally transmitting the religious meanings contained in the Qur'an made them available to those who could not read.

31. In northern Nigeria Hausa speakers traditionally identified various types of marriages based on the strictness of seclusion, typically differentiating *auren kulle* (marriage with strict seclusion) from *auren tsare* (marriage with partial seclusion) and *auren jahilai* (marriage of the ignorant, with no seclusion) (M. G. Smith 1955). In Dogondoutchi people differentiate simply between *armen kubli* (marriage with seclusion) and *armen sake* (marriage with no seclusion).

32. One should not exaggerate the benefits of seclusion, however. Not all the secluded women I met managed to set up a business. For women who had no daughter who could be sent hawking food door to door, having to pay a young girl to buy supplies and sell the prepared food cut into their earnings. They could not sell peanut oil, for instance, because buying peanuts (rather than growing them) would have similarly reduced their profits considerably.

33. It is noteworthy that in Nigeria many women were attracted to the movement because they saw its doctrines and practices as a move forward compared to the situation within the Sufi orders (Westerlund 1997). There, the Izala movement not only stressed the necessity of women's education but also promoted awareness of women's rights regarding inheritance and divorce (Loimeier 1997b).

34. Children's education, too, has been severely compromised by the lack of funds. In contrast to northern Nigeria, where having both men and women occupy the same space is seen by 'yan Izala as a "lesser evil" than keeping women ignorant of Islam (Umar 2001:137), Izala leaders in Dogondoutchi hope one day to have access to classrooms that will allow boys and girls to be taught separately. As of 2006, with only a few exceptions, most children were taught in open-air classes or under shelters made of woven grass. In one school I visited in 2000, children aged four to seven sat on mats (boys on one side, girls on the other) and the only chair was occupied by the teacher.

35. It is significant that most of the protests initiated by Izala (at times, in coalition with other Islamic associations) target policies aimed at regulating the rights and roles of women in Nigérien society. When, in 1991, the *Rassemblement Démocratique des Femmes du Niger* (RDFN), a new women's association, asked to participate in the Sovereign National Conference held to reform the Nigérien state, some leaders of the association were assaulted by 'yan Izala in Maradi and Zinder (Charlick 2004).

36. Following the National Conference on Family Health and Development that was held in Niamey in 1985, the French law of 1920, which prohibited the importation, sale, and advertisement of contraceptives, was repealed. Soon after, the Nigérien government approved a development plan that contained family-planning provisions. Family planning was eventually integrated into maternal and child health activities. Following the implementation of a family health action program, recommendations were approved to facilitate access to contraception in the national family-planning program. Although access to reproductive health services has expanded considerably in recent years, the use of modern methods of birth control remains extremely low, especially in rural areas where female illiteracy is high, clinics are overcrowded and poorly staffed, contraceptive shortages are frequent, and transportation to the nearest health centers is limited (Guengant and May 2001).

37. As one *'dan* Izala explained, "No one should practice birth control [based on limited resources] because it is God who feeds you and provides. God said to marry and have lots of children. Even if you have twenty children, God will provide for them."

38. In 2004 the Nigérien government held a series of seminars around the country to raise awareness of the serious problems facing the health care and educational systems as the population continues to expand rapidly. A World Bank–sponsored project currently seeks to decrease fertility in Niger by strengthening maternal health and family planning services, promoting women's status, supporting demographic data collection, and conducting policy research. In 2007 the government established a national plan to curb population growth through the promotion of information campaigns to educate religious leaders, and especially women, about the importance of family planning.

39. In June 1994 Muslim women's groups rejected the Family Code saying that 603 of its 906 articles were a breach of Qur'anic principles. The Code, which reformist Muslim activists oppose unanimously, was intended to eliminate gender bias in inheritance rights, land tenure, and child custody. It would have forbidden husbands from repudiating

their wives and allowed couples to officially choose a monogamous relationship. In a formal statement, women from six different Muslim organizations said that all the issues the Code intended to oversee were already regulated by the Muslim religion and should not suffer human interference (Mayer 1995:1). After Islamic associations condemned the Code, the government suspended discussions and has taken no further action.

40. That such critical discussions about society are primarily religious in nature is not surprising given Mawri society's persistent history of confrontation between Muslims and spirit devotees (Masquelier 1993). These debates that divide communities and families under different religious banners broaden our understanding of civil society's potential when it is exported to social contexts in which people are urged—through televised sermons, printed materials, taped admonitions, or unmediated confrontations—to reorder their lives, from matters of dress and commensalism to how they should earn and spend money.

4. When Charisma Comes to Town

1. Malam Awal orchestrated public confessions of individuals who had joined Awaliyya. The new converts were made to acknowledge in front of a crowd of assembled 'yan Awaliyya that they were wrong but had now found "true" Islam. A friend who attended one of these confessions heard a young man say that he was mistaken in thinking that Izala was *addinin kwarai* (true religion). He later asked God's forgiveness for his sin. Those who were assembled prayed for him and contributed money so he could buy new clothes.

2. Dar al-Islam is the "world of Islam" in which Muslims rule themselves.

3. Malam Awal, in one of his sermons, explained the greed of *malamai* as follows:

The Prophet said: "If you ask a *malami*, 'Where are you going?' he will respond, 'I am going to a *wa'azi.*' If you ask him again, 'What are you carrying?' he will respond that he is carrying a Qur'an. When you ask, 'And what is that?' he will answer, 'Oh, it is a bag to put whatever people give me.'" "This one," God said, "you must cut off his head. He is a pagan." If you are a *malami,* you should go to the *wa'azi* without thinking about what people are going to give you.

4. Women, too, saw Malam Awal as a threat to the community. During a conversation I was having with the three wives of a *'dan* Izala, one of them defiantly claimed that those who had not joined Izala—and whom in previous years she had severely criticized in my presence—were better Muslims than Malam Awal and his followers. By categorizing members of the Awaliyya as "bad" Muslims, she implicitly acknowledged a closer kinship between Muslims who accepted neither Izala nor Awaliyya values and 'yan Izala themselves. In her eyes, those who categorically rejected the Awaliyya ethos were "authentic" Muslims.

5. In the words of one of Malam Awal's close disciples:

At one point, the traditionalist imam and 'yan Izala got together to fight Malam Awal and bring him in front of the judge. When you hear distasteful things said about you, you know your opponents are spreading negative rumors. 'Yan Izala insisted on being heard by the mayor in Malam Awal's presence. They said, "Your sermon is not what God asked. You are just confusing people." They wanted him to sign a paper that said he agreed to stop preaching. Of course, Malam Awal refused.

Although it is doubtful that the judge in question acceded to Muslim officials' request that Malam Awal be banned from preaching—at the time, the preacher enjoyed the protection of Ibrahim Bare Maïnassara, the then president of Niger—what is significant is that Awal's religious adversaries would try to censor him at all. With the increase of Muslim associations in the past two decades, obtaining authorization to preach has become easier for anyone wishing to do so. Prior to the liberalization of Nigérien politics, however, the power to grant preaching permits was strictly in the hands of the *Association Islamique du Niger,* the state-regulated organization that, through its ability to weed out potential "troublemakers," could exert control over the nature and content of sermons.

6. Initially Awal's claims that other Muslims in Niger had started the fast "too early" were met with ferocious objections in Dogondoutchi. Eventually local Muslim leaders gave up trying to stop the preacher from establishing a different fasting schedule, despite the controversies his reforms generated among their own constituencies. Note that the activities of Muslim leaders who depart from their predecessors have come under increased scrutiny. In February 1997 Nigérien authorities arrested a reformist Muslim leader for celebrating the end of Ramadan on February 9 instead of the official date of February 8. Seven policemen and several civilians were ultimately injured and a police station destroyed when disciples of the imprisoned man attempted to free him from detention.

7. 'Yan Awaliyya are also called 'yan mandiri because they beat their chests like members of the Qadiriyya. The *mandiri* is a small drum played by 'yan Qadiriyya. According to a friend, "'yan Awaliyya do some singing and dancing—they whirl—like Qadiris. It is a way of communing with God. They beat their chests in unison, it's like Iranians who flagellate themselves or use swords as a form of penitence."

8. Thus, at the tomb of the Prophet, the religious police bar visitors from praying in the tomb chamber or touching the silver cage around it. At Hira'a Cave, in the mountains at the edge of Mecca where Muhammad is believed to have received the first verses of the Qur'an, a warning posted by the religious police warns pilgrims not to pray or "touch stones" to receive blessings.

9. The flurry of flash photography surrounding Malam Awal during the commemorative celebration was especially ironic to me, as I had purposefully left my camera at home that evening, never suspecting that taking photos was allowed and even encouraged.

10. The great majority of Dogondoutchi residents believed that Malam Awal hailed from Kano in Kano State, Nigeria. One person told me that he was from the border town of Maigatari in Jigawa State, Nigeria—a town that, thanks to the establishment of a Free Trade zone, enjoys brisk cross-border traffic.

11. One disciple said, in explaining Malam Awal's unparalleled experience, "he has seen absolutely everything."

12. Even outside the ranks of his disciples, the preacher's erudition was recognized as valuable. A young university-educated civil servant suggested to me that Malam Awal was more a historian than a religious man. From his perspective, the preacher's contributions to the religious debate were based not on his piety so much as his knowledge of Islam.

13. As the union of 3 (associated with maleness and male elements, cycles, and activities) and 4 (its female counterpart), the number 7 is extremely important in Mawri

society. It is the product of the joining of male and female principles that provide the foundation for local conceptions of the universe and its reproduction.

14. Following Weber and Mauss, Gaffney nevertheless notes that the distinction between priests (who are the recipients of divine blessings) and magicians (whose power is based on the knowledge of magic) may appear blurred, particularly in the case of Muslim saints who "display 'almost a total confusion of power and roles'" (Mauss, in Gaffney 1994:36–37).

15. A close disciple of Awal told me that the preacher at times looked like a young man and at other times appeared considerably older. Another disciple said that "one day you would find him short, and the next day you would find him tall. At times he was white, and on other days he looked black."

16. Based on current knowledge, it seems reasonable to infer that, in Niger, Muslim leaders who, like Malam Awal, vigorously resisted state-sponsored attempts to vaccinate children took their cues from their Nigerian counterparts who had, since 2002, forced the World Health Organization to delay or cancel several immunization drives. For a thorough account of how residents of Zaria, northern Nigeria, resisted polio vaccination initiatives, see Renne 2006.

17. Elsewhere in southern Niger, the 2003 polio campaign was similarly thwarted by alarmist claims that the vaccine passed on the AIDS virus and had been devised to deplete the world of its Muslim population.

18. As previously noted, Awaliyya and Izala share a concern for the rational utilization of resources. Both also condemn the excessive practice of *sadaka* (alms giving) in which surviving kin traditionally engage—by distributing bean flour cakes, kola nuts, and cash—during the mourning period. As one '*dan* Izala, a health counselor, pithily put it, "Why give your money or your millet to someone who has a much nicer outfit than you? It makes no sense."

19. In 2000, warnings circulated that those who spread (or listened to) rumors which cast the preacher in a bad light would automatically go to hell. A '*dan* Awaliyya explained that if an individual simply listened to the negative gossip spread about the preacher, when the gossiper accumulated ten sins, four of those would eventually become his or her own. Muslims, he implied, should not only avoid spreading disparaging gossip about Malam Awal but should also prevent its dissemination—especially if they wished to avoid the fires of hell.

20. The creation or expansion of transnational Islamic networks is not new, of course. Sufi orders such as the Tijaniyya and the Qadiriyya have long formed extensive linkages throughout North and Sub-Saharan Africa. As noted in chapter 2, these networks regularly exacerbated French and British anxieties over the dangers of subversive proselytism and the possibilities of Madhist revolts during the colonial period.

21. The first Sarauniya bore a daughter, but her successors were prevented by their priestly responsibilities from marrying and having children.

22. Sarauniya, the only daughter of the King of Daura (northern Nigeria), was forced to leave the kingdom. She was guided to Lougou by the Tunguma stone, the famed stone of justice still used today to render judgment.

23. The "stranger from the East" scenario has a long history in Hausaland. The spread of Islam in Kano, Nigeria, some ten centuries earlier is linked to the coming of a stranger who, wresting the land from its pagan inhabitants, became the first King of Kano (Paden 1973; Palmer 1928).

24. The attitude of Muslims who refuse to recognize Sarauniya's contribution to Nigérien culture and history is comparable to that of Ghanaian Pentecostals who adamantly reject the state's call to celebrate cultural heritage because they view that heritage as inseparable from demonic spirits (Meyer 1998b).

25. As one 'dan Izala put it, "in Mecca, they don't do zikiri. It is haram [forbidden]. In Mecca, no one walks around carrying prayer beads. God never said to walk around with prayer beads." From this perspective, prayer beads should be kept in one's pocket and taken out only during prayer.

26. 'Yan Awaliyya took pride in listing the places where Malam Awal had been invited to preach. Their testimonies of the preacher's globe-trotting enhanced the strategic importance of Dogondoutchi as a center of renewed religiosity. According to Malam Bassirou,

> Malam Awal stayed in many towns. He was given big houses with several stories but did not take them. Someone in Belgium was very surprised to learn that the preacher has settled in Dogondoutchi. How could he stay in Dogondoutchi after the lifestyle he enjoyed in Europe? Malam Awal was given two land parcels in Tahoua [Niger's fourth largest city] to build a house. In Agadez [a large desert town], too, people promised to build a house for him. He said no. He is more loved [in Dogondoutchi] than anywhere else.

27. The story, of course, does not end here. Having succeeded in antagonizing Tandja, Malam Awal had to leave town, to escape the president's wrath. The president allegedly requested that a warrant be issued for the preacher's arrest on the grounds that he had caused a public disturbance.

5. Building a Mosque in the Home of a Spirit

1. In the Nigérien town of Mirria, people similarly believed that the palace was inhabited by powerful, yet dangerous, spirits. Even devout Muslims expressed fears of the creatures, although, of course, they loudly proclaimed their contempt for bori (Saunders 1978).

2. As Piault (1972:465) puts it, the Arewa chief is "the owner of all spirits," and he must provide sacrificial victims for the spirits who live in and around Dogondoutchi.

3. Maizari was settled as an independent village before it was eventually incorporated as part of Dogondoutchi.

4. Paden (1973:141) notes that in Hausa-speaking communities zawiya traditionally referred to two things: first, in some villages situated on major transportation routes, the zawiya was a hut where travelers could seek lodging; second, in both rural and urban areas, Sufi orders maintained centers, or zawiya, "for the purpose of worship, teaching, and lodging for transient brothers."

5. Hajiya Salamatou, a devout follower of Malam Awal, told me that, when she was a young girl, she was scared each time she had to pass in front of the derga tree. She would always run in the hope of outdistancing the Doguwa, should the spirit try to catch her.

6. According to some witnesses, the swarming ants had been the Doguwa herself, as spirits can change their shape. Although they generally take on a human form to communicate with people, occasionally they transform themselves into animals—a cow, a donkey, a swarm of bees, and so on.

7. According to a senior woman and follower of Awal, the events unfolded as follows: "When people started building the mosque, the ants came out. Malam Awal said to the ants, 'I am building a house, and I will be your neighbor.' At that point the ants disappeared. Only Malam Awal could see the Doguwa."

8. "Chronotope," in Bakhtin's work, can be literally translated as "time-space." More specifically, chronotopes are "points in the geography of a community where time and space intersect and fuse. Time takes on flesh and becomes visible for human contemplation; likewise, space becomes charged and responsive to the movements of time and history and the enduring character of a people" (Bakhtin 1981:84).

9. Deforestation in this and other regions of Niger occurred in the context of the shift toward private property, aided by the spread of Islam which popularized the notion that trees and land were devoid of spiritual content. As Cooper (2006:354) perceptively notes, "One could argue that the loss of tree cover in the region is part of a massive desacralization of the landscape . . . made possible technologically through the promotion of the plough . . . and ideologically through the promotion of Islamic law . . . a massive act of conquest by the monotheists." In the Maradi and Dogondoutchi region, she continues, the few remaining stands of trees were protected because they were believed to be the homes of spirits.

10. Certain *malamai* specialize in amulets or supplicatory prayers (*addu'a*) that protect travelers along the way. Prayers are sometimes described as a force that moves across space, making the way safe for the person it is destined to protect. A *malami* told me that when he recited a protective prayer for a traveler going to Niamey, within moments the prayer was in Niamey, making the city safe for that person.

11. I was told on at least two occasions that the Awaliyya mosque had been built *precisely* where the tree that sheltered the Doguwa had been.

12. In 2004 a Muslim woman told me that the older brother of a prominent *'dan Izala* became blind after he had tried to rid the family compound of spirits. Their father had been an active member of *bori*. After the father died, his older son, a respected Qur'anic scholar, dug up the sacrificial stones on which his father had shed blood for the spirits and threw them into the bush. Soon afterward, he lost his sight. In Niamey, where he had gone to seek treatment for his affliction, he was told that his condition was irreversible. "Everyone in the neighborhood now says that his blindness has to do with the destruction of the spirit's sacrificial shrines," my friend stated. "Why did he have to dig up the stones and throw them away? He should have left them where they were," she concluded.

13. When asked what is the worst sin a Muslim can commit, most Muslims declare that it is *tsabi* (sacrifice; worship of spirits), which leads straight to hell if the offender does not repent before dying. One does not have to engage in spirit possession to commit this sin. The simple act of buying a hen or a wrapper for a spirit in the hope of placating that creature is a form of "idolatry."

14. Ignoring the persistent demands of a spirit can be difficult, especially when one's life is at stake. Whether or not *bori* is the work of Satan, as is routinely asserted, placating a spirit through an offering of perfume or a gift of cloth seems for some less sinful than wasting away.

15. For simplicity's sake, I refer to the Doguwa's master as male. In my experience, individuals accused of engaging in nefarious processes of wealth-making that involved a Doguwa spirit were often men.

16. Doguwa, by definition, are never totally gone. They may disappear for a while, but they eventually return to resume the work they were initially invited to perform. They can no longer work for the convicted *maye* (witch), but they can create wealth for his descendants. Children of convicted witches are widely suspected of engaging (often against their will) in sinister activities centering on the transformation of blood into wealth.

17. A *malami* once recounted that, while attending Qur'anic school, he felt that something was holding his hand. He could not write anymore. After reciting a Qur'anic verse, he felt better. He knew then that a spirit had been trying to interfere with his studies.

18. To the charge of "idolatry" brought by 'yan Izala against them, Muslims who made use of amulets responded that since the name of God was inscribed in the amulet, they were not creating an idol but demonstrating their belief in God.

19. Secrets may have some pharmaceutical elements, but these are usually combined with scriptural verses appropriate to the threat one is seeking protection against or the opportunities one is trying to capture.

20. One '*dan* Izala explained the danger of amulets in this way:

> Let's say you purchase a *laya* to get rid of your co-wife, to avoid being beaten, or to cause your neighbor to lose his job. Then, if [what you wished for] actually happens, you will think that the amulet works. You believe in God, but you also believe in the power of the amulet. One day something bad happens, and it was just the day that you forgot to wear the amulet. So now you are convinced of the efficacy of the *laya* but not of God's power. You've now put your trust in two Gods. This is wrong. God is unique.

21. In a somewhat different version, the child allegedly saw a man wearing a white outfit praying on the site of what is now the mosque. When he looked again, the man was gone. He ran to tell everyone what he had seen. Some people, among them Malam Awal, thought that the Prophet had appeared to the child and took it as a sign that a mosque should be built on that site.

22. According to yet another version of the mosque story,

> The little mosque had been there for a long time. But no one knew about it. When Malam Awal came, he showed the mosque to everyone. This is where he told people to go when they wanted to ask God something.

23. Predictably the miraculous mosque was the focus of heated discussions between skeptics and believers. Awaliyya members I met in 2000 were angered by doubters' claims. As one of them angrily said, "The little mosque is the mosque of God. It was built by God. Those who say that God didn't build it are lying!"

24. During the *haji* in Mecca pilgrims throw pebbles at a stone pillar representing the devil to symbolize rejection of temptation.

25. The *Kano Chronicle* is a written account of the history of the Hausa-speaking people of Kano, Nigeria, dating back to the tenth century AD.

26. Izala reformists described the West as a cradle of impiety and decadence long before 9/11. They drew a stark contrast between Muslim societies characterized by religious devotion and moral restraint and societies that did not "fear God." The events of 9/11 appear to have had a sizable impact on Muslim subjectivities. They helped focus what had been relatively dispersed recriminations about unemployment, poverty, and margin-

ality. Youths who had no connections to Izala now read their experience of crisis through the lens of 9/11 and the Manichaean world that has emerged in its wake.

6. How Is a Girl to Marry without a Bed?

1. Piety does not imply poverty, however. The language of austerity adopted by 'yan Izala is occasionally tempered by the recognition that their message is primarily addressed to those who are burdened by social obligations they cannot satisfy. Prosperous mothers can bestow wealth upon their daughters, but they should do so discreetly so as to avoid embarrassing less fortunate neighbors. "If you have a lot of money, you can buy gold jewelry for your daughter. But it is only to wear at home. If you don't have much to give your daughter, that's fine. One must not feel shame," one 'dan Izala explained.

2. My intent here is not to equate globalization with modernity. Rather, I wish to point out that globally circulating goods—whether laminated beds or prayer beads, Tupperware bowls or televisions—are identified locally as modern products precisely because they come from afar, even if they are considered old or out of date elsewhere. One is modern, in this context, when one is connected to a network of global consumers.

3. "Baptism" (baptême) is a commonly used term in Niger that refers to the naming ceremony held seven days after an infant's birth—not the Christian ceremony by which one is admitted as a full member of the Church body.

4. In a society where virtually no young woman remains single for any length of time, Callaway (1987:40) notes, based on her research in Kano, Nigeria, that "the social advantages of an early marriage outweigh the possibilities of anything else imaginable a daughter might do." Although more women are now pursuing secondary studies and contemplating careers, they do not view employment as an alternative to marriage and motherhood. Elite young women may postpone marriage to complete their studies, but they, too, see marriage as a social obligation and not an option.

5. Piault (1978:422) notes that around 1935 bridewealth payments could be as low as 20 francs.

6. In her rich analysis of wedding gifts in the Hausa town of Maradi, Cooper (1997a) points out that earlier accounts of marriage in Hausa society have generally described women's investments in kayan 'daki as labor-intensive activities from which wives and mothers reap no appreciable benefits, as they simply serve the social system that constrains female opportunities in the first place. The Dogondoutchi case demonstrates that women generate more than simply material value when they invest in commodities for the benefit of their newly married daughters.

7. One need only hear the self-conscious laughter that erupts among women at the mere mention of "mortar and pestle" to verify the sexual connotation still attached to these objects, despite the changing protocol in wedding gift acquisitions. I once saw a young woman pretend to hit her husband with her pestle in a moment of anger. Appalled by her boldness, the husband retaliated by threatening to divorce her. The story of their altercation quickly spread, causing shock and outrage. Yet, I believe that these intense reactions—including the husband's—were caused as much by the young woman's violent gesture as by its symbolic message: her act inverted their sexual roles, turning her husband into the mortar in which she was attempting to thrust her "phallic" implement.

8. Women similarly pointed out that the goats and sheep tethered in the marital compounds were their exclusive property. Because husbands are morally and legally obliged to support their wives (and children), the income wives may derive from cash-generating

activities is theirs alone. A wife can dispose of it however she wishes, even occasionally lending money to her husband so he can support her.

9. Once a source of womanly wealth and pride, the hand-woven cotton blankets (*sakala*) that brides traditionally acquired as wedding gifts are now considered antiquated and worthless by young women; *sakala* are now given to the groom's mother, and the bride receives the mass-produced, synthetic wall hangings (*tapis*) associated with a more cosmopolitan, modern identity.

10. It is assumed that parents who agree to a marriage of alms for their daughter, forgoing bridewealth, will be amply rewarded for their piety on Judgment Day.

11. In addition to providing his dependents with food and shelter, a husband must also buy clothes for them (Masquelier 1996), and failing to do so can be grounds for divorce. Bebe angrily told me that Hadiza's husband had not bought his wife a single *complet* (custom-made blouse, ankle-length wrapper, and head covering of matching fabric) during their short marriage. Even worse, Hadiza often had to ask her mother for food because her husband's family did not feed her adequately.

12. Beds, in the past, were made of *sabara* branches and covered with simple mats of interwoven palm leaves. In colonial times it was fashionable to add a straw mattress and sheets (Fala Habi Aboubacar 1988).

13. Izala restrictions on *sadaki* and gift exchange have potent implications not only for the creation but also for the circulation of women's wealth, when we consider that a mother's property may be used, indirectly, to finance her daughter's *kayan 'daki*. When a woman dies, her bed is sold and the money from the sale is used to buy a bed for her sister, if she is married; if she is not married, the bed is set aside until her wedding. The bowls and wall hangings that have never been used are given to her daughters (or sometimes her sisters), provided they are married. The bowls that have been used to serve food are given to the deceased woman's cousins. Perhaps it is too soon to know, but it may well be that women are bemoaning changing patterns of inheritance which, under Izala influence, have become more male-centered.

14. The sharp distinction I may have drawn between Western bourgeois ideology and reformist Muslim notions of restraint and asceticism does not imply that all Izala reformists live austere lives away from the temptations of consumer culture. Local members of Izala include wealthy merchants who live in two-story houses (the ultimate expression of wealth in Dogondoutchi), own cars, and equip their wives with luxurious furniture and electric appliances.

15. A similar situation has been described for elite Igbo-speaking women by Bastian (2002:3), who points out that although educated young women in Nigeria aspire to marriage, they often "find themselves wrestling with the multiple failures of nationalist political and western-based economic ideologies" in a society where marital and sexual practices remain essentially patriarchal.

16. Once, when talking with a friend about wedding gifts, her sister said she had heard that an Izala bride received a small metal bed purchased by the groom, which, in her opinion, no mother ever would have bought for her daughter. My friend, who knew the young bride's mother and actually had had a chance to inspect the wedding gifts, further pointed out that the mattress was of such poor quality that it would probably quickly deteriorate. More than a reproach of the mother's inability to generate wealth for her daughter, the two women's critical evaluation of the bed and mattress this bride had received was an indirect condemnation of the marriage reforms

that forced local women to undermine their own and their daughter's access to wealth and status.

17. At a time when Nigérien health officials and activists have been actively campaigning to discourage *le marriage précoce*—the marriage of young girls who face risks of serious complications (often leading to obstetric fistula, infant mortality, or maternal death) during childbirth because their pelvis is not fully developed—the preacher's campaign to marry off young girls proved controversial among the educated elite. The girls whose unions Awal negotiated were rarely older than sixteen and sometimes as young as thirteen. Critics who disapproved of the preacher's methods for facilitating marriage procedures derisively referred to these marriages as *armen kananen yara* (marriage of little girls).

18. Because women's investment in *kayan 'daki* ties capital into property that is transferable but generates no income, it has not been critically analyzed. Except for Cooper's (1997a) account of Maradi women's contribution to the local economy, the literature on Hausa women's income-generating strategies has been remarkably gender-biased (Callaway 1987; Raynaut 1977; Schildkrout 1982). Izala male-centered discourses about marriage and wealth apparently replicate these biases.

7. Fashioning Muslimhood

1. "Islamic Groups Banned in Fashion Row." BBC News, November 12, 2000. http://news.bbc.co.uk/hi/english/world/africa/newsid_1018000/1018858.stm (accessed 2/10/2001).

2. The first FIMA was held near the desert town of Agadez in 1998 and was hailed by the Nigérien Minister of Tourism and Artisanship as "an important contribution to the consolidation of peace, the promotion of African culture, the renewed growth of tourism, and the development of the economy of the North" (Camel Express 1998).

3. Available at http://www.parisparis.com/fr/journal/afp/mode.html (accessed 2/10/2001).

4. Thus, whereas in Egypt, Turkey, and for a while in Algeria, Muslim women were made to bear the burden of embodying modernity by shedding their veils (Fanon 1965), in France, for instance, the veil became a potent symbol of resistance against secular forms of female encompassment and vestmental control.

5. "Strategy" does not adequately describe the kind of moral agency I have in mind, for it presupposes a consciousness that is not always there. Nonetheless, I use the term to stress the critical role women play as interpreters of the Qur'anic message.

6. It was acknowledged in Izala circles that girls who started wearing the *hijabi* late were lax in the way they dressed. They could not develop the requisite sensibility that enabled them to experience the veil as an intimate part of their embodied selfhood.

7. Markets are public spaces par excellence, where people—largely men, youths, or postmenopausal women—converge to trade, share news, meet people, or see and be seen.

8. Limited space prevents an elaboration on the complex ways in which "knowing" and "seeing" presuppose each other for secluded women when they are exposed to male glares. Bebe's experience of being an object of men's attention, her testimony suggests, felt like a violation, because the men knew her and knew she should not be seen. Whether real or imagined, the knowledge of her transgression that she read in their eyes and the

more general sense in which sight is both recognition and revelation has interesting implications for an anthropology of gendered exposure inspired by the work of Berger (1972) and Mulvey (1989).

9. For a discussion of seclusion in Hausa society, see Callaway 1987; Cooper 1994, 1998; Hill 1972; and Mack 1991.

10. *"Kubli ya fi armen sake"* (seclusion is better than marriage in which a woman can leave her home), an Izala wife explained, because the secluded wife accumulates divine rewards.

11. Whether made from the printed cotton fabric used to tailor women's outfits or from lighter, clingy, and silky or opaque synthetic material, head coverings have many practical uses, for example, as mats when none is available or blankets during the night. They also act as padding when their wearers carry bulky items on their heads. Women use them as well to dry themselves after bathing, to wrap up their infants and tie them onto their backs, and occasionally to wipe off a baby's bodily excretions. When expertly used, head coverings can highlight the elegance of a particular coiffure.

12. In Maradi, some Izala women wear a *hijabi* fitted with a zipper in the back so their babies can catch some air when tied to their mother's back (Barbara Cooper, personal communication). Such patterns were not visible in Dogondoutchi, another reminder of the diversity in localized fashions and expressions of piety.

13. The same logic dictates that women should not wear heavy bracelets that make noise, because these would attract unwanted attention. Moussa, a *'dan* Izala, further elaborated:

> All the things that women wear to attract men are *haram* [forbidden]. Perfume, for instance. A woman can make herself beautiful but only within her compound and for the benefit of her husband. Not to attract another man; that's sinful.

14. I was routinely told that *'yan* Awaliyya wore white clothes because white was the color of Islam. "When someone dies," Hassana, a steady follower of Awal explained,

> you wrap the corpse in a white shroud. The Arabs of Mecca, they wear white clothes. The Prophet himself wore white clothes. It's because you are a Muslim that you wear white. We do what our fathers did, that is the way to do things properly.

15. In the 1990s men who had joined Izala would only marry girls from Izala households. For a *'dan* Izala to marry a girl from a non-Izala household was tantamount to abandoning his commitment to reformist ideals. A decade earlier, in northern Nigeria, Isma'ila Idris, the founder of Izala, appealed to his followers not to give their daughters away in marriage to *'yan darika* because the latter were "unbelievers" (Loimeier 1997b). In 1994 I heard of an Izala preacher who refused to let his daughter marry the father of her unborn child because he was not a *'dan* Izala. After the child was born, the father came to slaughter a ram as is customary on this occasion, but the preacher refused to let him hold a naming ceremony for the child. He allegedly told the young man that rams were not slaughtered for illegitimate children.

16. As Bassirou, a *'dan* Izala, put it, "There is no difference between Izala and *darika* dress. Every woman must wear the *hijabi*. Women must hide their bodies. Islam orders women to wear the *hijabi*."

17. Significantly, despite the pervasive rhetoric identifying Meccan women's dress as the original models that have inspired local Muslim fashions, Izala veils are worlds apart from the impractical modes of veiling embraced by Saudi women (and women in Iran or the Swahili Coast) that require using a hand to hold the head covering in place. If doing things "like in Mecca" has a particular cachet for Muslims in Dogondoutchi, it does not means slavishly imitating Saudi styles—sartorial and otherwise—but rather drawing a connection between local and Saudi expressions of Muslim identity.

18. In the Nigérien capital *gabdi*, unmarried women who live with their parents but primarily support themselves through discreet prostitution, use Qur'anic education to re-fashion themselves as good Muslims (Alidou 2005). Through their participation in female-based Qur'anic literacy classes, they adopt the mantle of piety to create a respectable (and thus marriageable) reputation. This veneer of religiosity enables them to enjoy the freedom (and material rewards) that married women are denied.

19. In post-abolition Zanzibar, Fair (2001:91) points out, veiling was also occasionally associated with the concealment of activities that ran counter to the image of respectability women tried to project. Under the cover of her veil, a woman could "rendezvous with a lover, enter a house known for selling alcohol, or go to a party uninvited and feel relatively secure that word of her activities would not get back to her parents or husband."

20. Prohibiting young women from entering the mosque, I was often told, was a measure intended to minimize distractions for the men who prayed. I was also reminded that menstruating women were barred access to prayer sites because of their polluted state.

21. For more on the relation between possession and prostitution, see Barkow 1971 and Masquelier 2001b.

22. This does not mean that the frontiers of modesty have not shifted. Izala dress practices helped modify notions of proper dress. In the past, a woman could expose certain parts of her body—for example, her neck and her arms—without incurring disapproval. If the scooped neckline of a woman's tailored top enabled a shoulder to occasionally emerge from under the fabric, it was not considered inappropriate as long as her stomach, buttocks, and legs were covered.

23. Girls who attend school and want to veil must wear a white head covering. In other words, although veiling is optional, schoolgirls wishing to veil cannot choose the color of their head coverings.

24. Rumors circulated in early 2000 that one of my neighbors, a *'dan* Izala, was wearing dozens of amulets around his waist. A number of Muslim women, who rejected Muslim reformism, told me that members of Izala were liars, intent on tricking good Muslims. "This is why they veil, to hide their secrets," one woman suggested.

25. For a detailed account of the place of transnationalism in African fashion, see Rabine 2002.

26. Fair (2001) similarly notes that one may hear young girls in Zanzibar chanting Hindi love songs even though they speak not a word of Hindi. See also Casey, in press.

27. Incidentally the popularity of the *bodi*, a tight, curve-enhancing top also known as *baya* ("behind"), is often linked to the advent of Brazilian television series that feature this attire. As one young civil servant explained: "When they see how actresses on these shows are dressed, girls rush to the supermarket in Niamey or to the "Habits Boston" shop and they buy clingy T-shirts like the *baya*."

28. The Habermasian model of the public sphere does not include nonverbal modes of communication but focuses exclusively on rational argumentation as the means through which people participate in the public sphere.

8. "The Fart Does Not Light the Fire"

1. To compete with Izala leaders' aggressively media-oriented preaching, Malam Awal made all his sermons available on cassette tapes for local consumption. Significantly, the dilution of the Awaliyya membership was accompanied by a gradual waning of the preacher's sermon recordings and their circulation in cassette form. During my 2006 stay in Dogondoutchi, the voice of Malam Awal, whose mixture of melodious tones and shrill inflections I had learned to recognize, was rarely heard escaping from the amplifiers that 'yan Awaliyya had initially installed in the center of town to disseminate the preacher's message.

2. "His students no longer study the Qur'an. They just sing songs. We don't think that songs are good. They have no usefulness," Malam Bassirou, a one-time disciple of Malam Awal, told me.

3. A youth's testimony aptly sums up what other residents were thinking at the time: "None of my friends are 'yan Awaliyya, but my grandmother follows Malam Awal. She is crazy, that's why she follows Malam Awal. She's old. Everything that's in her head has shrunk."

4. As noted, despite reformist claims that women can attend the Friday prayer at the mosque when they wear a *hijabi*, women pray in the privacy of their homes. Their relative invisibility from public life (and their limited capacity to display piety through public acts) generally means that they are held less accountable in the performance of religious duties (*ibada*). By praying indoors (with no one to witness their performance), women make it difficult for anyone to counter their claims of piety.

5. "Girls should learn the Qur'an," the traditionalist Imam of Dogondoutchi told me:

> Even after she has mastered the first level [memorizing the entire Qur'an], a girl can keep on studying and learning the Qur'an. But she must stop attending school if she marries. Then, if her father or her husband is a scholar, he can teach her. Her husband should teach her if he has the time and knowledge.

6. Although these interferences effectively mediate local audiences' understanding of the reformist message, they are not necessarily perceived as a hindrance to learning. Instead of blocking meaning, they become part of the experience, even part of the message. Women who attend Izala sermons, therefore, do not necessarily feel that they have missed something.

7. Ayouba, a civil servant who openly disapproved of Malam Awal's project of moral reform, told me that the preacher's presence led to many divorces in households where wives opted to openly disobey their husbands and continue to attend Awaliyya singing sessions. I was not able to verify this information, but I did speak with men who complained about their wives' "foolish" admiration for Malam Awal. As a practicing Muslim married to a woman employed in the local administration, Ayouba wondered how husbands tolerated their wives' insolent behavior: "How can they let their wives leave in the evening and spend half the night dancing and singing?"

8. Although Awal encouraged his followers to play the drum, he denied doing so when faced with accusations that Awaliyya practices were heretical. On one occasion when 'yan Awaliyya were accused of beating drums, they responded that they were simply stroking them and therefore not committing a heresy.

9. Chanted verses figure prominently in the daily experience of both male and female Hausa speakers despite the efforts of Muslim reformists to stamp out these supposedly sinful practices (Cooper 2001; Mack 2004).

10. Youths, particularly males, are often singled out as being too complacent (and at times downright dissolute) about their religious duties. They have not learned to fear God. Their youth hampers them from developing the requisite "anticipatory awareness of death" (Hirschkind 2006:190) that should ideally help them commit to a life of piety. In other words, they are prevented from worrying about the issue of death and afterlife by their immaturity and their chronological remoteness from death.

11. In Dogondoutchi, the translation of *salla* (prayer) into rewards that accumulate daily until the day of reckoning is the object of ongoing speculation. For instance, there is much debate as to whether praying alone results in fewer rewards than praying in a crowd. According to one Qur'anic teacher,

> Since the Prophet was born, we have prayed jointly. People must get together to pray. If people pray as a crowd, they each receive twenty-seven rewards. If you pray alone, you only receive one *lada*, whether you are a saint or a simple Muslim. If you are in the bush, however, and you pray alone, you will receive many rewards. If you manage not to think that a lion or a hyena could come and kill you, you will receive fifty rewards.

12. In the reckoning of good and evil, it is possible to attribute credit for a positive action such as performing the pilgrimage to Mecca to an individual who was not able to personally go on the *haji*. Conversely, one can accrue offenses unknowingly, as when the pain experienced by a mother in childbirth is perceived as a wrongdoing inflicted by the child. This offense can be lifted by burning the child's arm to compensate for the pain he caused his mother (Cooper 2006).

13. This is how Binta, a young wife of twenty-two, summarized the duties of a wife:

> Malam Awal tells women to respect their husbands. If he comes home, you must ask whether he needs water to wash himself. If he carries something, you must go and carry it for him. You must serve him food, you must serve him water. You must tell him, "*Sanu da zuwa* [welcome.]" You must not argue with him. You must treat him with respect and wish him well. When he comes home, you must ask: "*Ina gajiya?* [How are you?]" [Malam Awal] tells women to be patient. If there's a day when your husband has not brought food home, don't be angry. Don't leave. Tomorrow he will come with food.

14. By leaving the marital home to return to her father's home or stay with sympathetic kin, a woman signifies her desire to break away from the marriage (see Cooper 1997b) when she does not simply hope to compel her husband to agree to improve the terms of the relationship.

15. Women who divorce, or are divorced by, their husbands generally lose custody of their children once the latter are weaned.

16. In Dogondoutchi, I did not find that women saw their fate in the hereafter as dependent on a marital tie, unlike the women of Maradi, where marriage, as reported by Cooper (1992:393), is "a literal thread to a man who has the 'pull' to get them into heaven

through prayer." Today, with the democratization of Islamic knowledge, the emphasis is on personal accountability. At the same time, it is clear that men who share responsibility for the offenses committed by their wives will have to face the consequences on Judgment Day. Similarly, women who can be blamed for their husbands' or children's misdeeds will see these *alhuka* (offenses) heaped onto their scales when the total sum of their bad deeds is tallied up against good ones.

17. As Callaway (1987) notes in her study of Hausa women in Nigeria, any woman who displays too much independence and questions her husband's decisions is labeled quarrelsome.

18. Obviously one exception to this situation would include, for some women, the decision to follow Malam Awal's teaching against their husbands' wishes.

19. Widows cannot leave their homes during the period of mourning (*takaba*), and they follow a strict regimen destined to mark their new husband-less condition. *Takaba*, which lasts four months and ten days for women of childbearing age and three months if they are past menopause, corresponds to the ritual waiting period known as *idda* that follows the termination of marriage because of divorce. During *takaba*, a widow does not leave her home, she can only wash three times a week, and she cannot use perfumed soap or lotion. Her hair is not plaited and she wears no makeup. She cannot eat with the rest of the household. Her meatless food is prepared separately, and her cooking implements and eating utensils are washed separately from those used by the rest of the household.

20. As noted in chapter 7, fifteen years ago it was unheard of for a young girl to marry a member of Izala if she had not been raised in an Izala household, but in recent years it has become a more acceptable practice.

21. This is illustrated by the following passages from one of Malam Awal's sermons:

> If your wife commits adultery, God will not accept your prayer for forty days. If you go see some women to sleep with them and you ignore your wife's needs because you are too tired to make love to her, so much so that your wife ends up committing adultery herself, God will not accept your prayer for 40 days. If you let your wives walk around town, God will erase your prayers for 40 days.

Note here that the preacher blames the husband not only for committing adultery but for not being able to satisfy his wife sexually because of his adulterous activities.

22. Elsewhere I discuss at length the struggles of women who are married to Muslim men but, during possession ceremonies, are called by spirits to become their human hosts; as previously noted, these ceremonies are condemned by Islam (Masquelier 2001b).

23. A'i was hardly alone in entertaining these views. Women in the early 1990s told me that some prostitutes should (or would) experience eternal bliss in the hereafter despite their immoral activities on earth because they were basically generous and caring people.

24. By February 2000 Malam Awal had divorced the woman—allegedly of Saudi origin—whom he initially had brought to Dogondoutchi in 1997 as well as several local women he had married since settling in town. He had also married a woman from Agadez but the marriage did not last, according to a friend who knew many of his former wives' families. One of his followers told me at the time that these rumors of divorce were wildly exaggerated and that the preacher had only divorced three of his wives—in one

case, supposedly because the woman could only talk about the Izala doctrine. Yet others claimed that he had married more than thirty women and kept some of them for only two days before sending them back to their parents' homes.

25. This was still the reason given by Malam Awal's followers when I asked them in late 2004 why the marriages did not last.

26. Malam Awal was not the first (nor would he be the last) Qur'anic teacher to use his religious authority and social position to take advantage of women sexually. In the Dogondoutchi neighborhood where I have been staying since 1994, a *malami* was rumored to have sexually assaulted a young woman in 2000. She had fortunately managed to escape before being raped. Neighbors were outraged but not surprised by the incident. The would-be rapist, who boasted he was descended from one of the first Muslim families in the region, was a well-known womanizer.

27. In her ethnography of a Sufi cult of Pakistani origin, Werbner (2003:291) remarks that "usual yardsticks of judgment are suspended in favor of a world of teleologically inspired acts of supreme courage, selflessness, and faith."

28. The term "Islam" literally means "submission."

CLOSING REMARKS

1. Postpartum abstinence is the primary means through which Mawri women have traditionally ensured birth spacing, as is recommended by the Qur'an. This practice resonates with the belief—still prevalent despite health workers' efforts to dispel it—that the "milk of pregnancy" is not as nutritious as "regular" breast milk and that women must avoid becoming pregnant while they are still nursing a child. While Muslims of a literalist stripe insist that contraception is to be rejected since it is not mentioned in the Qur'an, more liberal-minded Muslims interpret the Qur'an's recommendation that women breast-feed for two years and the Prophet's enjoinment against pregnancy during lactation as an endorsement of child spacing.

2. In 1988 a law was passed to help women gain access to contraceptives. Prior to that time, a woman requesting contraception had to seek her husband's written authorization. When Mariama first asked for my assistance in procuring contraceptives, she operated under the assumption that my presence would render her husband's authorization unnecessary.

3. Rather than invoking religion or morality in their lectures about why family planning is "good" for families, local health workers appeal to people's "common sense." As one health worker explained to me,

> To people who are reluctant to practice birth spacing, I say, "Do you plant millet seeds real close to each other in the field? No, you don't because you know that these plants would not grow properly. Each plant needs *space*, aside from rain and sun. It's the same for children. They need space in order to grow healthy."

Bibliography

Abadie, Maurice. 1927. *La colonie du Niger.* Paris: Société d'Éditions Géographiques, Maritimes et Coloniales.

Abu-Lughod, Lila. 1986. *Veiled Sentiments: Honor and Poetry in a Bedouin Society.* Berkeley: University of California Press.

———. 1990. The Romance of Resistance: Tracing Transformations of Power through Bedouin Women. *American Ethnologist* 17(1): 41–55.

———. 1991. Writing Against Culture. In *Recapturing Anthropology: Working in the Present,* ed. Richard G. Fox, pp. 137–162. Santa Fe, N.M.: School of American Research Press.

———. 1997. Movie Stars and Islamic Moralism in Egypt. In *The Gender/Sexuality Reader: Culture, History, Political Economy,* ed. Roger N. Lancaster and Micaela di Leonardo, pp. 502–512. New York: Routledge.

———. 1998a. Introduction: Feminist Longings and Postcolonial Conditions. In *Remaking Women: Feminism and Modernity in the Middle East,* ed. Lila Abu-Lughod, pp. 3–31. Princeton, N.J.: Princeton University Press.

———. 1998b. The Marriage of Feminism and Islamism in Egypt: Selective Repudiation as a Dynamic of Postcolonial Cultural Politics. In *Remaking Women: Feminism and Modernity in the Middle East,* ed. Lila Abu-Lughod, pp. 243–269. Princeton, N.J.: Princeton University Press.

Adeleye, Remi. 1971. *Power and Diplomacy in Northern Nigeria (1804–1906).* London: Longman.

Ahmed, Leila. 1992. *Women and Gender in Islam: Historical Roots of a Modern Debate.* New Haven, Conn.: Yale University Press.

Al-Azmeh, Aziz. 1993. *Islams and Modernities.* London: Verso.

Alidou, Ousseina. 2005. *Engaging Modernity: Muslim Women and the Politics of Agency in Postcolonial Niger.* Madison: Wisconsin University Press.

Al-Karsani, Awad Al-Sid. 1993. Beyond Sufism: The Case of Millennial Islam in Sudan. In *Muslim Identity and Social Change in Sub-Saharan Africa,* ed. Louis Brenner, pp. 135–153. Bloomington: Indiana University Press.

Allman, Jean. 2001. Rounding Up Spinsters: Gender Chaos and Unmarried Women in Colonial Asante. In *Wicked Women and the Reconfiguration of Gender in Africa,* ed. Dorothy L. Hodgson and Sheryl A. McCurdy, pp. 130–148. Portsmouth, N.H.: Heinemann.

———. 2004. Fashioning Africa: Power and the Politics of Dress. In *Fashioning Africa: Power and the Politics of Dress,* ed. Jean Allman, pp. 1–10. Bloomington: Indiana University Press.

Amselle, Jean-Loup. 1985. Le Wahabisme à Bamako (1945–1985). *Canadian Journal of African Studies* 19(2): 345–357.

———. 1998. *Mestizo Logics: Anthropology of Identity in Africa and Elsewhere*. Stanford, Calif.: Stanford University Press.

Antoun, Richard. 1989. *Muslim Preacher in the Modern World: A Jordanian Case Study in Comparative Perspective*. Princeton, N.J.: Princeton University Press.

Appadurai, Arjun. 1996. *Modernity at Large: Cultural Dimensions of Globalization*. Minneapolis: University of Minnesota Press.

Appadurai, Arjun, and Carol A. Breckenridge. 1995. Public Modernity in India. In *Consuming Modernity: Public Culture in a South Asian World*, ed. Carol A. Breckenridge, pp. 1–22. Minneapolis: University of Minnesota Press.

Arji, Saïdou. 2000. 2eme Édition du FIMA: L'opposition musclée des barbus. *Alternative*, November 9. http://www.geocities.com.alterniger/html/227/fima.htm (accessed 2/10/2001).

Armbrust, Walter. 1999. Bourgeois Leisure and Egyptian Media Fantasies. In *New Media in the Muslim World: The Emerging Public Sphere*, ed. Dale F. Eickelman and Jon Anderson, pp. 106–132. Bloomington: Indiana University Press.

Arnaud, Robert. 1912. *L'Islam et la politique musulmane française en Afrique occidentale française*. Paris: Comité de l'Afrique Française.

Asad, Talal. 1986. *The Idea of an Anthropology of Islam*. Washington, D.C.: Georgetown University Center for Contemporary Arab Studies, Occasional Paper series.

———. 2003. *Formations of the Secular: Christianity, Islam, Modernity*. Stanford, Calif.: Stanford University Press.

Ashforth, Adam. 1998. Reflections on Spiritual Insecurity in a Modern African City (Soweto). *African Studies Review* 41(3): 39–67.

Ask, Karin, and Marit Tjomsland. 1998. Introduction. In *Women and Islamization: Contemporary Dimensions of Discourse on Gender Relations*, ed. Karin Ask and Marit Tjomsland, pp. 1–16. New York: Berg.

Awn, Peter J. 1994. Indian Islam: The Shah Bano Affair. In *Fundamentalism and Gender*, ed. John Stratton Hawley, pp. 63–78. New York: Oxford University Press.

Bakhtin, Mikhail. 1981. *The Dialogic Imagination*. Translated by Caryl Emerson and Michael Holquist. Edited by Michael Holquist. Austin: University of Texas Press.

Barkindo, Bawuro M. 1993. Growing Islamism in Kano since 1970: Causes, Form and Implications. In *Muslim Identity and Social Change in Sub-Saharan Africa*, ed. Louis Brenner, pp. 91–105. Bloomington: Indiana University Press.

Barkow, Jerome. 1971. The Institution of Courtesanship in the Northern States of Nigeria. *Genève-Afrique* 10(1): 1–16.

Barlow, Robin, and Wayne Snyder. 1993. Taxation in Niger: Problems and Proposals. *World Development* 21(7): 1179–1189.

Bastian, Misty L. 1993. "Bloodhounds Who Have No Friends": Witchcraft and Locality in the Nigerian Popular Press. In *Modernity and Its Malcontents: Ritual and Power in Postcolonial Africa*, ed. Jean Comaroff and John Comaroff, pp. 167–192. Chicago: University of Chicago Press.

———. 2002. Acadas and Fertilizer Girls: Young Nigerian Women and the Romance of Modernity. In *Gendered Modernities: Ethnographic Perspectives*, ed. Dorothy L. Hodgson, pp. 53–76. New York: Palgrave.

Bauer, Janet. 1985. Sexuality and the Moral Construction of Women in an Islamic Society. *Anthropological Quarterly* 58: 120–129.

———. 2005. Corrupted Alterities: Body Politics in the Time of the Iranian Diaspora. In *Dirt, Undress, and Difference: Critical Perspectives on the Body's Surface,* ed. Adeline Masquelier, pp. 122–148. Bloomington: Indiana University Press.

Behrend, Heike. 1999. *Alice Lakwena and the Holy Spirits: War in Northern Uganda 1986–97.* Athens: Ohio University Press.

Beik, Janet. 1991. Women's Roles in the Contemporary Hausa Theater of Niger. In *Hausa Women in the Twentieth Century,* ed. Catherine Coles and Beverly Mack, pp. 232–243. Madison: University of Wisconsin Press.

Berger, John. 1972. *Ways of Seeing.* London: Penguin.

Bernal, Victoria. 1994. Gender, Culture, and Capitalism: Women and the Remaking of Islamic "Tradition" in a Sudanese Village. *Comparative Studies in Society and History* 36(1): 36–67.

———. 1997. Islam, Transnational Culture, and Modernity in Rural Sudan. In *Gendered Encounters: Challenging Cultural Boundaries and Social Hierarchies in Africa,* ed. Maria Grosz-Ngate and O. H. Kokole, pp. 131–151. New York: Routledge.

Bernus, Edmond, Pierre Boilley, Jean Clauzel, and Jean-Louis Triaud. 1993. *Nomades et commandants: Administration et sociétés nomades dans l'ancienne A.O.F.* Paris: Éditions Karthala.

Bilu, Yoram, and Eyal Ben-Ari. 1992. The Making of Modern Saints: Manufactured Charisma and the Abu-Hatseiras of Israel. *American Ethnologist* 19(4): 672–687.

Birman, Patricia. 2006. Future in the Mirror: Media, Evangelicals, and Politics in Rio de Janeiro. In *Religion, Media, and the Public Sphere,* ed. Birgit Meyer and Annelies Moors, pp. 52–72. Bloomington: Indiana University Press.

Blunt, Robert. 2004. Satan Is an Imitator: Kenya's Recent Cosmology of Corruption. In *Producing African Futures: Ritual and Reproduction in a Neoliberal Age,* ed. Brad Weiss, pp. 294–328. Boston: Brill.

Bodman, Herbert L. 1998. Introduction. In *Women in Muslim Societies: Diversity Within Unity,* ed. Herbert L. Bodman and Nayereh Tohidi, pp. 1–18. Boulder, Colo.: Lynne Rienner.

Bourdieu, Pierre. 1977. *Outline of a Theory of Practice.* Translated by Richard Nice. Cambridge: Cambridge University Press.

———. 1984. *Distinction: A Social Critique of the Judgment of Taste.* Translated by Richard Nice. London: Routledge.

———. 1990. *The Logic of Practice.* Translated by Richard Nice. Stanford, Calif.: Stanford University Press.

Bowen, John R. 1993. *Muslims through Discourse: Religion and Ritual in Gayo Society.* Princeton, N.J.: Princeton University Press.

———. 1997. Modern Intentions: Reshaping Subjectivities in an Indonesian Muslim Society. In *Islam in an Era of Nation-States,* ed. Robert W. Hefner and Patricia Horvatich, pp. 157–182. Honolulu: University of Hawai'i Press.

Boyd, Jean. 1989. *The Caliph's Sister: Nana Asma'u, 1793–1865: Teacher, Poet, and Islamic Leader.* London: Frank Cass.

Boyd, Jean, and D. Murray Last. 1985. The Role of Women as "Agents Religieux" in Sokoto. *Canadian Journal of African Studies* 19(2): 283–300.

Boyd, Jean, and Beverly B. Mack. 1997. *The Collected Works of Nana Asma'u, 1793–1864.* East Lansing: Michigan State University Press.

Brenner, Louis. 1984. *West African Sufi: The Religious Heritage and Spiritual Search of Cerno Bokar Saalif Taal.* Berkeley: University of California Press.

———. 1985. *Réflexions sur le savoir islamique en Afrique de l'ouest.* Bordeaux: Centre d'Études d'Afrique Noire.

———. 1993a. Constructing Muslim Identity in Mali. In *Muslim Identity and Social Change in Sub-Saharan Africa,* ed. Louis Brenner, pp. 59–78. Bloomington: Indiana University Press.

———, ed. 1993b. *Muslim Identity and Social Change in Sub-Saharan Africa.* Bloomington: Indiana University Press.

———. 2001. *Controlling Knowledge: Religion, Power, and Schooling in a West African Muslim Society.* Bloomington: Indiana University Press.

Brevié, Jules. 1923. *Islamisme contre naturisme au Soudan français: Essai de psychologie politique coloniale.* Paris: Éditions Ernest Leroux.

Bush, George W. 2003. The State of the Union Address. Available at http://american rhetoric.com/speeches/stateoftheunion2003.html (accessed 2/13/2006).

Butler, Judith. 1997. *The Psychic Life of Power: Theories in Subjection.* Stanford, Calif.: Stanford University Press.

Butler, Noah. 2006. The Materialization of Magic: Islamic Talisman in West Africa. In *Studies in Witchcraft, Magic, War, and Peace in Africa: Nineteenth and Twentieth Centuries,* ed. Beatrice Nicolini, pp. 263–276. Lewiston, N.Y.: Edwin Mellen.

Callaway, Barbara. 1987. *Muslim Hausa Women in Nigeria: Tradition and Change.* Syracuse, N.Y.: Syracuse University Press.

Camel Express. 1998. Newsletter of the Friends of Niger, vol. 18.

Cardaire, Marcel. 1954. *L'Islam et le terroir africain.* Koulouba: IFAN.

Casanova, José. 1994. *Public Religions in the Modern World.* Chicago: University of Chicago Press.

Casey, Conerly. In press. Dancing Like They Do in Indian Film: Spirit Possession, Witchcraft Affliction, and the Media in Northern Nigeria. In *Cultural Sociology: An Introduction to Anthropology and Sociology in Nigeria,* ed. Salisu Abdullahi, Ismaila Zango, and Conerly Casey.

Charlick, Robert B. 1991. *Niger: Personal Rule and Survival in the Sahel.* Boulder, Colo.: Westview.

———. 2004. Niger. *African Studies Review* 47(2): 97–108.

Clarke, Peter. 1982. *West Africa and Islam: A Study of Religious Development from the 8th to the 20th Century.* London: Edward Arnold.

Cohen, Abner. 1969. *Custom and Politics in Urban Africa: A Study of Hausa Migrants in Yoruba Towns.* Berkeley: University of California Press.

Coles, Catherine, and Beverly Mack, eds. 1991. *Hausa Women in the Twentieth Century.* Madison: University of Wisconsin Press.

Comaroff, Jean. 1985. *Body of Power, Spirit of Resistance: The Culture and History of a South African People.* Chicago: University of Chicago Press.

Comaroff, Jean, and John Comaroff. 1993. Introduction. In *Modernity and Its Malcontents: Ritual and Power in Postcolonial Africa,* ed. Jean Comaroff and John Comaroff, pp. xi–xxxvii. Chicago: University of Chicago Press.

————. 1999. Occult Economies and the Violence of Abstraction: Notes from the South African Postcolony. *American Ethnologist* 26: 279–303.

Comaroff, John, and Jean Comaroff. 1992. *Ethnography and the Historical Imagination.* Boulder, Colo.: Westview.

————. 1997. *Of Revelation and Revolution: The Dialectics of Modernity on a South African Frontier.* Vol. 2. Chicago: University of Chicago Press.

Cooper, Barbara M. 1992. From the "Time of Cowries" to the "Time of Searching for Money": A History of Women in the Maradi Region of Niger, 1900–1989. Ph.D. diss., Boston University.

————. 1994. Reflections on Slavery, Seclusion, and Female Labor in the Maradi Region of Niger in the Nineteenth and Twentieth Centuries. *Journal of African History* 35: 61–78.

————. 1997a. *Marriage in Maradi: Gender and Culture in a Hausa Society in Niger, 1900–1989.* Portsmouth, N.H.: Heinemann.

————. 1997b. Gender, Movement, and History: Social and Spatial Transformations in 20th Century Maradi (Niger). *Environment and Planning D: Society and Space* 15: 195–221.

————. 1998. Gender and Religion in Hausaland: Variations in Islamic Practice in Niger and Nigeria. In *Women in Muslim Societies,* ed. Herbert L. Bodman and Nayereh Tohidi, pp. 21–38. Boulder, Colo.: Lynne Rienner.

————. 2001. The Strength in the Song: Muslim Personhood, Audible Capital, and Hausa Women's Performance of the Hajj. In *Gendered Modernities: Ethnographic Perspectives,* ed. Dorothy L. Hodgson, pp. 79–104. New York: Palgrave.

————. 2006. *Evangelical Christians in the Muslim Sahel.* Bloomington: Indiana University Press.

Copans, Jean. 1980. *Les marabouts de l'arachide: La confrérie mouride et les paysans du Sénégal.* Paris: Le Sycomore.

Corten, Andrew, and Ruth Marshall-Fratani. 2001. *Between Babel and Pentecost: Transnational Pentecostalism in Africa and Latin America.* London: Hurst.

Coulon, Christian. 1981. *Le marabout et le prince: Islam et pouvoir au Sénégal.* Paris: Pédone.

————. 1988. Women, Islam, and Baraka. In *Charisma and Brotherhood in African Islam,* ed. Donald B. Cruise O'Brien and Christian Coulon, pp. 113–134. Oxford: Clarendon.

Crapanzano, Vincent. 1973. *The Hamadsha: A Study in Moroccan Ethnopsychiatry.* Berkeley: University of California Press.

Crowder, Michael. 1968. *West Africa under Colonial Rule.* Evanston, Ill.: Northwestern University Press.

Cruise O'Brien, Donald B. 1967. Toward an "Islamic Policy" in French West Africa 1854–1914. *Journal of African History* 8(2): 303–316.

————. 1971. *The Mourides of Senegal.* Oxford: Clarendon.

Cruise O'Brien, Donald B., and Christian Coulon, eds. 1988. *Charisma and Brotherhood in African Islam.* Oxford: Clarendon.

Darrah, Allan C. 1980. Hermeneutic Approach to Hausa Therapeutics: The Allegory of the Living Fire. Ph.D. diss., Department of Anthropology, Northwestern University.

de Certeau, Michel. 1984. *The Practice of Everyday Life.* Translated by S. F. Rendall. Berkeley: University of California Press.

de Latour, Éliane. 1982. La paix destructrice. In *Guerres de lignages et guerrres d'états en Afrique,* ed. Jean Bazin and Emmanuel Terray, pp. 237–266. Paris: Éditions des Archives Contemporaines.

———. 1987. Le futur antérieur. In *La colonisation: Rupture ou parenthèse?* ed. Marc-Henri Piault, pp. 123–176. Paris: Éditions L'Harmattan.

———. 1992. *Les temps du pouvoir.* Paris: Éditions de l'École des Hautes Études en Sciences Sociales.

de Latour Dejean, Éliane. 1980. Shadows Nourished by the Sun: Rural Social Differentiation among the Mawri of Niger. In *Peasants in Africa: Historical and Contemporary Perspectives,* ed. Martin Klein, pp. 104–141. Beverly Hills, Calif.: Sage.

Deeb, Lara. 2006. *An Enchanted Modern: Gender and Public Piety in Shi'i Lebanon.* Princeton, N.J.: Princeton University Press.

Delafosse, Maurice. 1922. L'animisme nègre et sa résistance à l'islamisation en Afrique occidentale. *Revue du Monde Musulman* 49: 121–163.

Delaney, Carol. 1990. The Hajj: Sacred and Secular. *American Ethnologist* 17(3): 513–530.

———. 1991. *The Seed and the Soil: Gender and Cosmology in Turkish Village Society.* Berkeley: University of California Press.

Dilley, Roy. 2004. Global Connections, Local Ruptures: The Case of Islam in Senegal. In *Situating Globality: African Agency in the Appropriation of Global Culture,* ed. Wim van Binsbergen and Rijk van Dijk, pp. 190–219. Leiden: Brill.

Donnelly, John. 2004. Headway Seen in Africa on Polio Immunizations: Progress Renews Hope for Eradication of Virus. *The Boston Globe,* 3 August, A8.

Dunbar, Roberta Ann. 1991. Islamic Values, the State, and "the Development of Women": The Case of Niger. In *Hausa Women in the Twentieth Century,* ed. Catherine Coles and Beverly Mack, pp. 69–89. Madison: University of Wisconsin Press.

Durham, Deborah. 1999. The Predicament of Dress: Polyvalency and the Ironies of Cultural Identity. *American Ethnologist* 26(2): 389–412.

Eickelman, Dale F. 1976. *Moroccan Islam.* Austin: University of Texas Press.

———. 1989. National Identity and Religious Discourse in Contemporary Oman. *International Journal of Islamic and Arabic Studies* 6(1): 1–20.

———. 1997. Trans-State Islam and Security. In *Transnational Religion and Fading States,* ed. Susanne Hoeber Rudolph and James Piscatori, pp. 27–46. Boulder, Colo.: Westview.

Eickelman, Dale F., and Jon W. Anderson, eds. 1999. *New Media in the Muslim World: The Emerging Public Sphere.* Bloomington: Indiana University Press.

Eickelman, Dale F., and James Piscatori. 1990. Social Theory in the Study of Muslim Societies. In *Muslim Travelers: Pilgrimage, Migration, and the Religious Imagination,* ed. Dale F. Eickelman and James Piscatori, pp. 3–25. Berkeley: University of California Press.

———. 1996. *Muslim Politics.* Princeton, N.J.: Princeton University Press.

El Guindi, Fadwa. 1999. Veiling Resistance. *Fashion Theory* 3(1): 51–80.

El Saadawi, Nawa. 1980. *The Hidden Face of Eve: Women in the Arab World.* Boston: Beacon.

Ellis, Stephen. 2004. Briefing: The Pan-Sahel Initiative. *African Affairs* 103: 459–464.

el-Zein, Abdul H. 1977. Beyond Ideology and Theology: The Search for the Anthropology of Islam. *Annual Review of Anthropology* 6: 227–254.

Englund, Harri. 1996. Witchcraft, Modernity, and the Person: The Morality of Accumulation in Central Malawi. *Critique of Anthropology* 16(3): 257–279.

Errington, Frederick K., and Deborah B. Gewertz. 1995. *Articulating Change in the "Last Unknown."* Boulder, Colo.: Westview.

Esposito, John L. 1992. *The Islamic Threat: Myth or Reality?* New York: Oxford University Press.

Ewing, Katherine Pratt. 1997. *Arguing Sainthood: Modernity, Psychoanalysis, and Islam.* Durham, N.C.: Duke University Press.

Fair, Laura. 2001. *Pastimes and Politics: Culture, Community, and Identity in Post-Abolition Urban Zanzibar, 1890–1945.* Athens: Ohio University Press.

Fala Habi Aboubacar, Gisèle. 1988. L'art traditionnel de décorer l'habitat chez la femme Haoussa dans l'Ader à Tahoua au Niger. Mémoire de fin d'étude (CAEMTP), École Normale Supérieure d'Enseignement Technique et Professionnel, Université Cheikh Anta Diop, Dakar, Senegal.

Fanon, Frantz. 1965. *A Dying Colonialism.* Translated by Haakon Chevalier. New York: Grove.

Fatton, Robert, Jr. 1995. Africa in the Age of Democratization: The Civic Limitations of Civil Society. *African Studies Review* 38: 67–100.

Ferguson, James. 1999. *Expectations of Modernity: Myths and Meanings of Urban Life on the Zambian Copperbelt.* Berkeley: University of California Press.

Ferme, Mariane. 1994. What Alhaji Airplane Saw in Mecca and What Happened When He Came Home: Ritual Transformation in a Mende Community (Sierra Leone). In *Syncretism/Anti-Syncretism: The Politics of Religious Synthesis,* ed. Charles Stewart and Rosalind Shaw, pp. 27–44. New York: Routledge.

———. 2001. *The Underneath of Things: Violence, History, and the Everyday in Sierra Leone.* Berkeley: University of California Press.

Fischer, Michael M. J., and Mehdi Abedi. 1990. *Debating Muslims: Cultural Dialogues in Postmodernity and Tradition.* Madison: University of Wisconsin Press.

Fisher, H. S. 1973. Conversion Reconsidered: Some Historical Aspects of Religious Conversion in Black Africa. *Africa* 43: 27–40.

Fisher, I. 2000. Young Man Decides to Wive It Wealthily in Uganda. *Wobulenzi Journal.* Available http://www.nytimes.com/library/world/africa/070500uganda-marriage.html (accessed 2/15/2002).

Fisiy, Ciprian F., and Peter Geschiere. 2001. Witchcraft, Development, and Paranoia in Cameroon: Interactions between Popular, Academic, and State Discourse. In *Magical Interpretations, Material Realities: Modernity, Witchcraft, and the Occult in Postcolonial Africa,* ed. Henrietta L. Moore and Todd Sanders, pp. 226–246. London: Routledge.

Foucault, Michel. 1972. *The Archaeology of Knowledge.* Translated by Rupert Swyer. New York: Pantheon.

———. 1977. *Discipline and Punish: The Birth of the Prison.* Translated by Alan Sheridan. New York: Vintage Books.

———. 1980. Two Lectures: Lecture One: 7 January 1976. In *Power/Knowledge: Selected Interviews and Other Writings.* New York: Pantheon.

Friedman, Jonathan. 1994. *Cultural Identity and Global Process.* London: Sage.

———. 2002. Globalization and Localization. In *The Anthropology of Globalization: A Reader*, ed. Javier X. Inda and Renato Rosaldo, pp. 233–246. Malden, Mass.: Blackwell.

Fuglestad, Finn. 1983. *A History of Niger, 1850–1960*. New York: Cambridge University Press.

Gaffney, Patrick D. 1994. *The Prophet's Pulpit: Islamic Preaching in Contemporary Egypt*. Berkeley: University of California Press.

Gaspard, Françoise, and Farhad Khosrokhavar. 1995. *Le foulard et la république*. Paris: Éditions la Découverte.

Geertz, Clifford. 1968. *Islam Observed: Religious Development in Morocco and Indonesia*. Chicago: University of Chicago Press.

———. 1983. Centers, Kings, and Charisma: Reflections on the Symbolics of Power. In *Local Knowledge*, pp. 121–146. London: Fontana Press.

Gellner, Ernest. 1981. *Muslim Society*. Cambridge: Cambridge University Press.

Geschiere, Peter. 1997. *The Modernity of Witchcraft: Politics and the Occult in Postcolonial Africa*. Charlottesville: University of Virginia Press.

Gilsenan, Michael. 1973. *Saint and Sufi in Modern Egypt*. Oxford: Clarendon.

Glew, Robert S. 1996. Islamic Associations in Niger. *Islam et Sociétés au Sud du Sahara* 10: 187–204.

Göle, Nilüfer. 2002. Islam in Public: New Visibilities and New Imaginaries. *Public Culture* 14(1): 173–190.

Goody, Jack. 1968. Restricted Literacy in Northern Ghana. In *Literacy in Traditional Societies*, ed. Jack Goody, pp. 198–204. Cambridge: Cambridge University Press.

———. 1987. *The Interface between the Written and the Oral*. Cambridge: Cambridge University Press.

Gouilly, Alphonse. 1952. *L'Islam dans l'Afrique occidentale*. Paris: Larose.

Graeber, David. 1996. Beads and Money: Notes Towards a Theory of Wealth and Power. *American Ethnologist* 23(1): 4–24.

Gramsci, Antonio. 1971. *Selections from the Prison Notebooks*. New York: International.

Grégoire, Emmanuel. 1992. *The Alhazai of Maradi: Traditional Hausa Merchants in a Changing Sahelian City*. Translated by Benjamin H. Hardy. Boulder, Colo.: Lynne Rienner.

———. 1993. Islam and the Identity of Merchants in Maradi (Niger). In *Muslim Identity and Social Change in Sub-Saharan Africa*, ed. Louis Brenner, pp. 106–115. Bloomington: Indiana University Press.

Guengant, Jean-Pierre, and John F. May. 2001. Impact of the Proximate Determinants on the Future Course of Fertility in Sub-Saharan Africa. Paper presented at a workshop on "Prospects for Fertility Decline in High Fertility Countries." United Nations Secretariat, New York, July 9–11.

Gumi, Sheikh Abubakar. 1992. *Where I Stand*. Lagos, Nigeria: Spectrum Books.

Habermas, Jürgen. 1989. *The Structural Transformation of the Public Sphere: Inquiring into a Category*. Translated by Thomas Burger. Boston: MIT Press.

Hale, Sondra. 1996. *Gender Politics in Sudan: Islamism, Socialism, and the State*. Boulder, Colo.: Westview.

Hansen, Karen Tranberg. 2004. The World in Dress: Anthropological Perspectives on Clothing, Fashion, and Culture. *Annual Review of Anthropology* 33: 369–392.

Hanson, John H. 1996. *Migration, Jihad, and Muslim Authority in West Africa*. Bloomington: Indiana University Press.

Hardy, Georges. 1940. *Le problème religieux dans l'empire français.* Paris: Presses Universitaires de France.

Harris, Jay M. 1994. "Fundamentalism": Objections from a Modern Jewish Historian. In *Fundamentalism and Gender,* ed. John Stratton Hawley. New York: Oxford University Press.

Hassane, Souley. 2005. Les nouvelles élites islamiques du Niger et du Nigeria du Nord: Itinéraires et prédications fondatrices (1950–2003). In *Entreprises religieuses transnationales en Afrique de l'Ouest,* ed. Laurent Fourchard, André Mary, and René Otayek, pp. 373–394. Paris: Karthala.

Hawley, John Stratton, and Wayne Proudfoot. 1994. Introduction. In *Fundamentalism and Gender,* ed. John Stratton Hawley, pp. 3–44. New York: Oxford University Press.

Hefner, Robert, and Patricia Horvatich, eds. 1997. *Islam in an Era of Nation-States.* Honolulu: University of Hawai'i Press.

Hill, Polly. 1972. *Rural Hausa: A Village and a Setting.* Cambridge: Cambridge University Press.

Hirschkind, Charles. 1997. What Is Political Islam? *Middle East Report* 27: 4.

———. 2006. *The Ethical Soundscape: Cassette Sermons and Islamic Counterpublics.* New York: Columbia University Press.

Hiskett, Mervyn. 1973. *The Sword of Truth.* New York: Oxford University Press.

———. 1987. The Maitatsine Riots in Kano 1980: An Assessment. *Journal of Religion in Africa* 17(3): 209–223.

Hobsbawm, Eric. 1983. Introduction: Inventing Traditions. In *The Invention of Traditions,* ed. Eric Hobsbawm and Terence Ranger, pp. 1–14. New York: Cambridge University Press.

Hodgkin, Elizabeth. 1998. Islamism and Islamic Research in Africa. In *Islam et islamismes au sud du Sahara,* ed. Ousmane Kane and Jean-Louis Triaud, pp. 197–262. Paris: Karthala.

Hodgson, Dorothy L., and Sheryl A. McCurdy. 2001. Introduction: Wicked Women and the Reconfiguration of Gender in Africa. In *Wicked Women and the Reconfiguration of Gender in Africa,* ed. Dorothy L. Hodgson and Sheryl A. McCurdy, pp. 1–24. Portsmouth, N.H.: Heinemann.

Hoffman, Valerie J. 1995. *Sufism, Mystics, and Saints in Modern Egypt.* Columbia: University of South Carolina Press.

Hogben, S. J., and Anthony Kirk-Greene. 1966. *The Emirates of Northern Nigeria.* Oxford: Oxford University Press.

Hollander, Anne. 1993. *Seeing Through Clothes.* Berkeley: University of California Press.

Honwana, Alcinda. 2003. Undying Past: Spirit Possession and the Memory of War in Southern Mozambique. In *Magic and Modernity: Interfaces of Revelation and Concealment,* ed. Birgit Meyer and Peter Pels, pp. 60–80. Stanford, Calif.: Stanford University Press.

Horowitz, Michael M., et al. 1983. *Niger: A Social and Institutional Profile.* Binghamton, N.Y.: Institute for Development Anthropology.

Horton, Robin. 1971. African Conversion. *Africa* 41: 85–108.

Hunt, Nancy R. 1991. Noise over Camouflaged Polygamy, Colonial Morality Taxation, and a Woman-Naming Crisis in Belgian Africa. *Journal of African History* 32: 471–494.

———. 1999. *A Colonial Lexicon: Of Birth Ritual, Medicalization, and Mobility in the Congo.* Durham, N.C.: Duke University Press.

Huntington, Samuel P. 1996. *The Clash of Civilizations and the New World Order.* New York: Simon and Schuster.

Hutchinson, Sharon. 1996. *Nuer Dilemmas: Coping with Money, War, and the State.* Berkeley: University of California Press.

Hutson, Alaine S. 1999. The Development of Women's Authority in the Kano Tijaniyya 1894–1963. *Africa Today* 46(3/4): 43–64.

Ibrahim, Jibrin. 1991. Religion and Political Turbulence in Nigeria. *Journal of Modern African Studies* 29: 115–136.

Idrissa, Kimba. 2001. La dynamique de la gouvernance: administration, politique, et ethnicité au Niger. In *Le Niger: État et démocratie,* ed. Kimba Idrissa, pp. 15–83. Paris: L'Harmattan.

Inda, Jonathan X., and Renato Rosaldo. 2002. *The Anthropology of Globalization: A Reader.* Malden, Mass.: Blackwell.

Institut National de la Statistique. 2006. Enquête Démographique et de Santé et à Indicateurs Multiples. Calverton, Md.: Macro International. Available at http://www.measuredhs.com/pubs/pdf/FR193/FR193-NI06.pdf (accessed 3/6/09).

Isichei, Elizabeth. 1987. The Maitatsine Risings in Nigeria 1980–85: A Revolt of the Disinherited. *Journal of Religion in Africa* 17: 194–208.

James, Wendy. 1988. *The Listening Ebony: Moral Knowledge, Religion and Power among the Uduk of Sudan.* Oxford: Oxford University Press.

Kaba, Lansiné. 1974. *The Wahhabiyya: Islamic Reform and Politics in French West Africa.* Evanston, Ill.: Northwestern University Press.

———. 2000. Islam in West Africa: Radicalism and the New Ethic of Disagreement, 1960–1990. In *The History of Islam in Africa,* ed. Nehemia Levtzion and Randall L. Pouwels, pp. 189–208. Athens: Ohio University Press.

Kandiyoti, Deniz. 1991. Islam and Patriarchy. In *Women in Middle Eastern History: Shifting Boundaries in Sex and Gender,* ed. Nikki R. Keddie and Beth Baron, pp. 23–42. New Haven, Conn.: Yale University Press.

Kane, Ousmane. 1994. Izala: The Rise of Muslim Reformism in Northern Nigeria. In *Accounting for Fundamentalisms,* ed. Martin E. Marty and R. Scott Appleby, pp. 488–510. Chicago: University of Chicago Press.

———. 2003. *Muslim Modernity in Postcolonial Nigeria: A Study of the Society for the Removal of Innovation and Reinstatement of Tradition.* Leiden: Brill.

Kepel, Gilles. 2002. *Jihad: The Trail of Political Islam.* Translated by Anthony F. Roberts. New York: I. B. Tauris.

Koutoudi, Idimama. 1988. Doutchi de toutes les religions. *Nigerama* 3: 47.

Labouret, Henri. 1931. *A la recherche d'une politique indigène dans l'Ouest africain.* Paris: Éditions du Comité de l'Afrique française.

Laitin, David D. 1986. *Hegemony and Culture: Politics and Religious Change among the Yoruba.* Chicago: University of Chicago Press.

Lambek, Michael. 1990. Certain Knowledge, Contestable Authority: Power and Practice on the Islamic Periphery. *American Ethnologist* 17(1): 23–40.

———. 1993. *Knowledge and Practice in Mayotte: Local Discourses of Islam, Sorcery, and Spirit Possession.* Toronto: Toronto University Press.

———. 2002. *The Weight of the Past: Living with History in Mahajanga, Madagascar.* New York: Palgrave.

Lan, David. 1985. *Guns and Rain: Guerrillas and Spirit Mediums in Zimbabwe*. Berkeley: University of California Press.

Larkin, Brian. 1996. The Holy Qur'an, Tafsir, and the Uncertain Development of Religious Media in Northern Nigeria. Paper presented at the African Studies Association Meeting, San Francisco.

———. 1997. Indian Films and Nigerian Lovers: Media and the Creation of Parallel Modernities. *Africa* 67(3): 406–439.

Last, Murray. 1967. *The Sokoto Caliphate*. London: Humanities Press.

———. 1979. Strategies against Time. *Sociology of Health and Illness* 1(3): 306–317.

Last, Murray D., and M. A. Al-Hajj. 1987. Attempts at Defining a Muslim in 19th Century Hausaland and Bornu. *Journal of the Historical Society of Nigeria* 3(2): 231–240.

Launay, Robert. 1990. Pedigrees and Paradigms: Scholarly Credentials among the Dyula of the Northern Ivory Coast. In *Muslim Travelers: Pilgrimage, Migration, and the Religious Imagination*, ed. Dale F. Eickelman and James Piscatori, pp. 175–199. Berkeley: University of California Press.

———. 1992. *Beyond the Stream: Islam and Society in a West African Town*. Berkeley: University of California Press.

———. 1997. Spirit Media: The Electronic Media and Islam among the Dyula of Northern Côte d'Ivoire. *Africa* 67(3): 441–453.

Launay, Robert, and Benjamin F. Soares. 1999. The Formation of an Islamic Sphere in French Colonial West Africa. *Economy and Society* 28(4): 497–519.

Lazreg, Marnia. 1988. Feminism and Difference: The Perils of Writing as a Woman on Women in Algeria. *Feminist Studies* 14(1): 81–107.

———. 1990. Gender and Politics in Algeria: Unraveling the Religion Paradigm. *Signs* 15(4): 755–780.

———. 1994. *The Eloquence of Silence: Algerian Women in Question*. New York: Routledge.

LeBlanc, Marie Nathalie. 2000. Versioning Womanhood and Muslimhood: "Fashion" and the Life Course in Contemporary Bouaké, Côte d'Ivoire. *Africa* 70(3): 442–481.

Lehman, David, and Batia Siebzehner. 2006. Holy Pirates: Media, Ethnicity, and Religious Renewal in Israel. In *Religion, Media, and the Public Sphere*, ed. Birgit Meyer and Annelies Moors, pp. 91–111. Bloomington: Indiana University Press.

Levtzion, Nehemia. 1968. *Muslims and Chiefs in West Africa: A Study of Islam in the Middle Volta Basin in the Pre-Colonial Period*. Oxford: Clarendon.

Lewis, I. M. 1986. *Religion in Context: Cults and Charisma*. New York: Cambridge University Press.

Loimeier, Roman. 1997a. Islamic Reform and Political Change: The Example of Abubakar Gumi and the 'Yan Izala Movement in Nigeria. In *African Islam and Islam in Africa: Encounters between Sufis and Islamists*, ed. David Westerlund and Eva E. Rosander, pp. 286–307. Athens: Ohio University Press.

———. 1997b. *Islamic Reform and Political Change in Northern Nigeria*. Evanston, Ill.: Northwestern University Press.

Lubeck, Paul. 1985. Islamic Protest under Semi-Industrial Capitalism: Yan Tatsine Explained. *Africa* 55(4): 369–389.

———. 1987. Islamic Protest and Oil-Based Capitalism. In *State, Oil, and Agriculture*, ed. Michael Watts, pp. 268–290. Berkeley: Institute of International Studies, University of California.

Mack, Beverly B. 1991. Royal Wives in Kano. In *Hausa Women in the Twentieth Century,* ed. Catherine Coles and Beverly Mack, pp. 109–129. Madison: University of Wisconsin Press.

———. 2004. *Muslim Women Sing: Hausa Popular Song.* Bloomington: Indiana University Press.

Mack, Beverly B., and Jean Boyd. 2000. *One Woman's Jihad: Nana Asma'u, Scholar and Scribe.* Bloomington: Indiana University Press.

MacLeod, Arlene E. 1991. *Accommodating Protest: Working Women, the New Veiling, and Change in Cairo.* New York: Columbia University Press.

Mahmood, Saba. 2005. *Politics of Piety: The Islamic Revival and the Feminist Subject.* Princeton, N.J.: Princeton University Press.

Mamdani, Mahmood. 2004. *Good Muslim, Bad Muslim: America, the Cold War, and the Roots of Terror.* New York: Pantheon Books.

Mandel, Ruth. 1990. Shifting Centers and Emergent Identities: Turkey and Germany in the lives of Turkish Gastarbeiter. In *Muslim Travelers: Pilgrimage, Migration, and the Religious Imagination,* ed. Dale F. Eickelman and James Piscatori, pp. 153–171. Berkeley: University of California Press.

Marsden, Magnus. 2005. *Living Islam: Muslim Religious Experience in Pakistan's North-West Frontier.* Cambridge: Cambridge University Press.

Marty, Paul. 1917. *Étude sur l'Islam au Sénégal.* Paris: Éditions Leroux.

Masquelier, Adeline. 1992. "The Doguwa Is Like the White Man": Images of "Others" in *Bori* and Muslim Discourses. Paper presented at the American Ethnological Society meeting, Memphis, Tenn.

———. 1993. Narratives of Power, Images of Wealth: The Ritual Economy of *Bori* in the Market. In *Modernity and Its Malcontents: Ritual and Power in Postcolonial Africa,* ed. Jean Comaroff and John Comaroff, pp. 3–33. Chicago: University of Chicago Press.

———. 1994. "When I Die, They Will Play the Drums at My Burial": Death, Burial Strategies, and the Politics of Identity in Niger. Unpublished manuscript.

———. 1996. Mediating Threads: Clothing and the Texture of Spirit/Medium Relations in Bori. In *Clothing and Difference: Embodied Identities in Colonial and Post-Colonial Africa,* ed. A. A. Hendrickson, pp. 66–93. Durham, N.C.: Duke University Press.

———. 1999. "Money and Serpents, Their Remedy Is Killing": The Pathology of Consumption in Southern Niger. *Research in Economic Anthropology* 20: 97–115.

———. 2000. Of Headhunters and Cannibals: Migrancy, Labor, and Consumption in the Mawri Imagination. *Cultural Anthropology* 15(1): 84–126.

———. 2001a. Powers, Problems, and Paradoxes of Twinship in Niger. *Ethnology* 40(1): 45–62.

———. 2001b. *Prayer Has Spoiled Everything: Possession, Power, and Identity in an Islamic Town of Niger.* Durham, N.C.: Duke University Press.

———. 2002. Road Mythographies: Space, Mobility, and the Historical Imagination in Postcolonial Niger. *American Ethnologist* 29(4): 829–856.

———. 2005. The Naked Spirit: Disrobing, Deviancy, and Dissent in *Bori* Possession. In *Dirt, Undress, and Difference: Critical Perspectives on the Body's Surface,* ed. Adeline Masquelier, pp. 122–148. Bloomington: Indiana University Press.

———. 2007. Negotiating Futures: Islam, Youth, and the State in Niger. In *Islam and Muslim Politics in Africa,* ed. Benjamin F. Soares and René Otayek, pp. 243–262. New York: Palgrave.

———. 2008. When Female Spirits Start Veiling: The Case of Aldjana Mai Hidjab in a Muslim Town of Niger. *Africa Today* 54(3): 39–64.

———. In press. Prayer, Piety, and Pleasure: Contested Models of Islamic Worship in Dogondoutchi, Niger. In *Religious Modernities in West Africa: New Moralities in Colonial and Postcolonial Societies,* ed. John Hanson and Rijk van Dijk. Bloomington: Indiana University Press.

———. n.d. Public Health or Public Threat? Polio Eradication Campaigns and the Materialization of State Power in Niger. Unpublished manuscript.

Mauss, Marcel. 1967. *The Gift: Forms and Functions of Exchange in Archaic Societies.* Translated by Ian Cunnison. New York: W. W. Norton.

———. 1973. Techniques of the Body. Translated by B. Brewster. *Economy and Society* 2(1): 70–88.

Mayer, Joel. 1995. Nouvelles du Niger. *Camel Express: Newsletter of the Friends of Niger,* vol. 12.

———. 2000a. Protests against FIMA. Niger News Kakaki, November 11. Available at http://users.idworld.net/jmayer/kakai/k001111.htm (accessed 12/1/2000).

———. 2000b. Islamic Organization Seeks to Have Ban Lifted, 240 Demonstrators Released, 30 to Face Charges. Niger News Kakaki, November 18. Available at http://users.idworld.net/jmayer/kakai/k001118.htm (accessed 2/10/2001).

Mbembe, Achille. 1992. Provisional Notes on the Postcolony. *Africa* 62: 3–37.

Meneley, Anne. 2007. Fashions and Fundamentalisms in Fin-de-Siècle Yemen: Chador Barbie and Islamic Socks. *Cultural Anthropology* 22(2): 214–243.

Mernissi, Fatima. 1987. *Beyond the Veil: Male-Female Dynamics in Modern Muslim Society.* Bloomington: Indiana University Press.

Mertens, Hugo, and Joseph Frigola. 2002. *Dogondoutchi: Une petite ville du Sahel nigérien.* Niamey: Micro Édition.

Metcalf, Barbara D. 1987. Islamic Arguments in Contemporary Pakistan. In *Islam and the Political Economy of Meaning: Comparative Studies of Muslim Discourse,* ed. William R. Roff, pp. 132–159. London: Croom Helm.

Meunier, Olivier. 1997. *Dynamique de l'enseignement islamique au Niger.* Paris: L'Harmattan.

———. 1998. Marabouts et courants religieux en pays hawsa: dynamique de l'islamisation de la ville de Maradi à la fin du XIXème siècle et durant le XXème siècle. *Revue Canadienne d'Études Africaines* 32(3): 521–557.

Meyer, Birgit. 1998a. Commodities and the Power of Prayer: Pentecostalist Attitudes towards Consumption in Contemporary Ghana. *Development and Change* 29(4): 751–776.

———. 1998b. "Make a Complete Break with the Past": Memory and Post-colonial Modernity in Ghanaian Pentecostalist Discourse. *Journal of Religion in Africa* 28(3): 316–349.

———. 1999. *Translating the Devil: Religion and Modernity among the Ewe in Ghana.* Trenton, N.J.: Africa World Press.

———. 2006. Impossible Representations: Pentecostalism, Vision, and Video Technology in Ghana. In *Religion, Media, and the Public Sphere,* ed. Birgit Meyer and Annelies Moors, pp. 290–312. Bloomington: Indiana University Press.

Meyer, Birgit, and Peter Geschiere, eds. 1999. *Globalization and Identity: Dialectics of Flow and Closure.* Malden, Mass.: Blackwell.

Bibliography

Meyer, Birgit, and Annelies Moors, eds. 2006. *Religion, Media, and the Public Sphere.* Bloomington: Indiana University Press.

Meyer, Birgit, and Peter Pels, eds. 2003. *Magic and Modernity: Interfaces of Revelation and Concealment.* Stanford, Calif.: Stanford University Press.

Miles, William F. S. 1994. *Hausaland Divided: Colonialism and Independence in Nigeria and Niger.* Ithaca, N.Y.: Cornell University Press.

———. 2003. Shari'a as De-Africanization: Evidence from Hausaland. *Africa Today* 50(1): 50–75.

Miller, Daniel. 1994. *Modernity, an Ethnographic Approach: Dualism and Mass Consumption in Trinidad.* New York: Berg.

———. 2005. Introduction. In *Clothing as Material Culture,* ed. Susanne Küchler and Daniel Miller, pp. 1–20. New York: Berg.

Monga, Celestin. 1995. Civil Society and Democratization in Francophone Africa. *Journal of Modern African Studies* 33: 359–379.

Monteil, Parfait-Louis. 1894. *De Saint-Louis à Tripoli par le lac Tchad: Voyage au travers du Soudan et du Sahara accompli pendant les années 1890–91–92.* Paris: Alcan.

Moore, Henrietta L. 1994. *A Passion for Difference: Essays in Anthropology and Gender.* Bloomington: Indiana University Press.

Moore, Henrietta L., and Todd Sanders. 2001. *Magical Interpretations, Material Realities: Modernity, Witchcraft, and the Occult in Postcolonial Africa.* London: Routledge.

Moors, Annelies. 2006. Representing Family Law Debates in Palestine: Gender and the Politics of Presence. In *Religion, Media, and the Public Sphere,* ed. Birgit Meyer and Annelies Moors, pp. 115–131. Bloomington: Indiana University Press.

Mulvey, Laura. 1989. Visual Pleasure and Narrative Cinema. In *Visual and Other Pleasures,* ed. Laura Mulvey, pp. 14–38. Bloomington: Indiana University Press.

Munson, Henry, Jr. 1993. *Religion and Power in Morocco.* New Haven, Conn.: Yale University Press.

Mustaphawas, Aliyu. 1991. The New Niger: A Reporter's Notebook by a VOA Hausa Broadcaster. *Camel Express* 7.

Niandou-Souley, Abdoulaye, and Gado Alzouma. 1996. Islamic Renewal in Niger: From Monolith to Plurality. *Social Compass* 43(2): 249–265.

Nicolas, Guy. 1975. *Dynamique sociale et appréhension du monde au sein d'une société hausa.* Paris: Institut d'Ethnologie.

———. 1978. L'expansion de l'influence arabe en Afrique sud saharienne. *L'Afrique et l'Asie Modernes* 117: 23–46.

———. 1981. *Dynamique de l'Islam au sud du Sahara.* Paris: Publications Orientalistes de France.

———. 1986. *Don rituel et échange marchand dans une société sahélienne.* Paris: Institut d'Ethnologie.

———. 1987. L'Islam au sud du Sahara aujourd'hui. *L'Afrique et l'Asie Modernes* 153: 4–45.

Norris, Lucy. 2005. Cloth That Lies: The Secrets of Recycling in India. In *Clothing as Material Culture,* ed. Susanne Küchler and Daniel Miller, pp. 83–105. New York: Berg.

Nyamnjoh, Francis B. 2001. Delusions of Development and the Enrichment of Witchcraft Discourses in Cameroon. In *Magical Interpretations, Material Realities: Moder-*

nity, Witchcraft, and the Occult in Postcolonial Africa, ed. Henrietta L. Moore and Todd Sanders, 28–49. New York: Routledge.

O'Brien, Susan. 1999. Pilgrimage, Power, and Identity: The Role of the Hajj in the Lives of Nigerian Hausa Bori Adepts. *Africa Today* 46(3/4): 7–40.

O'Fahey, R. S. 1990. *Enigmatic Saint: Ahmad Ibn Idris and the Idrisi Tradition.* Evanston, Ill.: Northwestern University Press.

———. 1993. Islamic Hegemonies in the Sudan: Sufism, Madhism, and Islamism. In *Muslim Identity and Social Change in Sub-Saharan Africa,* ed. Louis Brenner, pp. 21–35. Bloomington: Indiana University Press.

Oloruntemehin, Olatunji. 1972. Theories and Realities in the Administration of Colonial French West Africa from 1890 to the First World War. *Journal of the Historical Society of Nigeria* 6(3): 289–312.

Öncü, Ayse. 2006. Becoming "Secular Muslims": Yasar Buri Öztürk as a Super-subject in Turkish Television. In *Religion, Media, and the Public Sphere,* ed. Birgit Meyer and Annelies Moors, pp. 227–250. Bloomington: Indiana University Press.

Ong, Aihwa. 1987. *Spirit of Resistance and Capitalist Discipline: Factory Women in Malaysia.* Albany: State University of New York Press.

———. 1995. State Versus Islam: Malay Families, Women's Bodies, and the Body Politic in Malaysia. In *Bewitching Women, Pious Men: Gender and Body Politics in Southeast Asia,* ed. Aihwa Ong and Michael Peletz, pp. 54–94. Berkeley: University of California Press.

Otayek, René. 1988. Muslim Charisma in Burkina Faso. In *Charisma and Brotherhoods in African Islam,* ed. Donald B. Cruise O'Brien and Christian Coulon, pp. 90–112. Oxford: Clarendon.

Otayek, René, and Benjamin F. Soares. 2007. Introduction: Islam and Muslim Politics in Africa. In *Islam and Muslim Politics in Africa,* ed. Benjamin F. Soares and René Otayek, pp. 1–24. New York: Palgrave.

Paden, John N. 1973. *Religion and Political Culture in Kano.* Berkeley: University of California Press.

Palmer, H. R., ed. and trans. 1928. *Sudanese Memoirs.* 3 vols. Lagos: Government Printer.

Papanek, Hanna. 1973. Purdah: Separate Worlds and Symbolic Shelter. *Comparative Studies in Society and History* 15: 289–325.

Peletz, Michael. 1993. Sacred Texts and Dangerous Worlds: The Politics of Law and Cultural Rationalization in Malaysia. *Comparative Studies in Society and History* 34(1): 66–109.

———. 1997. "Ordinary Muslims" and Muslim Resurgents in Contemporary Malaysia: Notes on an Ambivalent Relationship. In *Islam in an Era of Nation-States,* ed. Robert W. Hefner and Patricia Horvatich, pp. 231–274. Honolulu: University of Hawai'i Press.

Pellow, Deborah. 1977. *Women in Accra: Options of Autonomy.* Algonac, Mich.: Reference.

Périé, Jean, and Henri Sellier. 1946. Histoire du peuplement du cercle de Dosso. Document 5.1.9. Aix-en-Provence: Archives d'Outre-Mer.

Peterson, Sara Ann. 1999. Marriage Structure and Contraception in Niger. *Journal of Biosocial Science* 31: 93–104.

Piault, Colette. 1963. Contribution à l'étude de la vie quotidienne de la femme Maouri. *Études Nigériennes* 10 IFAN-CNRS.

Piault, Marc-Henri. 1970. *Histoire Mawri: Introduction à l'étude des processus constitutifs d'un état*. Paris: Éditions du Centre National de la Recherche Scientifique.

———. 1972. La personne du pouvoir ou la souveraineté du souverain en pays Mawri (Hausa du Niger). Colloques Internationaux du C. N. R. S. 544 La notion de personne en Afrique noire.

———. 1978. Mariage en pays Hausa. In *Systèmes de signes*, ed. A. Adler, Michel Cartry, Michel Izard, Marc-Henri Piault, and Jean Rouch, pp. 419–433. Paris: Hermann.

Piot, Charles. 1999. *Remotely Global: Village Modernity in West Africa*. Durham, N.C.: Duke University Press.

Pittin, Renée. 1979. Marriage and Alternative Strategies: Career Patterns of Hausa Women in Katsina City. Ph.D. diss., Department of Anthropology, University of London.

Popenoe, Rebecca. 2004. *Feeding Desire: Fatness, Beauty, and Sexuality among a Saharan People*. New York: Routledge.

Quellien, Alain. 1910. *La politique musulmane dans l'Afrique occidentale*. Paris: Larose.

Rabine, Leslie W. 2002. *The Global Circulation of African Fashion*. New York: Berg.

Rahman, Fazlur. 1966. *Islam*. Chicago: University of Chicago Press.

Ranger, Terence O. 1987. Taking Hold of the Land: Holy Places and Pilgrimages in Twentieth-Century Zimbabwe. *Past and Present* 117: 158–194.

Rasmussen, Susan. 2001. Betrayal or Affirmation? Transformation in Witchcraft, Technologies of Power, Danger, and Agency among the Tuareg of Niger. In *Magical Interpretations, Material Realities: Modernity, Witchcraft and the Occult in Postcolonial Africa*, ed. Henrietta L. Moore and Todd Sanders, pp. 136–159. New York: Routledge.

Raynaut, Claude. 1976. Transformation du système de production et inégalité économique: le cas d'un village haoussa (Niger). *Canadian Journal of African Studies* 2: 279–306.

———. 1977. Aspects socio-économiques de la préparation et de la circulation de la nourriture dans un village hausa (Niger). *Cahiers d'Études Africaines* 68(17): 569–597.

Renne, Elisha. 2006. Perspectives on Polio and Immunization in Northern Nigeria. *Social Science and Medicine* 63: 1857–1869.

Renne, Elisha, and D. S. Usman. 1999. Bicycle Decoration and Everyday Aesthetics in Northern Nigeria. *African Arts* 32(2): 46–51.

République du Niger. 1936. Étude sur les coutumes fétishistes maouris (signée par le chef de subdivision à Doutchi, le 25 juillet). Cercle de Dosso. Document 5.1.1. Niamey: Archives Nationales du Niger.

Roberts, Allen R., and Mary Nooter Roberts, with Gassia Armenian and Ousmane Geye. 2003. *A Saint in the City: Sufi Arts of Urban Senegal*. Los Angeles: University of California, Fowler Museum of Cultural History.

Robinson, David. 1985. *The Holy War of Umar Tal*. Oxford: Clarendon.

———. 2000. *Paths of Accommodation: Muslims Societies and French Colonial Authorities in Senegal and Mauritania 1880–1920*. Athens: Ohio University Press.

Roff, William R. 1987. *Islam and the Political Economy of Meaning: Comparative Studies of Muslim Discourse*. London: Croom Helm.

Rosenthal, Judith. 1998. *Possession, Ecstasy, and Law in Ewe Voodoo*. Charlottesville: Virginia University Press.

Rowlands, Michael, and Jean-Pierre Warnier. 1988. Sorcery, Power, and the Modern State in Cameroon. *Man* 23: 118–132.

Roy, Olivier. 1994. *The Failure of Political Islam.* Translated by Carol Volk. London: I. B. Tauris.

———. 2004. *Globalized Islam: The Search for a New Ummah.* New York: Columbia University Press.

Rugh, Andrea B. 1986. *Reveal and Conceal: Dress in Contemporary Egypt.* Syracuse, N.Y.: Syracuse University Press.

Sahlins, Marshall. 1981. *Historical Metaphors and Mythical Realities: Structure in the Early History of the Sandwich Islands Kingdom.* Ann Arbor: University of Michigan Press.

Salvatore, Armando. 1998. Staging Virtue: The Disembodiment of Self-Correctness and the Making of Islam as Correct Norm. In *Yearbook of the Sociology of Islam,* ed. Georg Stauth, pp. 87–120. New Brunswick, N.J.: Transaction.

Sanders, Todd. 2001. Save Our Skins: Structural Adjustment, Morality, and the Occult in Tanzania. In *Magical Interpretations, Material Realities: Modernity, Witchcraft, and the Occult in Postcolonial Africa,* ed. Henrietta L. Moore and Todd Sanders, pp. 160–183. London: Routledge.

———. 2003. Reconsidering Witchcraft: Postcolonial Africa and Analytic (Un)Certainties. *American Anthropologist* 105(2): 338–352.

Sandickci, Özlem, and Güliz Ger. 2005. Aesthetics, Ethics, and Politics of the Turkish Headscarf. In *Clothing as Material Culture,* ed. Suzanne Kuechler and Daniel Miller, pp. 61–82. London: Berg.

Saunders, Margaret. 1978. Marriage and Divorce in a Muslim Hausa Town (Mirria, Niger). Ph.D. diss., Department of Anthropology, Indiana University.

Schildkrout, Enid. 1982. Dependence and Autonomy: The Economic Activities of Secluded Hausa Women in Kano, Nigeria. In *Women and Work in Africa,* ed. Edna Bay, pp. 55–83. Boulder, Colo.: Westview.

Schulz, Dorothea E. 2003. "Charisma and Brotherhood" Revisited: Mass-Mediated Forms of Spirituality in Urban Mali. *Journal of Religion in Africa* 33(2): 146–171.

———. 2006. Morality, Community, Publicness: Shifting Terms of Public Debate in Mali. In *Religion, Media, and the Public Sphere,* ed. Birgit Meyer and Annelies Moors, pp. 132–151. Bloomington: Indiana University Press.

Séré de Rivières. 1946. Rapport de tournée effectué par Séré de Rivières, chef de subdivision de Dogondoutchi. Document 6.3.38. Niamey: Archives Nationales du Niger.

Sermaye, Jean. 1937. *Barga: Maître de la brousse.* Casablanca: Les Éditions du Maghreb.

Shaw, Rosalind. 2002. *Memories of the Slave Trade: Ritual and the Historical Imagination in Sierra Leone.* Chicago: University of Chicago Press.

Shaw, Rosalind, and Charles Stewart, eds. 1994. *Syncretism/Anti-Syncretism: The Politics of Religious Synthesis.* New York: Routledge.

Shils, Edward A. 1965. Charisma, Order, and Status. *American Sociological Review* 30: 199–213.

Smith, Daniel Jordan. 2001. Ritual Killing, 419, and Fast Wealth: Inequality and the Popular Imagination in Southeastern Nigeria. *American Ethnologist* 28(4): 803–826.

Smith, James H. 2004. Of Spirit Possession and Structural Adjustment Programs: Government Downsizing, Education, and their Enchantments in Neoliberal Kenya. In *Producing African Futures: Ritual and Reproduction in a Neoliberal Age,* ed. Brad Weiss, pp. 262–293. Boston: Brill.

Smith, Mary F. 1955. *Baba of Karo: A Woman of the Muslim Hausa.* London: Faber & Faber.

Smith, M. G. 1955. *The Economy of Hausa Communities of Zaria: A Report to the Colonial Social Science Research Council*. London: Her Majesty's Stationary Office.

Smith, Wilfred Cantwell. 1957. *Islam in Modern History*. Princeton, N.J.: Princeton University Press.

Soares, Benjamin F. 2004a. Muslim Saints in the Age of Neoliberalism. In *Producing African Futures: Ritual and Reproduction in a Neoliberal Age*, ed. Brad Weiss, pp. 79–105. Boston: Brill.

———. 2004b. Islam and Public Piety in Mali. In *Public Islam and the Common Good*, ed. Armando Salvatore and Dale F. Eickelman, pp. 205–226. Boston: Brill.

———. 2005. *Islam and the Prayer Economy: History and Authority in a Malian Town*. Ann Arbor: University of Michigan Press.

———. 2007a. Saint and Sufi in Contemporary Mali. In *Sufism and the "Modern" in Islam*, ed. Martin Van Bruinessen and Julia Day Howell, pp. 76–91. New York: I. B. Tauris.

———. 2007b. Rethinking Islam and Muslim Societies in Africa. *African Affairs* 106: 319–336.

Sounaye, Abdoulaye. 2005. Les politiques de l'islam au Niger dans l'ère de la démocratisation de 1991 à 2002. *L'Islam politique au sud du Sahara: Identités, discours, et enjeux*, ed. Muriel Perez-Gomez, pp. 503–525. Paris: Karthala.

———. 2006. Structuring Islam in a Context of Democratization: A Case Study of Niger. Unpublished manuscript.

———. n.d. Islam, État et société: À la recherche d'une éthique publique au Niger. Unpublished manuscript.

Steedly, Mary M. 1993. *Hanging without a Rope: Narrative Experience in Colonial and Postcolonial Karoland*. Princeton, N.J.: Princeton University Press.

Stengs, Irene, Hilton White, C. Lynch, and J. A. Zimmermann. 2000. Millennial Transitions. *Public Culture* 12(2): 344–350.

Stoller, Paul. 1995. *Embodying Colonial Memories: Spirit Possession, Power, and the Hauka in West Africa*. New York: Routledge.

Straight, Bilinda. 2002. From Samburu Heirloom to New Age Artifacts: The Cross-Cultural Consumption of Mporo Marriage Beads. *American Anthropologist* 104(1): 7–21.

Sule, Balaraba B., and Priscilla E. Starratt. 1991. Islamic Leadership Positions for Women in Contemporary Kano Society. In *Hausa Women in the Twentieth Century*, ed. Catherine Coles and Beverly Mack, pp. 29–49. Madison: University of Wisconsin Press.

Sutter, John. 1979. Social Analysis of the Nigerien Rural Producer, Niger Agricultural Sector Assessment 2 (part D). Niamey: USAID.

Taussig, Michael T. 1987. *Shamanism, Colonialism, and the Wild Man: A Study in Terror and Healing*. Chicago: University of Chicago Press.

Thaiss, Gustav. 1994. Contested Meanings and the Politics of Authenticity: The "Hosay" of Trinidad. In *Islam, Globalization and Postmodernity*, ed. Akbar S. Ahmed and Hastings Donnan, pp. 38–62. New York: Routledge.

Thorold, Alan. 1993. Metamorphoses of the Yao Muslims. In *Muslim Identity and Social Change in Sub-Saharan Africa*, ed. Louis Brenner, pp. 79–90. Bloomington: Indiana University Press.

Triaud, Jean-Louis. 1974. La question musulmane en Côte d'Ivoire (1893–1939). *Revue Française d'Histoire d'Outre-Mer* 61(225): 542–571.

————. 1981. L'Islam et l'État en République du Niger (Première partie). *Le Mois en Afrique* 192: 9–26.

————. 2000. Islam in Africa under French Colonial Rule. In *The History of Islam in Africa*, ed. Nehemia Levtzion and Randall L. Pouwels, pp. 169–187. Athens: Ohio University Press.

Trimingham, John S. 1959. *Islam in West Africa*. Oxford: Clarendon.

————. 1962. *A History of Islam in West Africa*. New York: Oxford University Press.

————. 1971. *The Sufi Orders in Islam*. Oxford: Clarendon.

Tsing, Anna Lowenhaupt. 1993. *In the Realm of the Diamond Queen: Marginality in an Out-of-the-Way Place*. Princeton, N.J.: Princeton University Press.

Turner, Terence. 1980. The Social Skin. In *Not Work Alone: A Cross-Cultural View of Activities Superfluous to Survival*, ed. Jeremy Cherfas and Roger Lewin, pp. 112–140. London: Temple Smith.

Turner, Victor. 1972. The Center Out There: Pilgrim's Goal. *History of Religions* 12: 191–230.

Umar, Muhammad Sani. 1993. Changing Islamic Identity in Nigeria from the 1960s to the 1980s: From Sufism to Anti-Sufism. In *Muslim Identity and Social Change in Sub-Saharan Africa*, ed. Louis Brenner, pp. 154–178. Bloomington: Indiana University Press.

————. 2001. Education and Islamic Trends in Northern Nigeria: 1970s–1990s. *Africa Today* 48(2): 127–150.

Vaughan, Meghan. 1991. *Curing Their Ills: Colonial Power and African Illness*. Stanford, Calif.: Stanford University Press.

Vikør, Knut S. 2000. Sufi Brotherhoods in Africa. In *The History of Islam in Africa*, ed. Nehemia Levtzion and Randall L. Pouwels, pp. 441–476. Athens: Ohio University Press.

Watts, Michael. 1996. Islamic Modernities? Citizenship, Civil Society, and Islamism in a Nigerian City. *Public Culture* 8: 251–289.

Weber, Max. 1958. *The Protestant Ethic and the Spirit of Capitalism*. Translated by Talcott Parsons. New York: Scribner.

————. 1978. *Economy and Society: An Outline of Interpretive Sociology*. Translated by Ephraim Fischoff et al. Edited by Guenther Roth and Claus Wittich. Berkeley: University of California Press.

Weiss, Anita M. 1997. The Slow Yet Steady Path to Women's Empowerment in Pakistan. In *Islam, Gender, and Social Change*, ed. Yvonne Yazbeck Haddad and John L. Esposito, pp. 124–143. New York: Oxford University Press.

Weiss, Brad. 1996. *The Making and Unmaking of the Haya Lived World: Consumption, Commoditization, and Everyday Practice*. Durham, N.C.: Duke University Press.

————. 1998. Electric Vampires: Haya Rumors of the Commodified Body. In *Bodies and Persons: Comparative Perspectives from Africa and Melanesia*, ed. Michael Lambek and Andrew Strathern, pp. 172–196. New York: Cambridge University Press.

————. 2002. Thug Realism: Inhabiting Fantasy in Urban Tanzania. *Cultural Anthropology* 17(1): 93–124.

Werbner, Pnina. 1996. Stamping the Earth with the Name of Allah: Zikr and the Sacralizing of Space among British Muslims. In *Making Muslim Space in North America and Europe*, ed. Barbara D. Metcalf, pp. 167–185. Berkeley: University of California Press.

———. 2003. *Pilgrims of Love: The Anthropology of a Global Sufi Cult*. Bloomington: Indiana University Press.

Werbner, Pnina, and Ellen Bassu, eds. 1998. *Embodying Charisma: Modernity, Locality, and the Performance of Emotion in Sufi Cults*. New York: Routledge.

West, Harry. 2001. Sorcery of Construction and Socialist Modernization: Ways of Understanding Power in Postcolonial Mozambique. *American Ethnologist* 28(1): 119–150.

Westerlund, David. 1997. Reaction and Action: Accounting for the Rise of Islamism. In *African Islam and Islam in Africa,* ed. David Westerlund and Eva Evers Rosander. Athens: Ohio University Press.

Westerlund, David, and Eva Evers Rosander, eds. 1997. *African Islam and Islam in Africa: Encounters between Sufis and Islamists*. Athens: Ohio University Press.

White, Luise. 2000. *Speaking with Vampires: Rumor and History in Colonial Africa*. Berkeley: University of California Press.

Whitsitt, Novian. 2003. Islamic Hausa Feminism Meets Northern Nigerian Romance: The Cautious Rebellion of Bilkisu Funtuwa. *African Studies Review* 46(1): 137–153.

Woodward, Sophie. 2005. Looking Good: Feeling Right—Aesthetics of the Self. In *Clothing as Material Culture,* ed. Susanne Küchler and Daniel Miller, pp. 21–39. New York: Berg.

Works, John A. 1976. *Pilgrims in a Strange Land: Hausa Communities in Chad*. New York: Columbia University Press.

Zuhur, Sherifa. 1992. *Revealing Reveiling: Islamist Gender Ideology in Contemporary Egypt*. Albany: State University of New York Press.

Index

Abadie, Maurice, 290n31
Abedi, Mehdi, 81
Abidjan, 188
Abraham, 91, 252
Abu-Lughod, Lila, 34, 179, 246
adashi (rotating credit association), 196
addini (religion), 1, 22, 29, 225, 286n16, 297n1. *See also* Islam; Muslims
Afghanistan, 19, 31
Africa, xii, xix, xxii, 20, 40, 42, 43–44, 47, 48–49, 51, 54, 58, 72, 110, 121, 136, 154, 176, 180, 286n12, 305n2; North Africa, 40, 44, 54, 141; religion in, 2, 23, 37, 38, 81; Sub-Saharan Africa, 26, 72, 291n47, 299n20; West Africa, xxiii, 1–2, 13, 18, 20, 23–25, 36–37, 39, 40–44, 51–52, 71, 92, 94, 104, 115–16, 127, 135, 138, 141, 172, 238, 279, 285n3 (preface), 286nn10,15, 287n3, 288nn7,13, 289nn15,19, 290n33, 293n16. *See also* colonial period; Islam, in Africa; Muslims; postcolonial period; precolonial period
Agadez, xiv, 300n26, 305n2, 310n24
agriculture, xxii, 46, 47, 74, 99, 106, 155. *See also* farming
Ahmadu Bello University, 126
Ahmed, Leila, 209
AIDS, 87, 243, 299n17
alcohol, 62, 63, 307; alcoholism, 43
Algeria, xiv, 3; Algerian war of independence, 43, 213; Algerian women, 213–14, 216, 305n4
alhazai (persons who have made pilgrimage to Mecca), xvi, 56, 138. *See also* haji; Mecca
Alidou, Ousseina, 27, 249, 295n28
alms, 28, 53, 61, 95, 133, 167, 191, 222, 243, 253, 255, 260, 264, 299n18, 304n10
Alphadi, 207
al-Qaeda, 286n15
al-Tijani, Ahmad, 3. *See also* Tijaniyya
Amadou, Hama, 207

Amulets (*layu*), 2, 38, 53, 80, 88, 89, 123, 127, 152, 157, 160, 161, 166–67, 293n13, 301n10, 302nn18,20, 307n24; amulet makers, 41, 53, 96, 127, 162, 288n9. *See also* Idolatry; *rubutu*
animism, 20, 23, 37, 49, 52, 54, 127, 134, 136, 155, 159, 160. *See also* fetishism; naturism
anthropology, xxiii, 33, 178, 186, 205, 212; anthropological literature, 153, 154, 278; of Islam, xix, xxiii, 9, 20–21, 154; and Weber, 17, 18
Antoun, Richard, 21
Appadurai, Arjun, 145
Arabic language, 12, 13, 44, 53, 56, 79, 80, 81, 94–95, 130, 248–50, 254
Arewa, xv, 46–47, 49, 50, 58, 59, 66, 134, 146–49, 151, 162, 165, 287n3, 289nn16,21, 290nn33,41, 300n2; and Islam, xix, 10, 27, 38–39, 45, 48, 51, 53, 55, 81, 88, 105, 135, 137, 155
Argungu, 125, 128
Armbrust, Walter, 228
Asad, Talal, 8–9, 24–25
Ashforth, Adam, 245
Asma'u, Nana, 27, 287n20
Association Islamique du Niger (AIN), 57, 297n5
Assoumi, Aboubacar, 288n10
austerity, xx, 7, 31, 89, 90, 144, 153, 177, 180, 181, 198, 218, 226, 228, 278, 303
autonomy, 18; women's, xvii, 5, 10, 97, 99–100, 102, 175, 203, 205, 213, 214, 231, 267, 273, 278
Awal, Mahamane (Shehu Muhammadu Awalu), xii, xix, 5–8, 15, 31, 34–35, 111, 112–13, 116, 125–26, 129–35, 140, 143–45, 160, 245, 274–75, 285n5, 286n7,12, 287n24, 297nn1,5, 298nn10,11, 299nn15,16,19, 300nn26,27, 302n21, 309n8; charisma of, 30, 114–15, 124–26, 132, 135, 137, 142–44, 153, 168, 174, 203, 250; and Dogondoutchi, 118, 133, 135–38,

333

Index

Index

Adeline Masquelier is Professor of Anthropology and Director of the Religious Studies Program at Tulane University. She is author of *Prayer Has Spoiled Everything: Possession, Power, and Identity in an Islamic Town of Niger* and editor of *Dirt, Undress, and Difference: Critical Perspectives on the Body's Surface* (Indiana University Press, 2005).